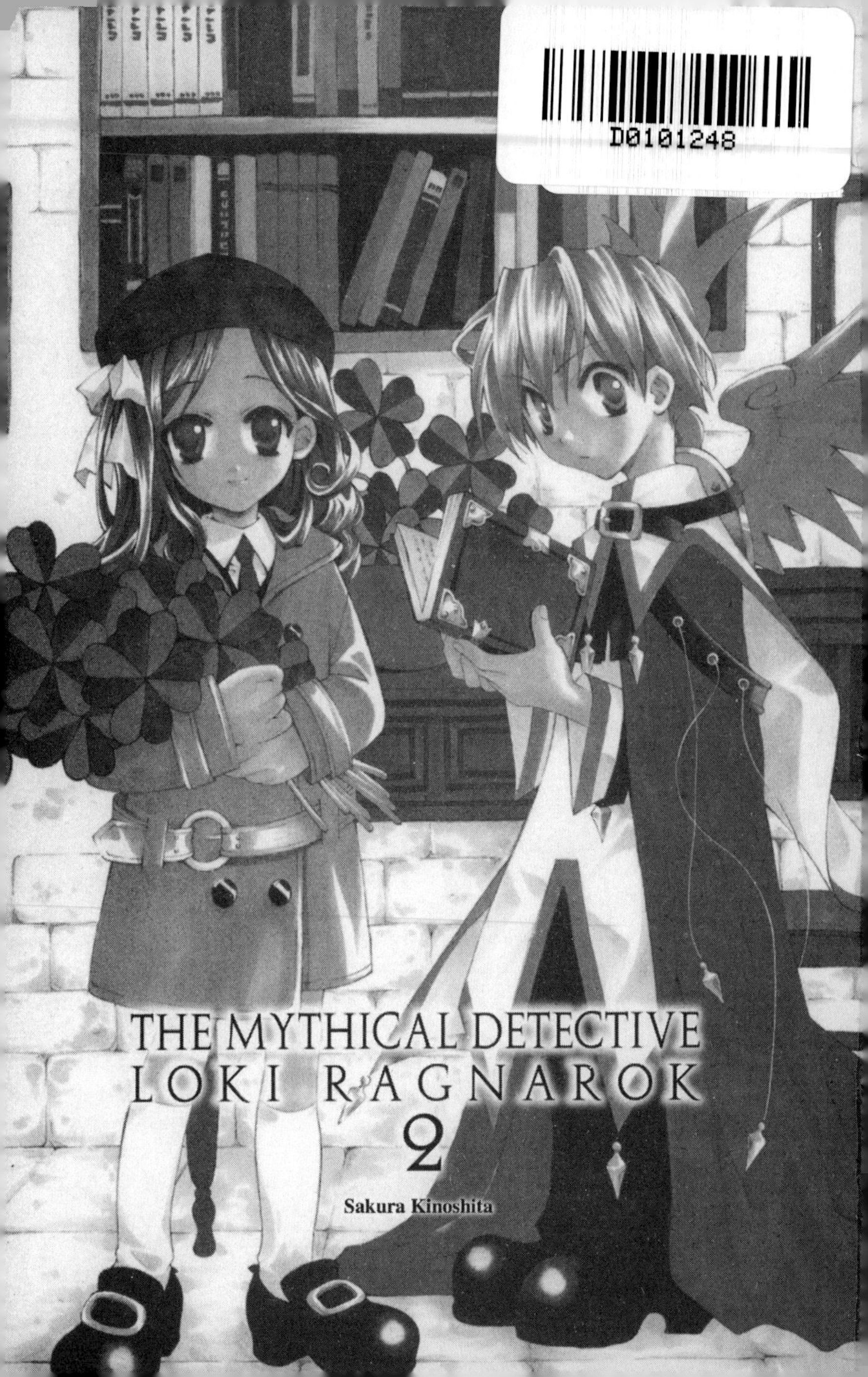
THE MYTHICAL DETECTIVE
LOKI RAGNAROK
2
Sakura Kinoshita

THE
MYTHICAL
DETECTIVE
LOKI
RAGNAROK

❖ Contents ❖

CHAPTER 5

The Ghost of Cat Mansion

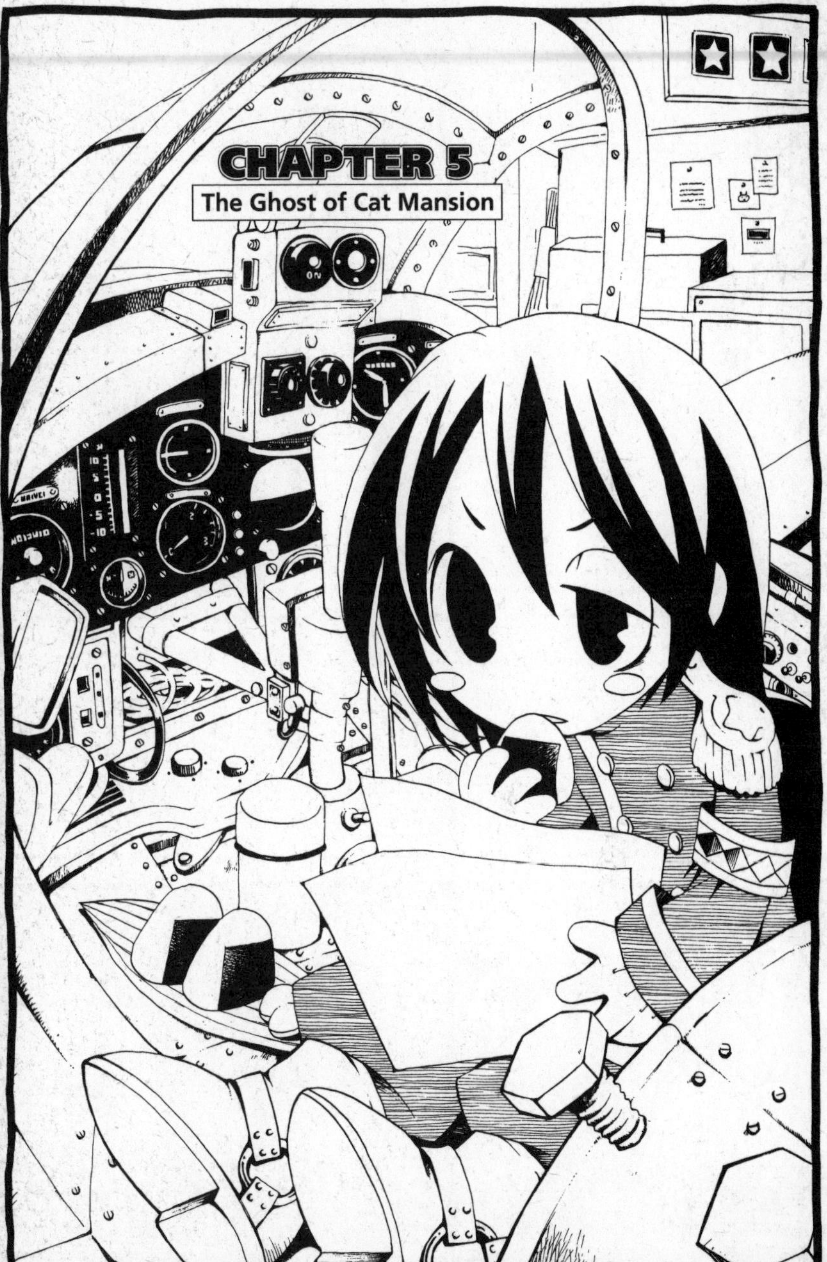

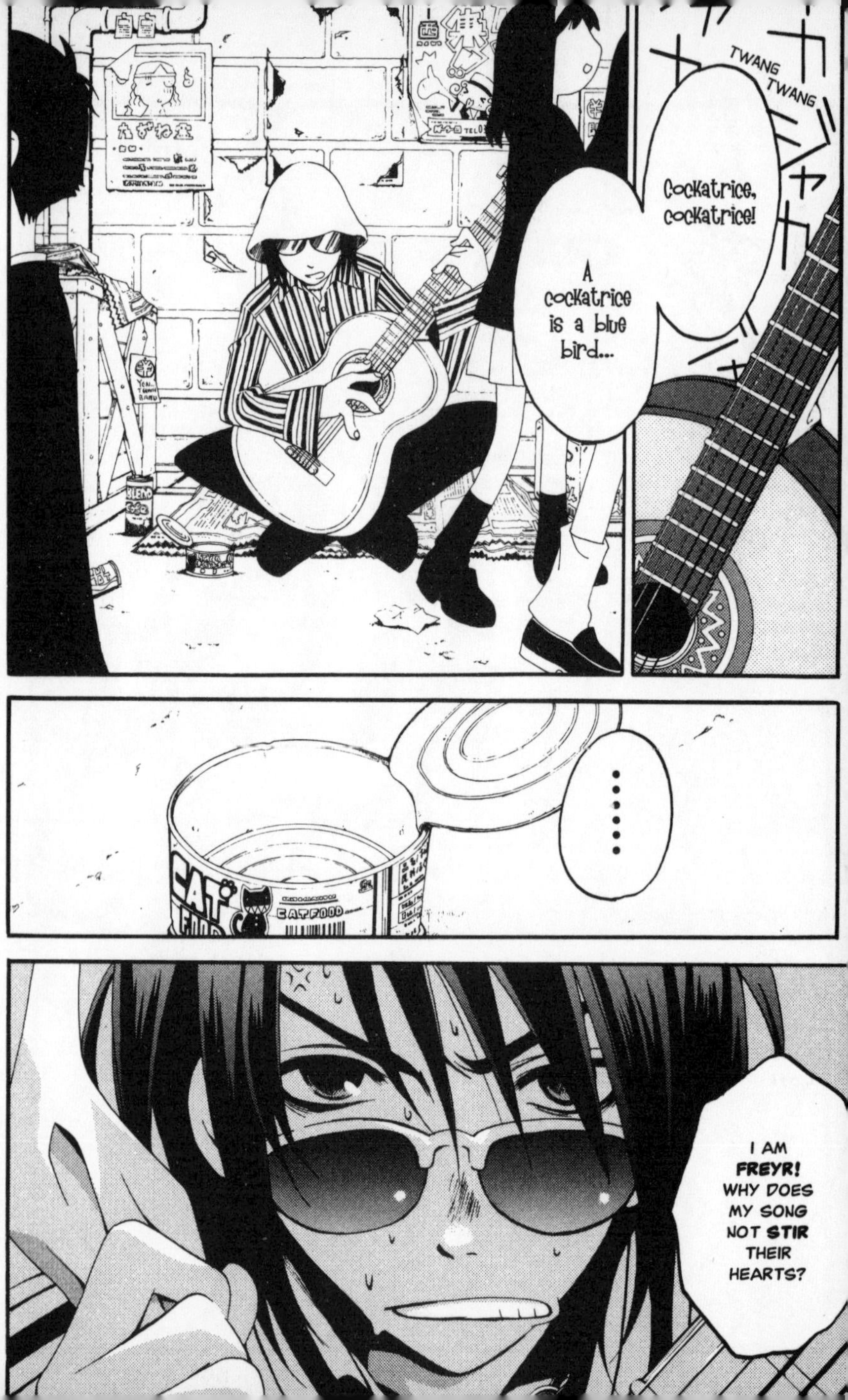
TWANG TWANG
Cockatrice, cockatrice!
A cockatrice is a blue bird...
......
I AM FREYR! WHY DOES MY SONG NOT STIR THEIR HEARTS?

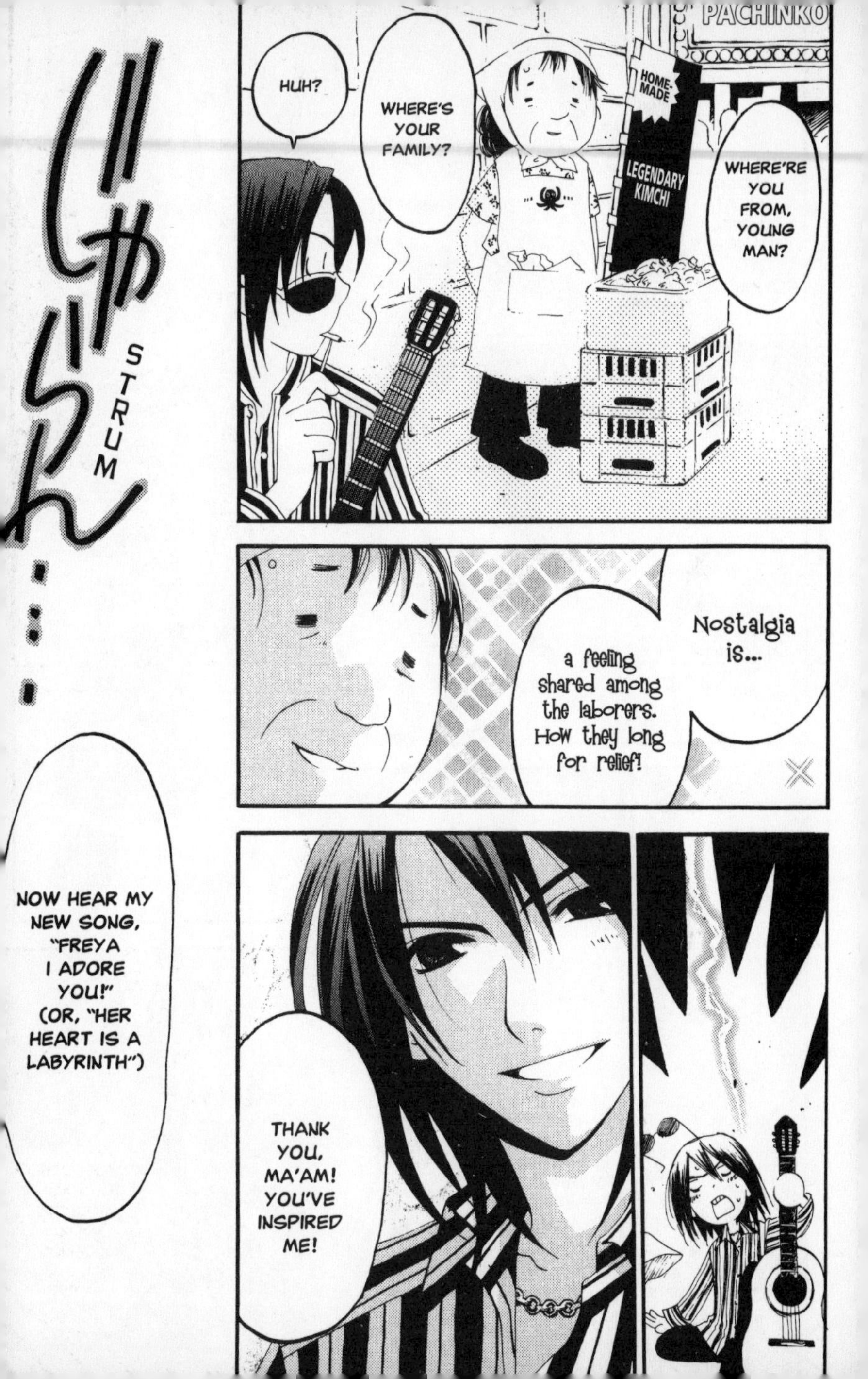
PACHINKO
HOME-MADE
LEGENDARY KIMCHI
WHERE'RE YOU FROM, YOUNG MAN?
WHERE'S YOUR FAMILY?
HUH?
Nostalgia is...
a feeling shared among the laborers. How they long for relief!
THANK YOU, MA'AM! YOU'VE INSPIRED ME!
じゃらん……
STRUM
NOW HEAR MY NEW SONG, "FREYA I ADORE YOU!" (OR, "HER HEART IS A LABYRINTH")

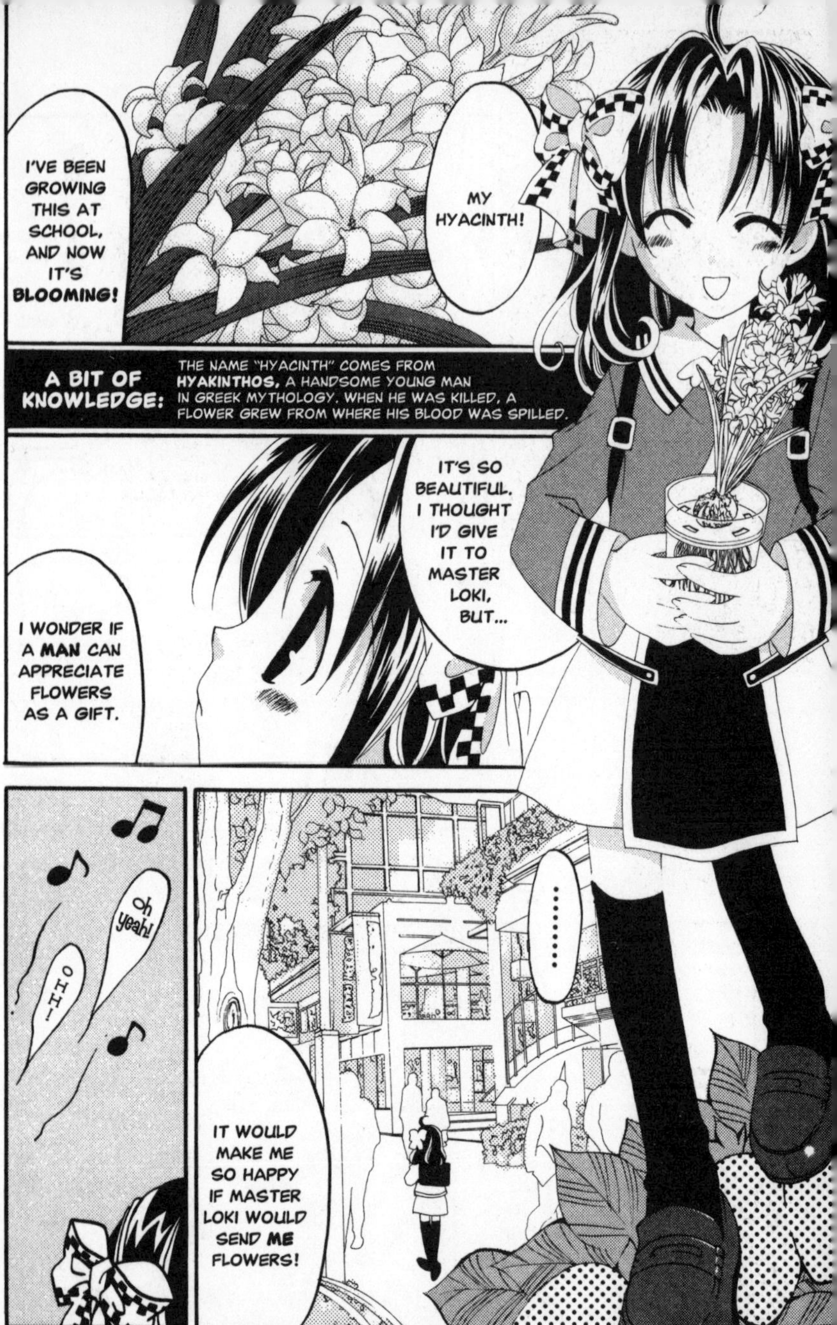
MY HYACINTH!
I'VE BEEN GROWING THIS AT SCHOOL, AND NOW IT'S BLOOMING!
A BIT OF KNOWLEDGE:
THE NAME "HYACINTH" COMES FROM HYAKINTHOS, A HANDSOME YOUNG MAN IN GREEK MYTHOLOGY. WHEN HE WAS KILLED, A FLOWER GREW FROM WHERE HIS BLOOD WAS SPILLED.
IT'S SO BEAUTIFUL. I THOUGHT I'D GIVE IT TO MASTER LOKI, BUT...
I WONDER IF A MAN CAN APPRECIATE FLOWERS AS A GIFT.
......
IT WOULD MAKE ME SO HAPPY IF MASTER LOKI WOULD SEND ME FLOWERS!
oh yeah!
OHH!

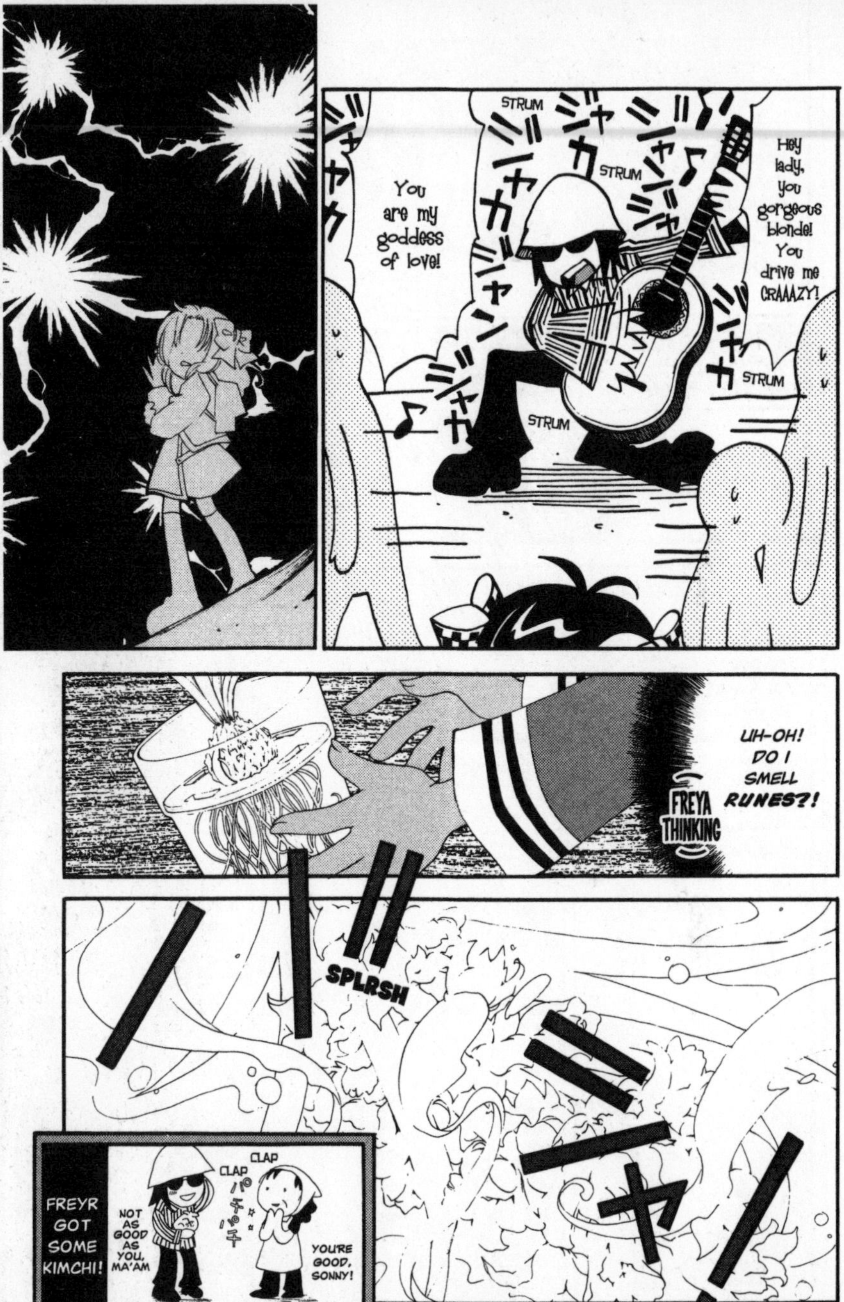

Hey lady, you gorgeous blonde! You drive me CRAAAZY!
You are my goddess of love!
STRUM
STRUM
STRUM
STRUM
UH-OH! DO I SMELL RUNES?!
FREYA THINKING
SPLRSH
FREYR GOT SOME KIMCHI!
CLAP
CLAP
YOU'RE GOOD, SONNY!
NOT AS GOOD AS YOU, MA'AM

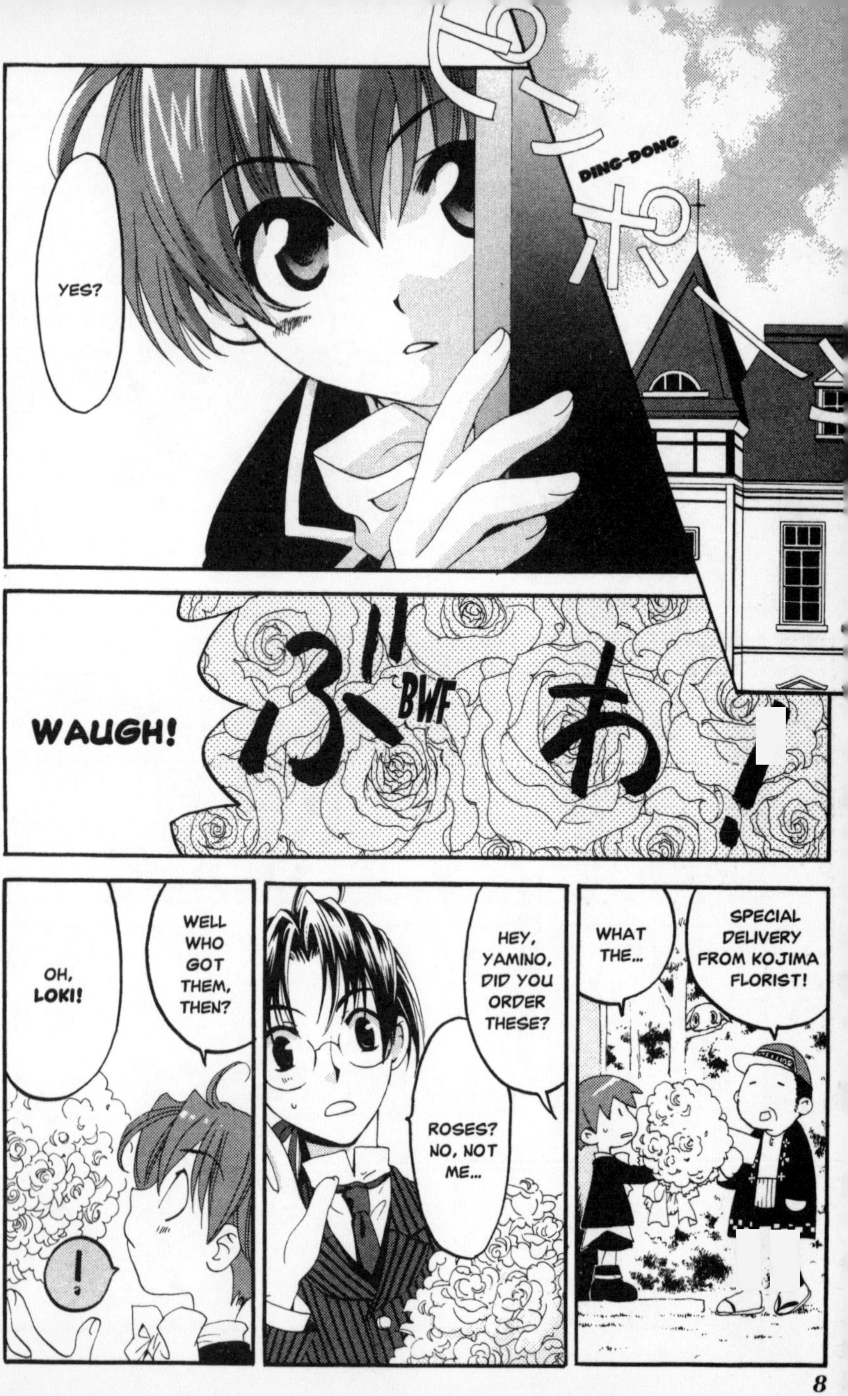
DING-DONG
YES?
WAUGH!
BWF
SPECIAL DELIVERY FROM KOJIMA FLORIST!
WHAT THE...
HEY, YAMINO, DID YOU ORDER THESE?
ROSES? NO, NOT ME...
WELL WHO GOT THEM, THEN?
OH, LOKI!
!

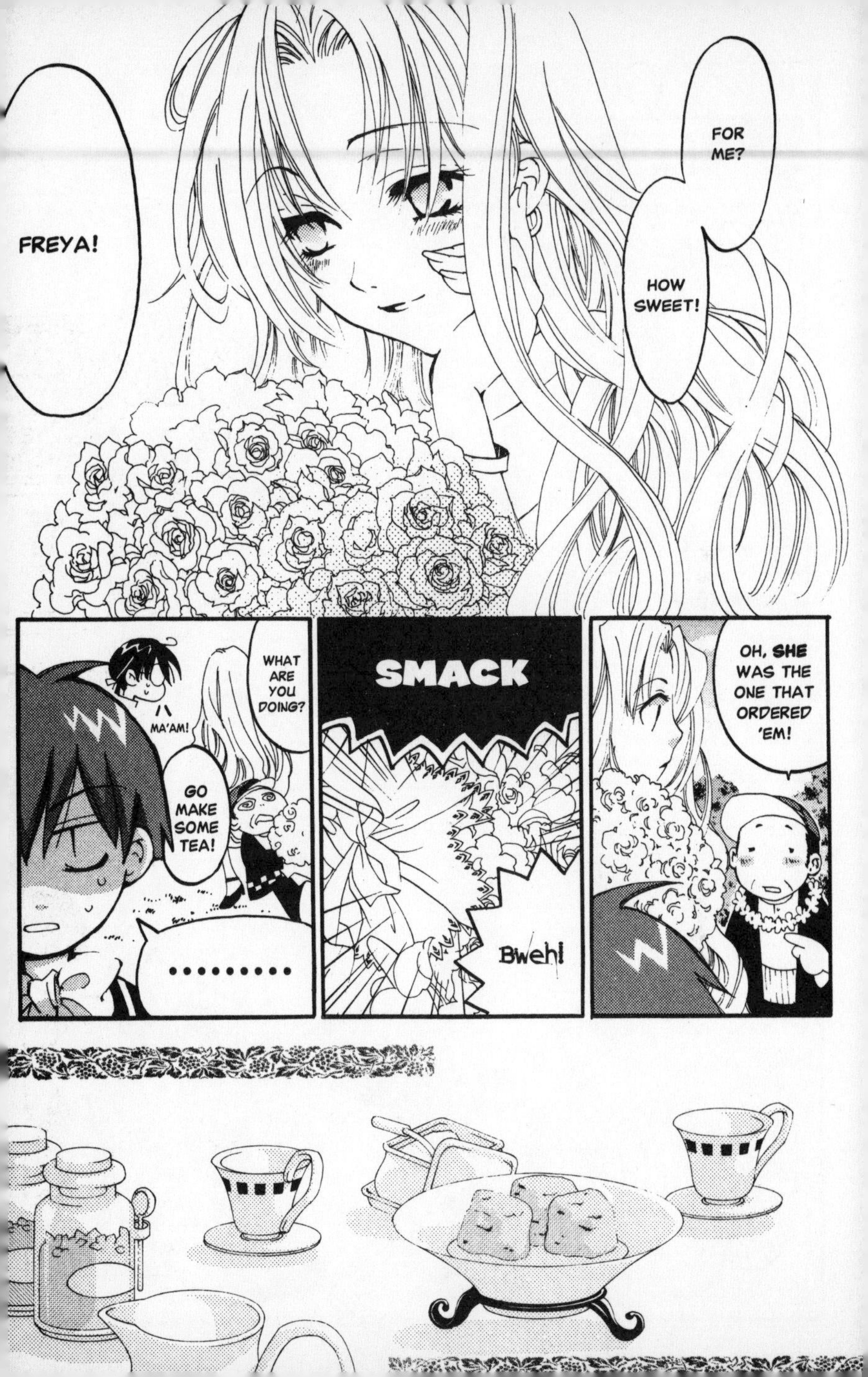
FOR ME?
HOW SWEET!
FREYA!
OH, SHE WAS THE ONE THAT ORDERED 'EM!
SMACK
Bweh!
WHAT ARE YOU DOING?
MA'AM!
GO MAKE SOME TEA!
....

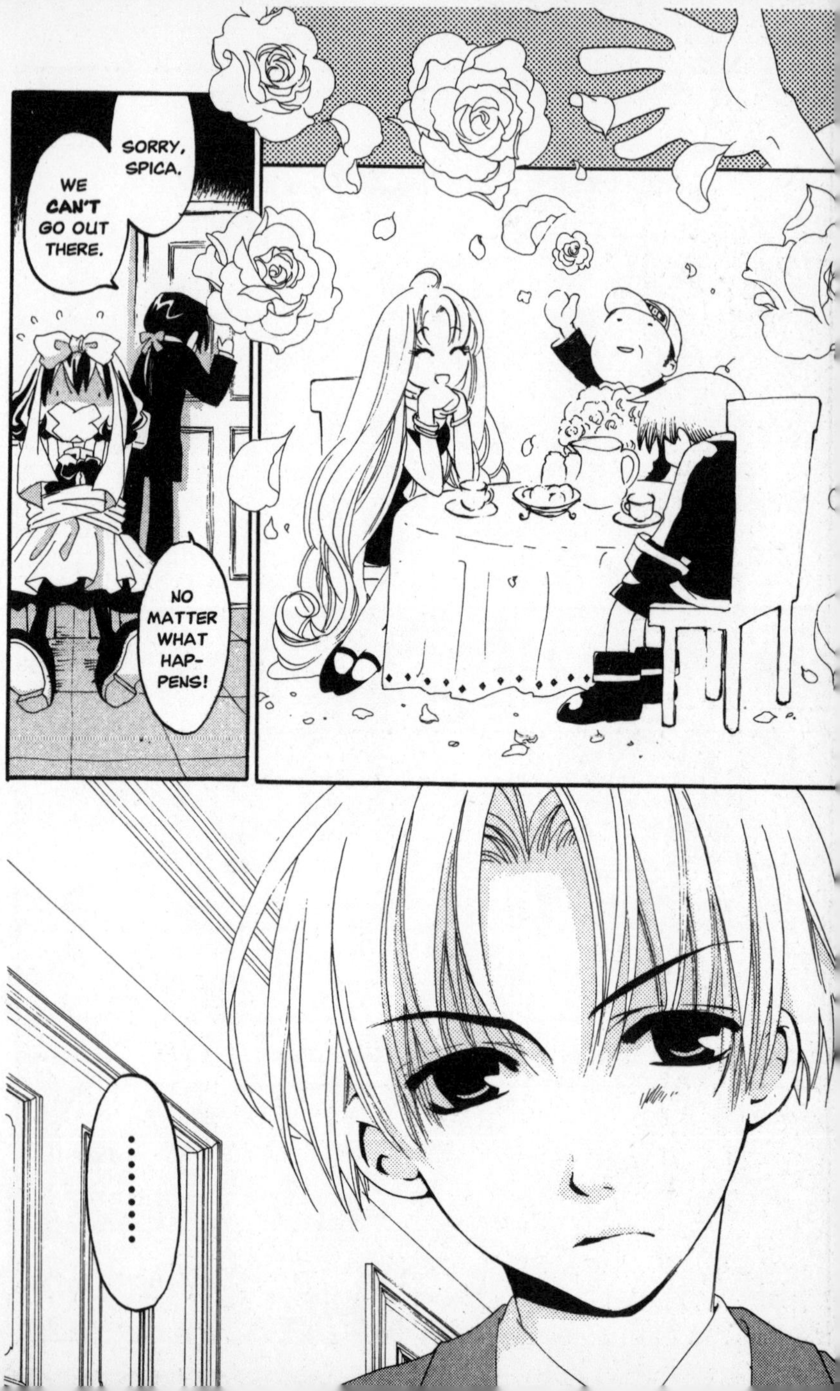
SORRY, SPICA.
WE CAN'T GO OUT THERE.
NO MATTER WHAT HAP-PENS!
....

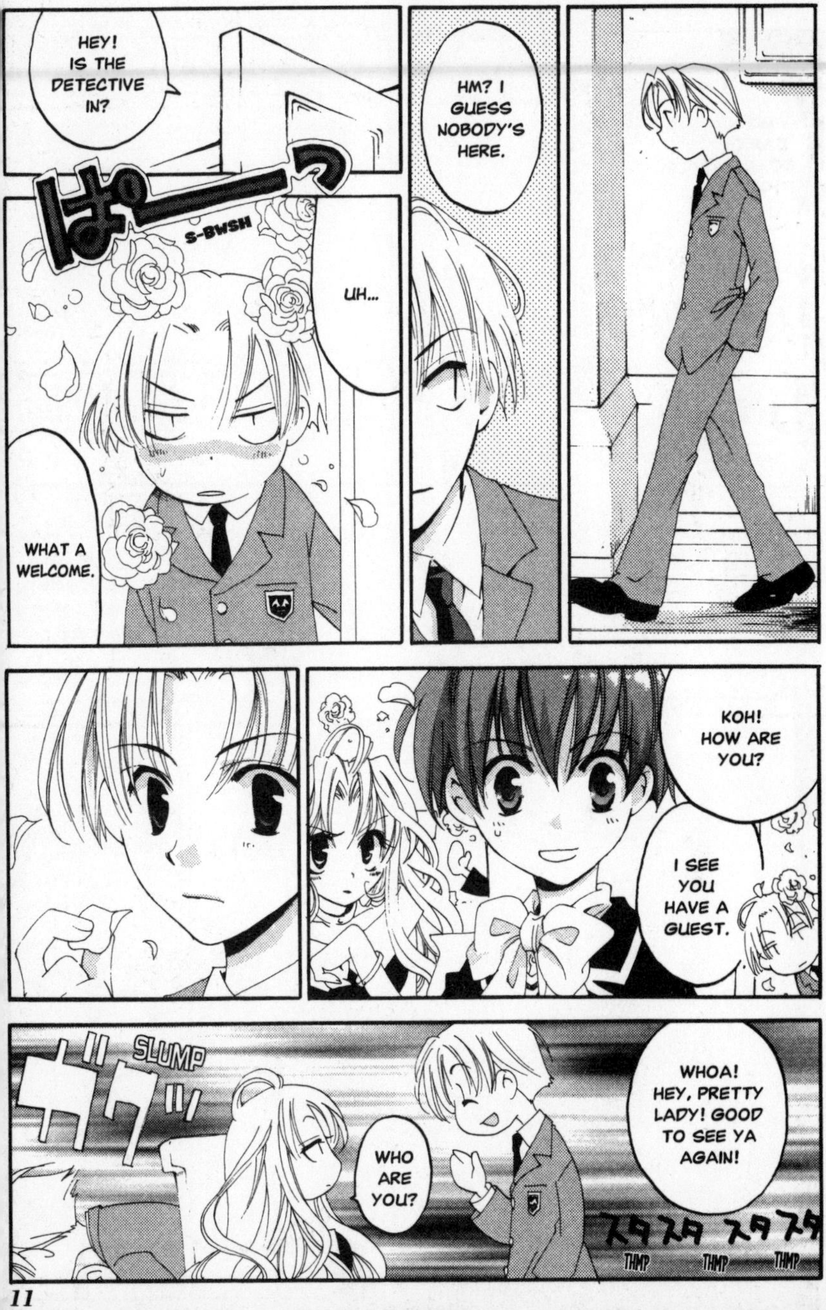
HM? I GUESS NOBODY'S HERE.
HEY! IS THE DETECTIVE IN?
ぱーっ
S-BWSH
UH...
WHAT A WELCOME.
KOH! HOW ARE YOU?
I SEE YOU HAVE A GUEST.
WHOA! HEY, PRETTY LADY! GOOD TO SEE YA AGAIN!
スタスタ スタスタ
THMP THMP THMP
WHO ARE YOU?
ガクッ
SLUMP

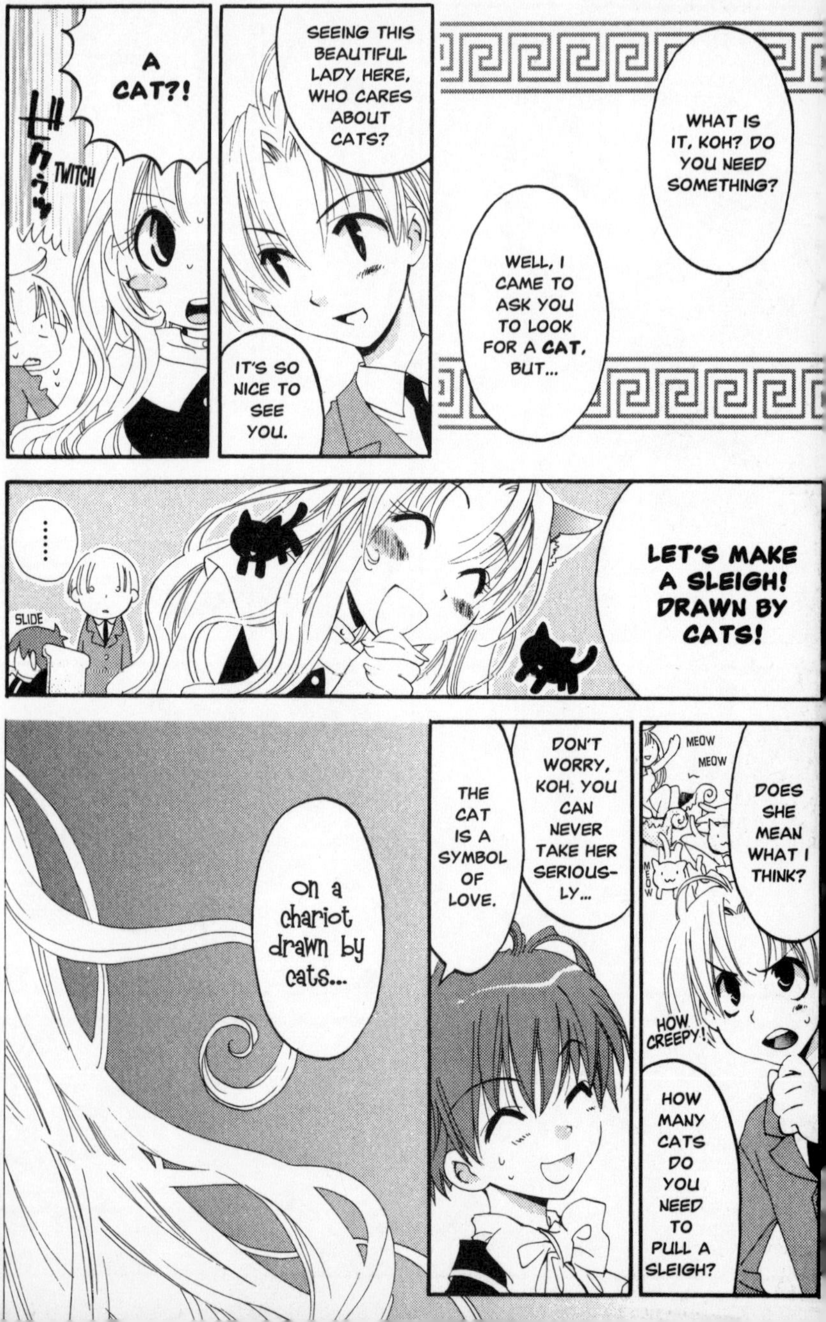
WHAT IS IT, KOH? DO YOU NEED SOMETHING?
WELL, I CAME TO ASK YOU TO LOOK FOR A **CAT**, BUT...
SEEING THIS BEAUTIFUL LADY HERE, WHO CARES ABOUT CATS?
IT'S SO NICE TO SEE YOU.
A CAT?!
TWITCH
LET'S MAKE A SLEIGH! DRAWN BY CATS!
......
SLIDE
DOES SHE MEAN WHAT I THINK?
MEOW
MEOW
MEOW
HOW CREEPY!
HOW MANY CATS DO YOU NEED TO PULL A SLEIGH?
DON'T WORRY, KOH. YOU CAN NEVER TAKE HER SERIOUS-LY...
THE CAT IS A SYMBOL OF LOVE.
on a chariot drawn by cats...

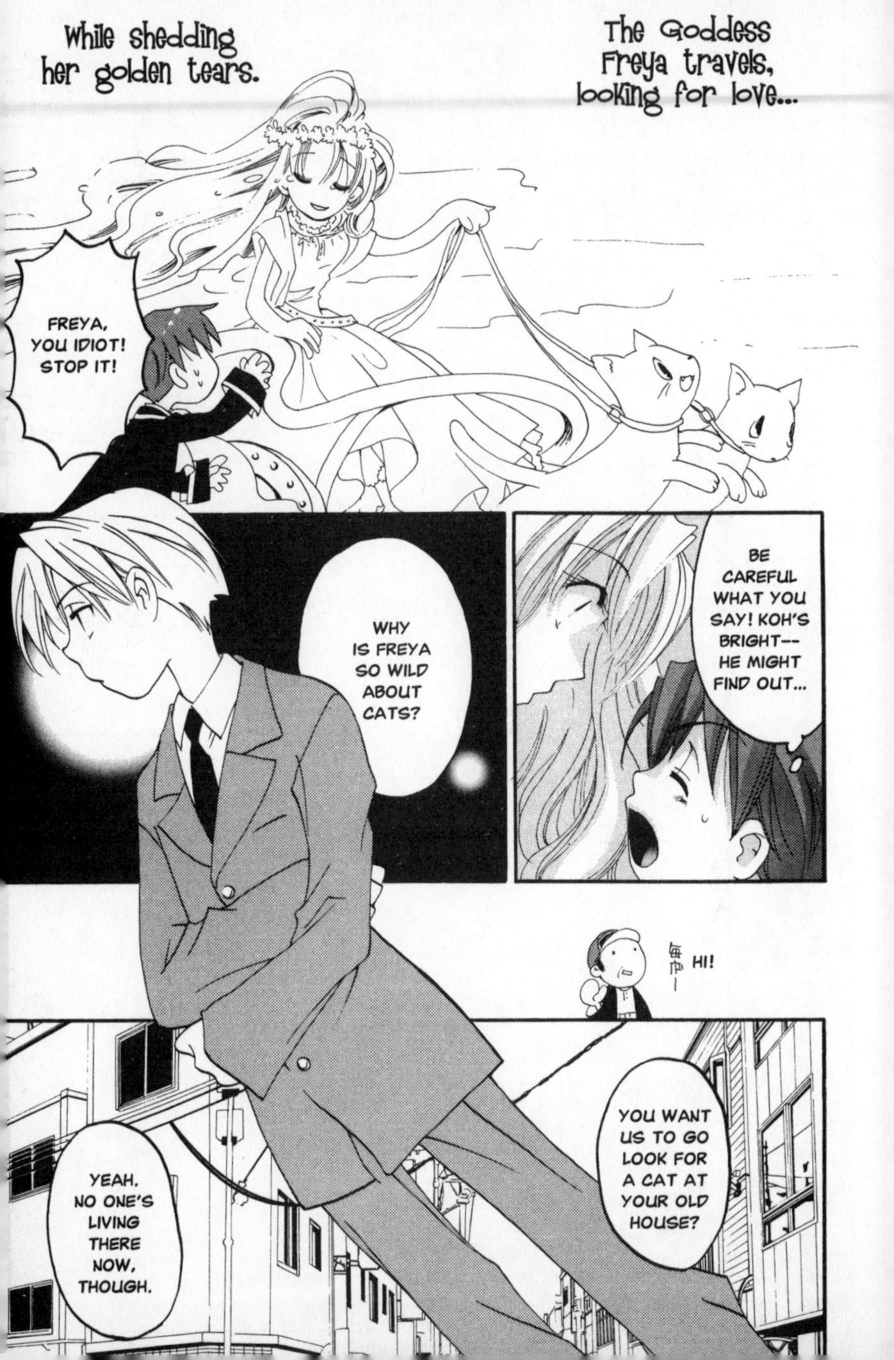
The Goddess Freya travels, looking for love...
While shedding her golden tears.
FREYA, YOU IDIOT! STOP IT!
BE CAREFUL WHAT YOU SAY! KOH'S BRIGHT-- HE MIGHT FIND OUT...
WHY IS FREYA SO WILD ABOUT CATS?
HI!
YOU WANT US TO GO LOOK FOR A CAT AT YOUR OLD HOUSE?
YEAH. NO ONE'S LIVING THERE NOW, THOUGH.

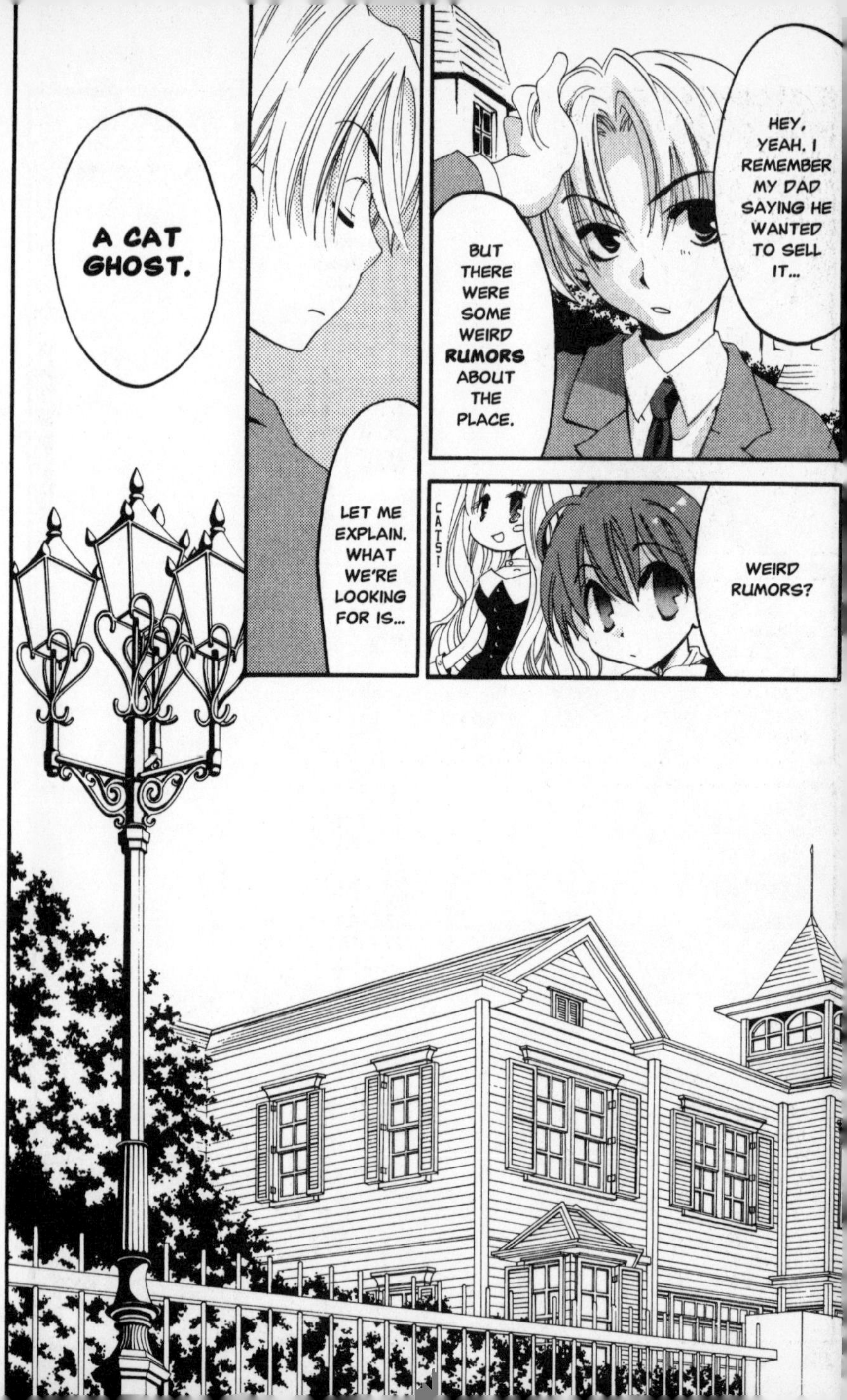
HEY, YEAH. I REMEMBER MY DAD SAYING HE WANTED TO SELL IT...
BUT THERE WERE SOME WEIRD RUMORS ABOUT THE PLACE.
A CAT GHOST.
WEIRD RUMORS?
CATS!
LET ME EXPLAIN. WHAT WE'RE LOOKING FOR IS...

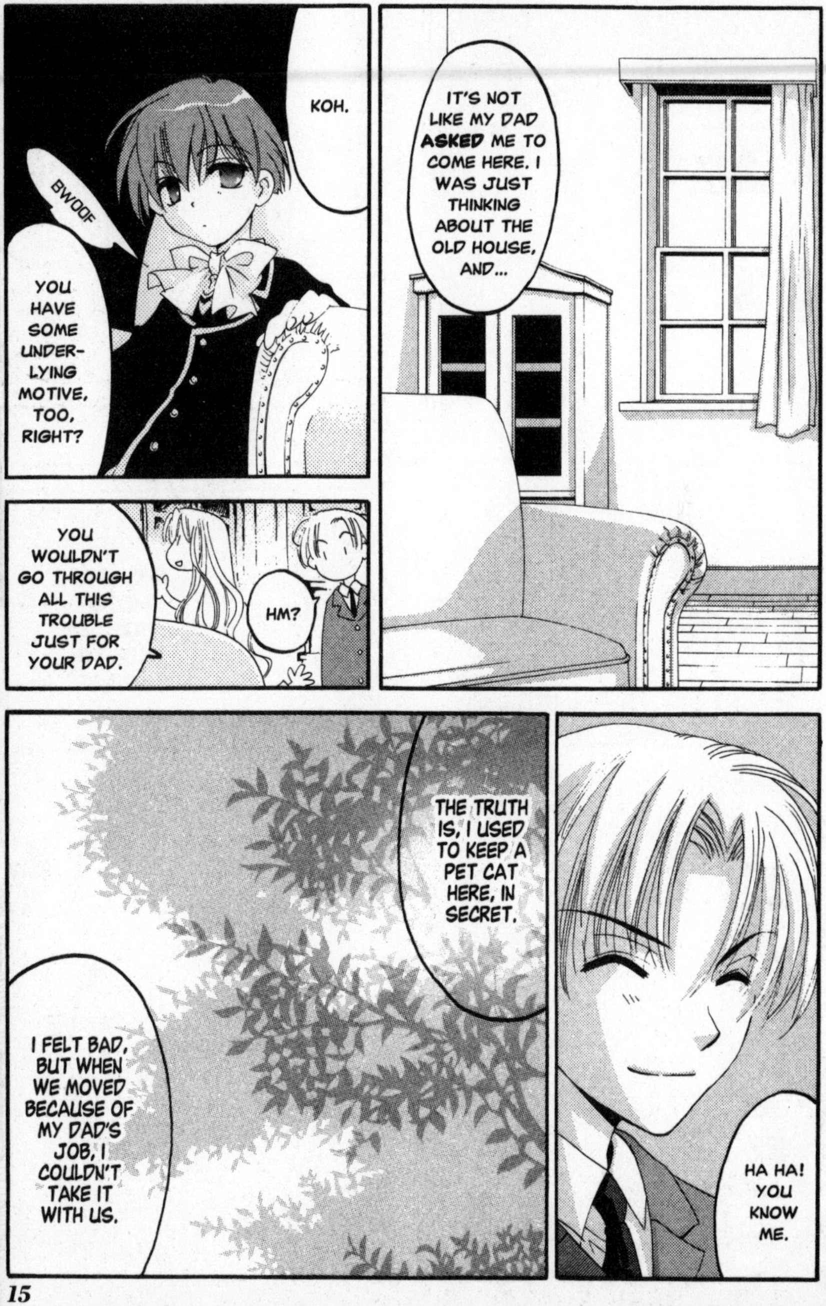
IT'S NOT LIKE MY DAD ASKED ME TO COME HERE. I WAS JUST THINKING ABOUT THE OLD HOUSE, AND...
KOH.
BWOOF
YOU HAVE SOME UNDER-LYING MOTIVE, TOO, RIGHT?
HM?
YOU WOULDN'T GO THROUGH ALL THIS TROUBLE JUST FOR YOUR DAD.
HA HA! YOU KNOW ME.
THE TRUTH IS, I USED TO KEEP A PET CAT HERE, IN SECRET.
I FELT BAD, BUT WHEN WE MOVED BECAUSE OF MY DAD'S JOB, I COULDN'T TAKE IT WITH US.

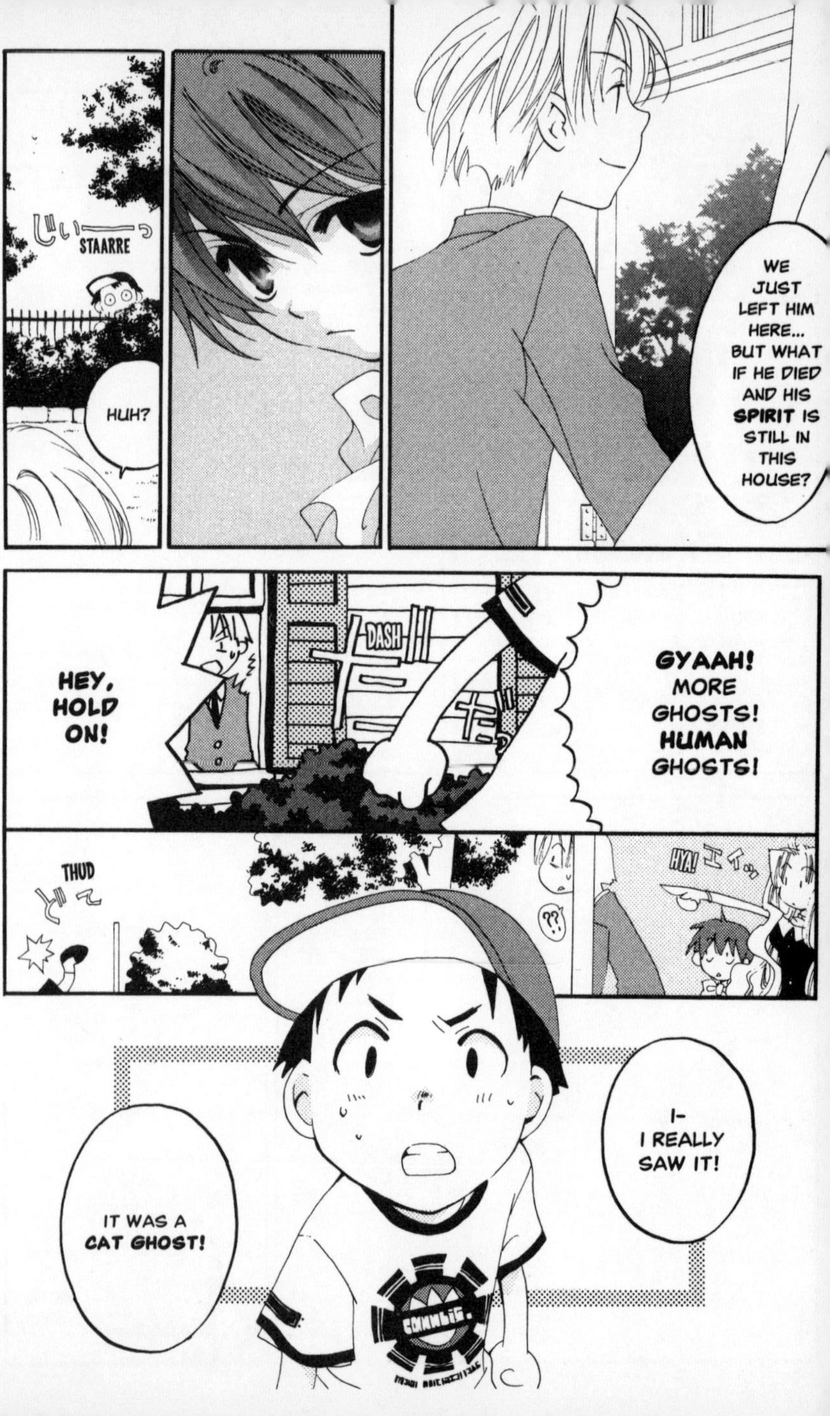

WE JUST LEFT HIM HERE... BUT WHAT IF HE DIED AND HIS SPIRIT IS STILL IN THIS HOUSE?
じぃーーっ
STAARRE
HUH?
GYAAH! MORE GHOSTS! HUMAN GHOSTS!
DASH
HEY, HOLD ON!
HYA!
エイッ
??
THUD
I- I REALLY SAW IT!
IT WAS A CAT GHOST!

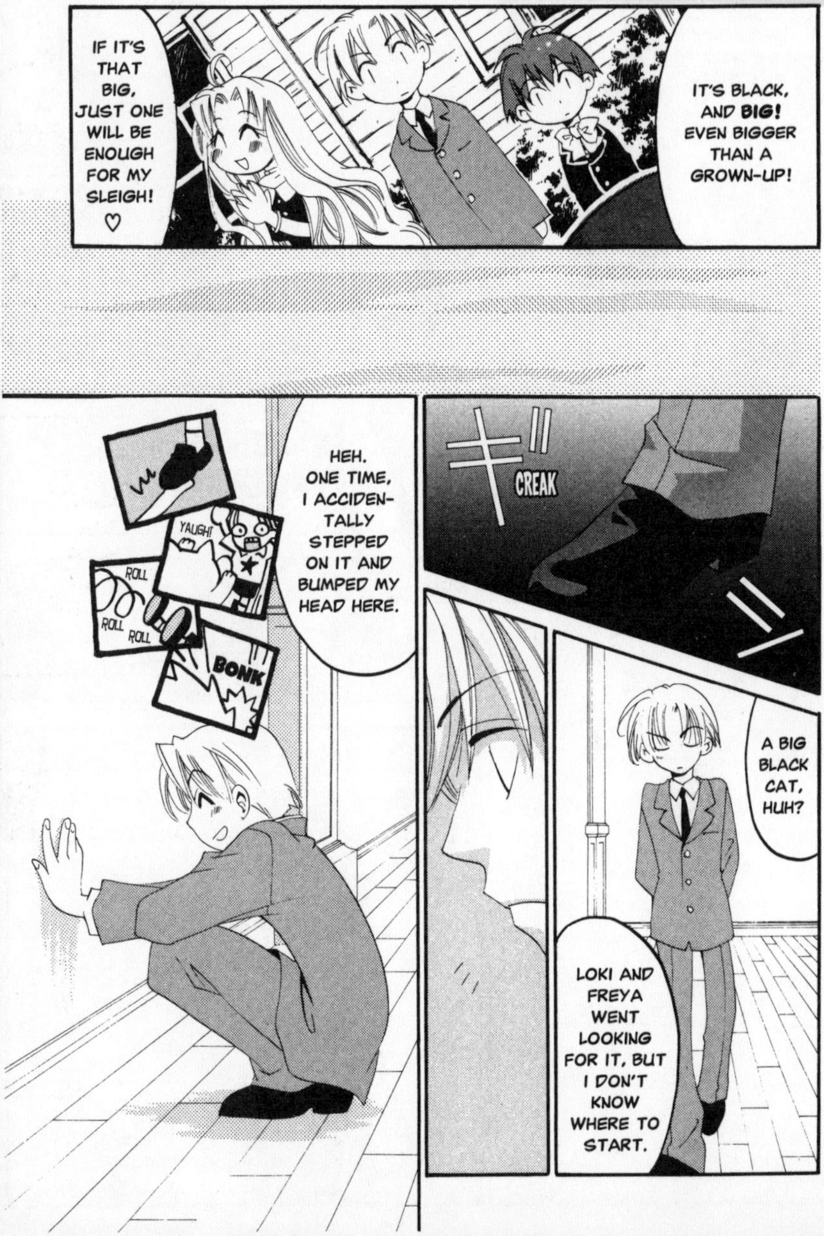
IT'S BLACK, AND **BIG!** EVEN BIGGER THAN A GROWN-UP!
IF IT'S THAT BIG, JUST ONE WILL BE ENOUGH FOR MY SLEIGH! ♡
CREAK
A BIG BLACK CAT, HUH?
LOKI AND FREYA WENT LOOKING FOR IT, BUT I DON'T KNOW WHERE TO START.
HEH. ONE TIME, I ACCIDENTALLY STEPPED ON IT AND BUMPED MY HEAD HERE.
YAUGH!
ROLL
ROLL
ROLL
BONK

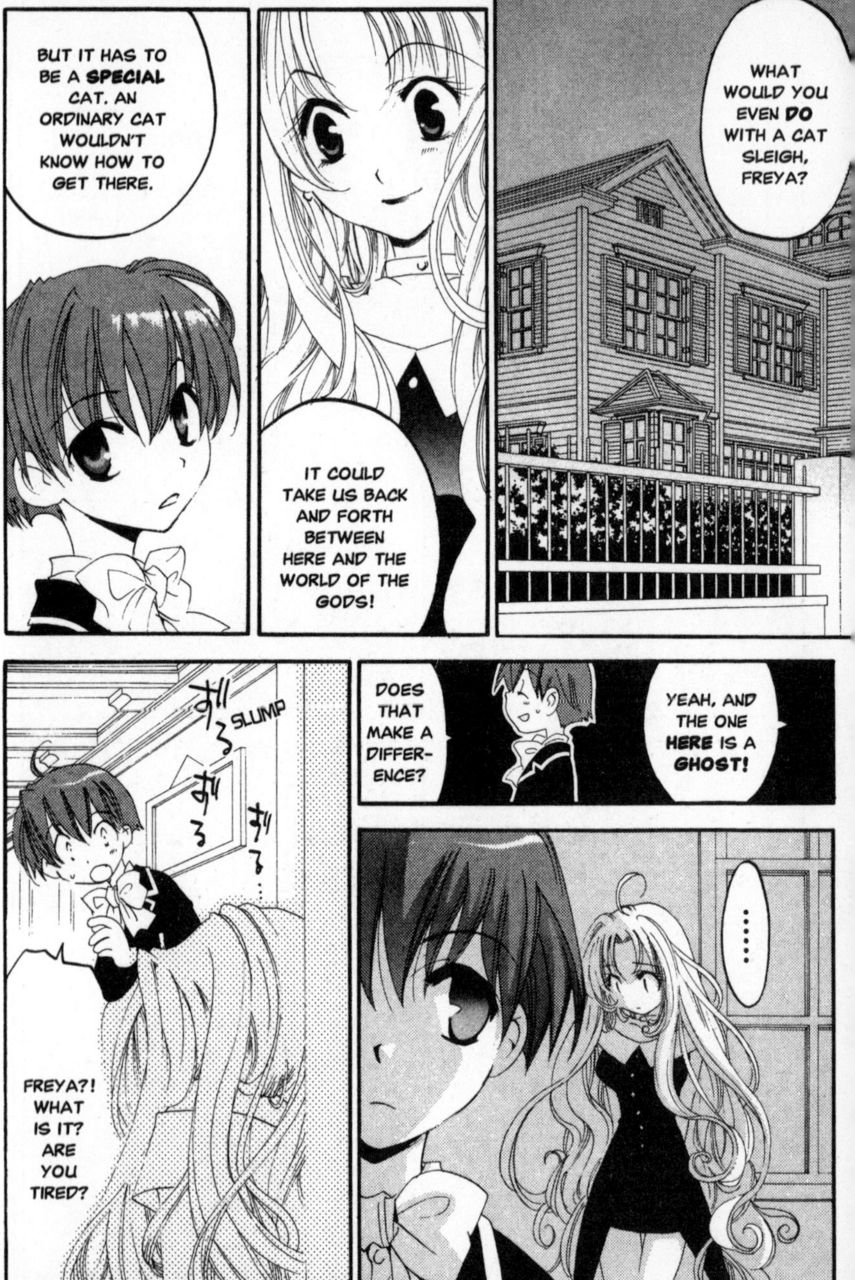
WHAT WOULD YOU EVEN DO WITH A CAT SLEIGH, FREYA?
IT COULD TAKE US BACK AND FORTH BETWEEN HERE AND THE WORLD OF THE GODS!
BUT IT HAS TO BE A SPECIAL CAT. AN ORDINARY CAT WOULDN'T KNOW HOW TO GET THERE.
YEAH, AND THE ONE HERE IS A GHOST!
DOES THAT MAKE A DIFFERENCE?
......
ずるずるずる…
SLUMP
FREYA?! WHAT IS IT? ARE YOU TIRED?

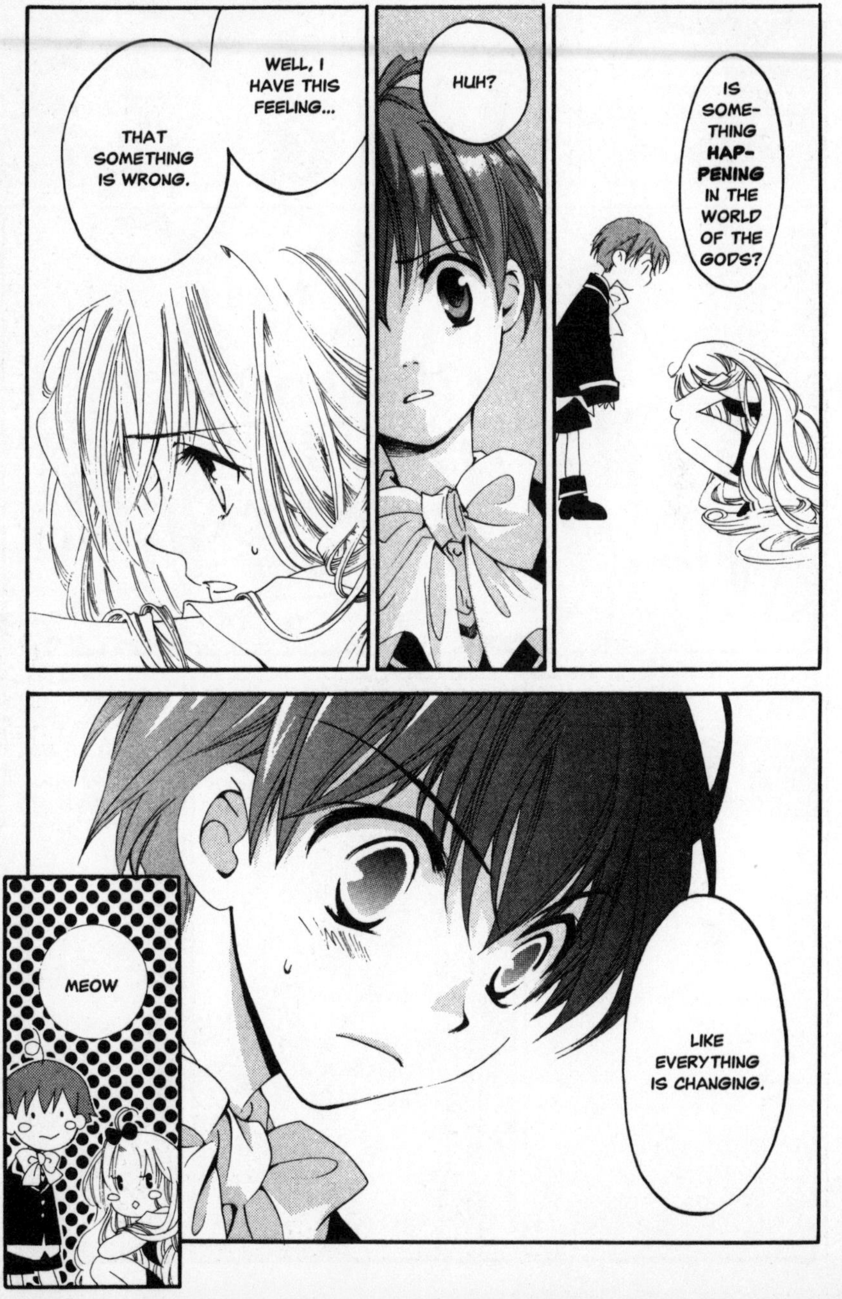
IS SOME-THING HAP-PENING IN THE WORLD OF THE GODS?
HUH?
WELL, I HAVE THIS FEELING...
THAT SOMETHING IS WRONG.
LIKE EVERYTHING IS CHANGING.
MEOW

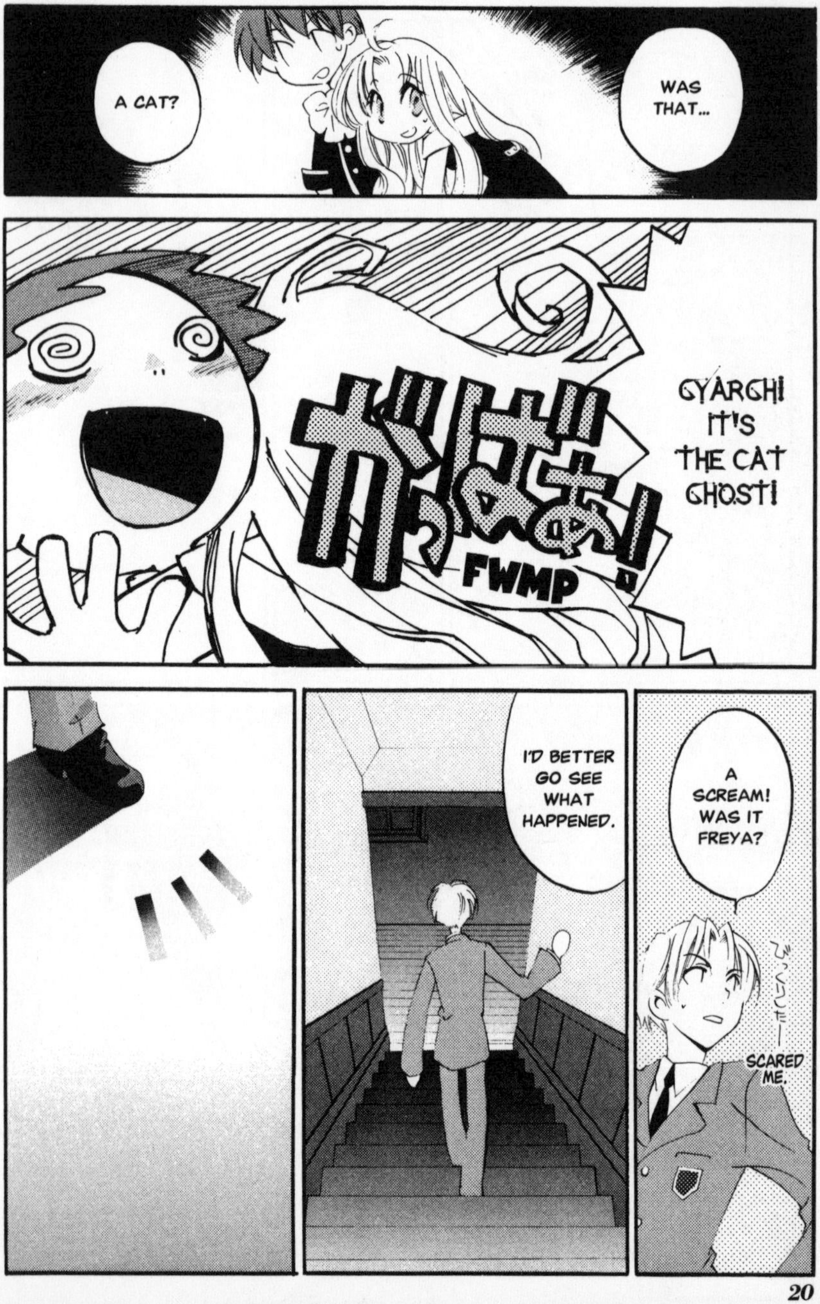
WAS THAT...
A CAT?
GYARGH! IT'S THE CAT GHOST!
FWMP
A SCREAM! WAS IT FREYA?
SCARED ME.
I'D BETTER GO SEE WHAT HAPPENED.

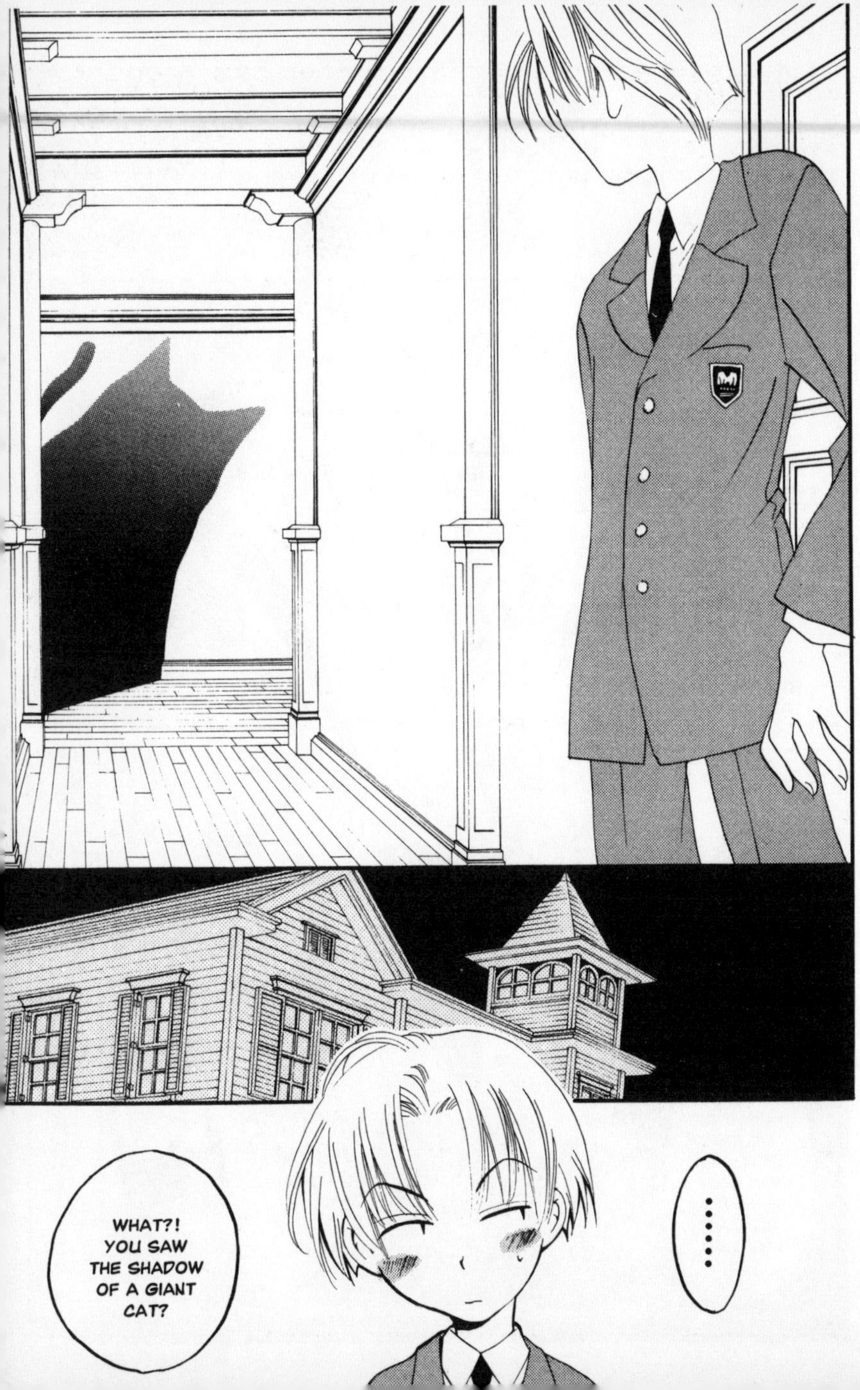
……
WHAT?! YOU SAW THE SHADOW OF A GIANT CAT?

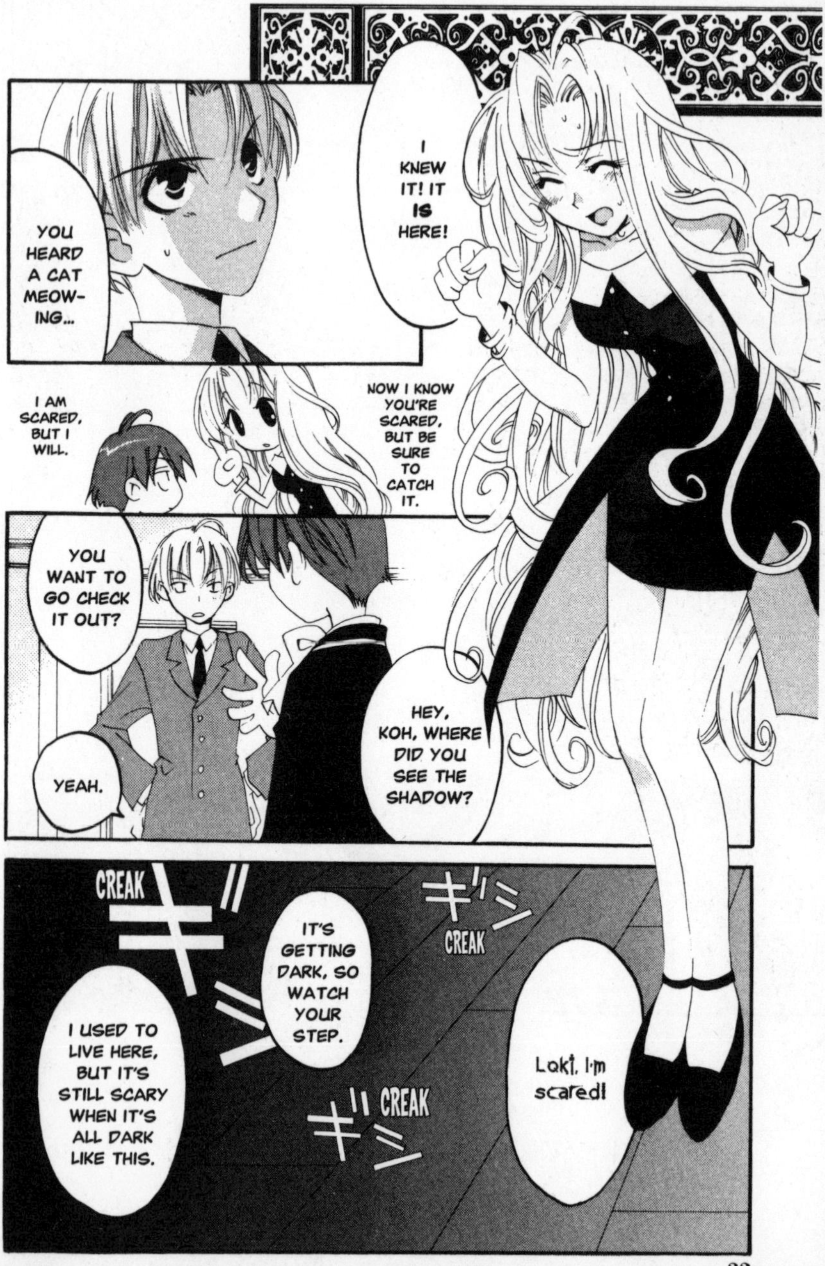
I KNEW IT! IT IS HERE!
YOU HEARD A CAT MEOWING...
NOW I KNOW YOU'RE SCARED, BUT BE SURE TO CATCH IT.
I AM SCARED, BUT I WILL.
HEY, KOH, WHERE DID YOU SEE THE SHADOW?
YOU WANT TO GO CHECK IT OUT?
YEAH.
Loki, I'm scared!
CREAK
CREAK
IT'S GETTING DARK, SO WATCH YOUR STEP.
CREAK
I USED TO LIVE HERE, BUT IT'S STILL SCARY WHEN IT'S ALL DARK LIKE THIS.

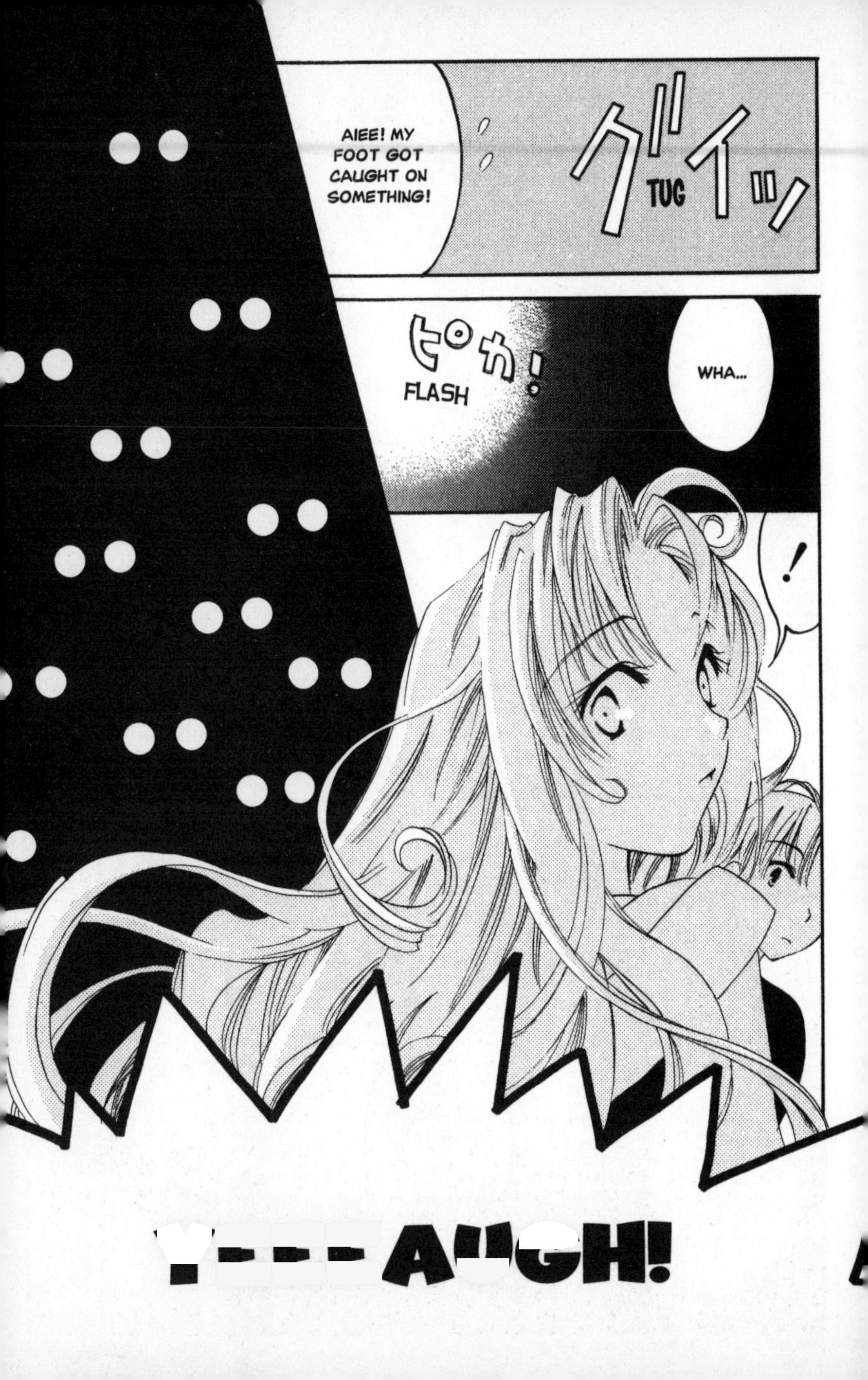
グイッ
TUG
AIEE! MY FOOT GOT CAUGHT ON SOMETHING!
WHA...
ピカ!
FLASH
!

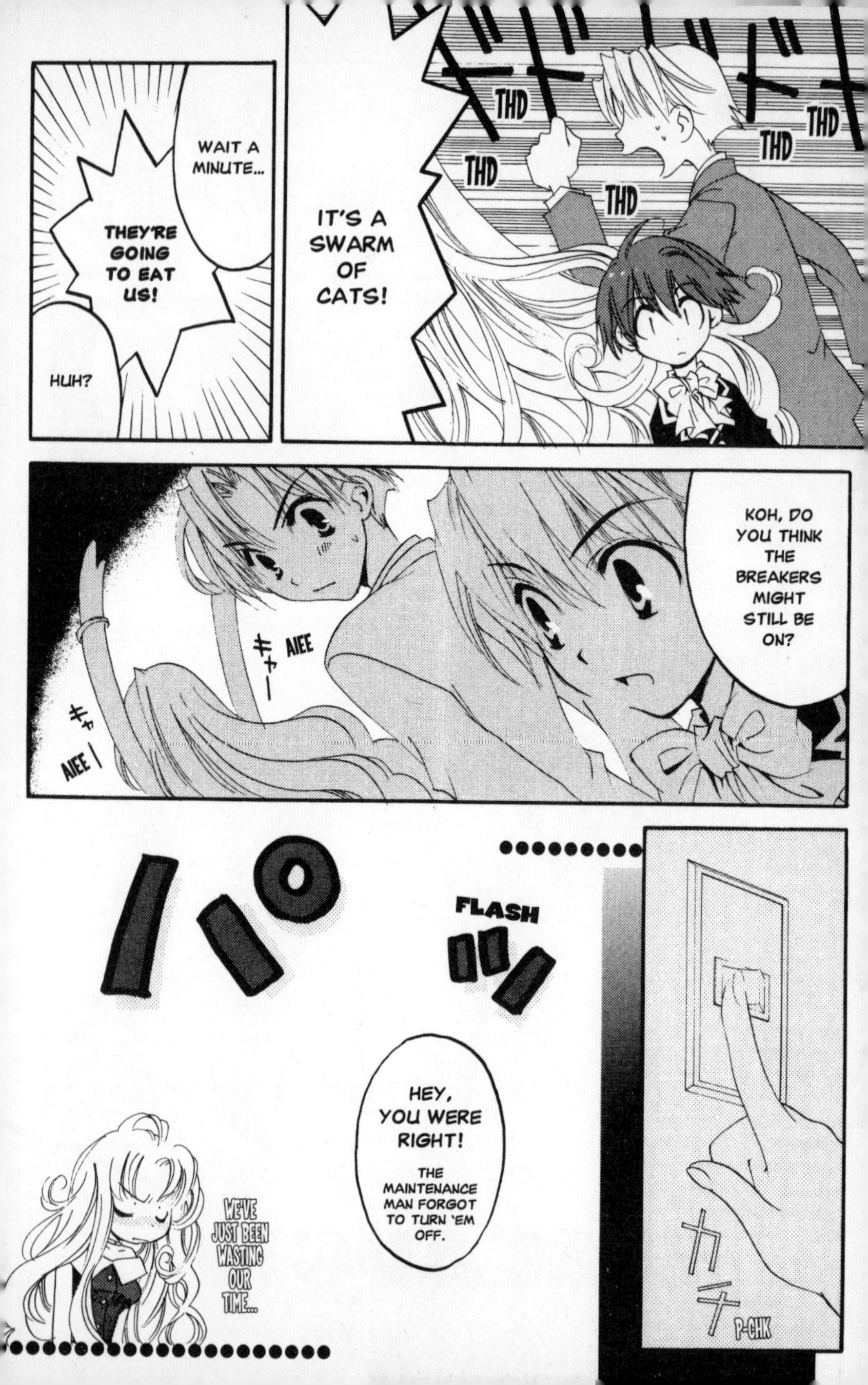
THD
THD
THD
THD
THD
IT'S A SWARM OF CATS!
WAIT A MINUTE...
THEY'RE GOING TO EAT US!
HUH?
KOH, DO YOU THINK THE BREAKERS MIGHT STILL BE ON?
AIEE
AIEE
P-CHK
FLASH
HEY, YOU WERE RIGHT!
THE MAINTENANCE MAN FORGOT TO TURN 'EM OFF.
WE'VE JUST BEEN WASTING OUR TIME...

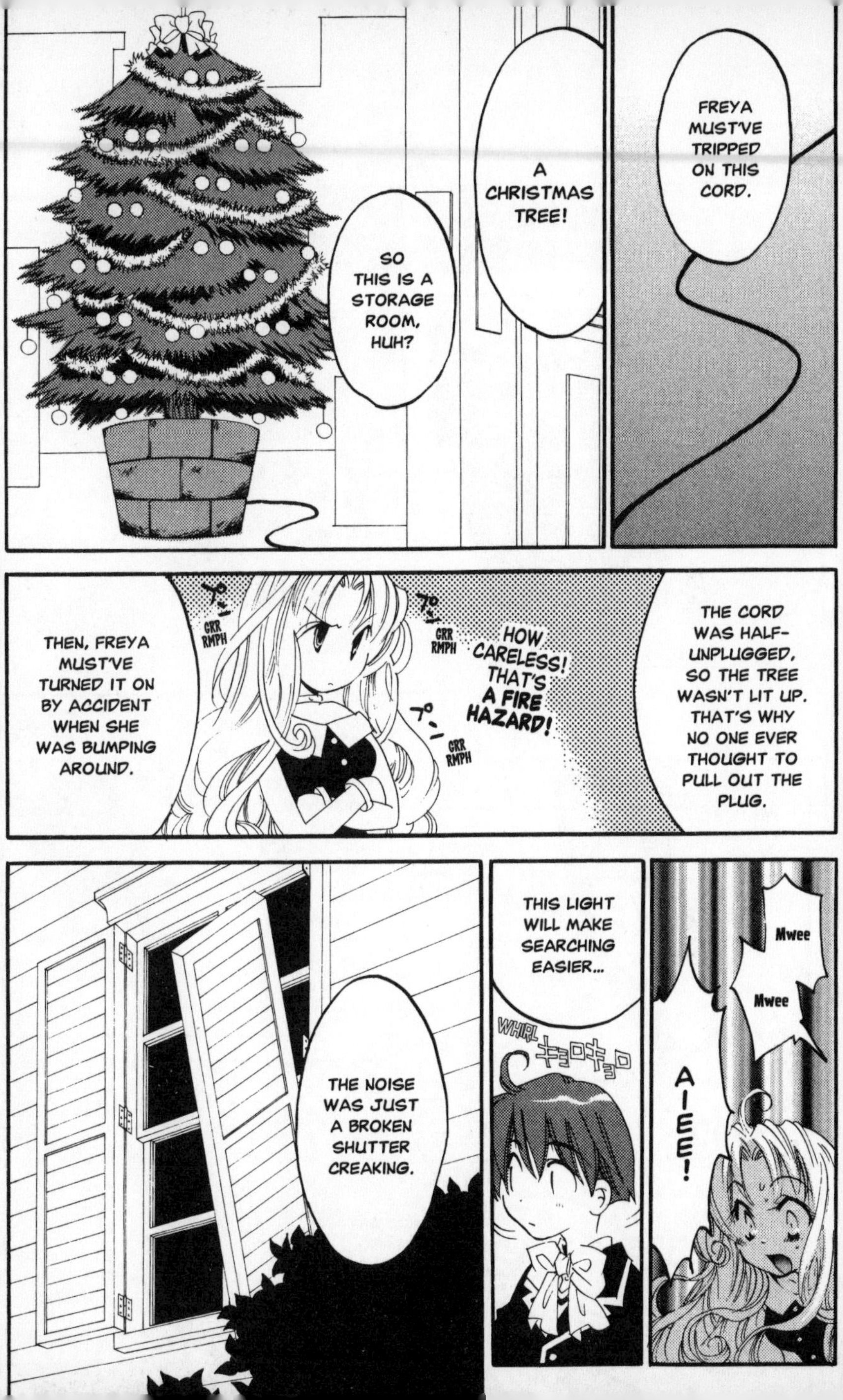
FREYA MUST'VE TRIPPED ON THIS CORD.
A CHRISTMAS TREE!
SO THIS IS A STORAGE ROOM, HUH?
THE CORD WAS HALF-UNPLUGGED, SO THE TREE WASN'T LIT UP. THAT'S WHY NO ONE EVER THOUGHT TO PULL OUT THE PLUG.
GRR RMPH
HOW CARELESS! THAT'S A FIRE HAZARD!
GRR RMPH
GRR RMPH
THEN, FREYA MUST'VE TURNED IT ON BY ACCIDENT WHEN SHE WAS BUMPING AROUND.
Mwee
Mwee
AIEE!
THIS LIGHT WILL MAKE SEARCHING EASIER...
WHIRL
THE NOISE WAS JUST A BROKEN SHUTTER CREAKING.

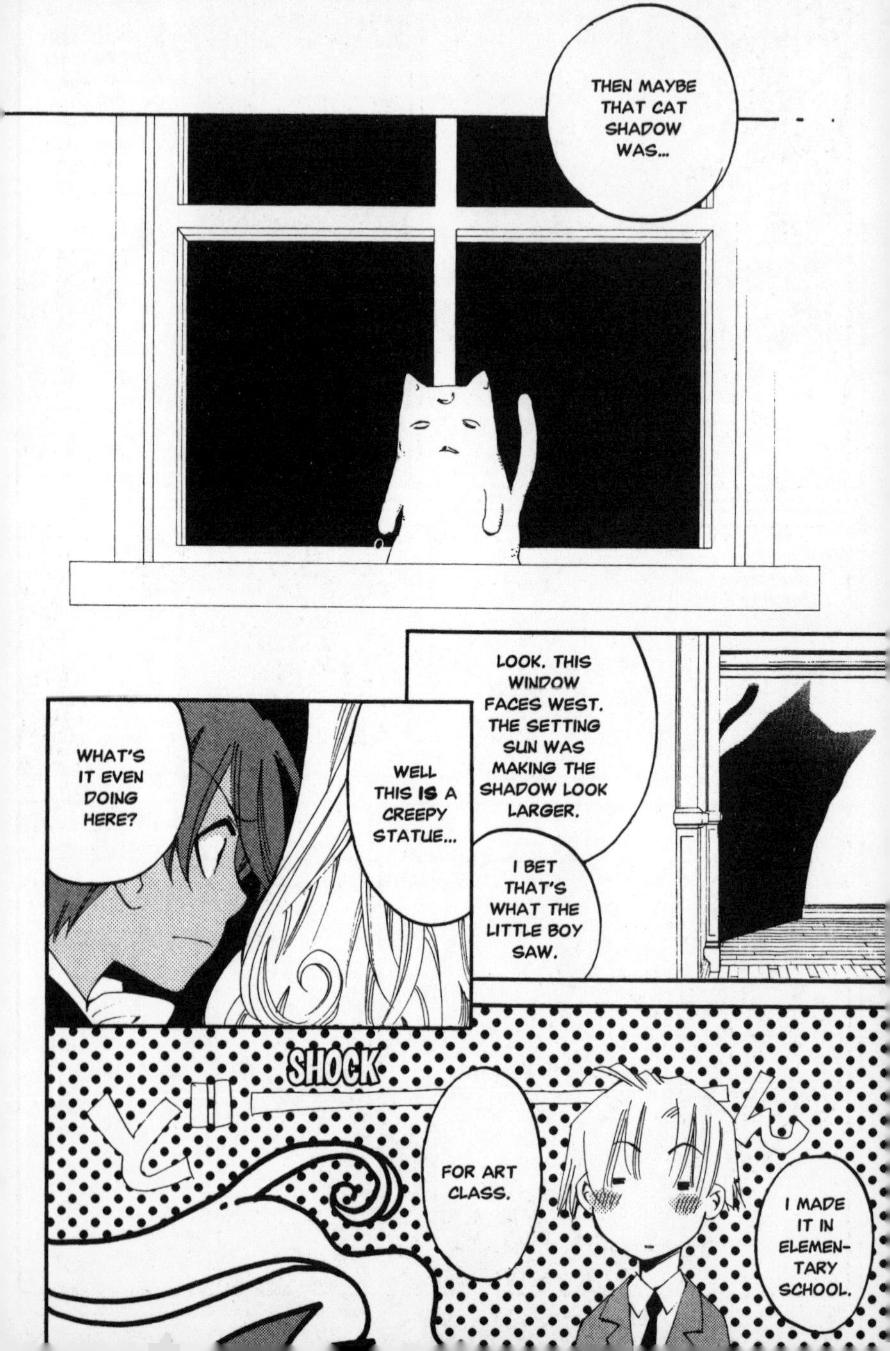
THEN MAYBE THAT CAT SHADOW WAS...
LOOK. THIS WINDOW FACES WEST. THE SETTING SUN WAS MAKING THE SHADOW LOOK LARGER.
I BET THAT'S WHAT THE LITTLE BOY SAW.
WELL THIS **IS** A CREEPY STATUE...
WHAT'S IT EVEN DOING HERE?
SHOCK
I MADE IT IN ELEMENTARY SCHOOL.
FOR ART CLASS.

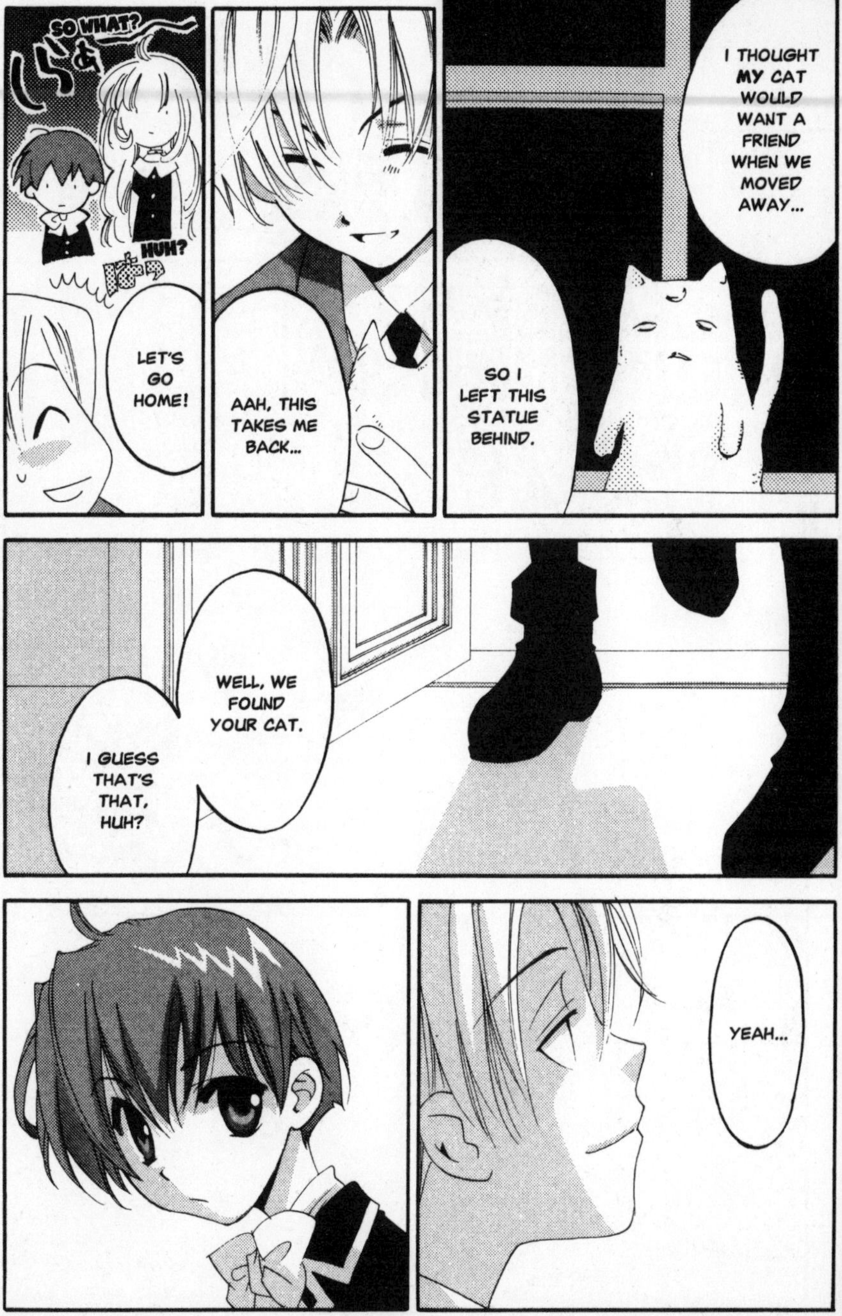
I THOUGHT MY CAT WOULD WANT A FRIEND WHEN WE MOVED AWAY...
SO I LEFT THIS STATUE BEHIND.
AAH, THIS TAKES ME BACK...
SO WHAT?
HUH?
LET'S GO HOME!
WELL, WE FOUND YOUR CAT.
I GUESS THAT'S THAT, HUH?
YEAH...

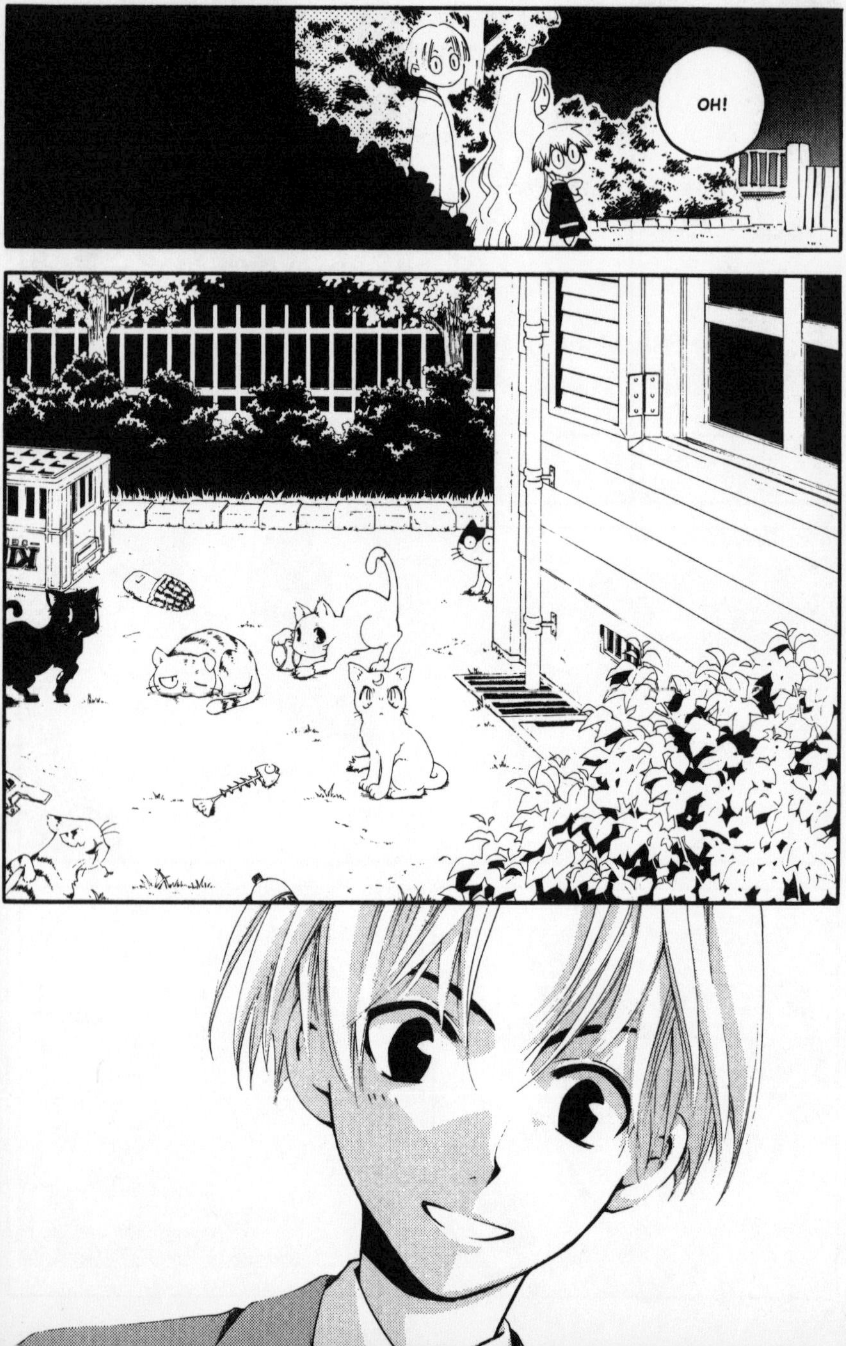
OH!

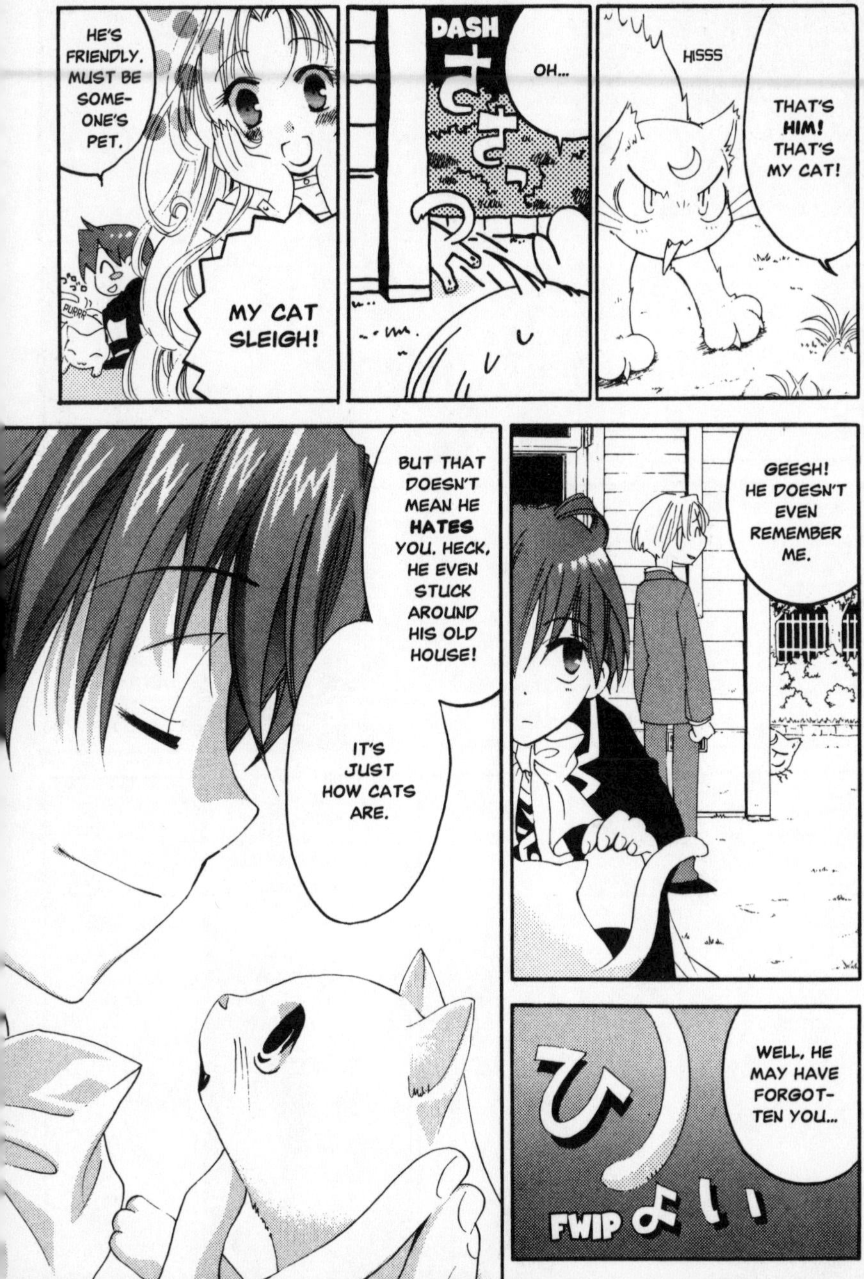
THAT'S **HIM!** THAT'S MY CAT!
HISSS
OH...
DASH
ささ
HE'S FRIENDLY. MUST BE SOME-ONE'S PET.
MY CAT SLEIGH!
PURRR
GEESH! HE DOESN'T EVEN REMEMBER ME.
WELL, HE MAY HAVE FORGOT-TEN YOU...
ひょい
FWIP
BUT THAT DOESN'T MEAN HE **HATES** YOU. HECK, HE EVEN STUCK AROUND HIS OLD HOUSE!
IT'S JUST HOW CATS ARE.

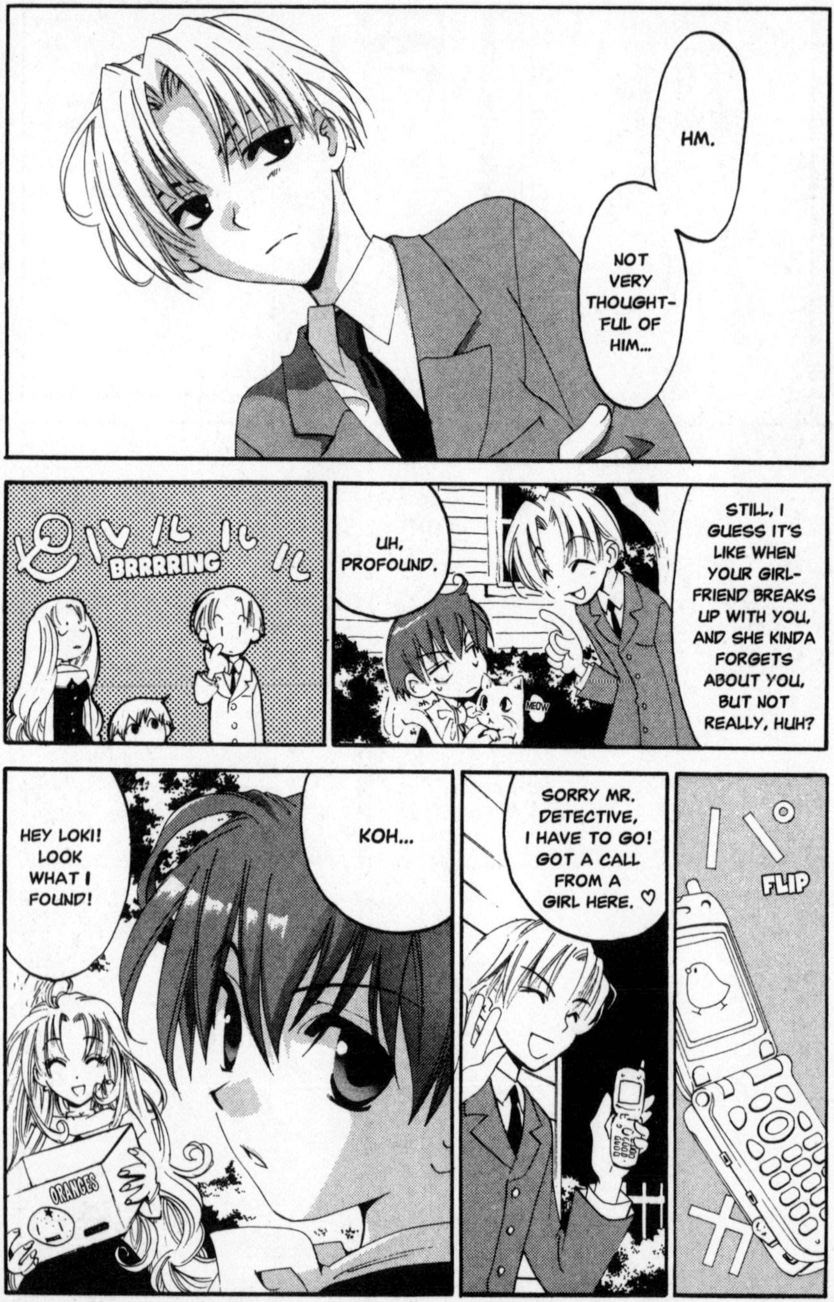
HM.
NOT VERY THOUGHT-FUL OF HIM...
STILL, I GUESS IT'S LIKE WHEN YOUR GIRL-FRIEND BREAKS UP WITH YOU, AND SHE KINDA FORGETS ABOUT YOU, BUT NOT REALLY, HUH?
UH, PROFOUND.
MEOW
BRRRRING
FLIP
SORRY MR. DETECTIVE, I HAVE TO GO! GOT A CALL FROM A GIRL HERE. ♡
KOH...
HEY LOKI! LOOK WHAT I FOUND!
ORANGES

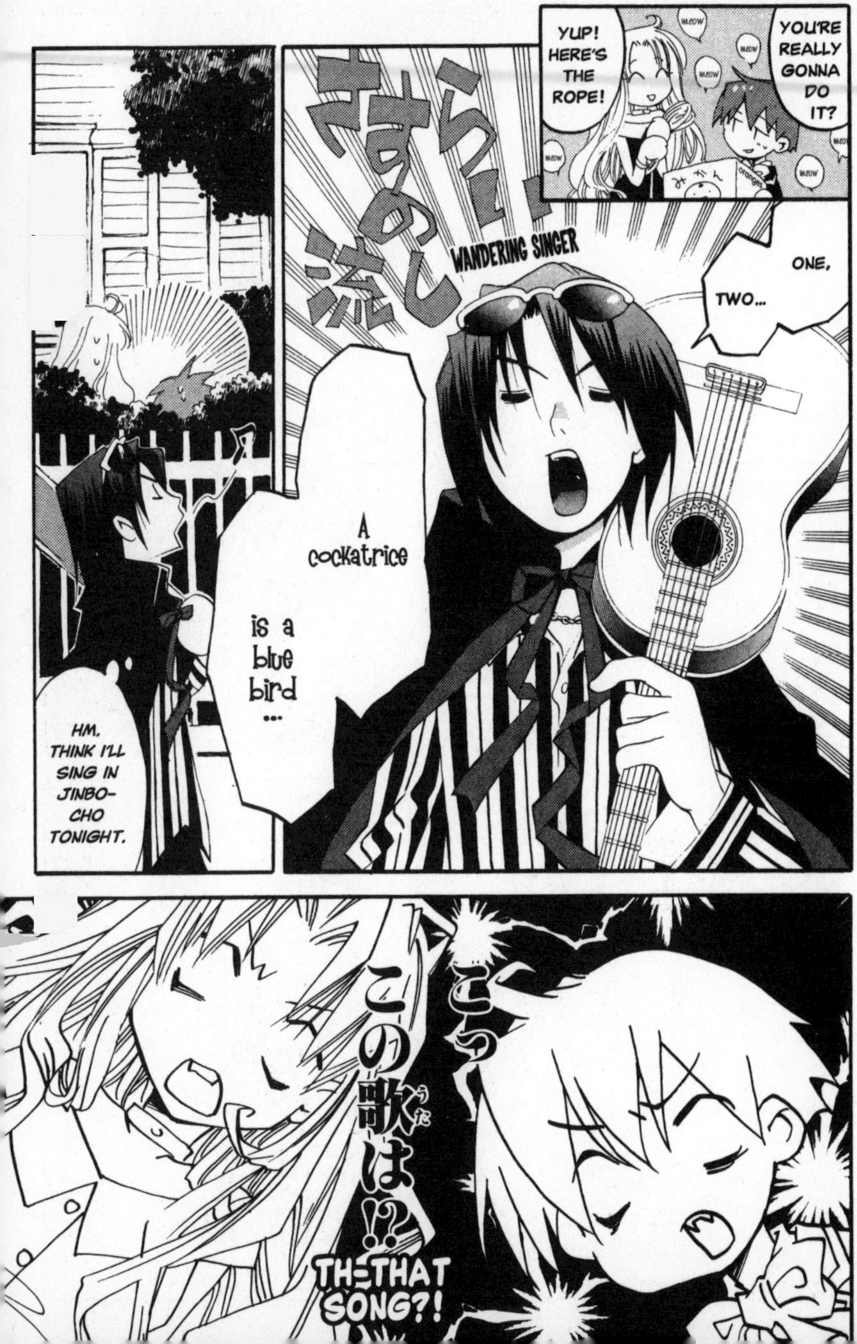
YOU'RE REALLY GONNA DO IT?
YUP! HERE'S THE ROPE!
meow
みかん
oranges
さすらいの流し
WANDERING SINGER
ONE, TWO...
A cockatrice is a blue bird ...
HM. THINK I'LL SING IN JINBO-CHO TONIGHT.
こ この歌は!?
TH-THAT SONG?!

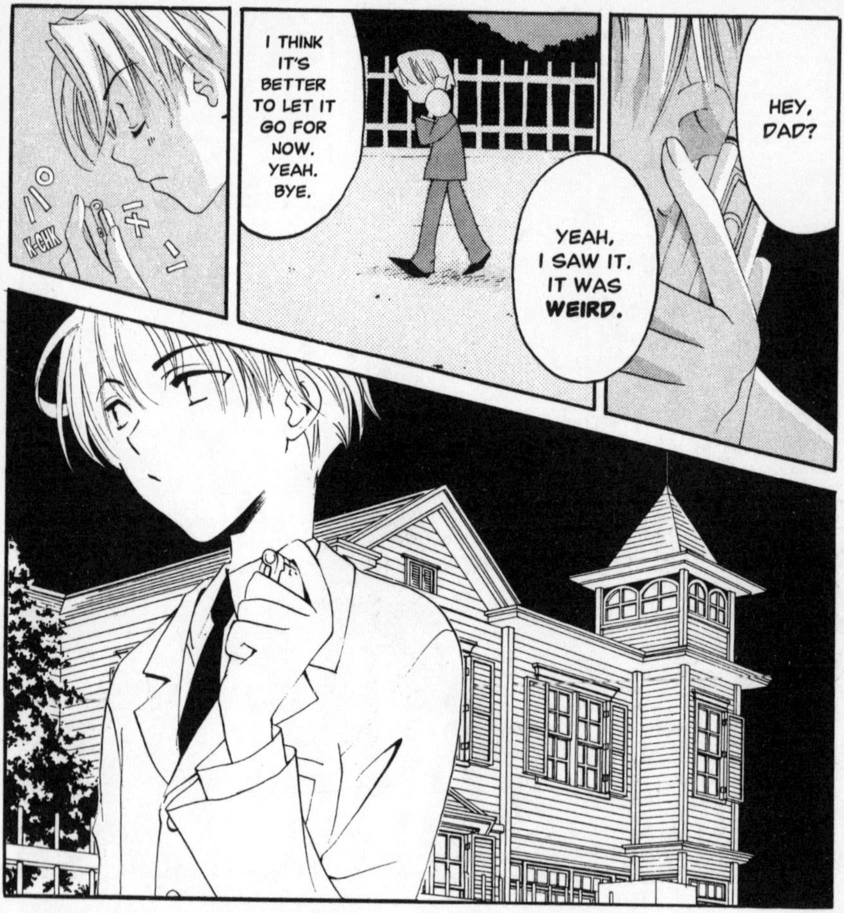
HEY, DAD?
YEAH, I SAW IT. IT WAS WEIRD.
I THINK IT'S BETTER TO LET IT GO FOR NOW. YEAH. BYE.
K-CHK

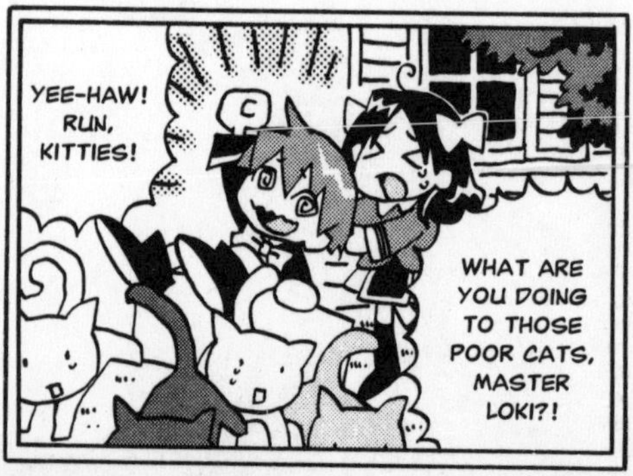
WHAT ARE YOU DOING TO THOSE POOR CATS, MASTER LOKI?!
YEE-HAW! RUN, KITTIES!

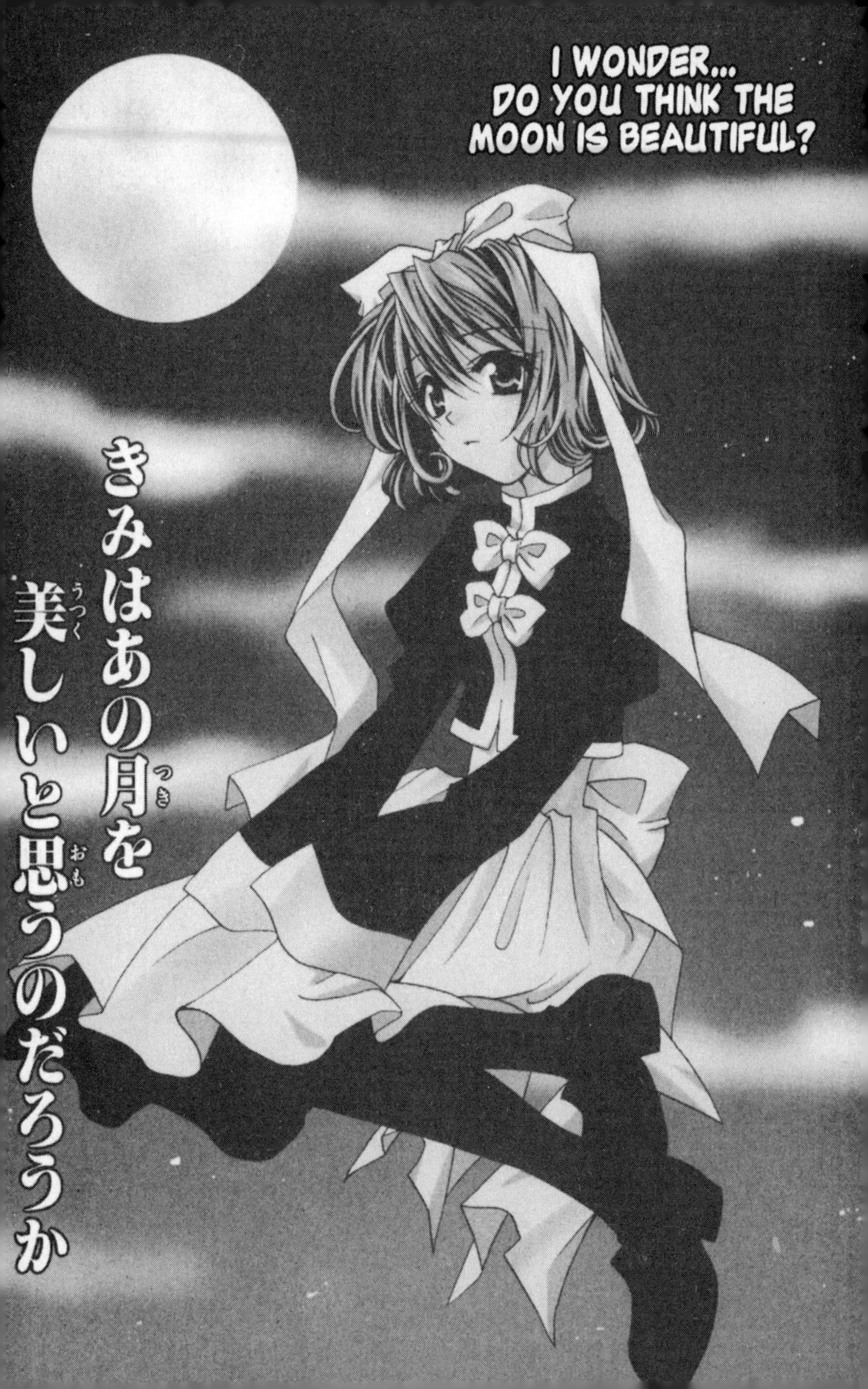
I WONDER...
DO YOU THINK THE
MOON IS BEAUTIFUL?
きみはあの月を
美しいと思うのだろうか

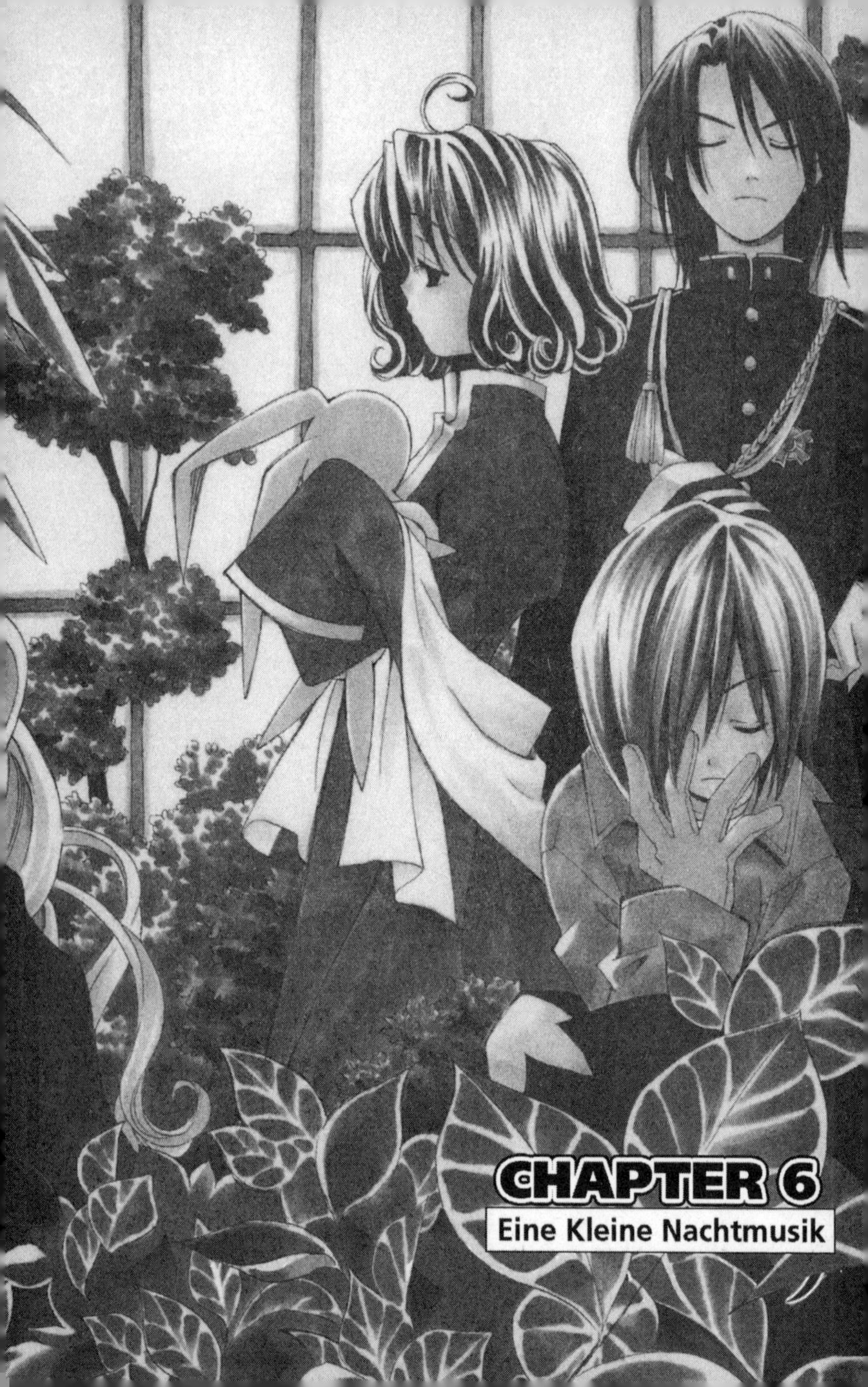
CHAPTER 6
Eine Kleine Nachtmusik

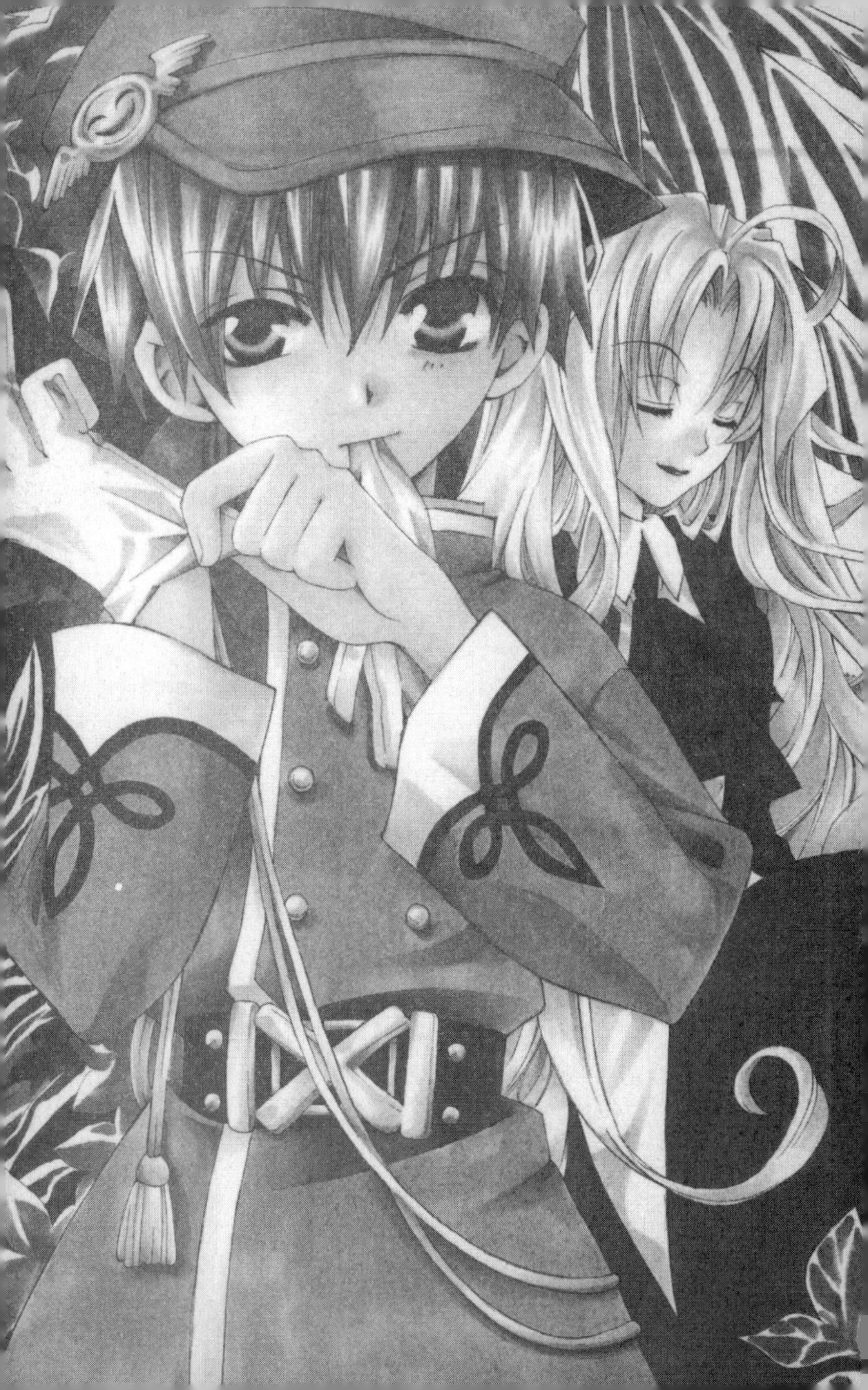

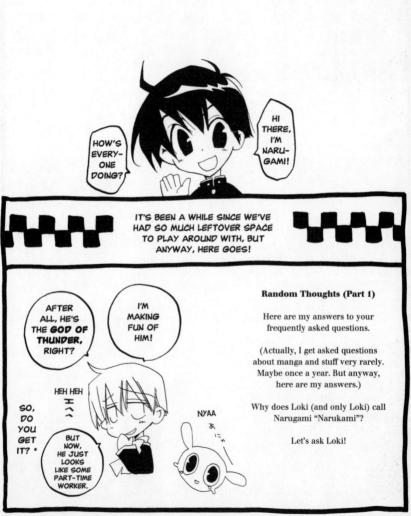

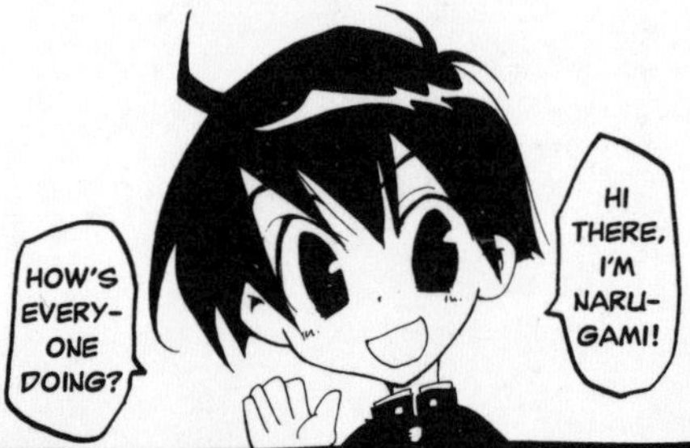
HI THERE, I'M NARU-GAMI!
HOW'S EVERY-ONE DOING?

IT'S BEEN A WHILE SINCE WE'VE HAD SO MUCH LEFTOVER SPACE TO PLAY AROUND WITH, BUT ANYWAY, HERE GOES!

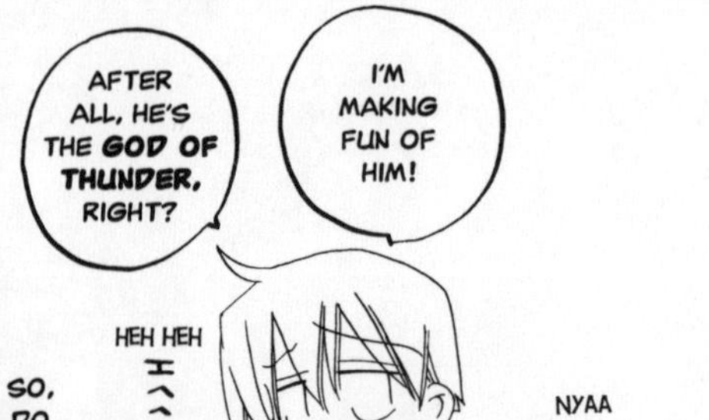
I'M MAKING FUN OF HIM!
AFTER ALL, HE'S THE **GOD OF THUNDER,** RIGHT?
NYAA
HEH HEH
BUT NOW, HE JUST LOOKS LIKE SOME PART-TIME WORKER.
SO, DO YOU GET IT? *

Random Thoughts (Part 1)

Here are my answers to your frequently asked questions.

(Actually, I get asked questions about manga and stuff very rarely. Maybe once a year. But anyway, here are my answers.)

Why does Loki (and only Loki) call Narugami "Narukami"?

Let's ask Loki!

PEOPLE ASK ME FOR NARU'S FIRST NAME A LOT, TOO. MAYBE HE'S THE MOST MYSTERIOUS CHARACTER OF ALL!

* Please see notes.

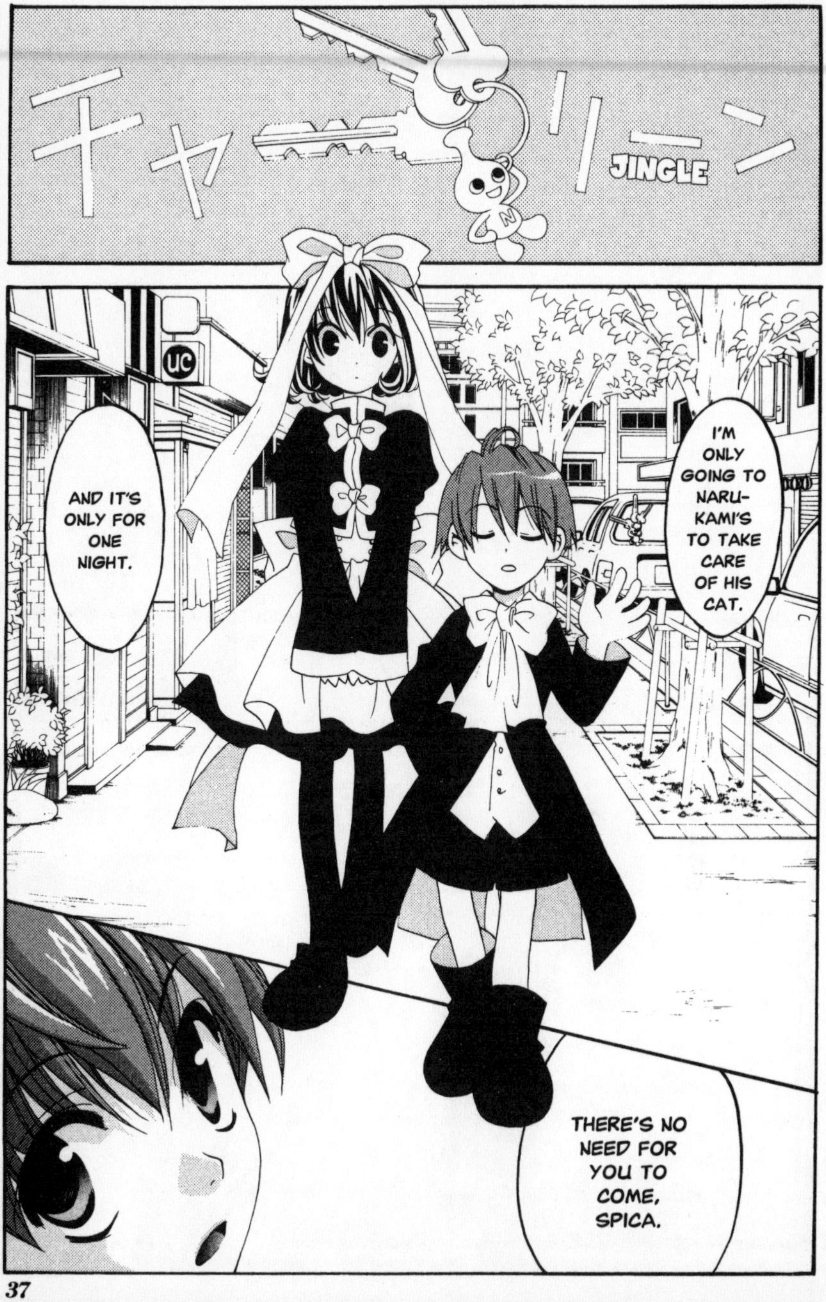

チャリーン
JINGLE
I'M ONLY GOING TO NARU-KAMI'S TO TAKE CARE OF HIS CAT.
AND IT'S ONLY FOR ONE NIGHT.
THERE'S NO NEED FOR YOU TO COME, SPICA.

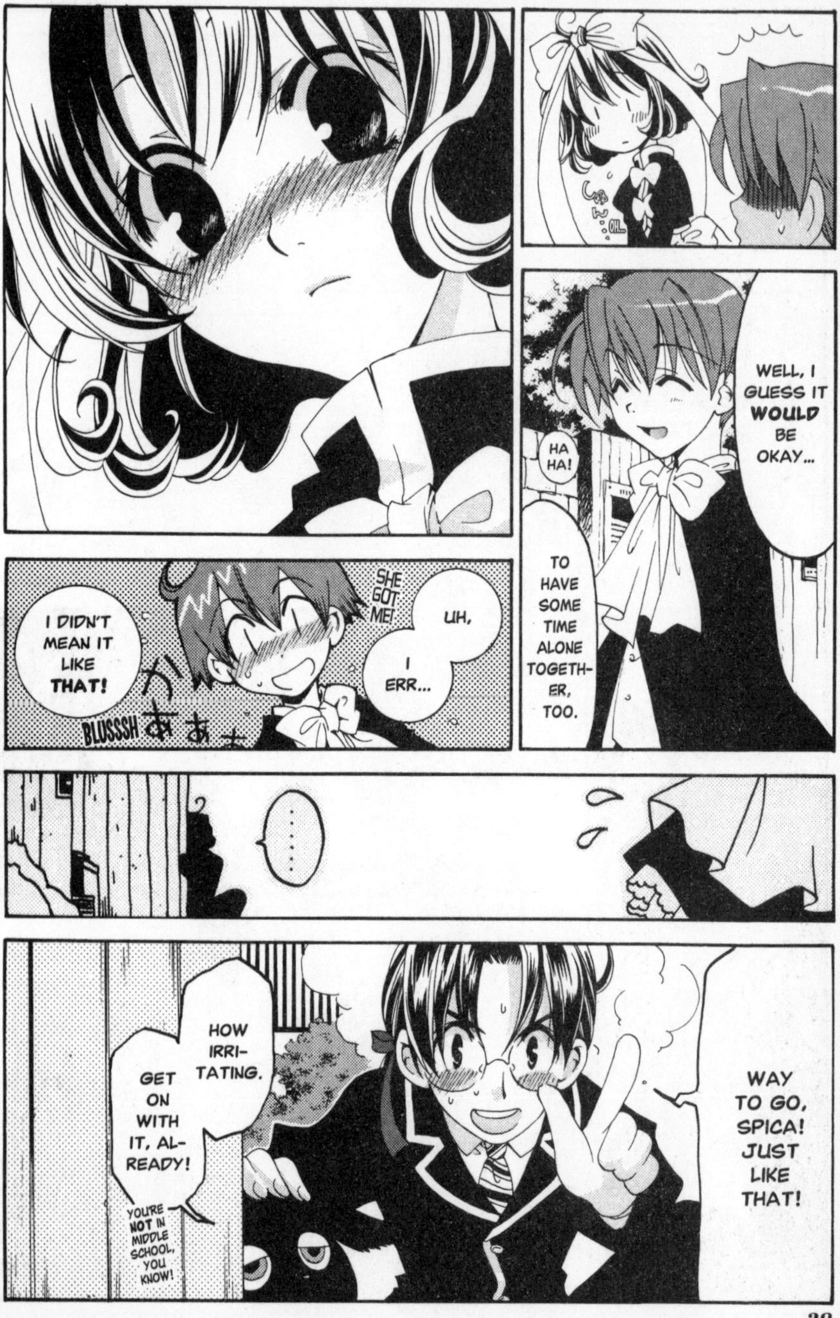
OH...
HA HA!
WELL, I GUESS IT **WOULD** BE OKAY...
TO HAVE SOME TIME ALONE TOGETH-ER, TOO.
SHE GOT ME!
UH, I ERR...
I DIDN'T MEAN IT LIKE **THAT!**
BLUSSSH
......
WAY TO GO, SPICA! JUST LIKE THAT!
HOW IRRI-TATING.
GET ON WITH IT, AL-READY!
YOU'RE **NOT** IN MIDDLE SCHOOL, YOU KNOW!

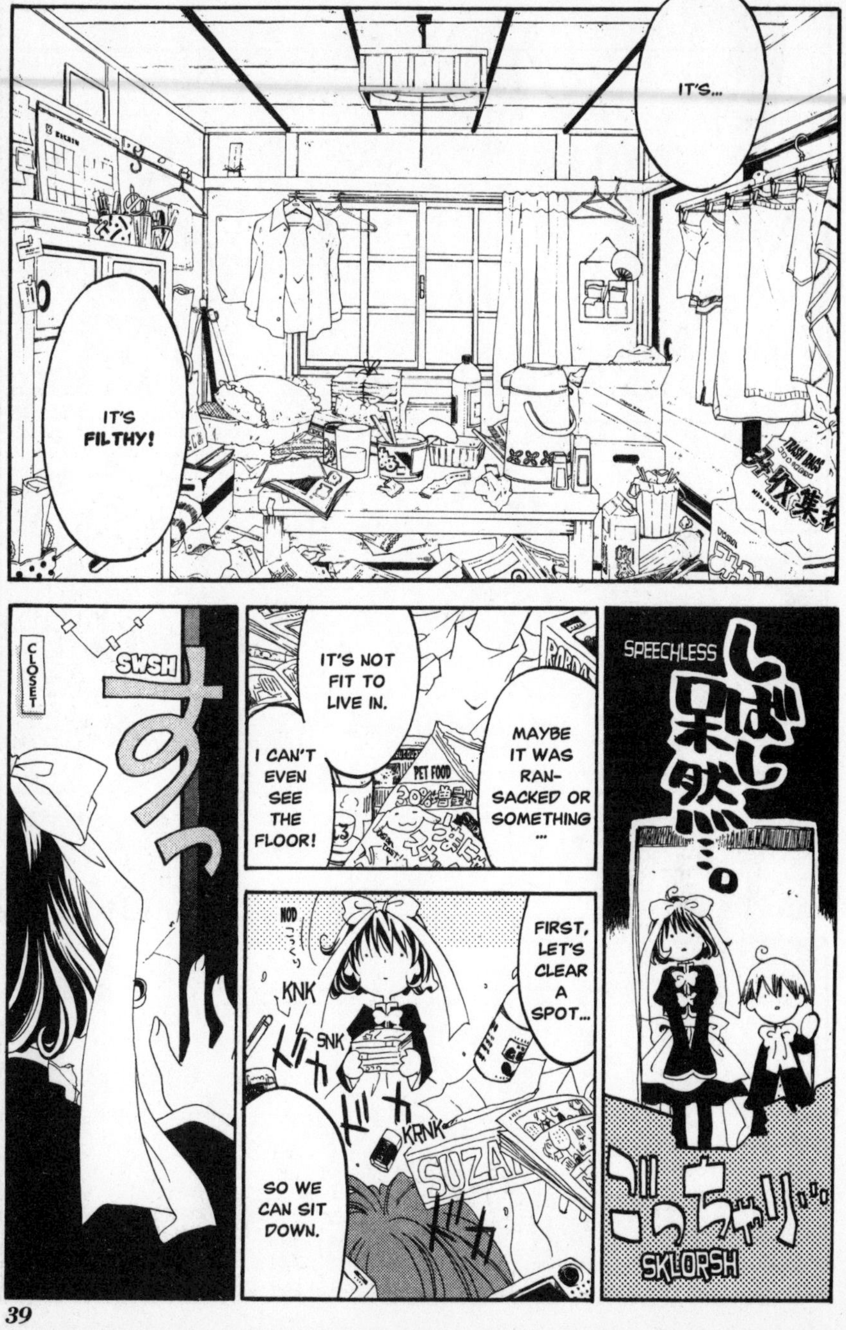
IT'S...
IT'S FILTHY!
TRASH BAGS
SPEECHLESS
SKLORSH
MAYBE IT WAS RAN-SACKED OR SOMETHING...
IT'S NOT FIT TO LIVE IN.
I CAN'T EVEN SEE THE FLOOR!
PET FOOD
FIRST, LET'S CLEAR A SPOT...
NOD
KNK
SNK
KRNK
SO WE CAN SIT DOWN.
CLOSET
SWSH

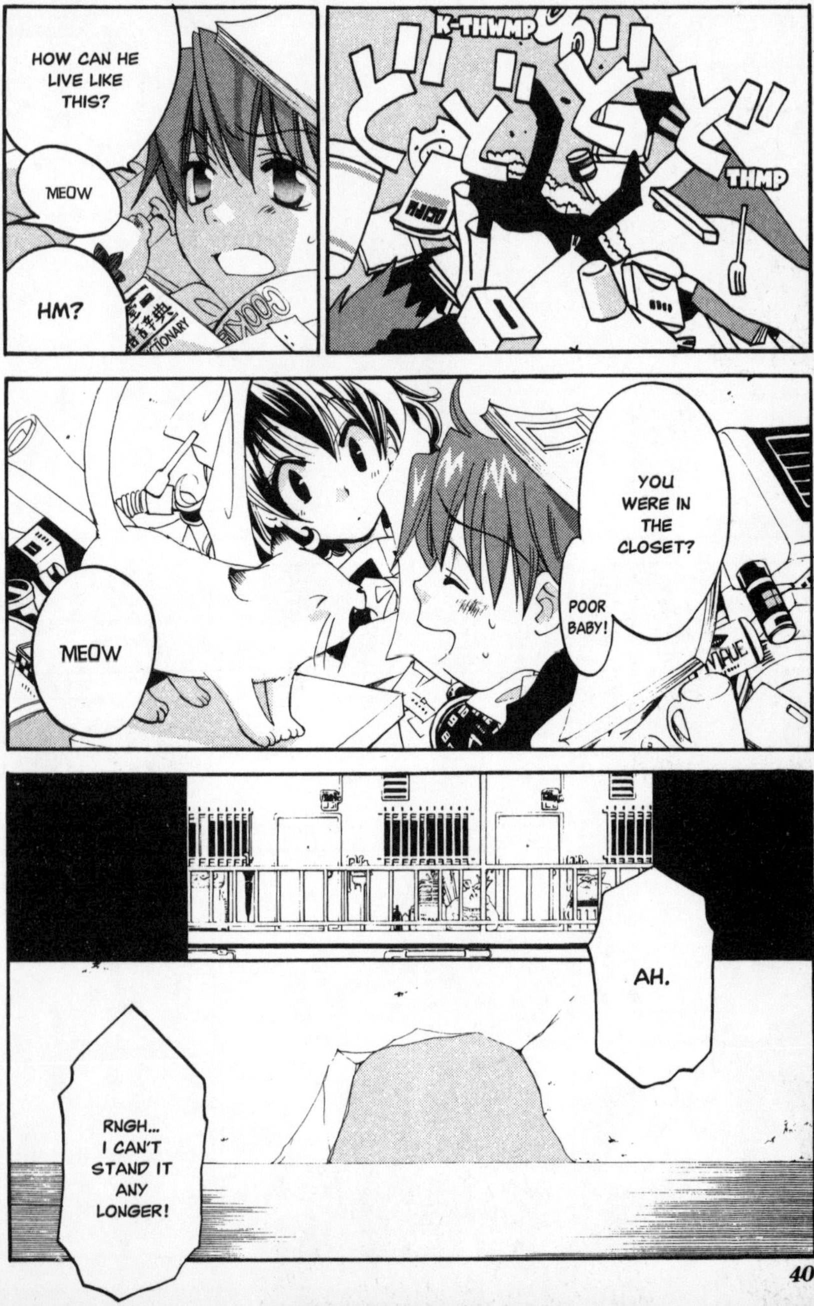
K-THWMP
THMP
HOW CAN HE LIVE LIKE THIS?
MEOW
HM?
YOU WERE IN THE CLOSET?
POOR BABY!
MEOW
AH.
RNGH... I CAN'T STAND IT ANY LONGER!

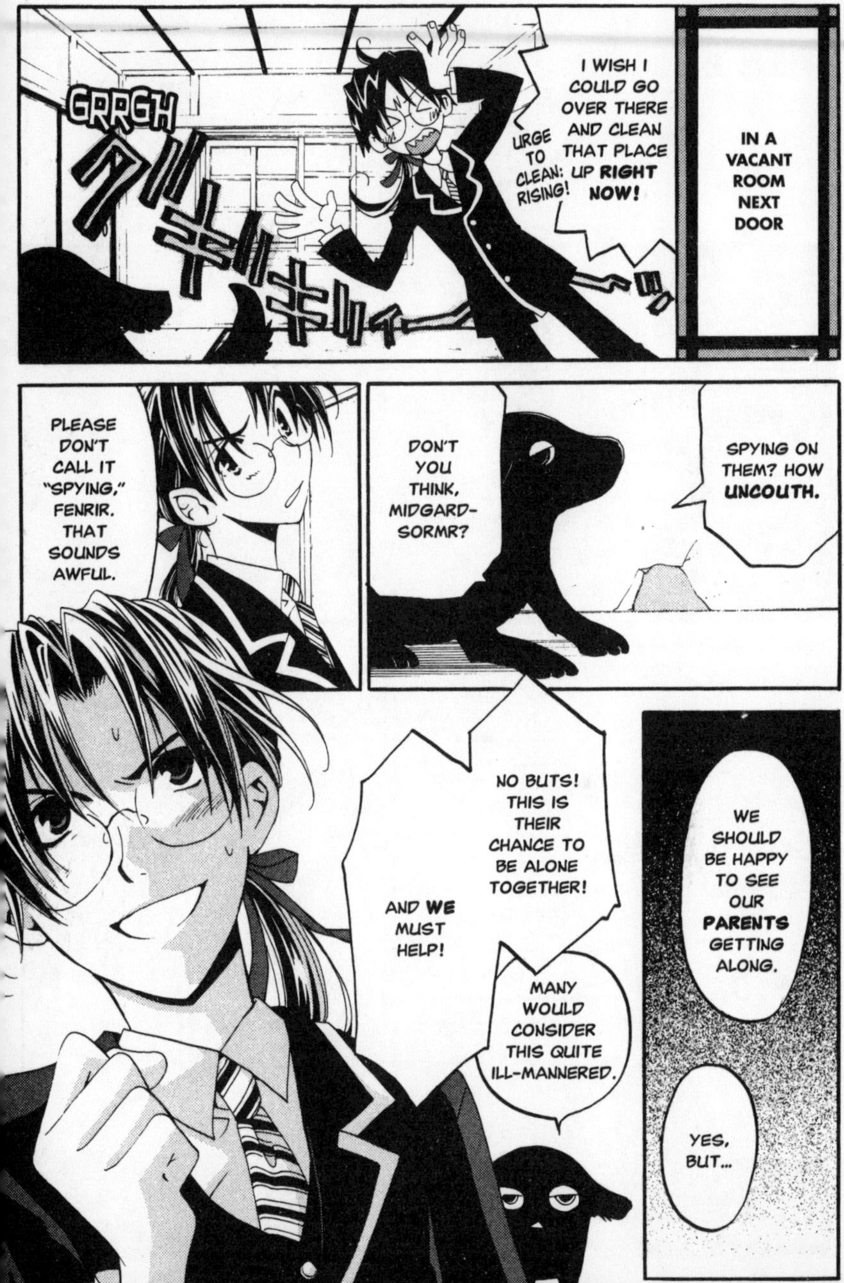
IN A VACANT ROOM NEXT DOOR
I WISH I COULD GO OVER THERE AND CLEAN THAT PLACE UP RIGHT NOW!
URGE TO CLEAN: RISING!
GRRGH
SPYING ON THEM? HOW UNCOUTH.
DON'T YOU THINK, MIDGARD-SORMR?
PLEASE DON'T CALL IT "SPYING," FENRIR. THAT SOUNDS AWFUL.
WE SHOULD BE HAPPY TO SEE OUR PARENTS GETTING ALONG.
YES, BUT...
NO BUTS! THIS IS THEIR CHANCE TO BE ALONE TOGETHER!
AND WE MUST HELP!
MANY WOULD CONSIDER THIS QUITE ILL-MANNERED.

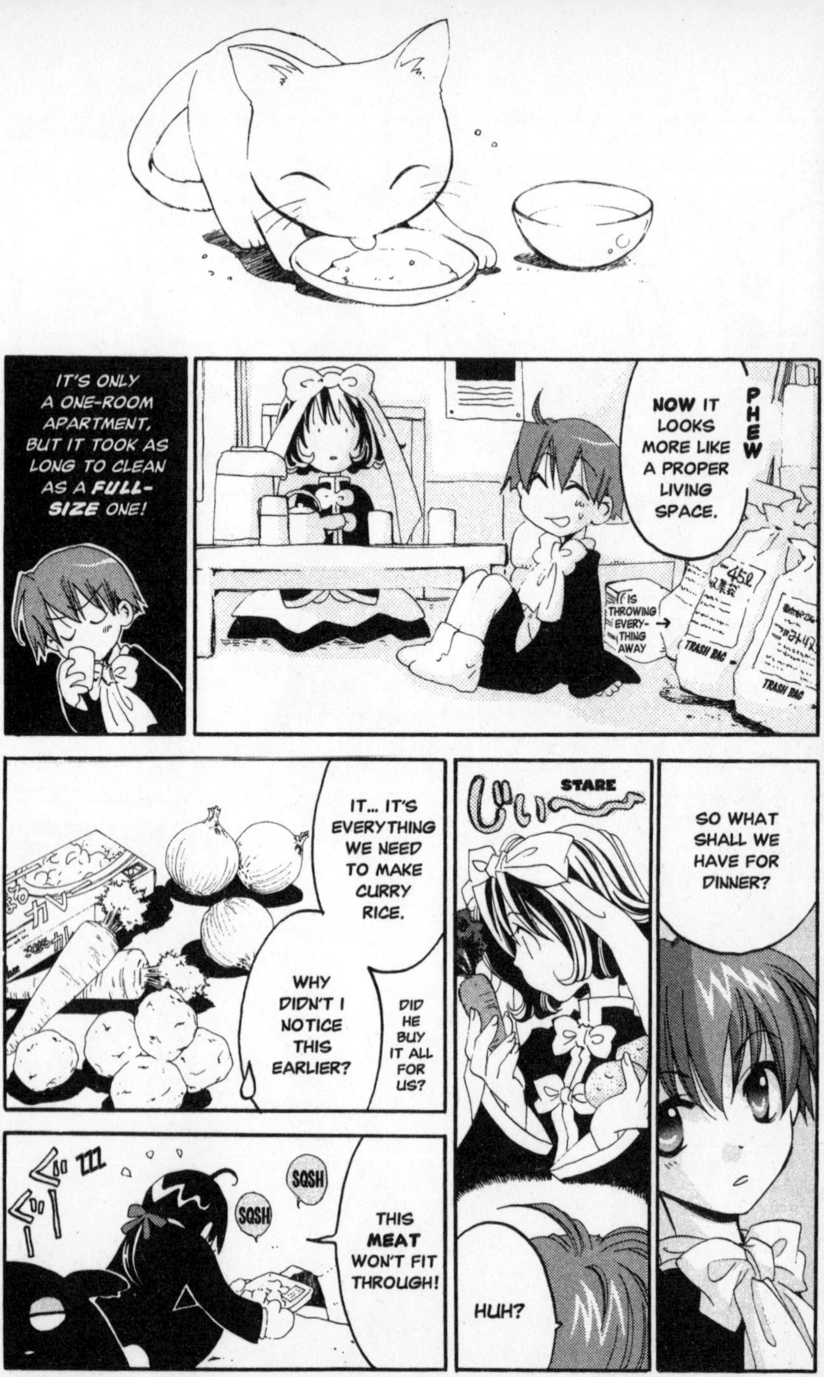
PHEW
NOW IT LOOKS MORE LIKE A PROPER LIVING SPACE.
IS THROWING EVERYTHING AWAY
TRASH BAG
TRASH BAG
IT'S ONLY A ONE-ROOM APARTMENT, BUT IT TOOK AS LONG TO CLEAN AS A FULL-SIZE ONE!
SO WHAT SHALL WE HAVE FOR DINNER?
HUH?
STARE
IT... IT'S EVERYTHING WE NEED TO MAKE CURRY RICE.
DID HE BUY IT ALL FOR US?
WHY DIDN'T I NOTICE THIS EARLIER?
THIS MEAT WON'T FIT THROUGH!
SQSH
SQSH
ZZZ

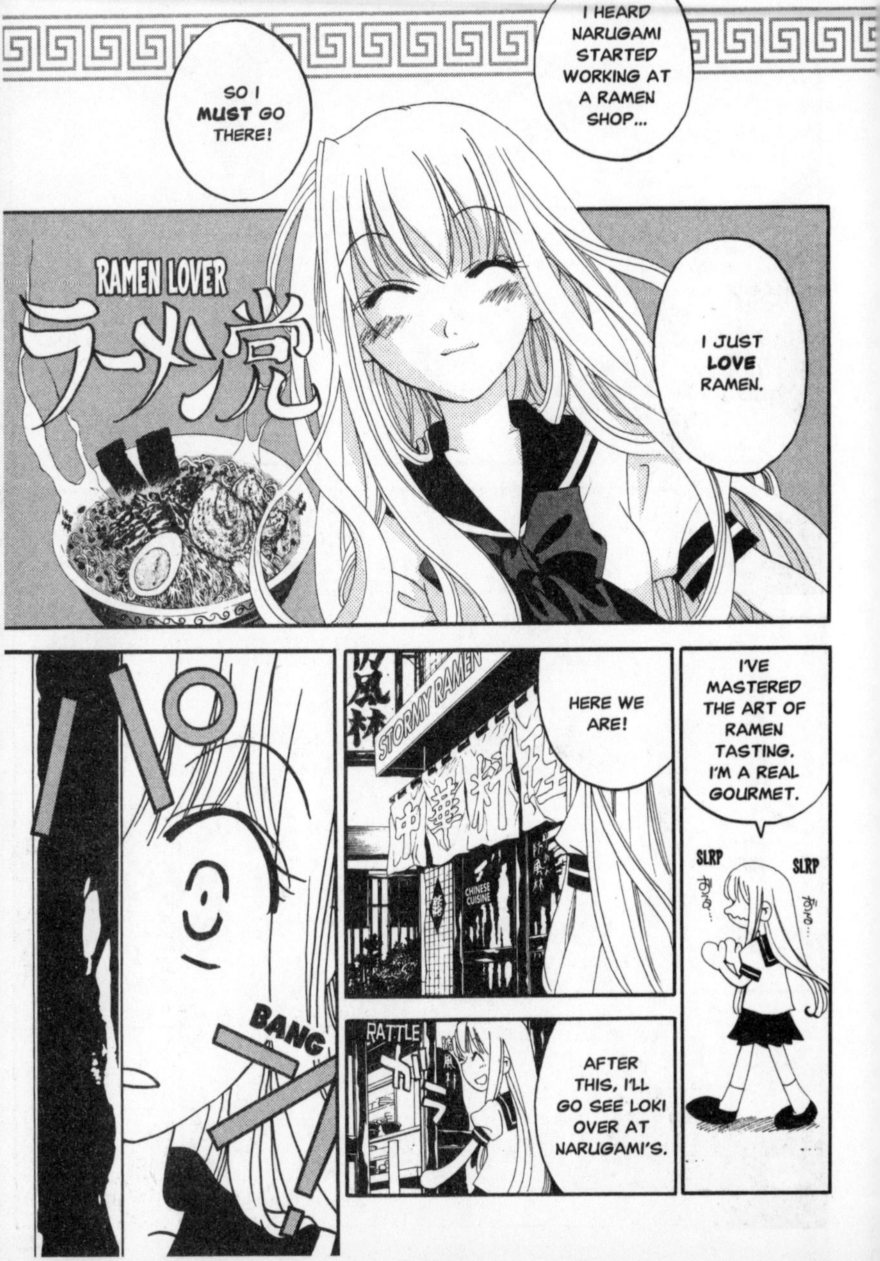
I HEARD NARUGAMI STARTED WORKING AT A RAMEN SHOP...
SO I MUST GO THERE!
RAMEN LOVER
I JUST LOVE RAMEN.
I'VE MASTERED THE ART OF RAMEN TASTING. I'M A REAL GOURMET.
SLRP
SLRP
STORMY RAMEN
HERE WE ARE!
CHINESE CUISINE
RATTLE
AFTER THIS, I'LL GO SEE LOKI OVER AT NARUGAMI'S.
BANG

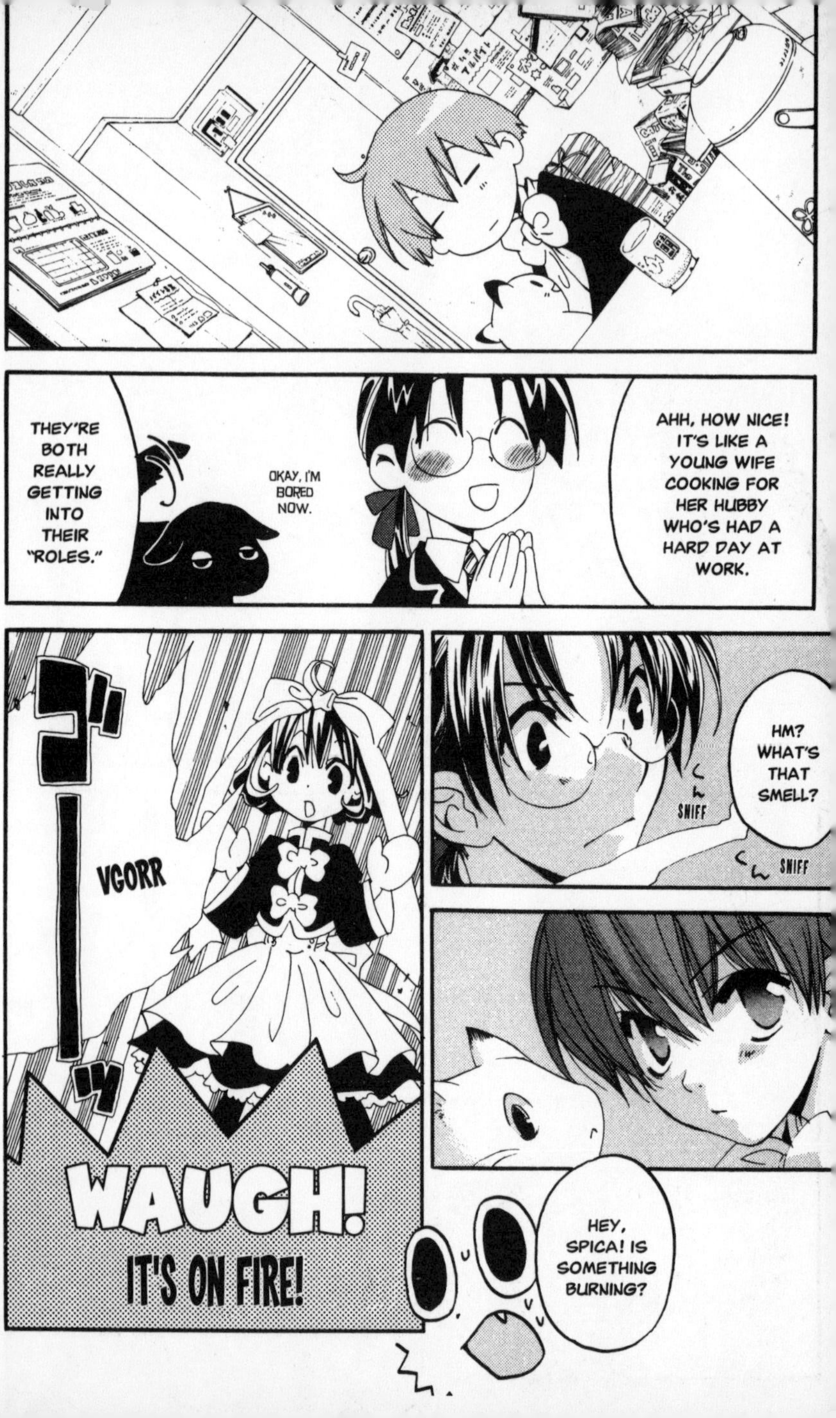
AHH, HOW NICE! IT'S LIKE A YOUNG WIFE COOKING FOR HER HUBBY WHO'S HAD A HARD DAY AT WORK.
OKAY, I'M BORED NOW.
THEY'RE BOTH REALLY GETTING INTO THEIR "ROLES."
HM? WHAT'S THAT SMELL?
SNIFF
SNIFF
VGORR
HEY, SPICA! IS SOMETHING BURNING?
WAUGH!
IT'S ON FIRE!

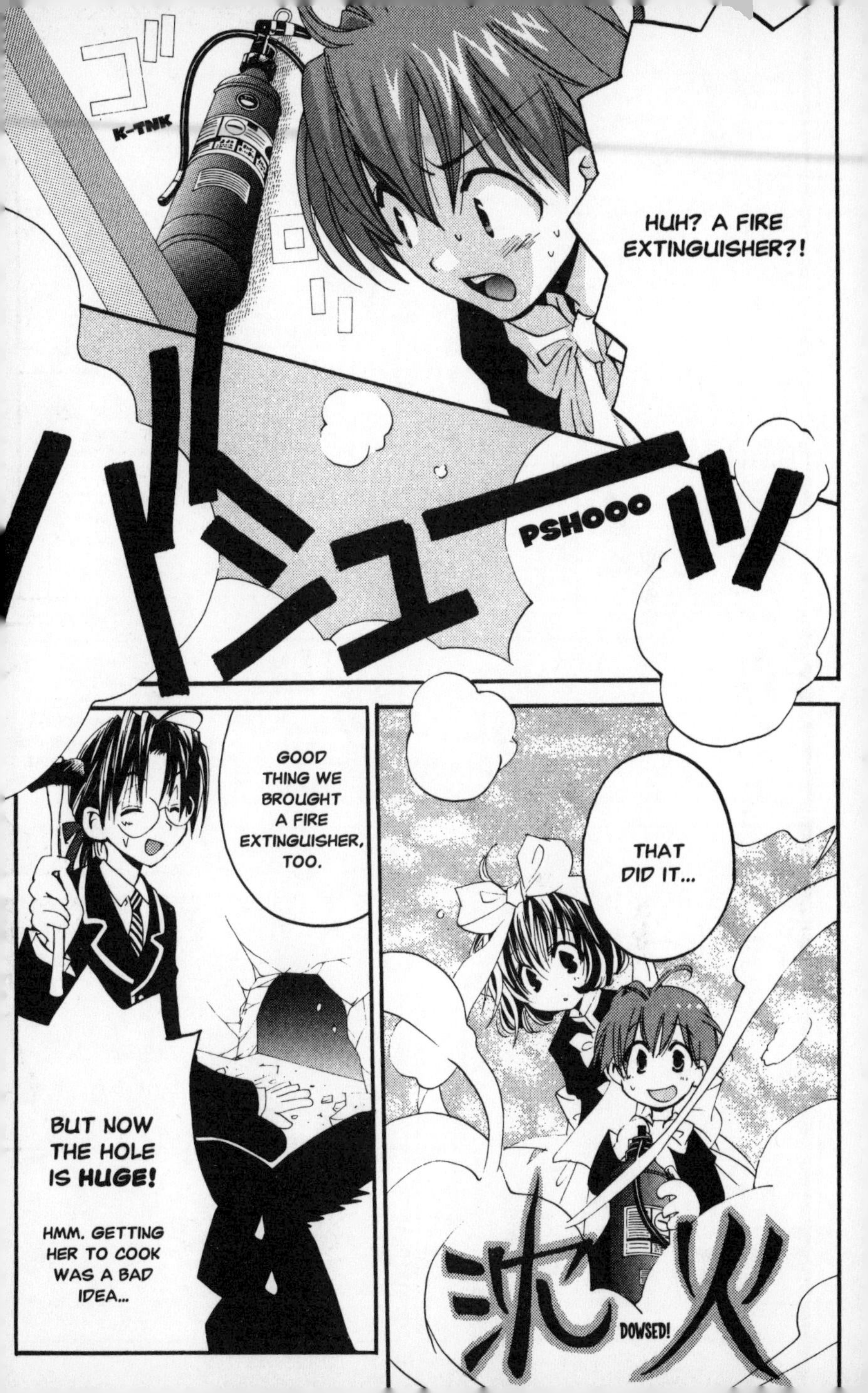
HUH? A FIRE EXTINGUISHER?!
K-TNK
PSHOOO
THAT DID IT...
DOWSED!
GOOD THING WE BROUGHT A FIRE EXTINGUISHER, TOO.
BUT NOW THE HOLE IS HUGE!
HMM. GETTING HER TO COOK WAS A BAD IDEA...

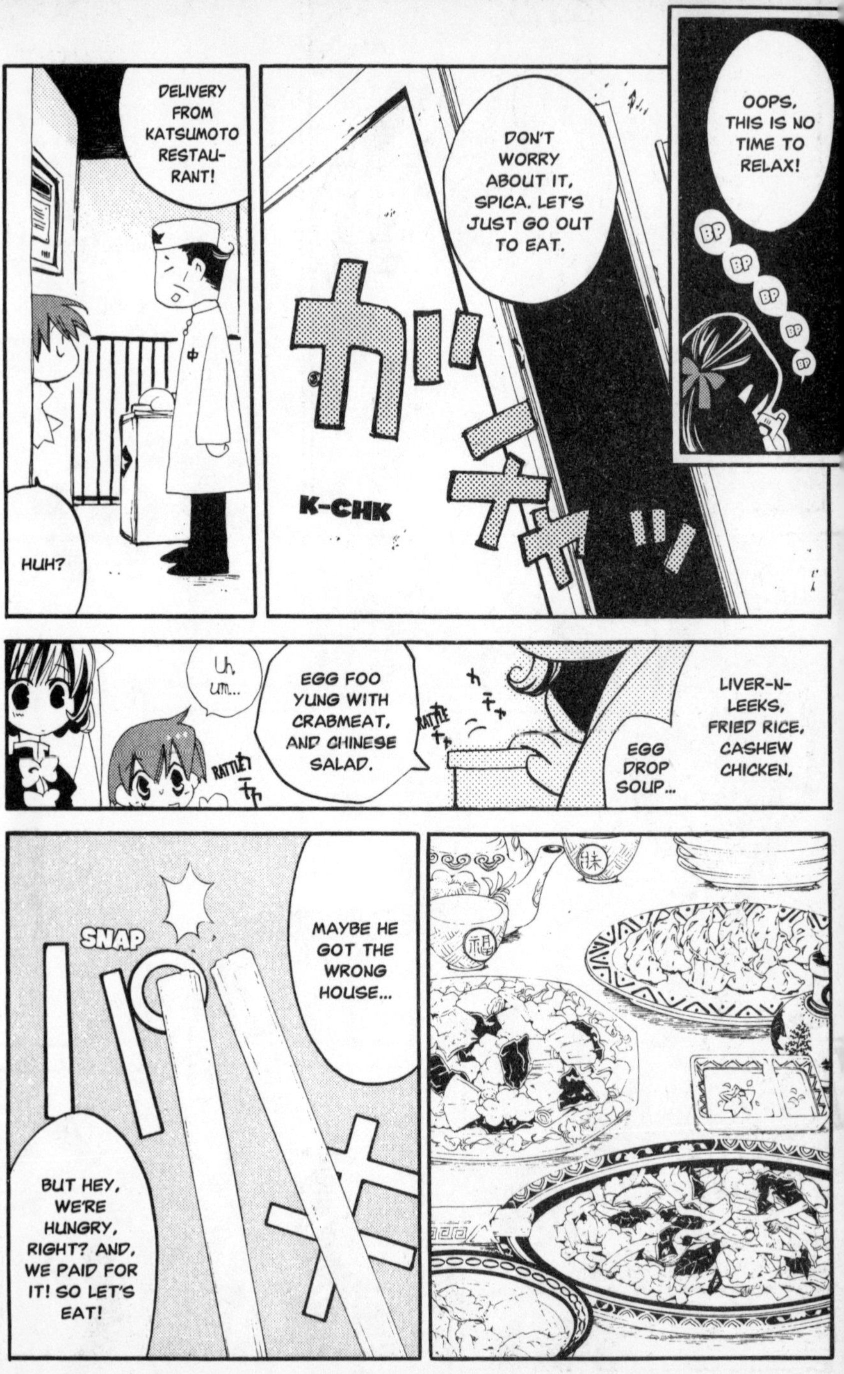
OOPS, THIS IS NO TIME TO RELAX!
BP
BP
BP
BP
BP
DON'T WORRY ABOUT IT, SPICA. LET'S JUST GO OUT TO EAT.
K-CHK
DELIVERY FROM KATSUMOTO RESTAU-RANT!
HUH?
LIVER-N-LEEKS, FRIED RICE, CASHEW CHICKEN,
EGG DROP SOUP...
RATTLE
EGG FOO YUNG WITH CRABMEAT, AND CHINESE SALAD.
RATTLE
Uh, um...
MAYBE HE GOT THE WRONG HOUSE...
SNAP
BUT HEY, WE'RE HUNGRY, RIGHT? AND, WE PAID FOR IT! SO LET'S EAT!

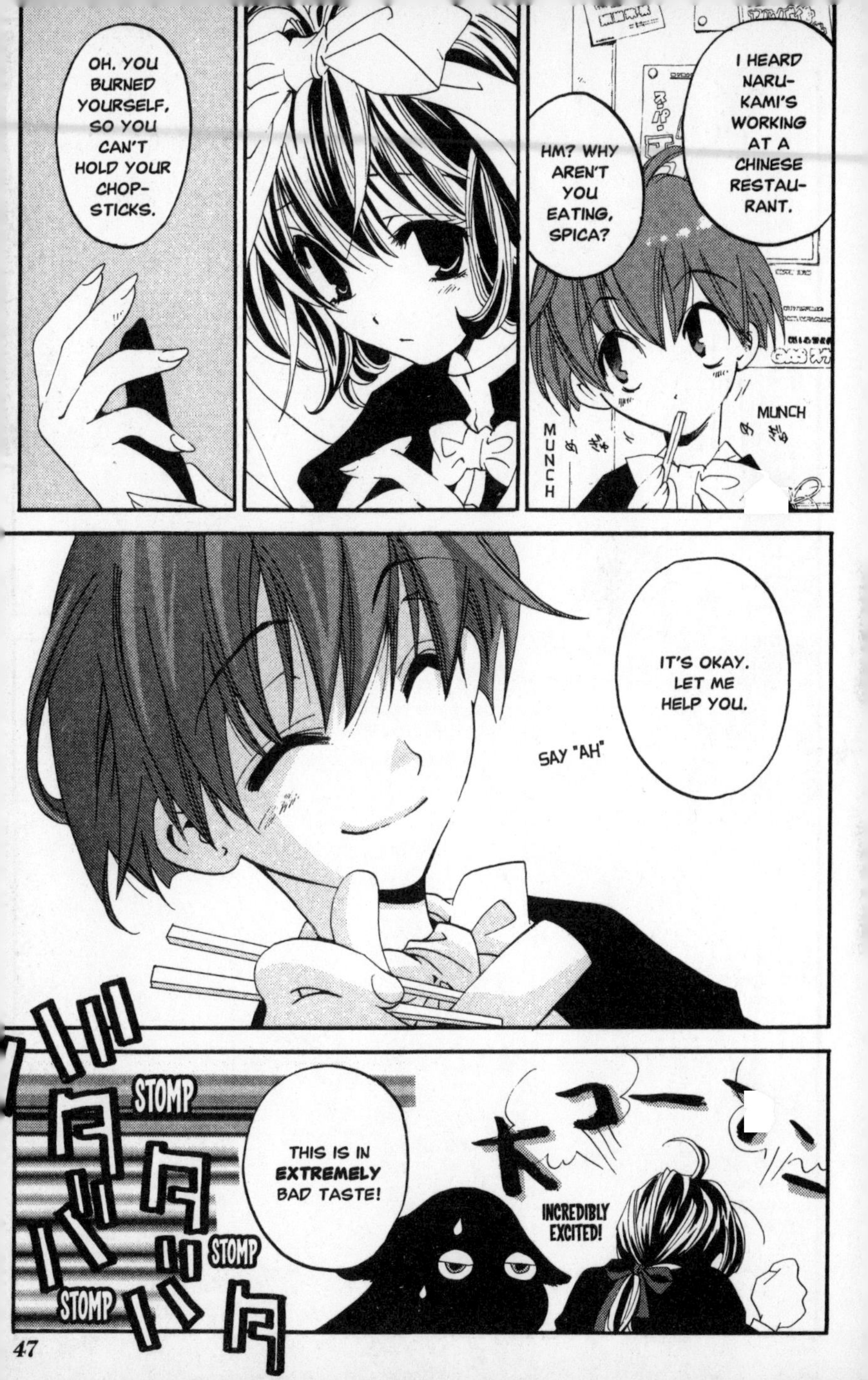
I HEARD NARU-KAMI'S WORKING AT A CHINESE RESTAU-RANT.
HM? WHY AREN'T YOU EATING, SPICA?
MUNCH
MUNCH
OH. YOU BURNED YOURSELF, SO YOU CAN'T HOLD YOUR CHOP-STICKS.
IT'S OKAY. LET ME HELP YOU.
SAY "AH"
INCREDIBLY EXCITED!
THIS IS IN EXTREMELY BAD TASTE!
STOMP
STOMP
STOMP

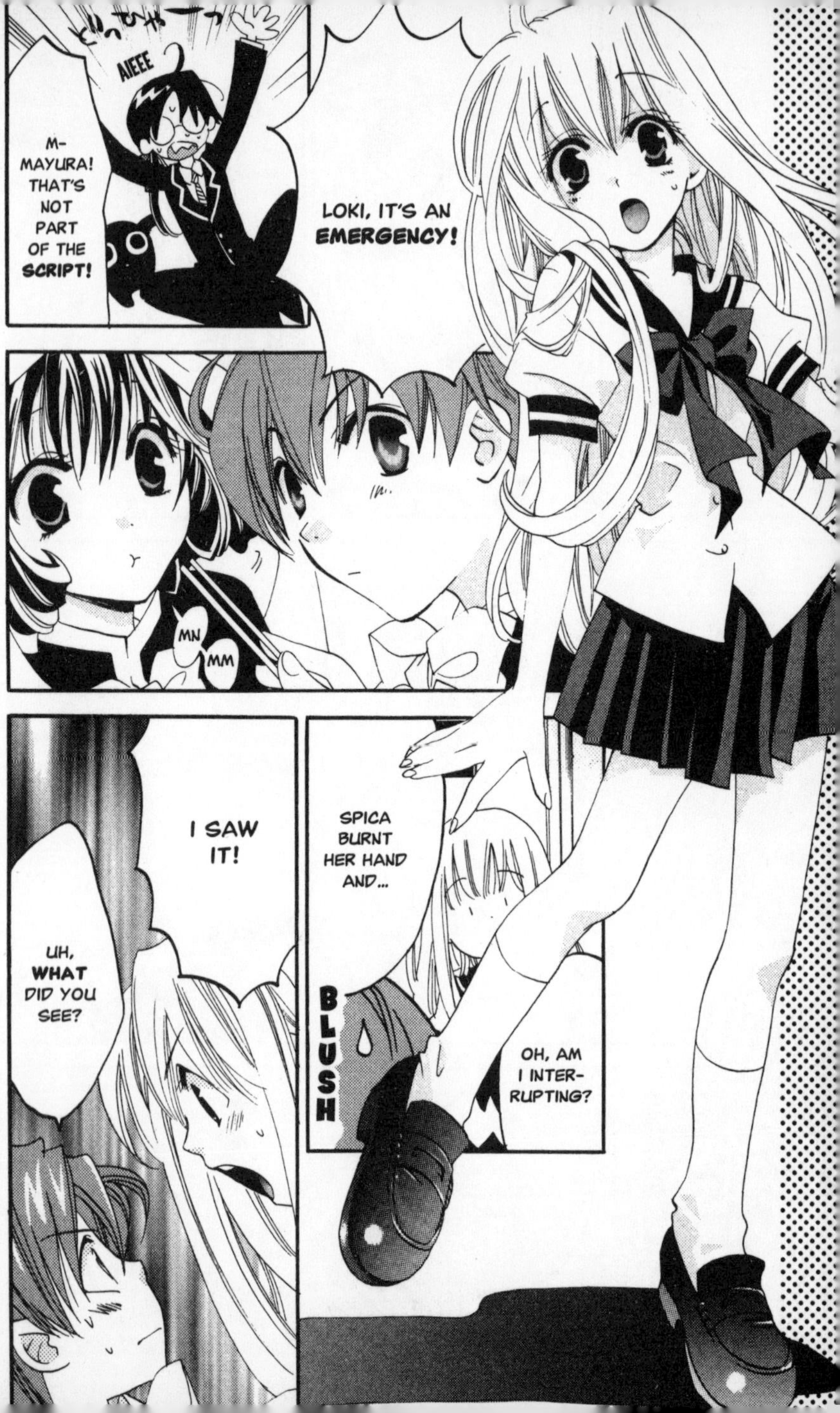
LOKI, IT'S AN EMERGENCY!
AIEEE
M-MAYURA! THAT'S NOT PART OF THE SCRIPT!
MN
MM
OH, AM I INTER-RUPTING?
BLUSH
SPICA BURNT HER HAND AND...
I SAW IT!
UH, WHAT DID YOU SEE?

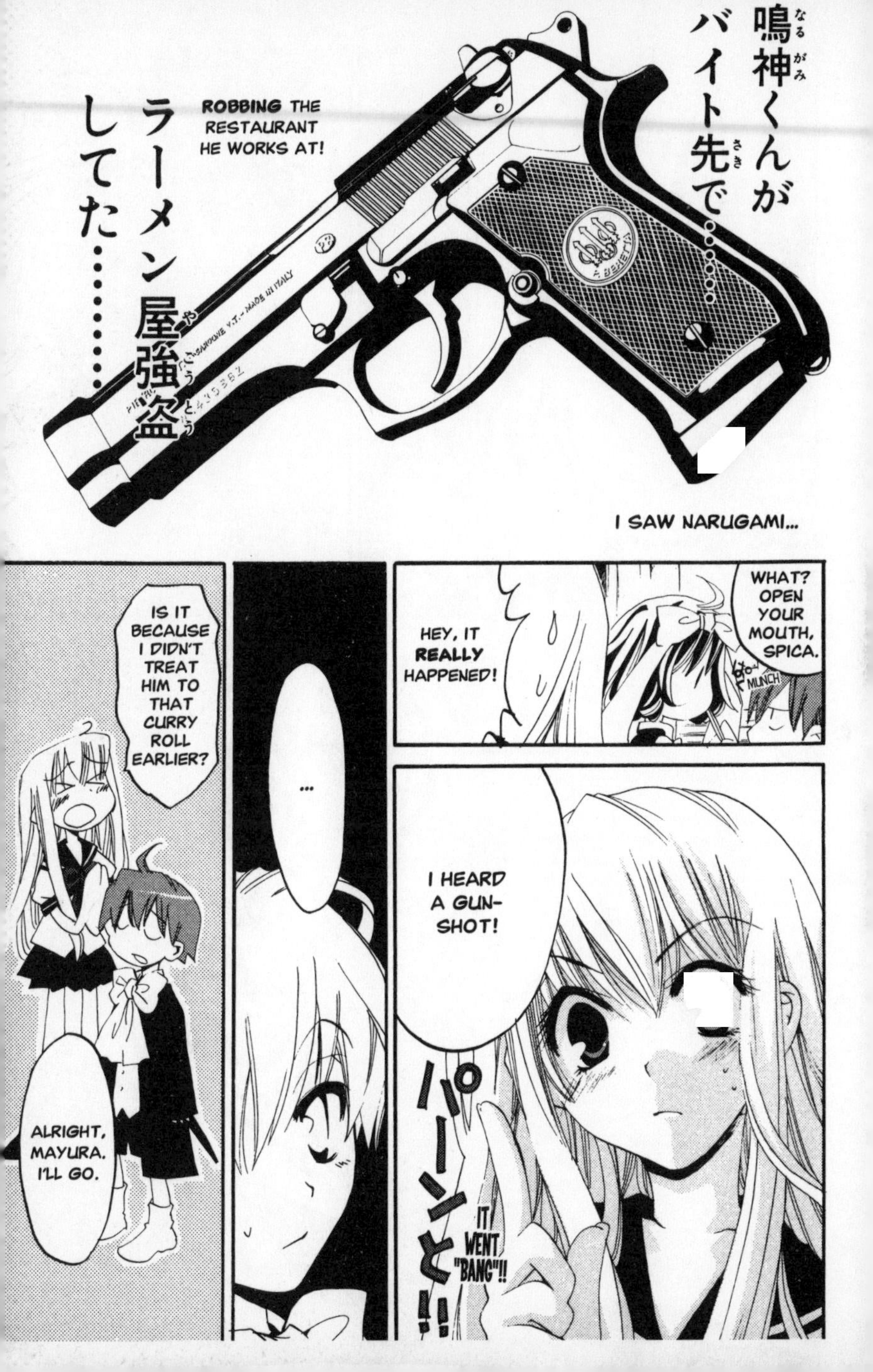

鳴神くんがバイト先で……
I SAW NARUGAMI...
ラーメン屋強盗してた……
ROBBING THE RESTAURANT HE WORKS AT!
WHAT? OPEN YOUR MOUTH, SPICA.
MUNCH
HEY, IT REALLY HAPPENED!
I HEARD A GUN-SHOT!
パーンと!!
IT WENT "BANG"!!
...
IS IT BECAUSE I DIDN'T TREAT HIM TO THAT CURRY ROLL EARLIER?
ALRIGHT, MAYURA. I'LL GO.

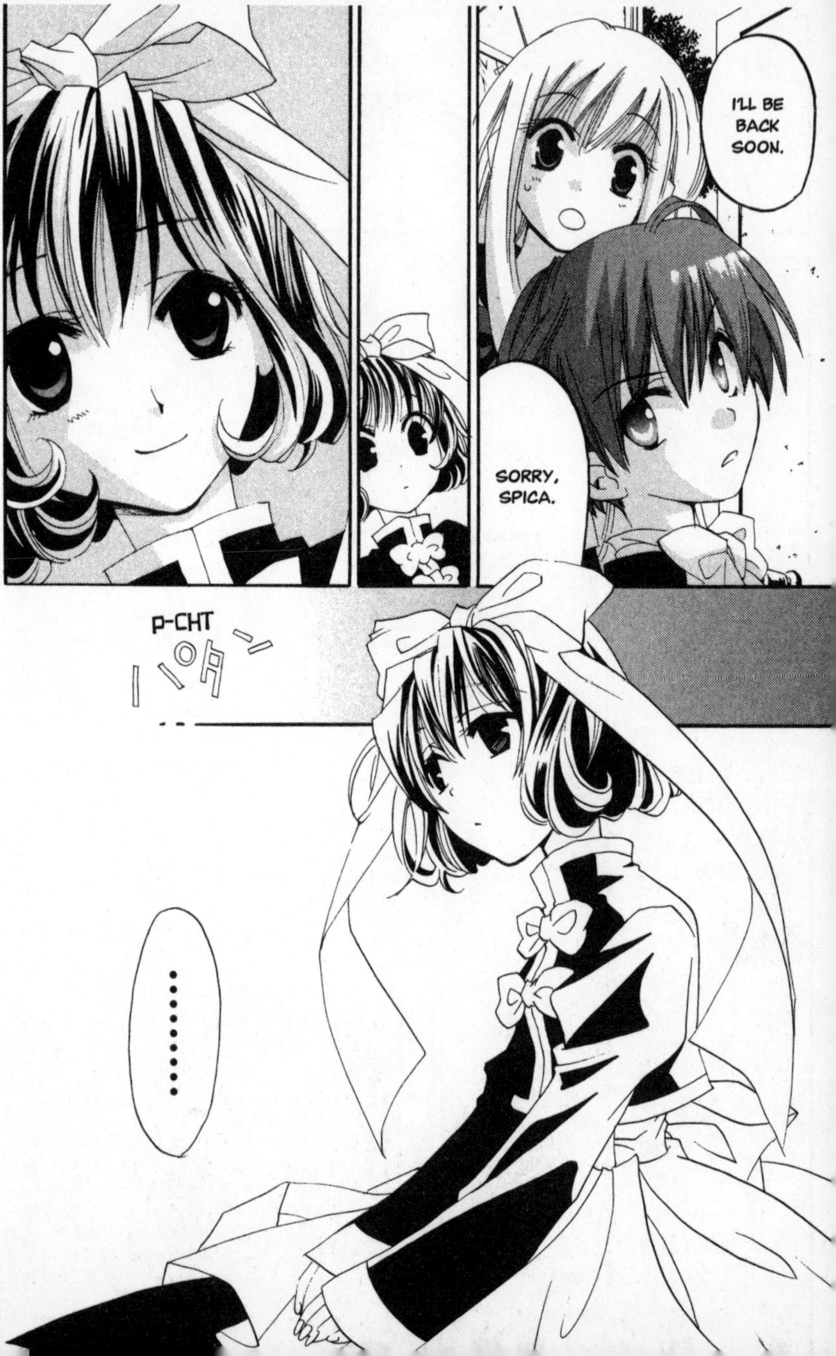
I'LL BE BACK SOON.
SORRY, SPICA.
P-CHT
パタン
......

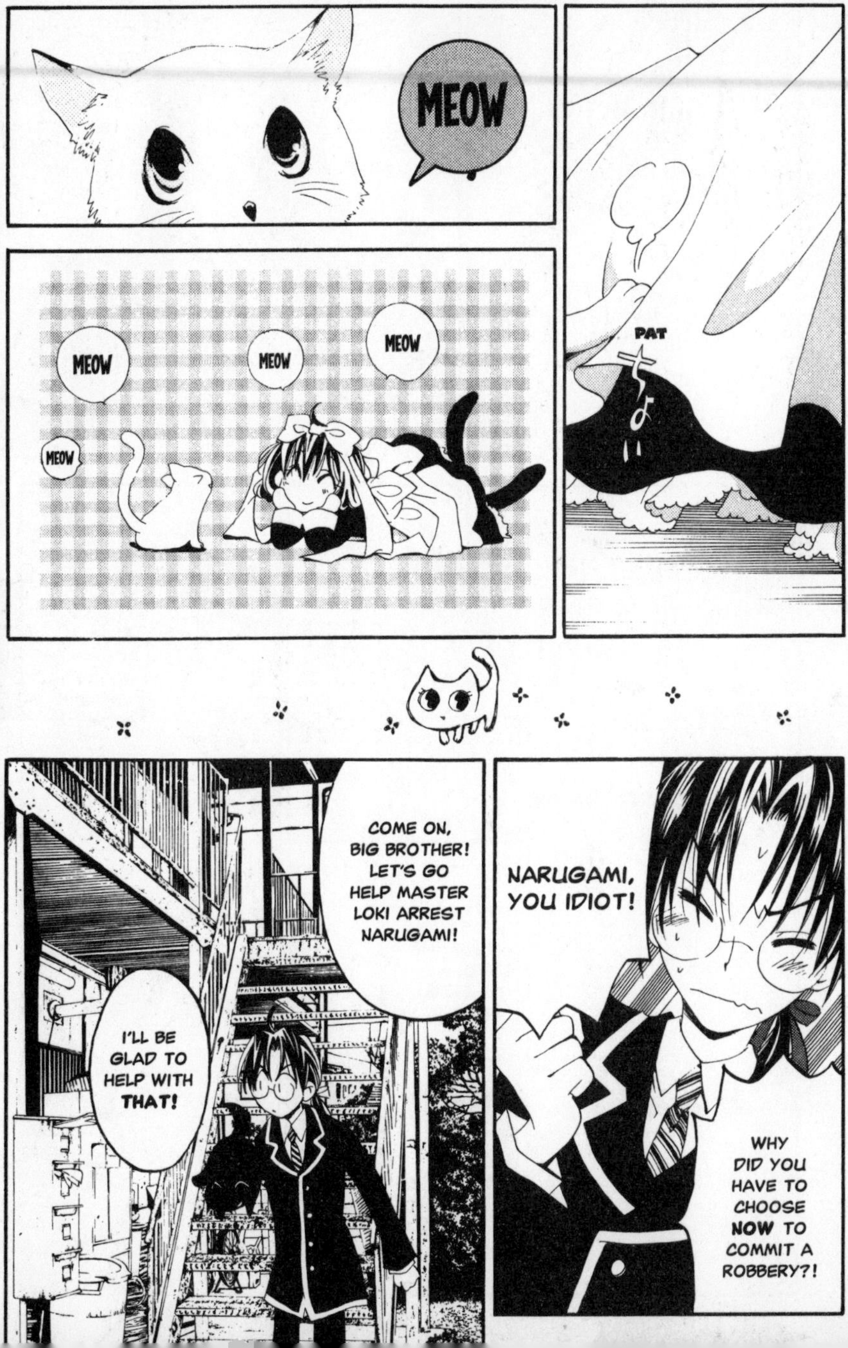
PAT
ちょい
MEOW
MEOW
MEOW
MEOW
MEOW
NARUGAMI, YOU IDIOT!
WHY DID YOU HAVE TO CHOOSE **NOW** TO COMMIT A ROBBERY?!
COME ON, BIG BROTHER! LET'S GO HELP MASTER LOKI ARREST NARUGAMI!
I'LL BE GLAD TO HELP WITH **THAT**!

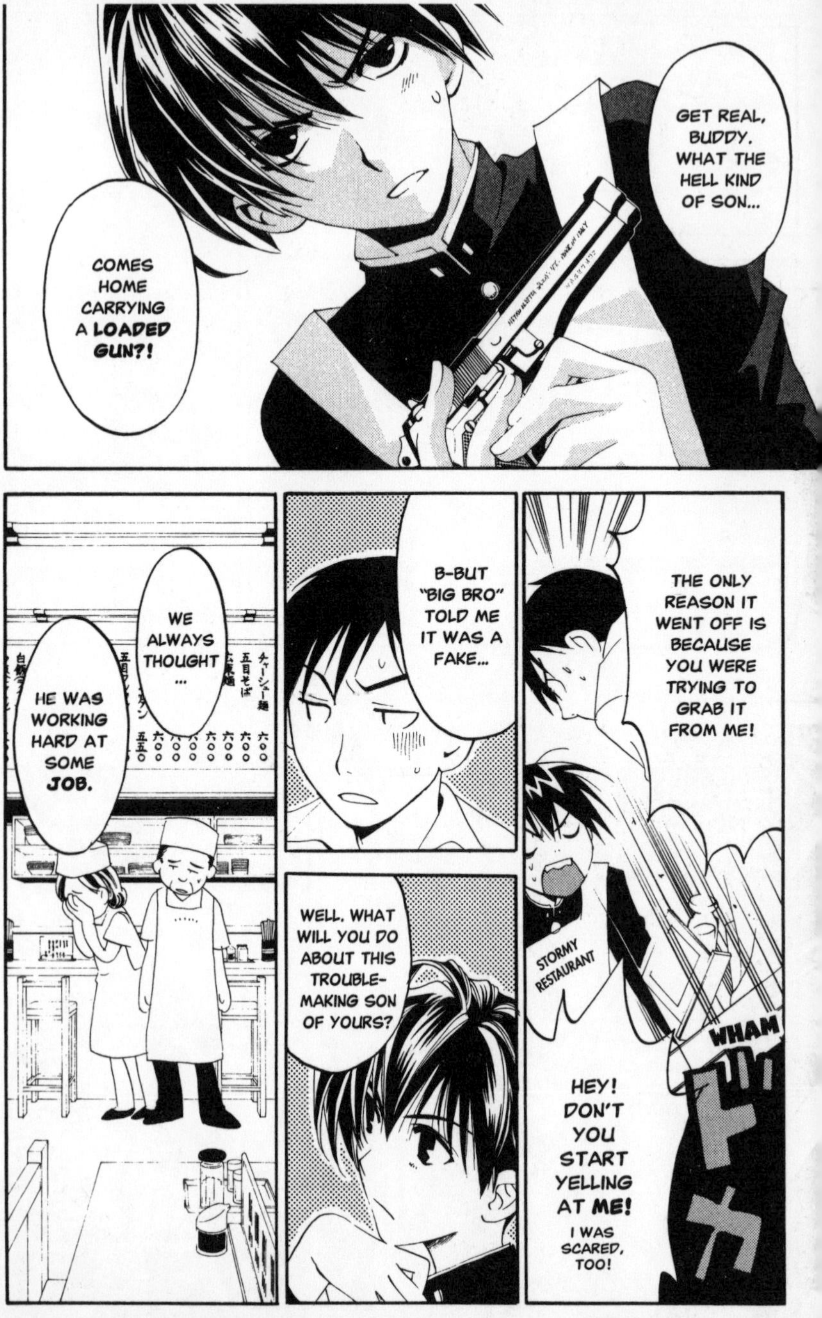
GET REAL, BUDDY. WHAT THE HELL KIND OF SON...
COMES HOME CARRYING A **LOADED GUN?!**
THE ONLY REASON IT WENT OFF IS BECAUSE YOU WERE TRYING TO GRAB IT FROM ME!
B-BUT "BIG BRO" TOLD ME IT WAS A FAKE...
STORMY RESTAURANT
WHAM
HEY! DON'T YOU START YELLING AT **ME!**
I WAS SCARED, TOO!
WELL, WHAT WILL YOU DO ABOUT THIS TROUBLE-MAKING SON OF YOURS?
WE ALWAYS THOUGHT...
HE WAS WORKING HARD AT SOME **JOB.**

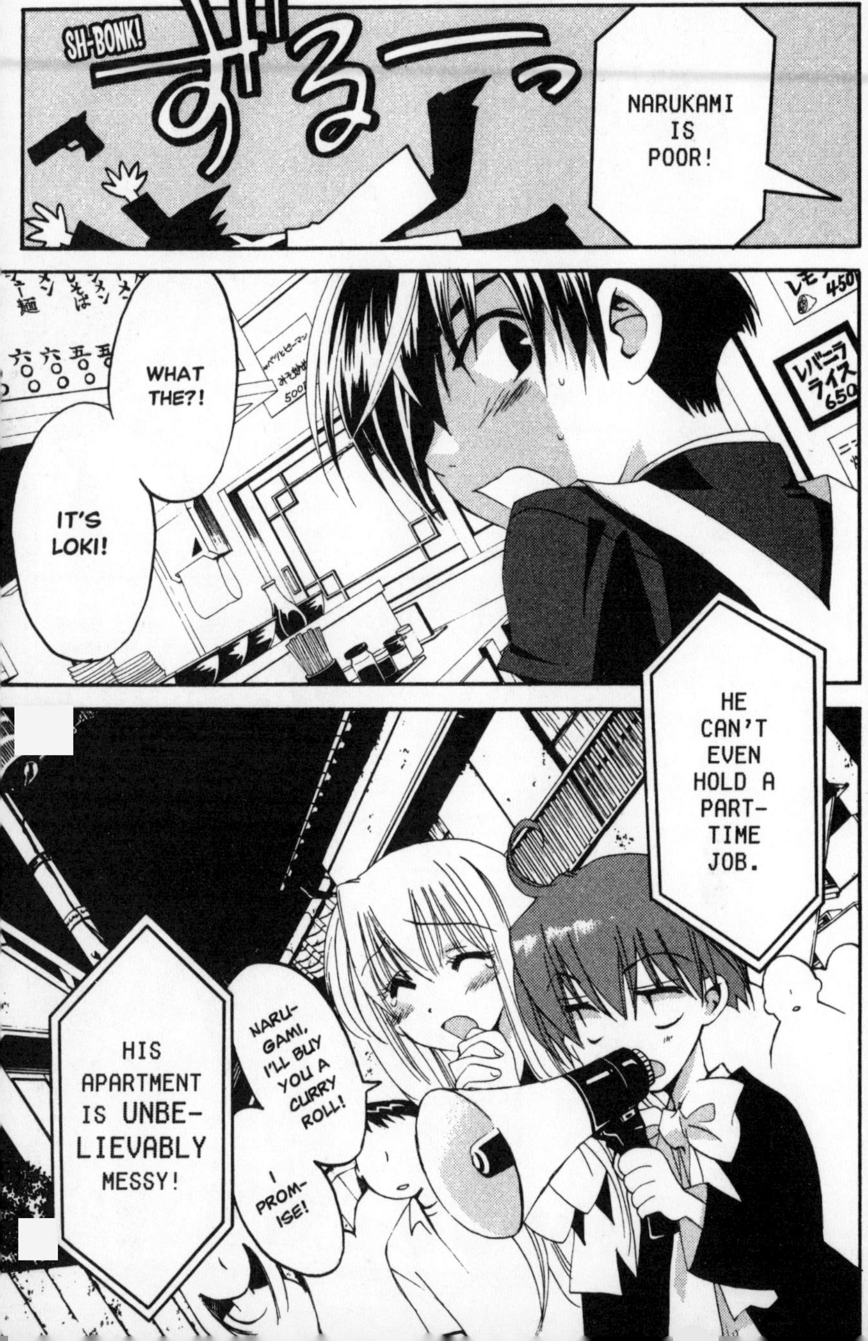
SH-BONK!
ずるーっ
NARUKAMI IS POOR!
WHAT THE?!
IT'S LOKI!
レバニラ ライス 650
HE CAN'T EVEN HOLD A PART-TIME JOB.
HIS APARTMENT IS UNBE-LIEVABLY MESSY!
NARU-GAMI, I'LL BUY YOU A CURRY ROLL!
I PROM-ISE!

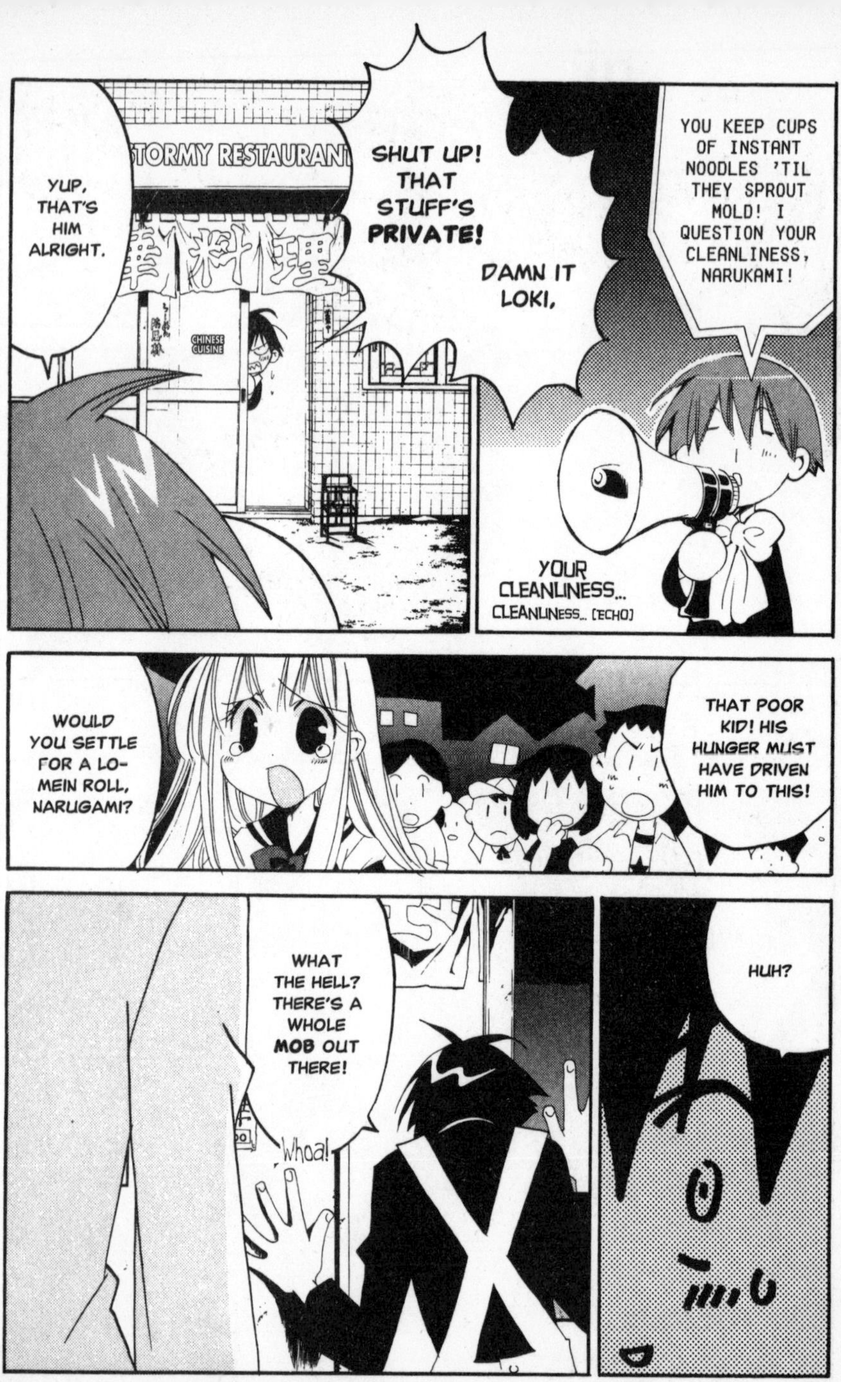
YOU KEEP CUPS OF INSTANT NOODLES 'TIL THEY SPROUT MOLD! I QUESTION YOUR CLEANLINESS, NARUKAMI!
YOUR CLEANLINESS...
CLEANLINESS... (ECHO)
DAMN IT LOKI,
SHUT UP! THAT STUFF'S **PRIVATE!**
STORMY RESTAURANT
華料理
CHINESE CUISINE
YUP, THAT'S HIM ALRIGHT.
THAT POOR KID! HIS HUNGER MUST HAVE DRIVEN HIM TO THIS!
WOULD YOU SETTLE FOR A LO-MEIN ROLL, NARUGAMI?
HUH?
WHAT THE HELL? THERE'S A WHOLE **MOB** OUT THERE!
Whoa!

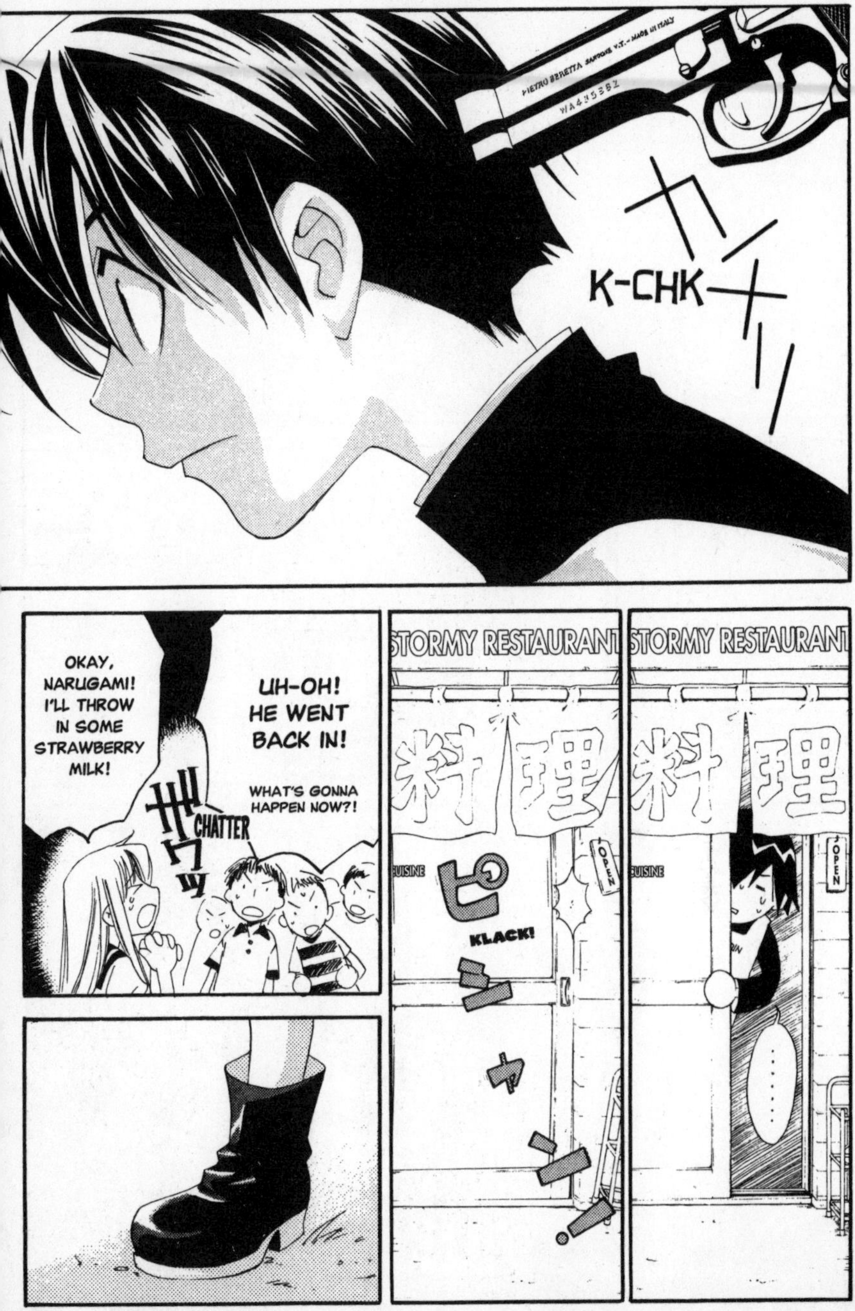
K-CHK
STORMY RESTAURANT
OPEN
CUISINE
......
STORMY RESTAURANT
CUISINE
OPEN
KLACK!
UH-OH! HE WENT BACK IN!
WHAT'S GONNA HAPPEN NOW?!
CHATTER
OKAY, NARUGAMI! I'LL THROW IN SOME STRAWBERRY MILK!

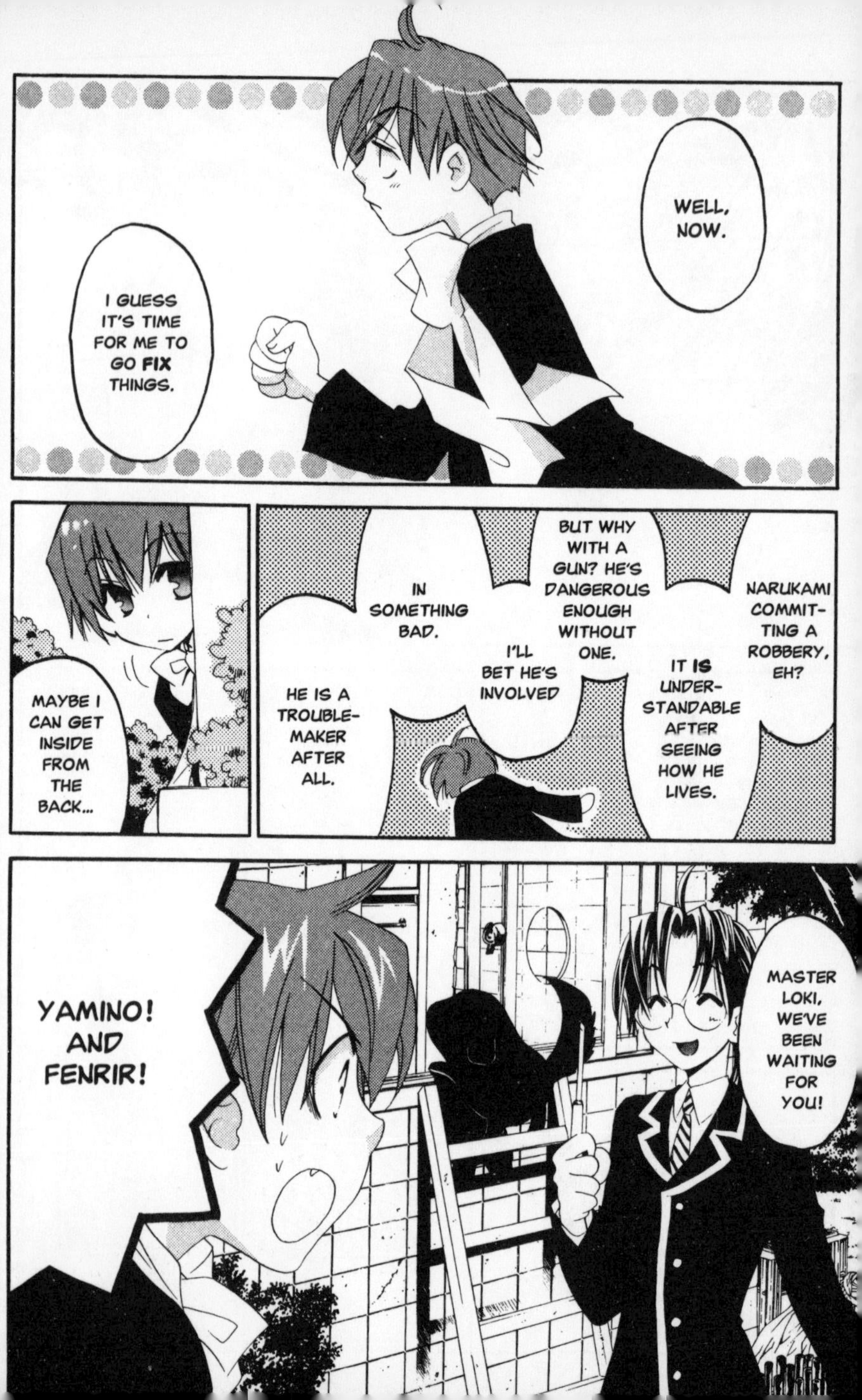
WELL, NOW.
I GUESS IT'S TIME FOR ME TO GO **FIX** THINGS.
NARUKAMI COMMITTING A ROBBERY, EH?
IT **IS** UNDERSTANDABLE AFTER SEEING HOW HE LIVES.
BUT WHY WITH A GUN? HE'S DANGEROUS ENOUGH WITHOUT ONE.
I'LL BET HE'S INVOLVED
IN SOMETHING BAD.
HE IS A TROUBLEMAKER AFTER ALL.
MAYBE I CAN GET INSIDE FROM THE BACK...
MASTER LOKI, WE'VE BEEN WAITING FOR YOU!
YAMINO! AND FENRIR!

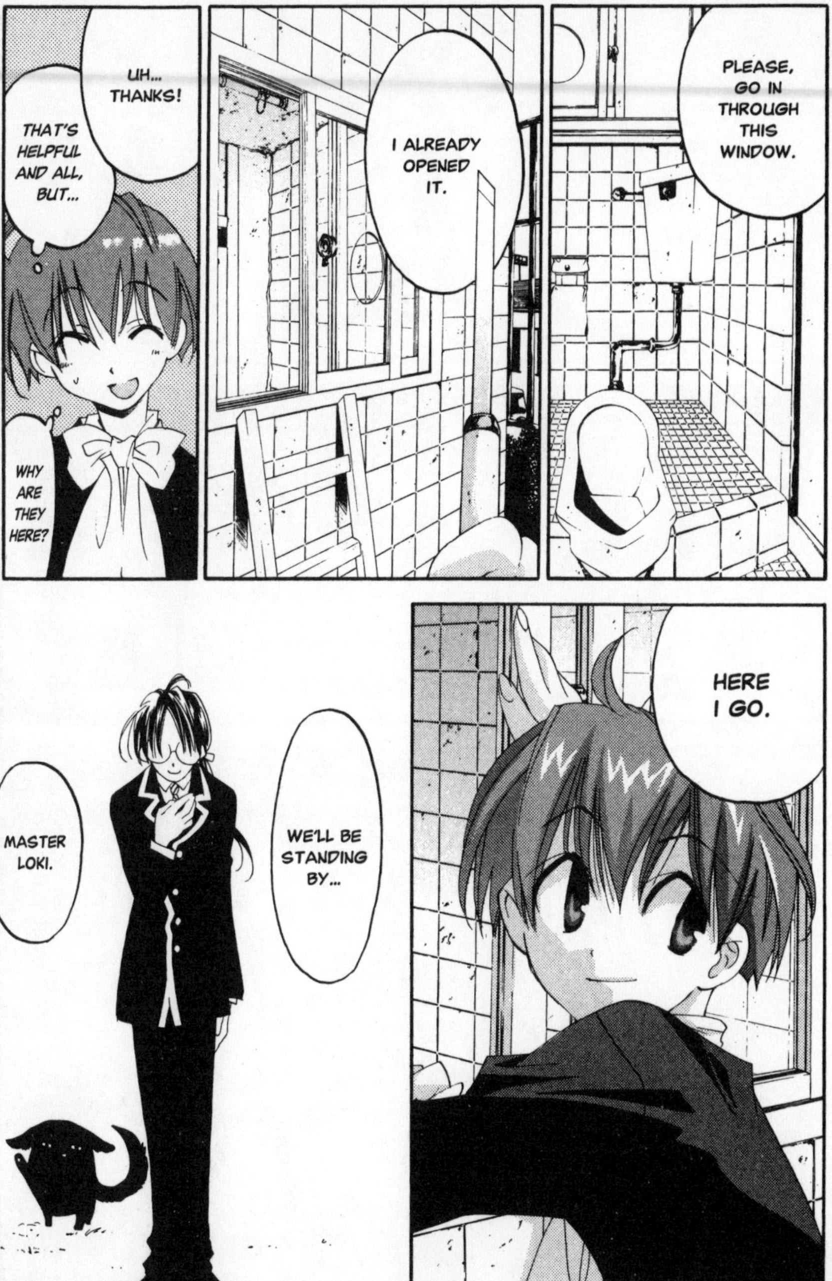
PLEASE, GO IN THROUGH THIS WINDOW.
I ALREADY OPENED IT.
UH... THANKS!
THAT'S HELPFUL AND ALL, BUT...
WHY ARE THEY HERE?
HERE I GO.
WE'LL BE STANDING BY...
MASTER LOKI.

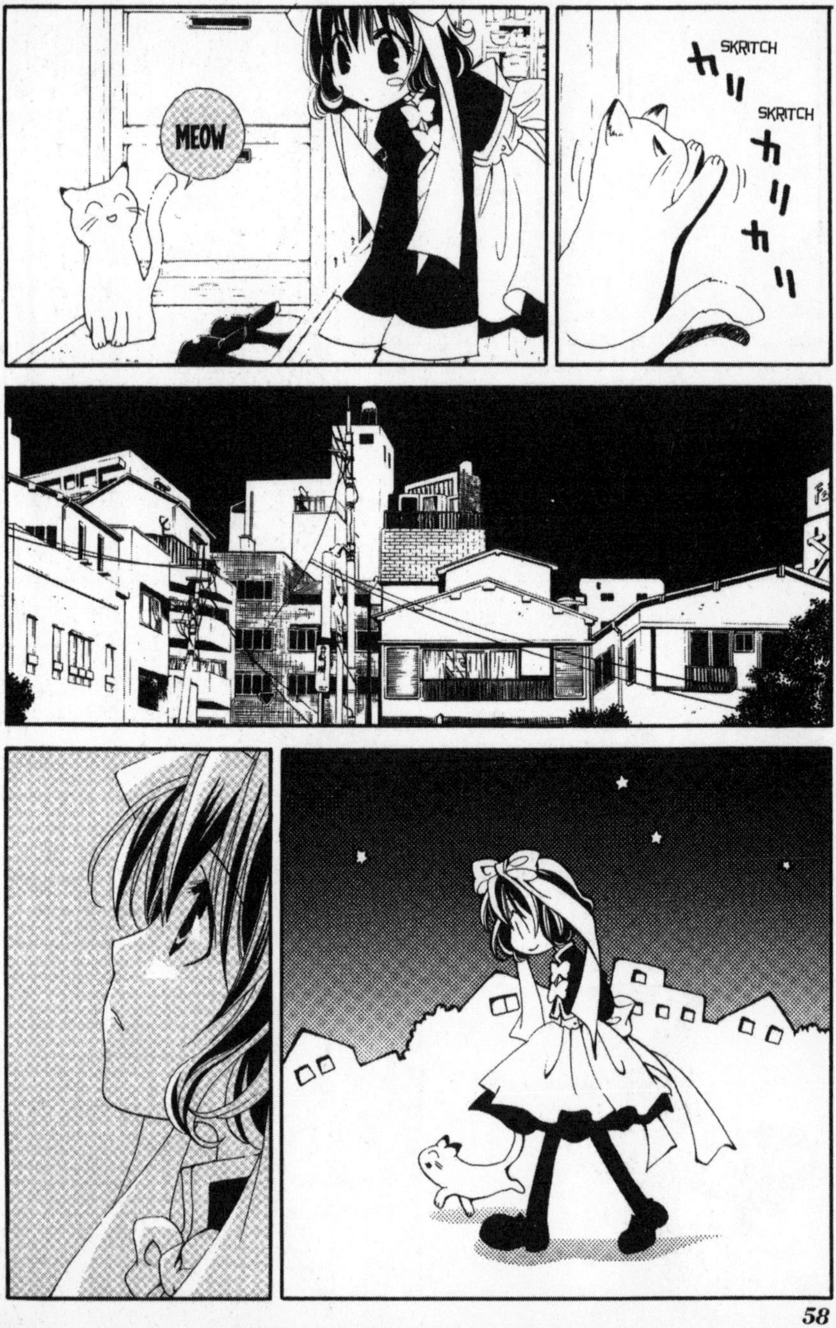
SKRITCH
カリ
SKRITCH
カリカリ
MEOW

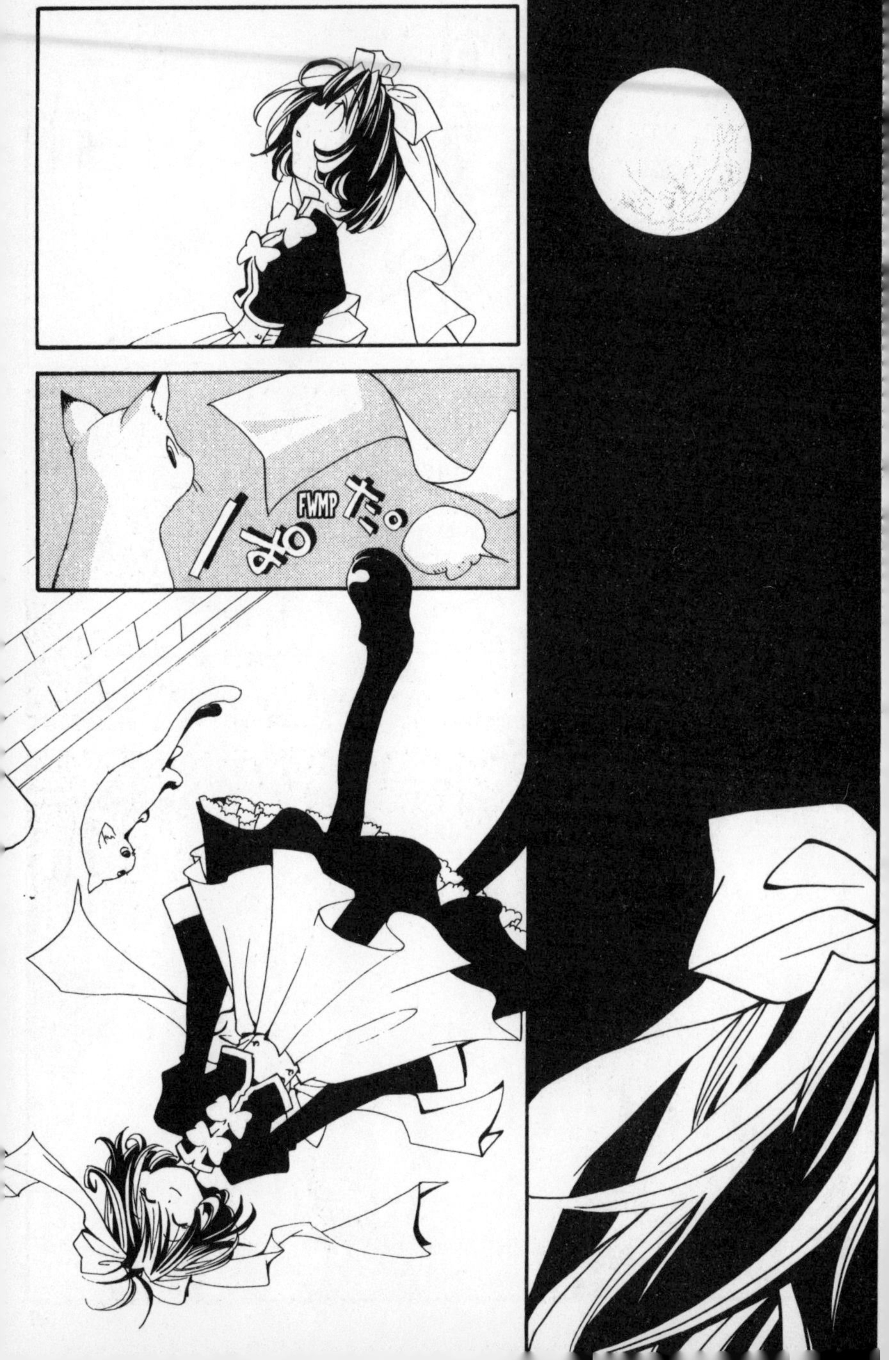
FWMP

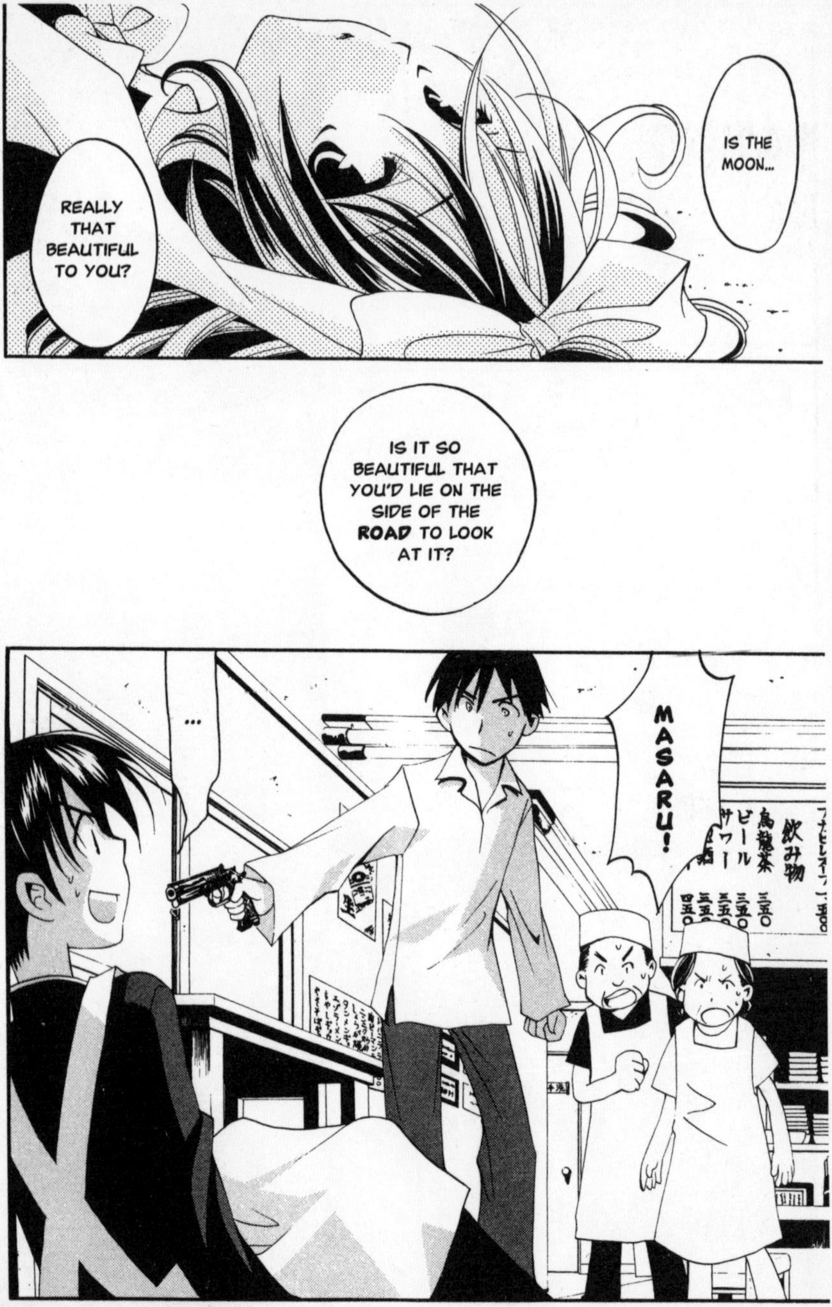
IS THE MOON...
REALLY THAT BEAUTIFUL TO YOU?
IS IT SO BEAUTIFUL THAT YOU'D LIE ON THE SIDE OF THE **ROAD** TO LOOK AT IT?
MASARU!
...

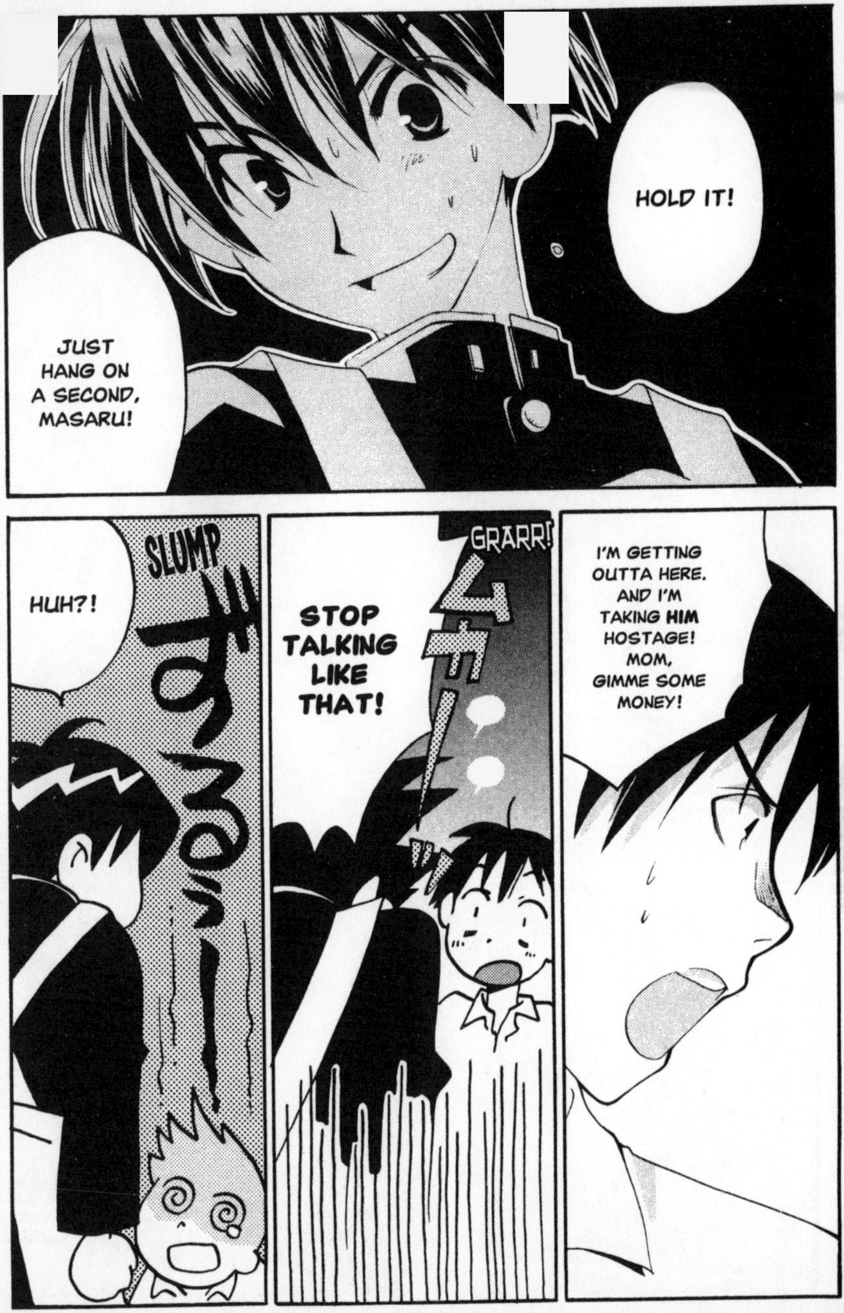
HOLD IT!
JUST HANG ON A SECOND, MASARU!
I'M GETTING OUTTA HERE. AND I'M TAKING HIM HOSTAGE! MOM, GIMME SOME MONEY!
GRARR!
STOP TALKING LIKE THAT!
SLUMP
HUH?!

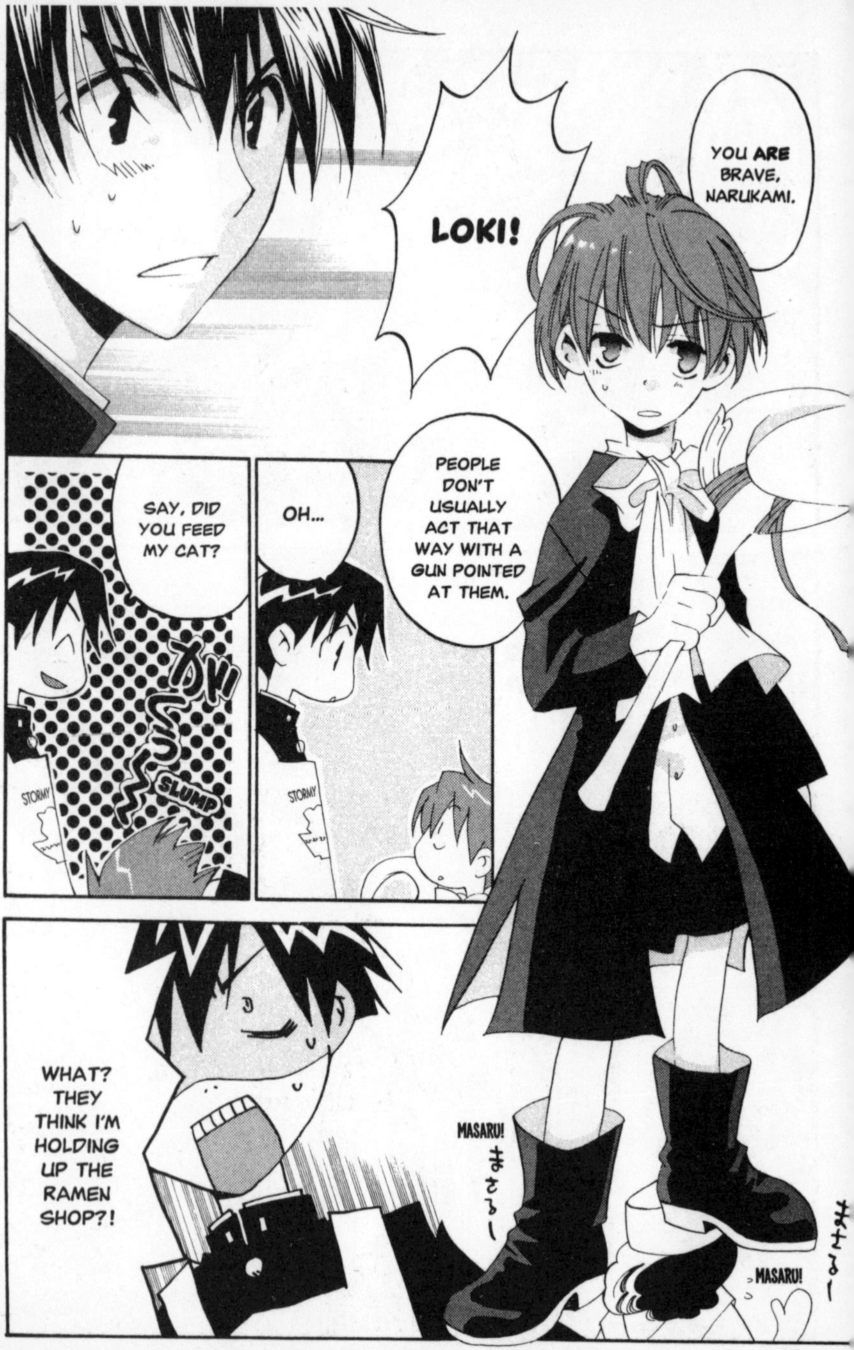

YOU ARE BRAVE, NARUKAMI.
LOKI!
PEOPLE DON'T USUALLY ACT THAT WAY WITH A GUN POINTED AT THEM.
OH...
SAY, DID YOU FEED MY CAT?
SLUMP
STORMY
STORMY
MASARU!
まさるー
MASARU!
WHAT? THEY THINK I'M HOLDING UP THE RAMEN SHOP?!

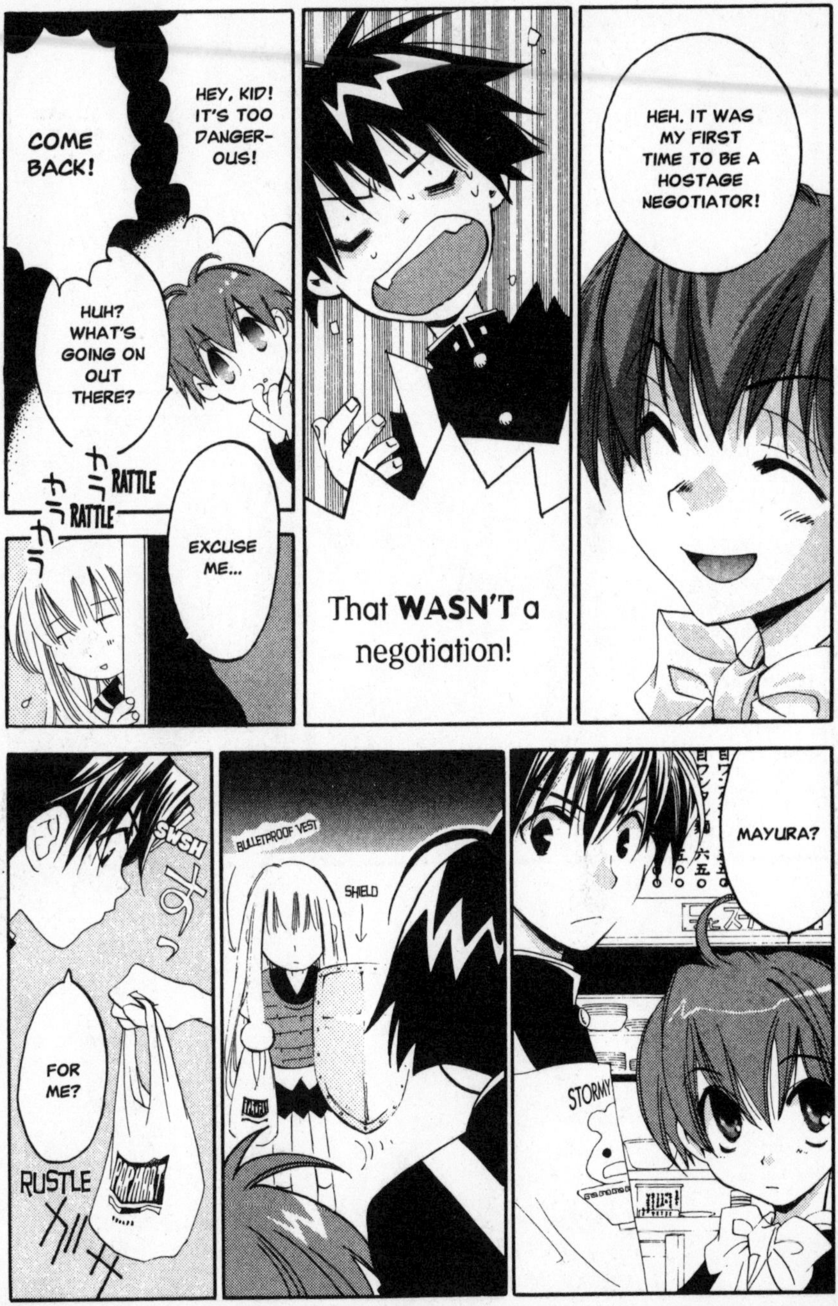
HEH. IT WAS MY FIRST TIME TO BE A HOSTAGE NEGOTIATOR!
That **WASN'T** a negotiation!
HEY, KID! IT'S TOO DANGER-OUS!
COME BACK!
HUH? WHAT'S GOING ON OUT THERE?
カラ RATTLE
カラ RATTLE
EXCUSE ME...
MAYURA?
STORMY
BULLETPROOF VEST
SHIELD
SWSH
FOR ME?
RUSTLE

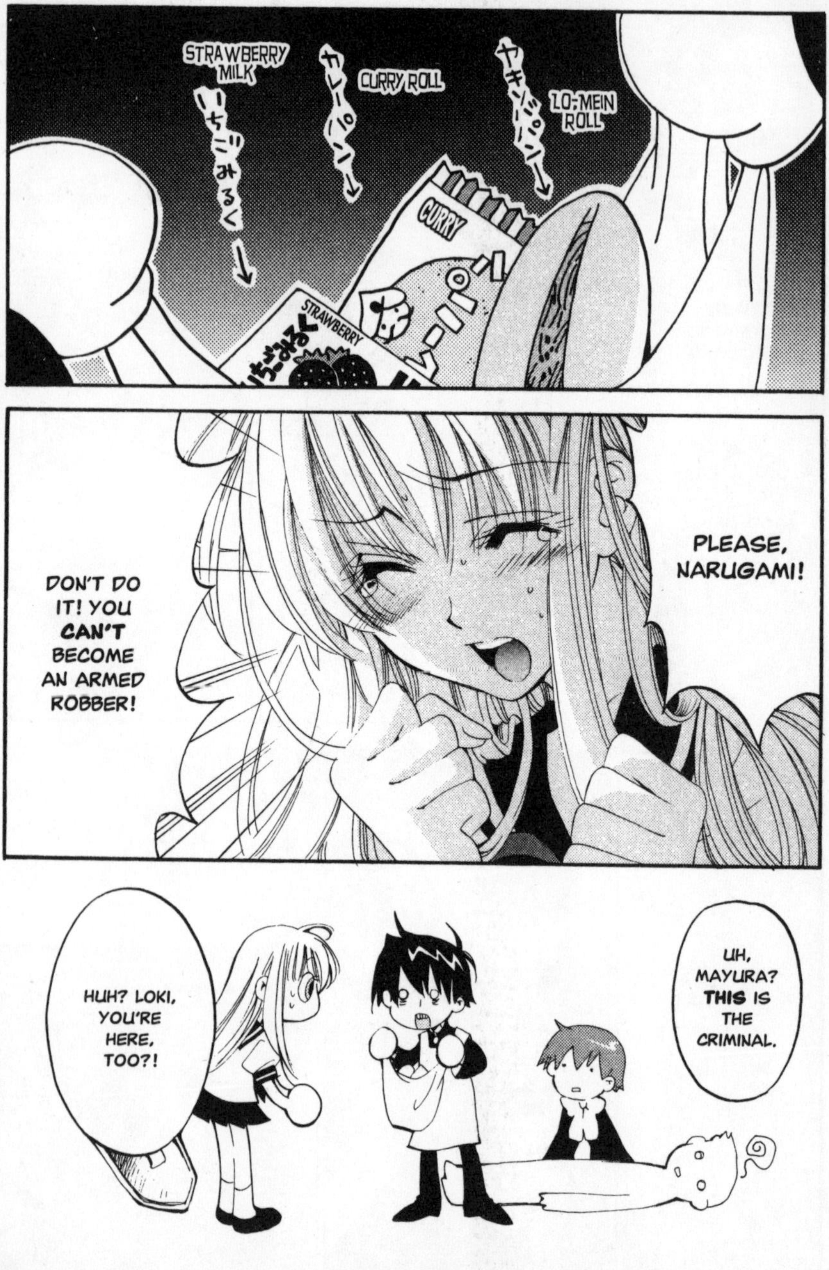

LO-MEIN ROLL
CURRY ROLL
STRAWBERRY MILK
CURRY
STRAWBERRY
PLEASE, NARUGAMI!
DON'T DO IT! YOU **CAN'T** BECOME AN ARMED ROBBER!
UH, MAYURA? **THIS** IS THE CRIMINAL.
HUH? LOKI, YOU'RE HERE, TOO?!

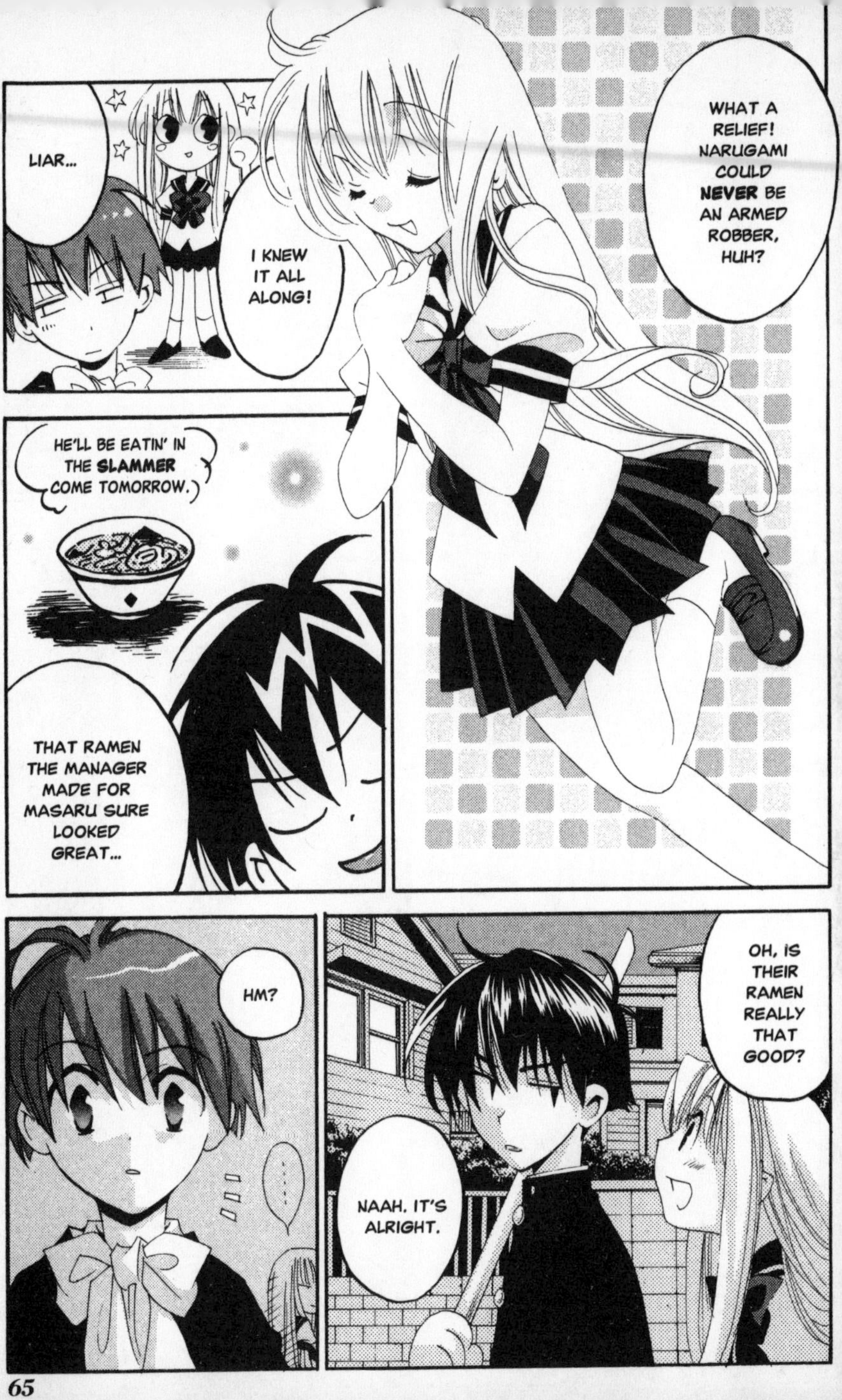
WHAT A RELIEF! NARUGAMI COULD NEVER BE AN ARMED ROBBER, HUH?
I KNEW IT ALL ALONG!
LIAR...
HE'LL BE EATIN' IN THE SLAMMER COME TOMORROW.
THAT RAMEN THE MANAGER MADE FOR MASARU SURE LOOKED GREAT...
OH, IS THEIR RAMEN REALLY THAT GOOD?
NAAH. IT'S ALRIGHT.
HM?
...

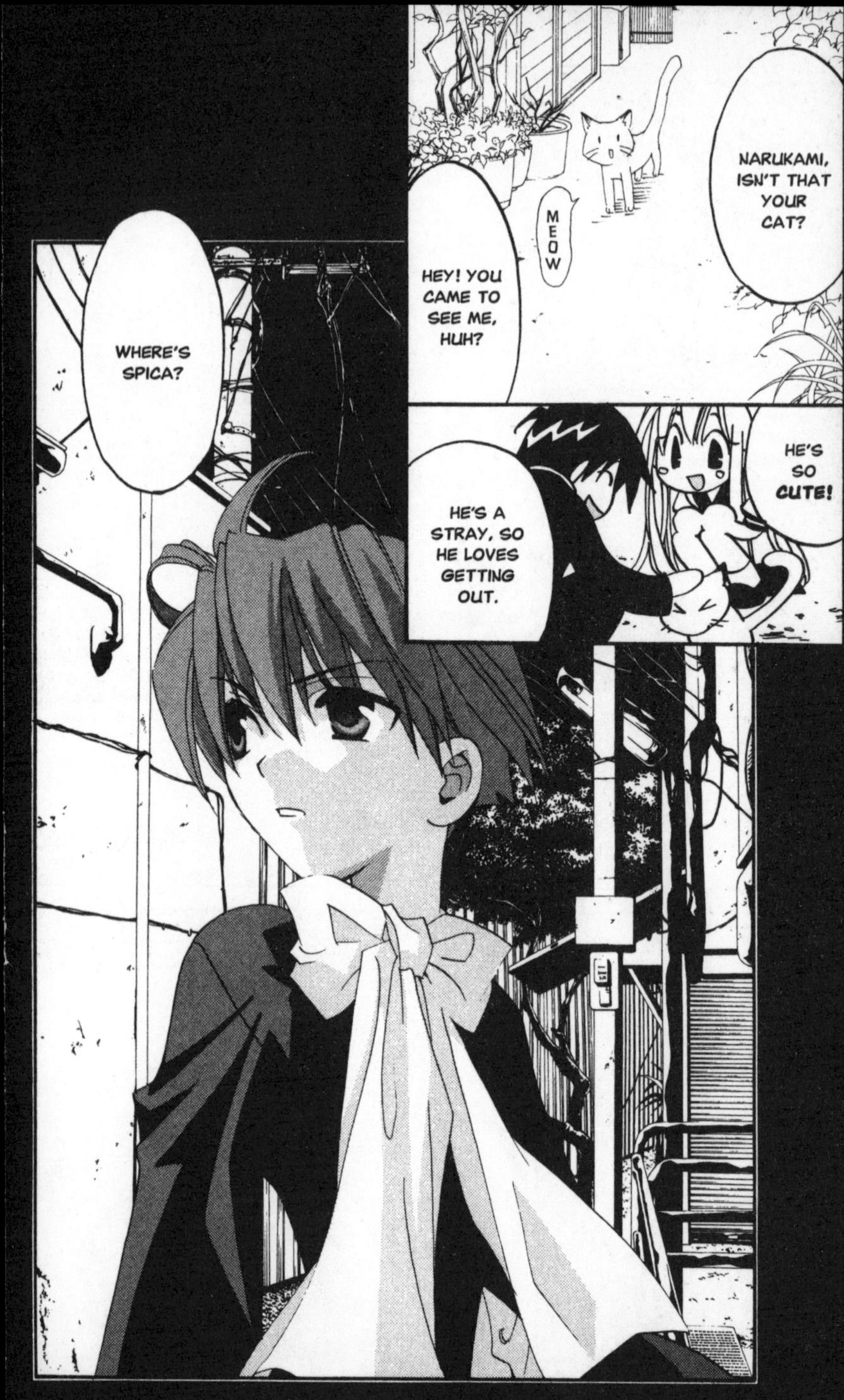
NARUKAMI, ISN'T THAT YOUR CAT?
MEOW
HEY! YOU CAME TO SEE ME, HUH?
HE'S SO CUTE!
HE'S A STRAY, SO HE LOVES GETTING OUT.
WHERE'S SPICA?

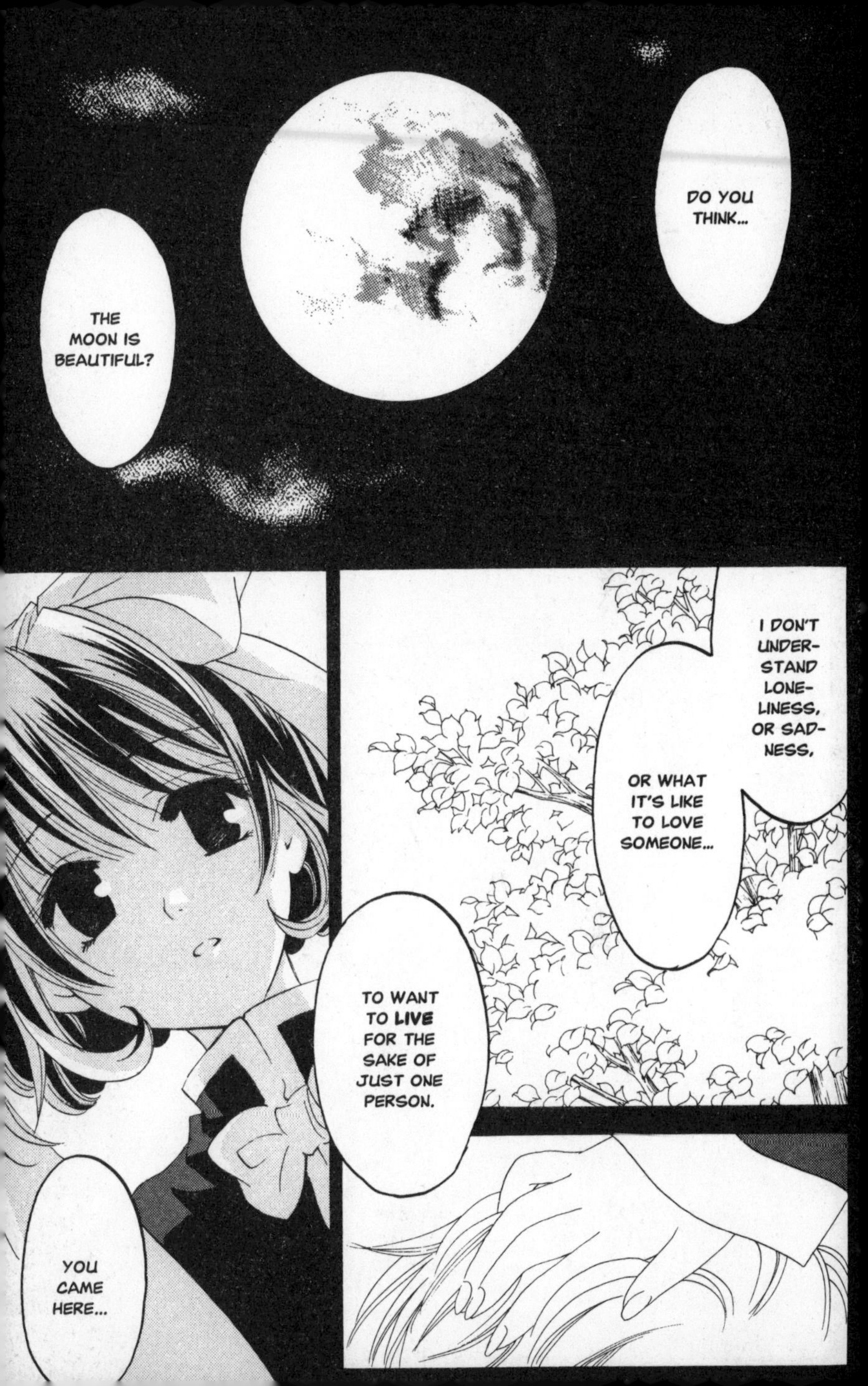
DO YOU THINK...
THE MOON IS BEAUTIFUL?
I DON'T UNDER-STAND LONE-LINESS, OR SAD-NESS,
OR WHAT IT'S LIKE TO LOVE SOMEONE...
TO WANT TO **LIVE** FOR THE SAKE OF JUST ONE PERSON.
YOU CAME HERE...

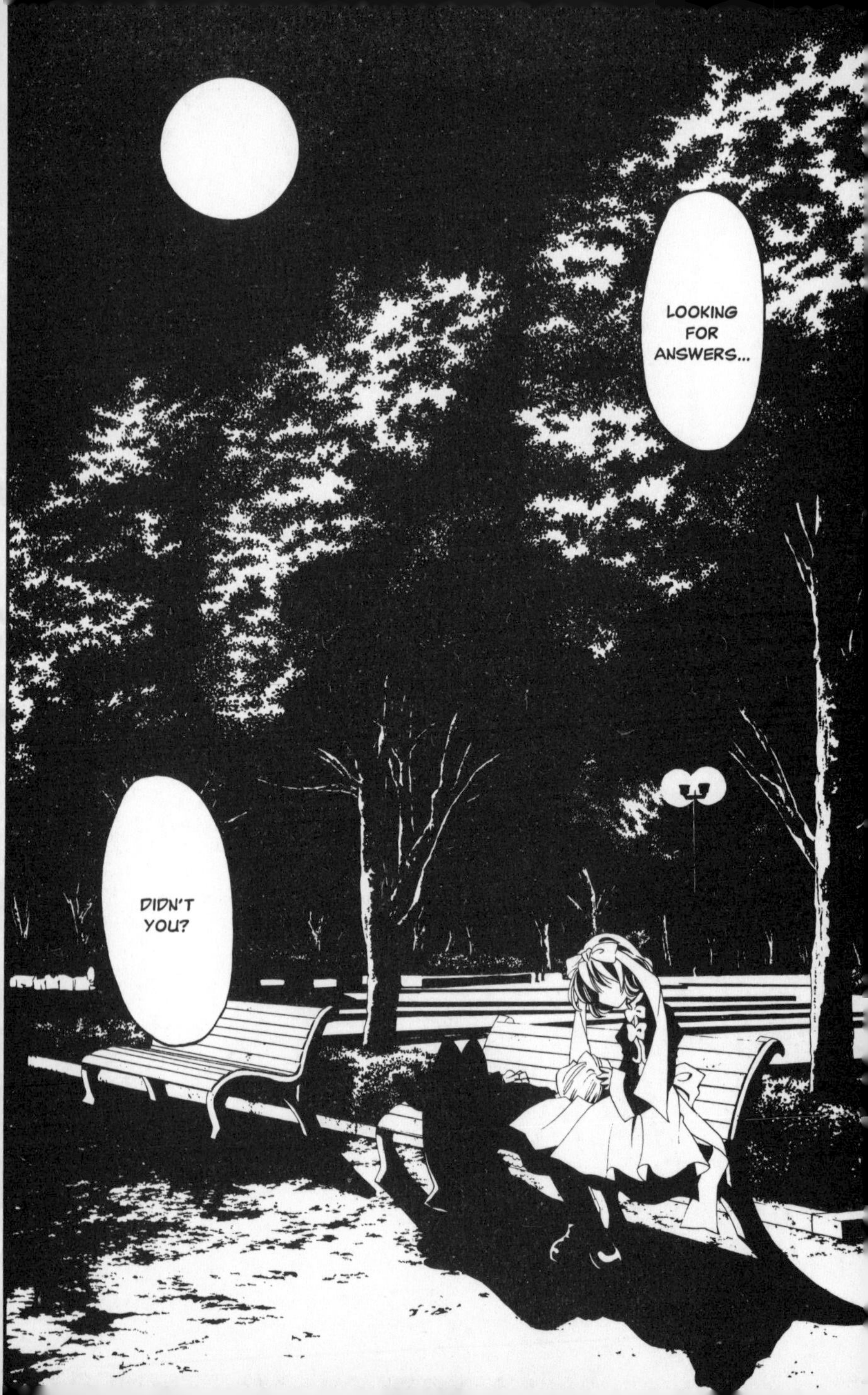
LOOKING FOR ANSWERS...
DIDN'T YOU?

CHAPTER 7

Moon Child

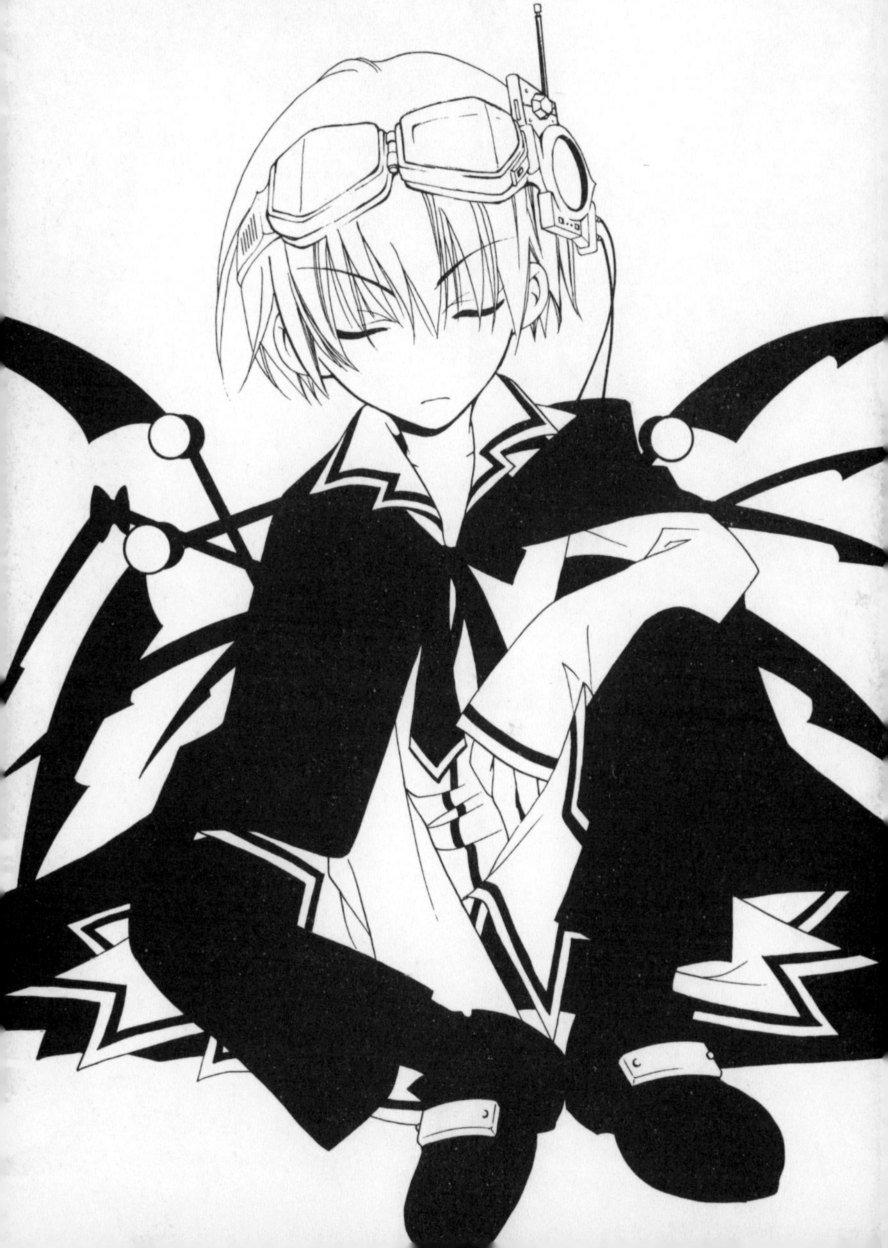

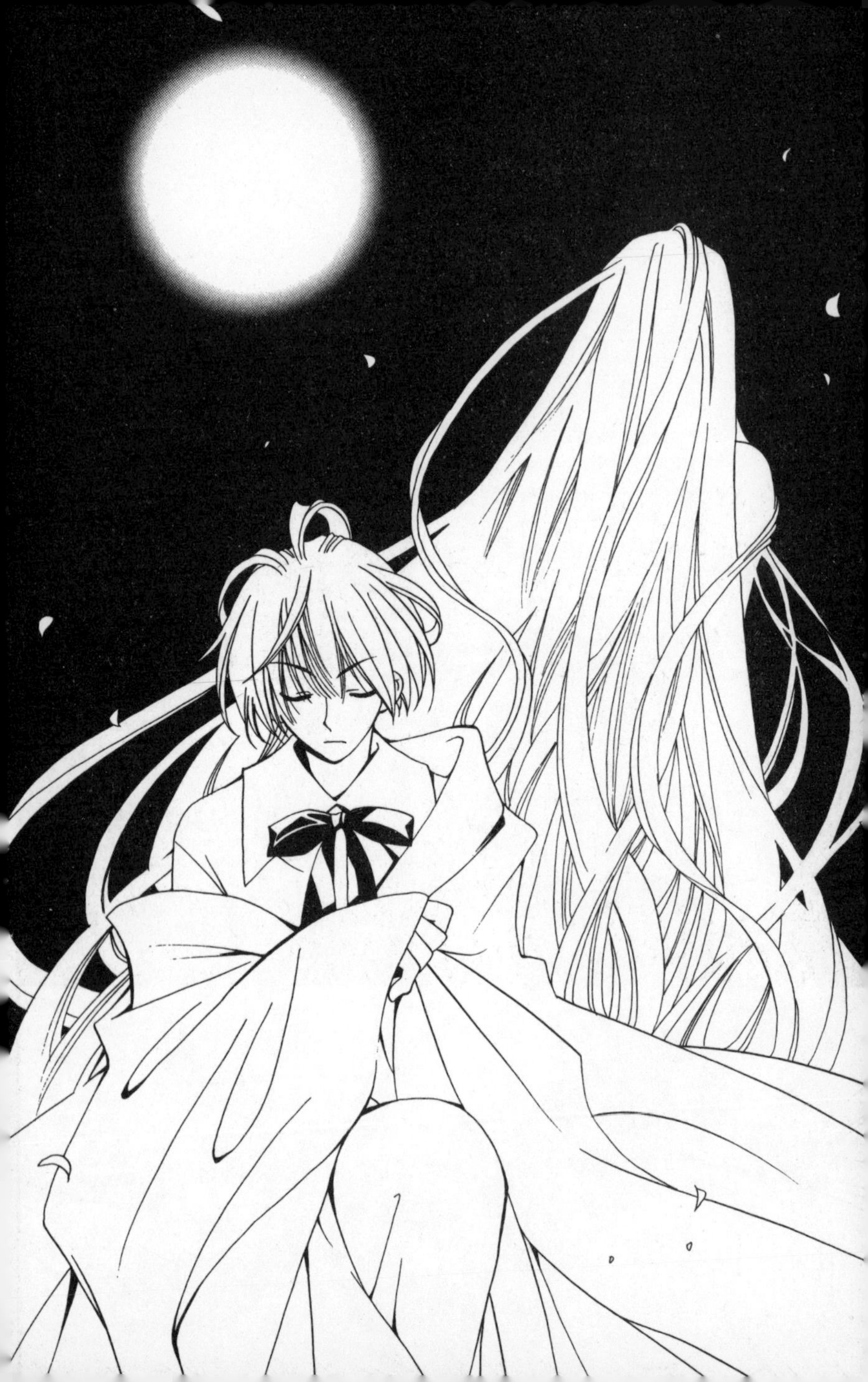

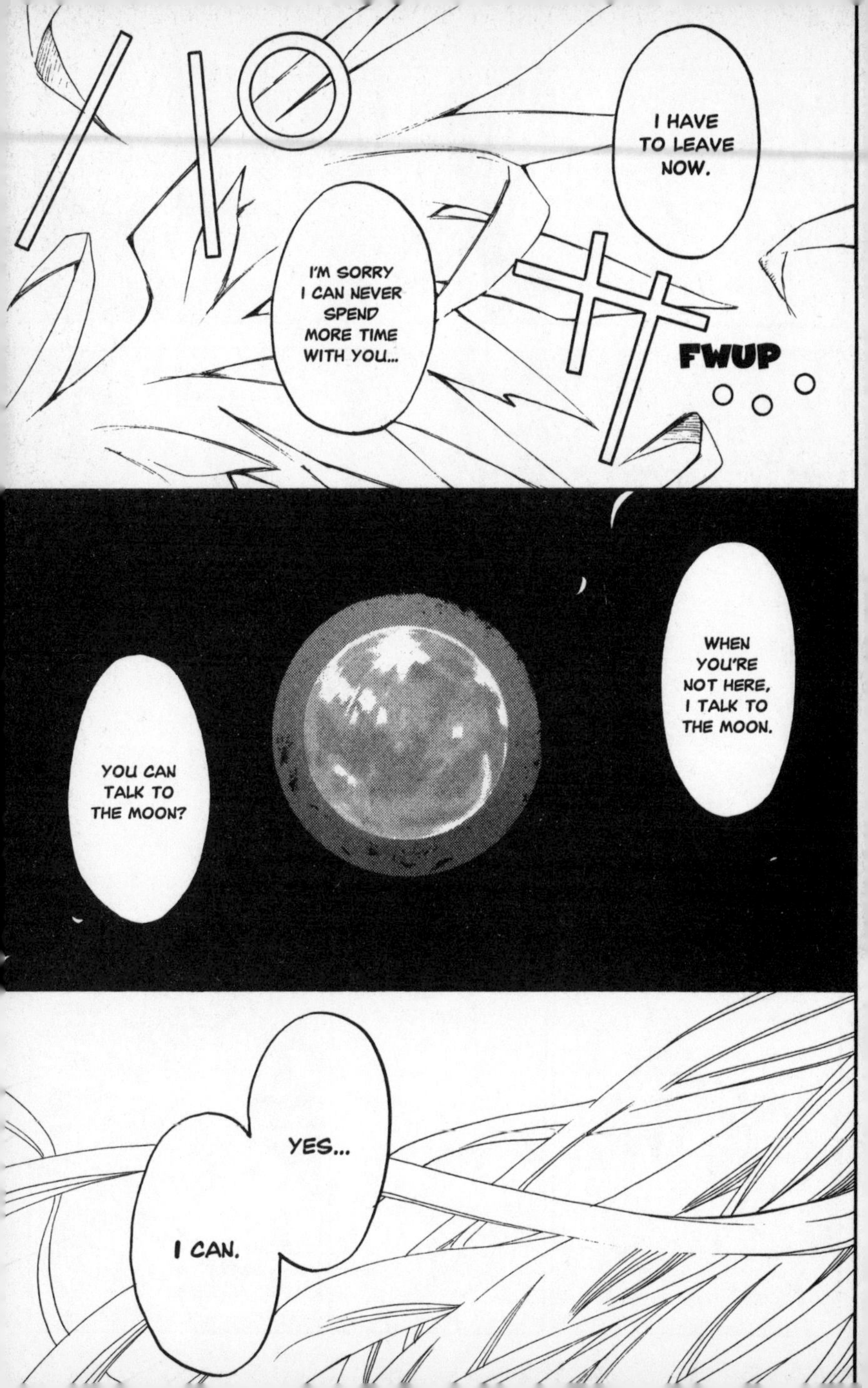
I HAVE TO LEAVE NOW.
I'M SORRY I CAN NEVER SPEND MORE TIME WITH YOU...
FWUP
WHEN YOU'RE NOT HERE, I TALK TO THE MOON.
YOU CAN TALK TO THE MOON?
YES...
I CAN.

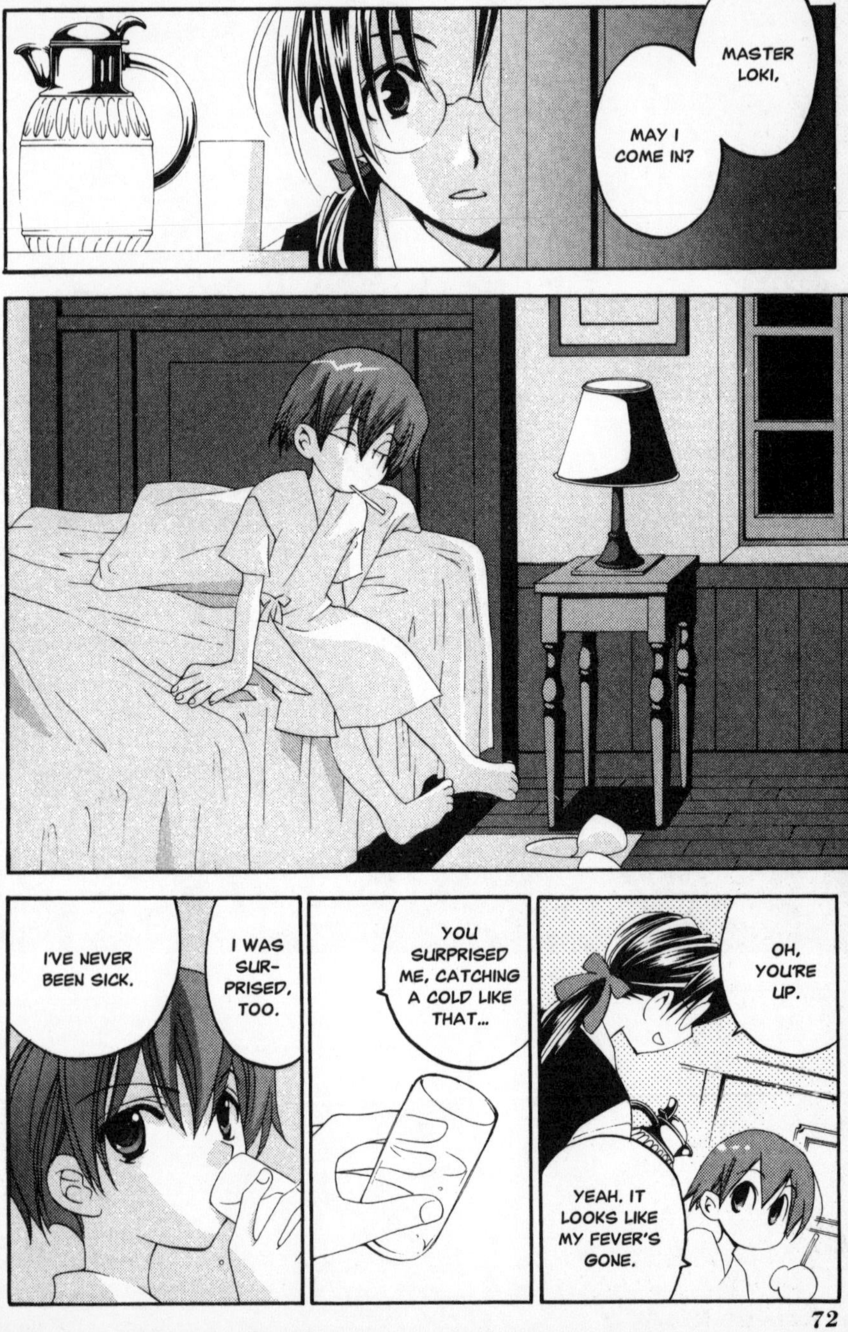
MASTER LOKI,
MAY I COME IN?
OH, YOU'RE UP.
YEAH. IT LOOKS LIKE MY FEVER'S GONE.
YOU SURPRISED ME, CATCHING A COLD LIKE THAT...
I WAS SUR-PRISED, TOO.
I'VE NEVER BEEN SICK.

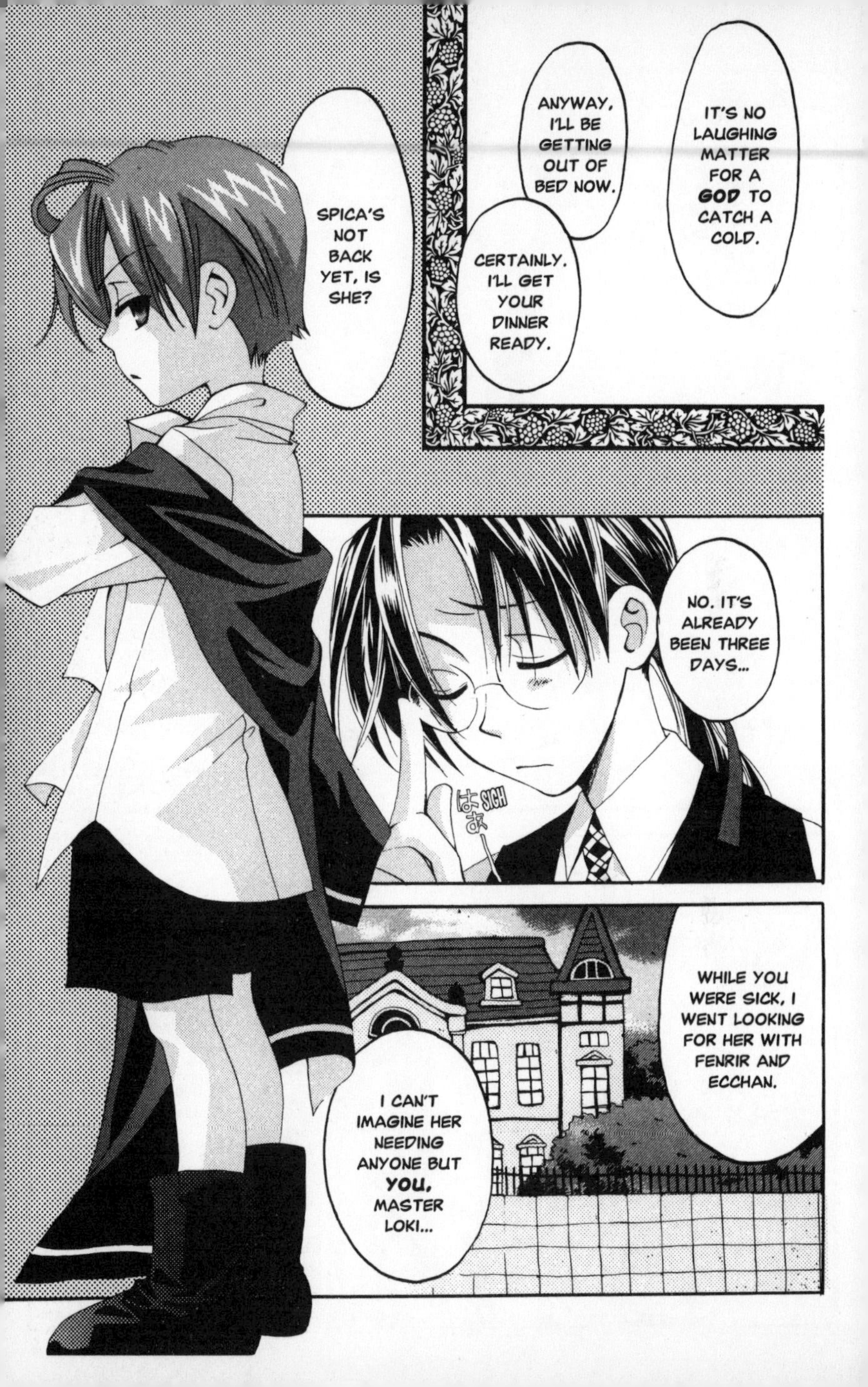
IT'S NO LAUGHING MATTER FOR A GOD TO CATCH A COLD.
ANYWAY, I'LL BE GETTING OUT OF BED NOW.
CERTAINLY. I'LL GET YOUR DINNER READY.
SPICA'S NOT BACK YET, IS SHE?
NO. IT'S ALREADY BEEN THREE DAYS...
はぁー SIGH
WHILE YOU WERE SICK, I WENT LOOKING FOR HER WITH FENRIR AND ECCHAN.
I CAN'T IMAGINE HER NEEDING ANYONE BUT YOU, MASTER LOKI...

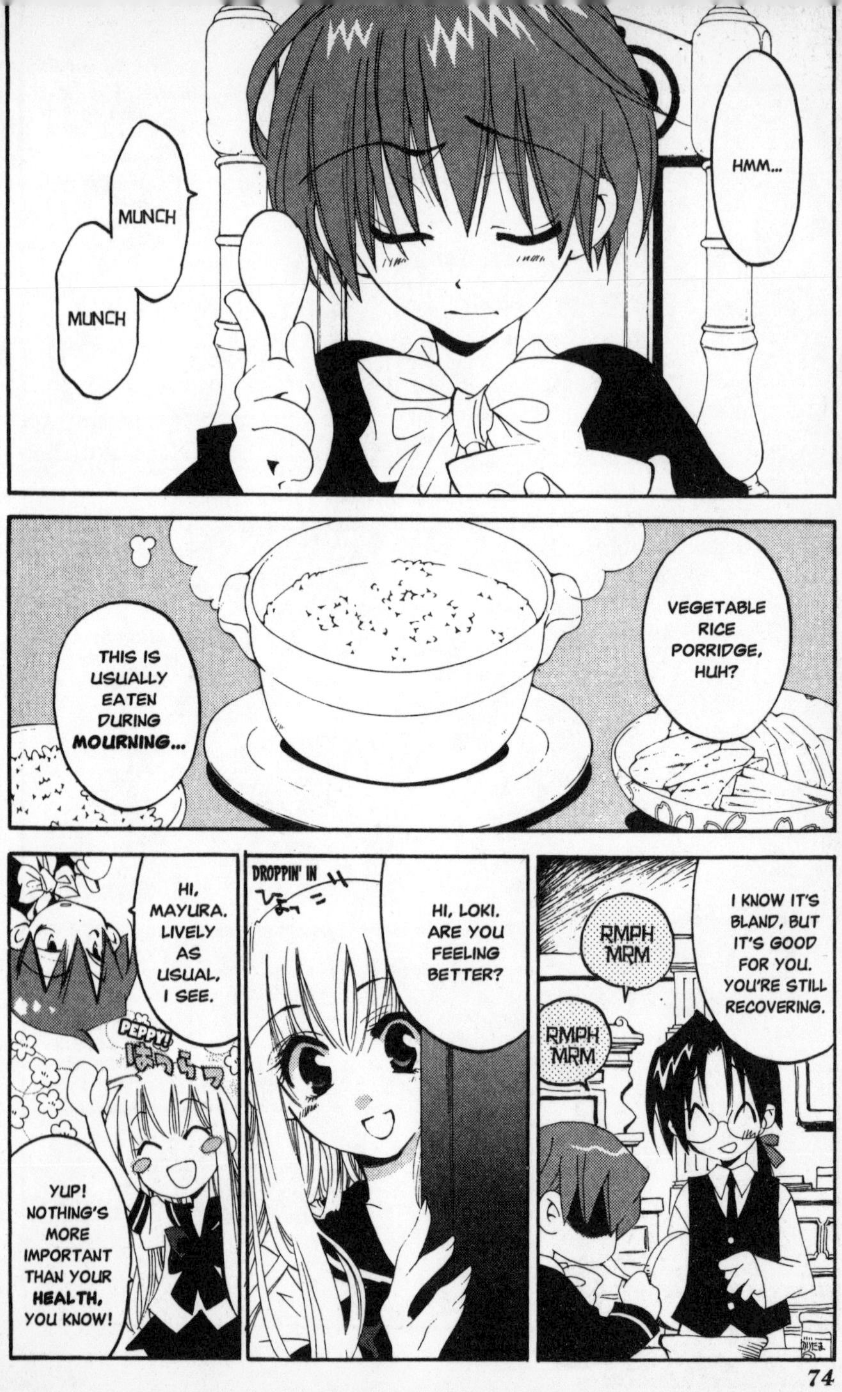

HMM...
MUNCH
MUNCH
VEGETABLE RICE PORRIDGE, HUH?
THIS IS USUALLY EATEN DURING **MOURNING...**
I KNOW IT'S BLAND, BUT IT'S GOOD FOR YOU. YOU'RE STILL RECOVERING.
RMPH MRM
RMPH MRM
DROPPIN' IN
HI, LOKI. ARE YOU FEELING BETTER?
HI, MAYURA. LIVELY AS USUAL, I SEE.
PEPPY!
YUP! NOTHING'S MORE IMPORTANT THAN YOUR **HEALTH,** YOU KNOW!

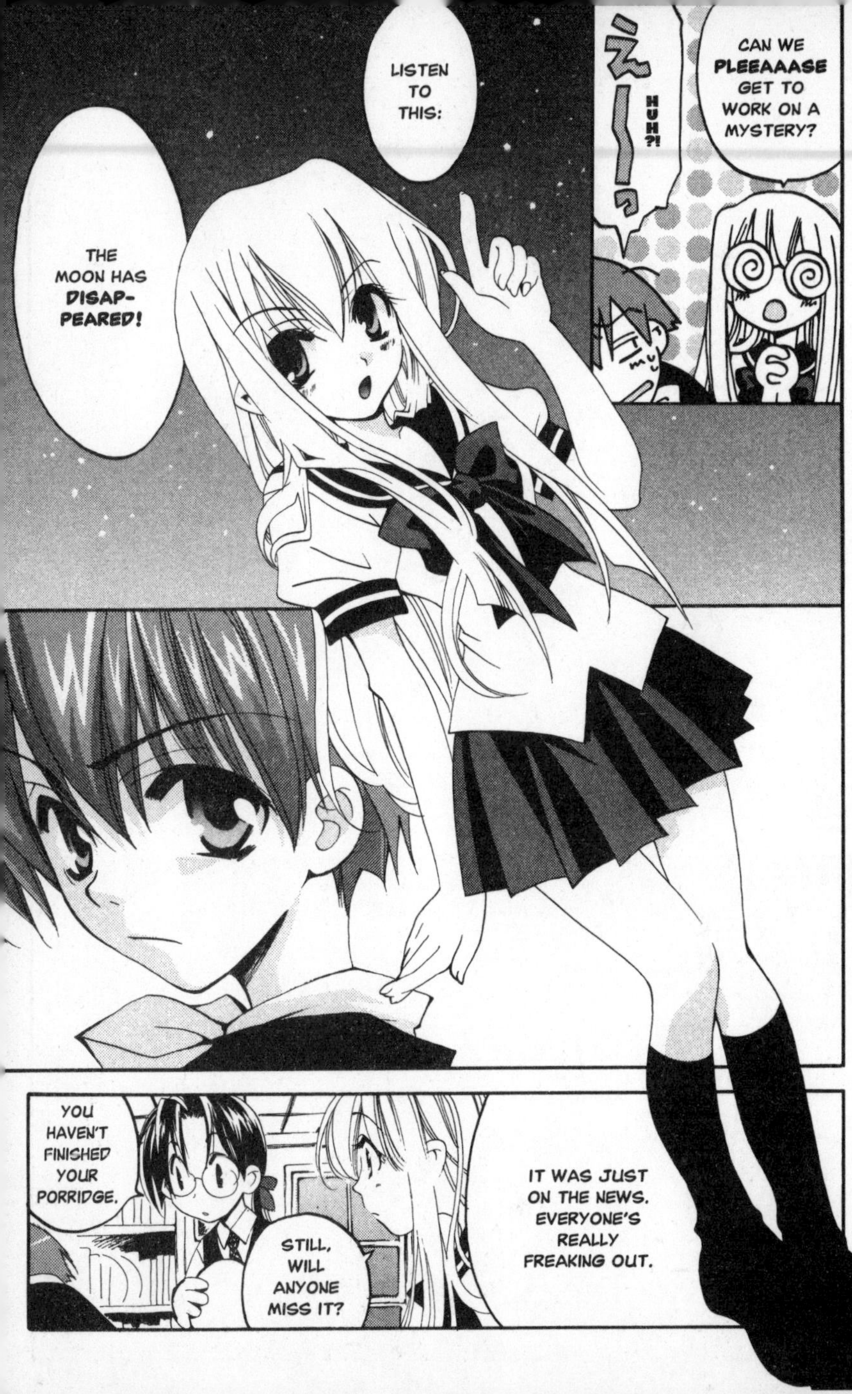
CAN WE PLEEAAASE GET TO WORK ON A MYSTERY?
えーっ
HUH?!
LISTEN TO THIS:
THE MOON HAS DISAPPEARED!
IT WAS JUST ON THE NEWS. EVERYONE'S REALLY FREAKING OUT.
STILL, WILL ANYONE MISS IT?
YOU HAVEN'T FINISHED YOUR PORRIDGE.

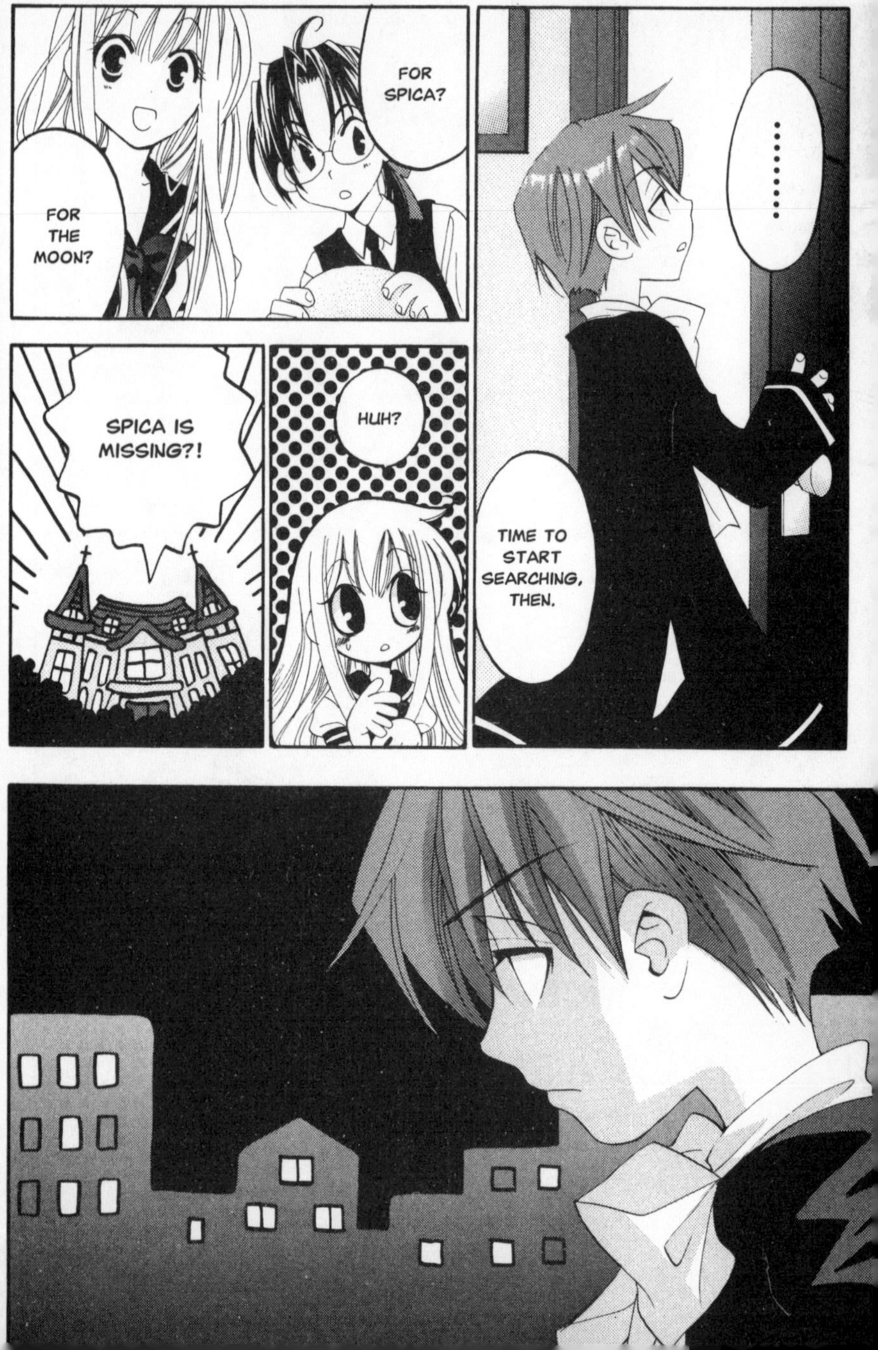

......
FOR SPICA?
FOR THE MOON?
TIME TO START SEARCHING, THEN.
HUH?
SPICA IS MISSING?!

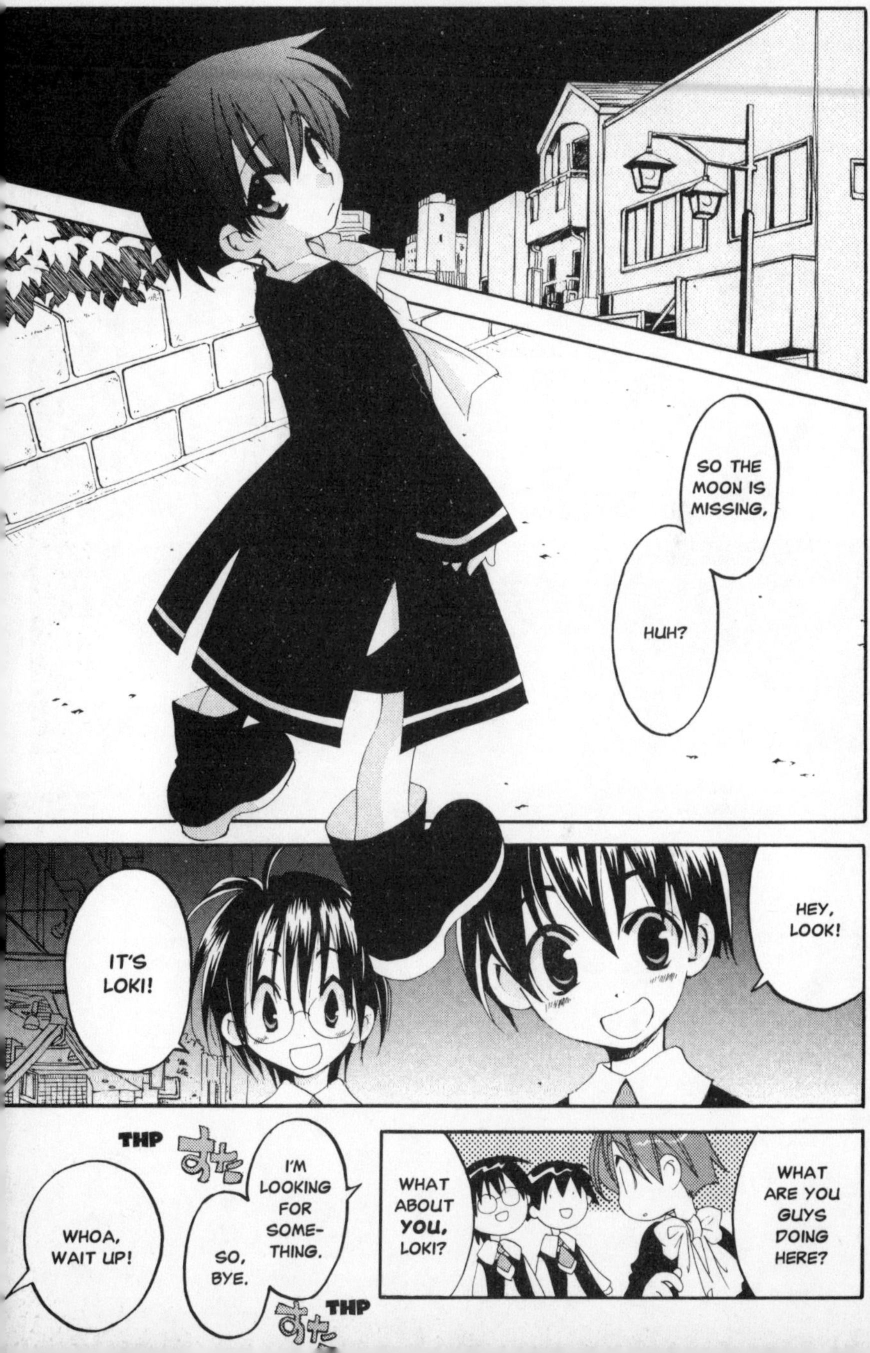
SO THE MOON IS MISSING,
HUH?
HEY, LOOK!
IT'S LOKI!
WHAT ARE YOU GUYS DOING HERE?
WHAT ABOUT YOU, LOKI?
I'M LOOKING FOR SOME-THING.
SO, BYE.
THP
THP
WHOA, WAIT UP!

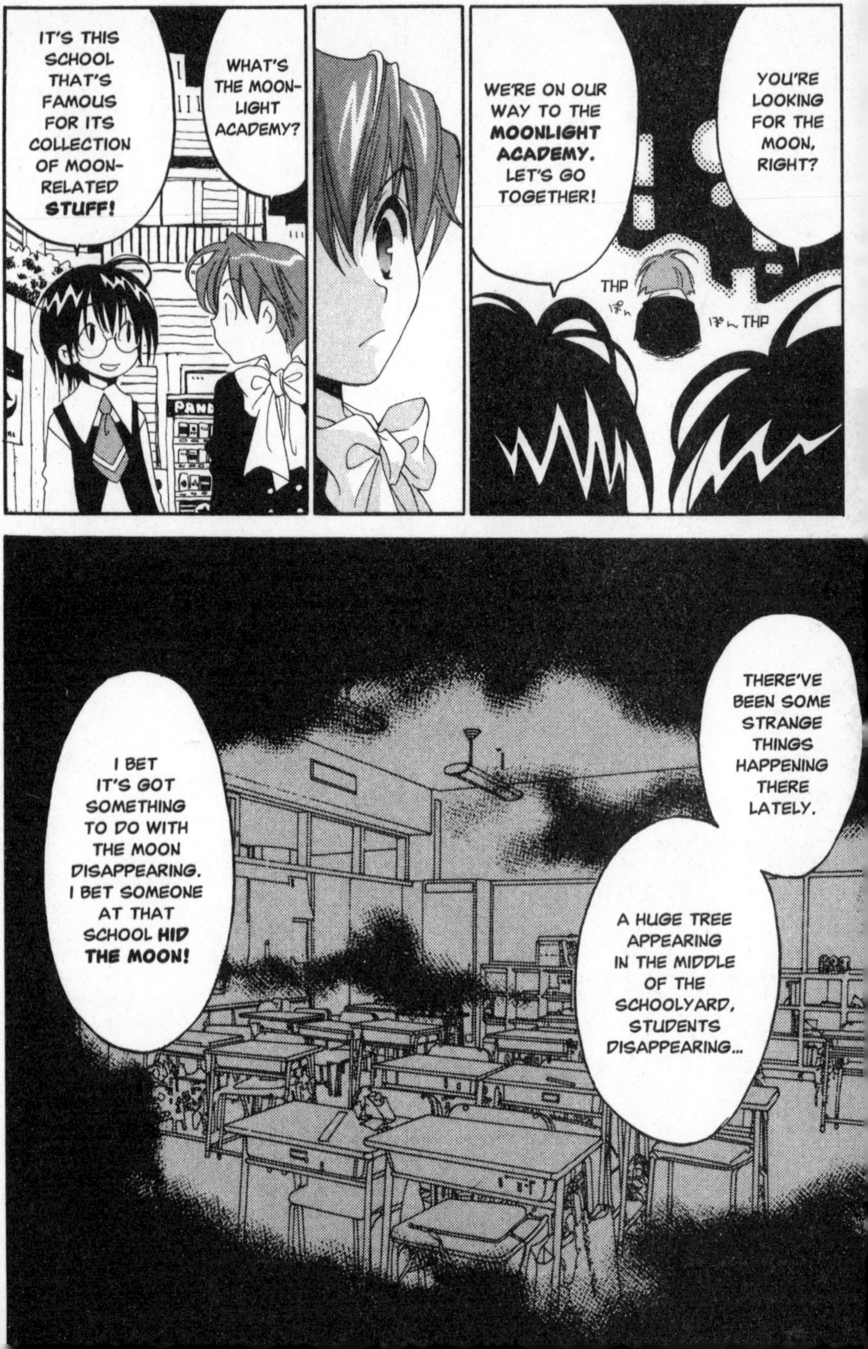
YOU'RE LOOKING FOR THE MOON, RIGHT?
WE'RE ON OUR WAY TO THE **MOONLIGHT ACADEMY.** LET'S GO TOGETHER!
THP
THP
WHAT'S THE MOON-LIGHT ACADEMY?
IT'S THIS SCHOOL THAT'S FAMOUS FOR ITS COLLECTION OF MOON-RELATED **STUFF!**
THERE'VE BEEN SOME STRANGE THINGS HAPPENING THERE LATELY.
A HUGE TREE APPEARING IN THE MIDDLE OF THE SCHOOLYARD, STUDENTS DISAPPEARING...
I BET IT'S GOT SOMETHING TO DO WITH THE MOON DISAPPEARING. I BET SOMEONE AT THAT SCHOOL **HID THE MOON!**

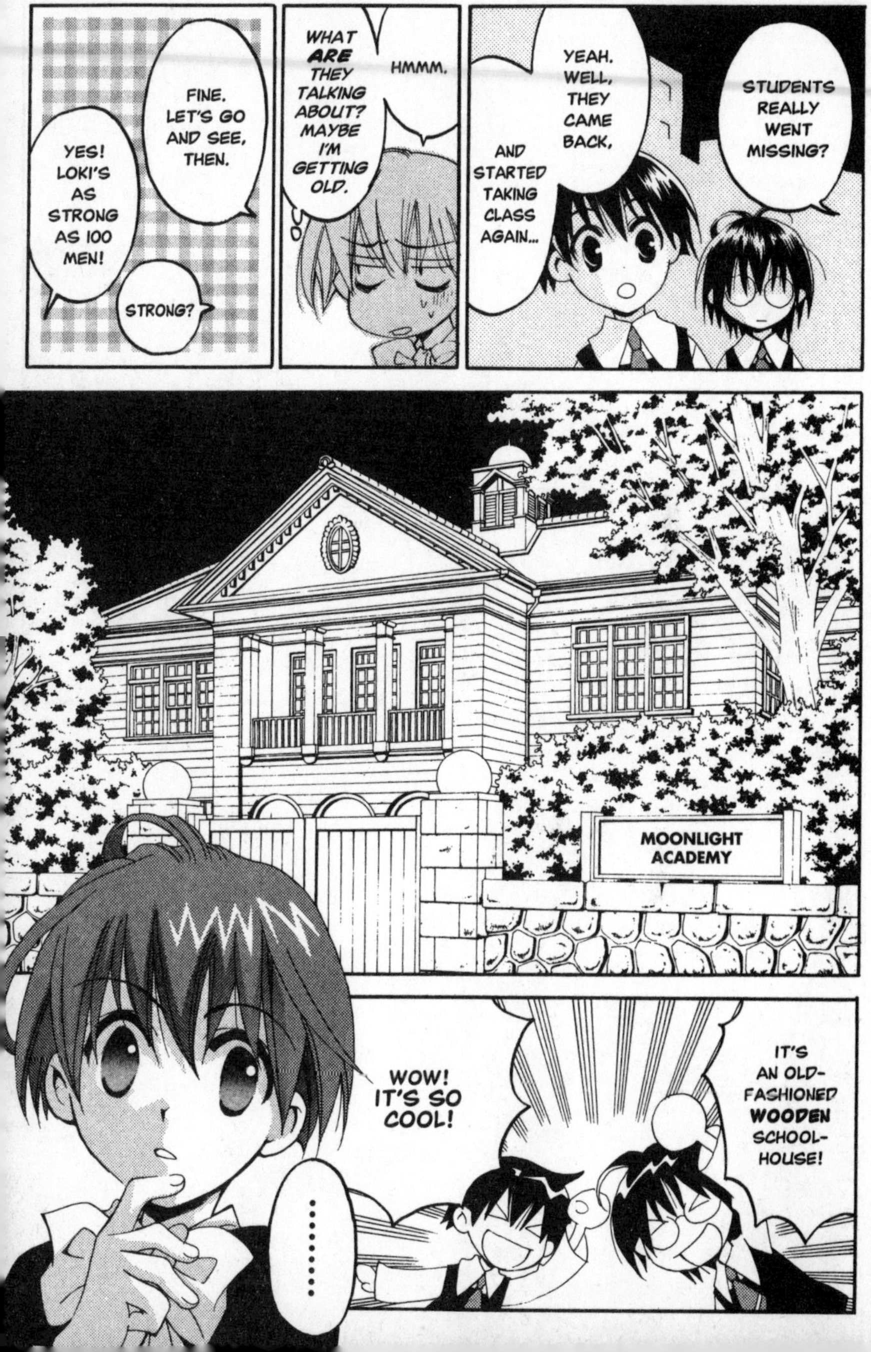
STUDENTS REALLY WENT MISSING?
YEAH. WELL, THEY CAME BACK,
AND STARTED TAKING CLASS AGAIN...
HMMM.
WHAT **ARE** THEY TALKING ABOUT? MAYBE I'M GETTING OLD.
FINE. LET'S GO AND SEE, THEN.
YES! LOKI'S AS STRONG AS 100 MEN!
STRONG?
MOONLIGHT ACADEMY
IT'S AN OLD-FASHIONED **WOODEN** SCHOOL-HOUSE!
WOW! IT'S SO COOL!
......

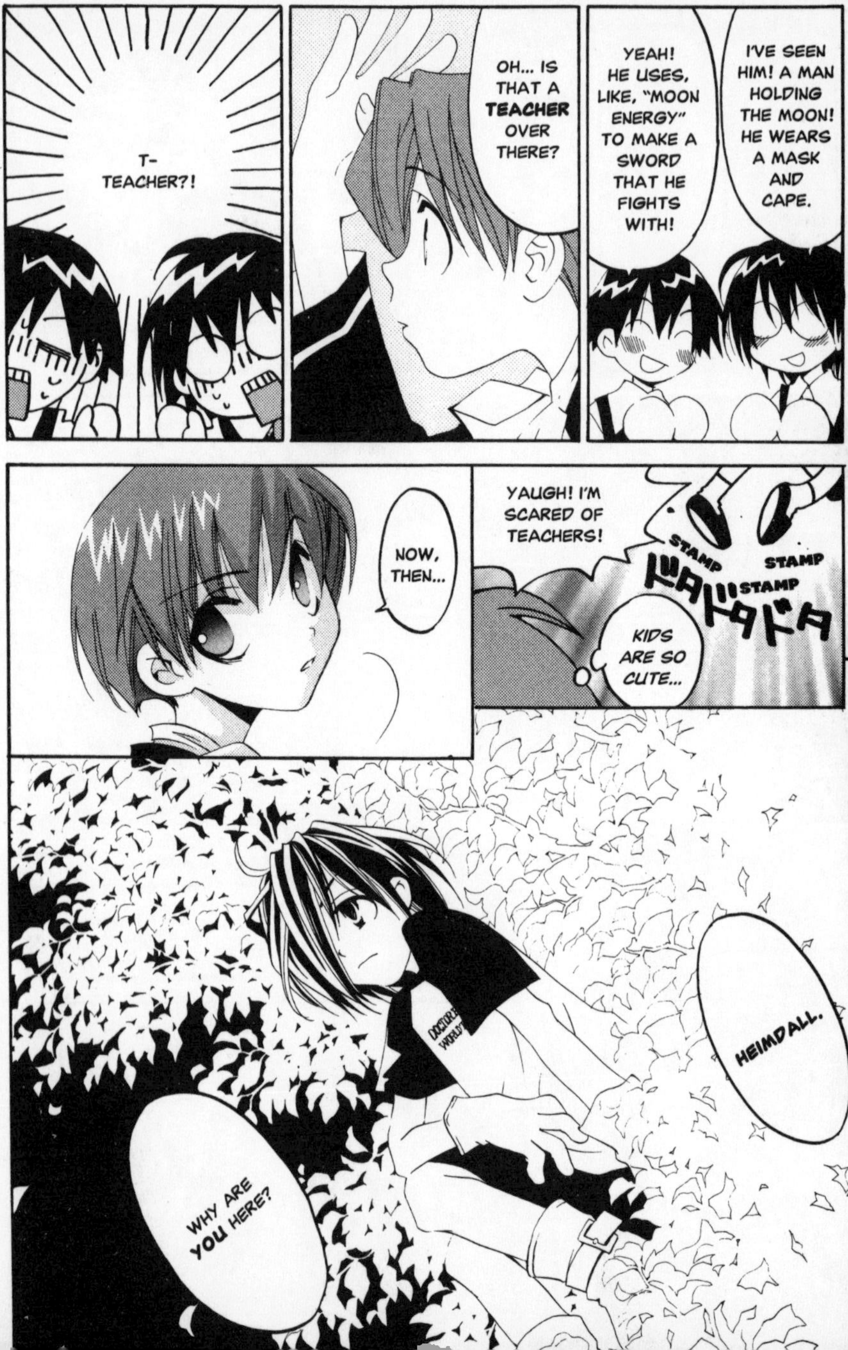

I'VE SEEN HIM! A MAN HOLDING THE MOON! HE WEARS A MASK AND CAPE.
YEAH! HE USES, LIKE, "MOON ENERGY" TO MAKE A SWORD THAT HE FIGHTS WITH!
OH... IS THAT A **TEACHER** OVER THERE?
T-TEACHER?!
YAUGH! I'M SCARED OF TEACHERS!
STAMP STAMP STAMP
ドタドタドタ
KIDS ARE SO CUTE...
NOW, THEN...
HEIMDALL.
WHY ARE **YOU** HERE?

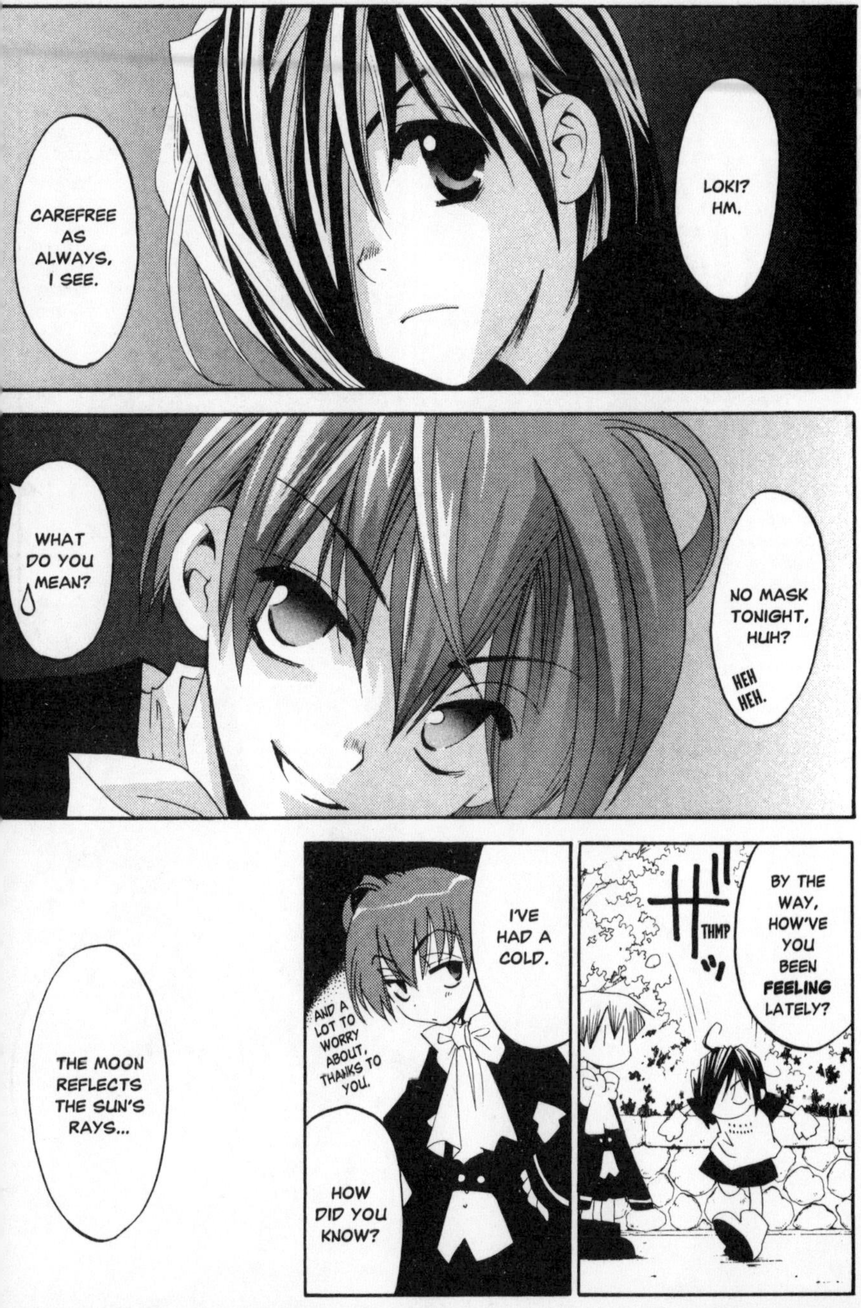
LOKI? HM.
CAREFREE AS ALWAYS, I SEE.
NO MASK TONIGHT, HUH?
HEH HEH.
WHAT DO YOU MEAN?
BY THE WAY, HOW'VE YOU BEEN FEELING LATELY?
THMP
I'VE HAD A COLD.
AND A LOT TO WORRY ABOUT, THANKS TO YOU.
HOW DID YOU KNOW?
THE MOON REFLECTS THE SUN'S RAYS...

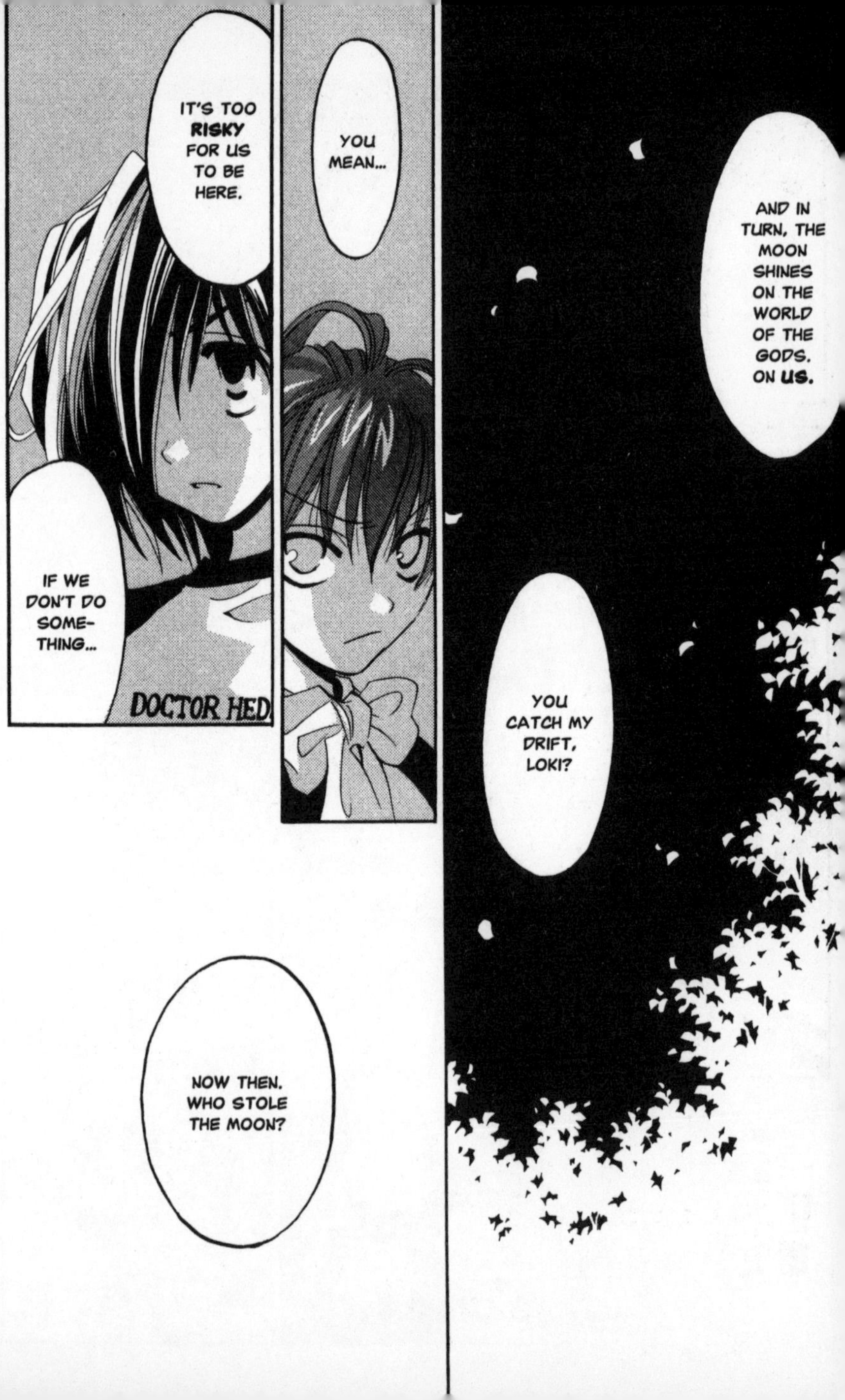
AND IN TURN, THE MOON SHINES ON THE WORLD OF THE GODS. ON **US**.
YOU CATCH MY DRIFT, LOKI?
YOU MEAN...
IT'S TOO **RISKY** FOR US TO BE HERE.
IF WE DON'T DO SOME-THING...
DOCTOR HED
NOW THEN. WHO STOLE THE MOON?

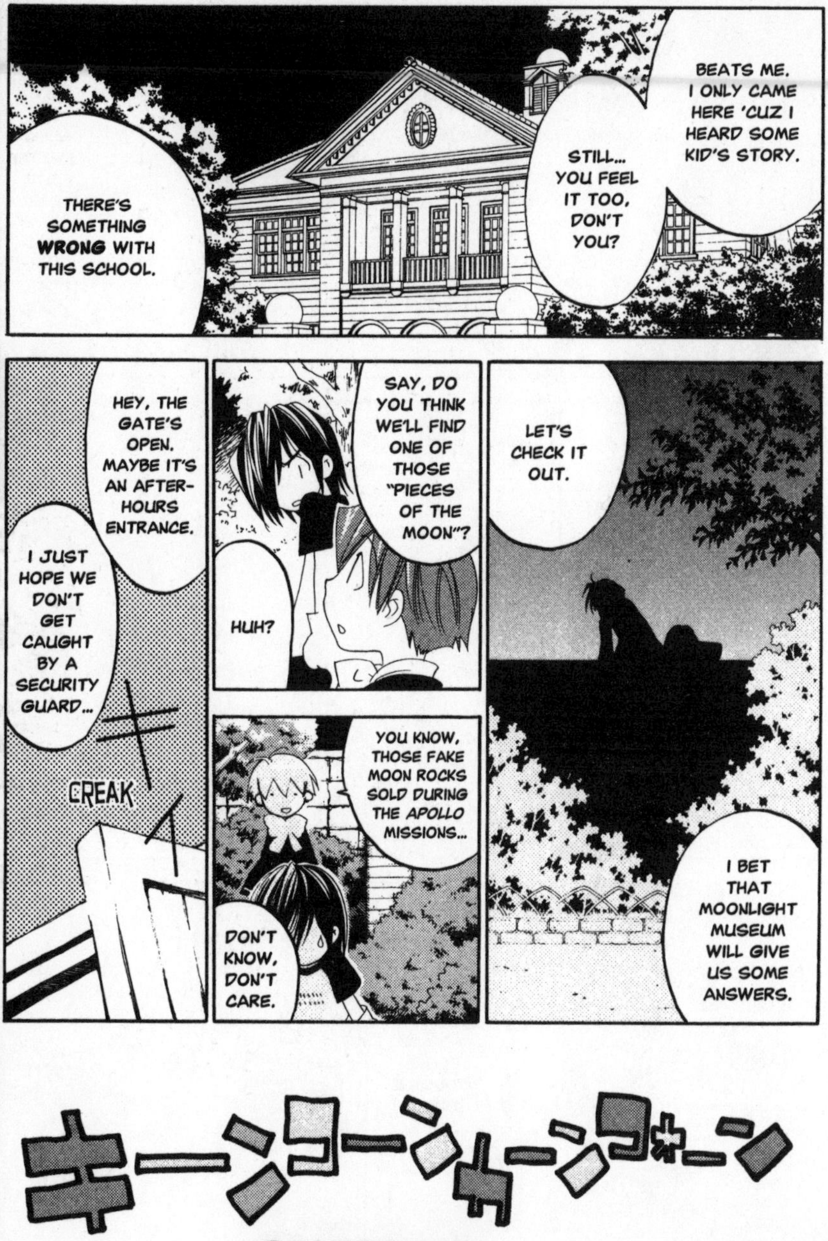
BEATS ME. I ONLY CAME HERE 'CUZ I HEARD SOME KID'S STORY.
STILL... YOU FEEL IT TOO, DON'T YOU?
THERE'S SOMETHING **WRONG** WITH THIS SCHOOL.
LET'S CHECK IT OUT.
I BET THAT MOONLIGHT MUSEUM WILL GIVE US SOME ANSWERS.
SAY, DO YOU THINK WE'LL FIND ONE OF THOSE "PIECES OF THE MOON"?
HUH?
YOU KNOW, THOSE FAKE MOON ROCKS SOLD DURING THE APOLLO MISSIONS...
DON'T KNOW, DON'T CARE.
HEY, THE GATE'S OPEN. MAYBE IT'S AN AFTER-HOURS ENTRANCE.
I JUST HOPE WE DON'T GET CAUGHT BY A SECURITY GUARD...
CREAK
BRRRRRING!

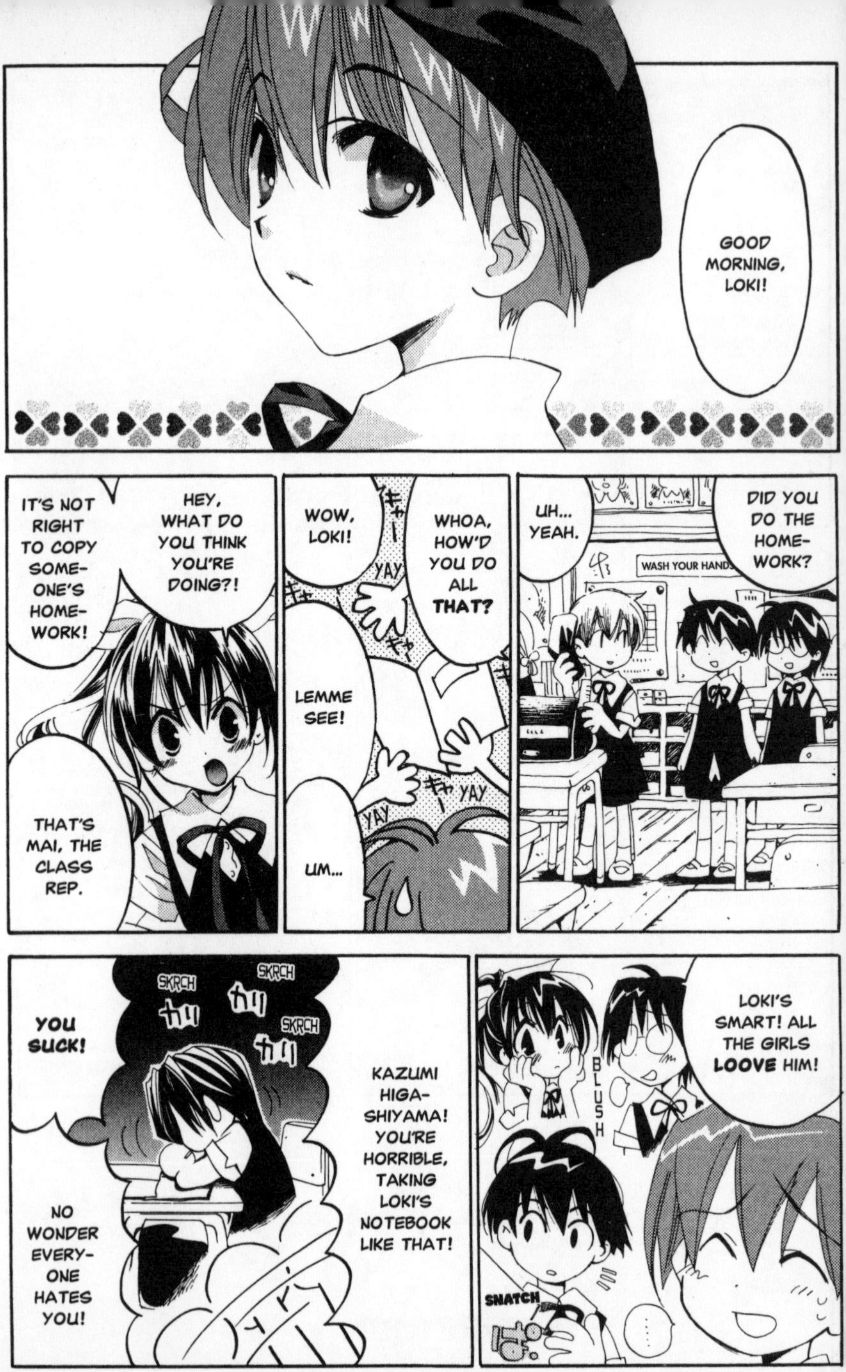

GOOD MORNING, LOKI!
DID YOU DO THE HOME-WORK?
UH... YEAH.
WASH YOUR HANDS
WHOA, HOW'D YOU DO ALL **THAT?**
WOW, LOKI!
YAY
LEMME SEE!
YAY
YAY
UM...
HEY, WHAT DO YOU THINK YOU'RE DOING?!
IT'S NOT RIGHT TO COPY SOME-ONE'S HOME-WORK!
THAT'S MAI, THE CLASS REP.
LOKI'S SMART! ALL THE GIRLS **LOOVE** HIM!
BLUSH
SNATCH
KAZUMI HIGA-SHIYAMA! YOU'RE HORRIBLE, TAKING LOKI'S NOTEBOOK LIKE THAT!
SKRCH
SKRCH
SKRCH
YOU SUCK!
NO WONDER EVERY-ONE HATES YOU!

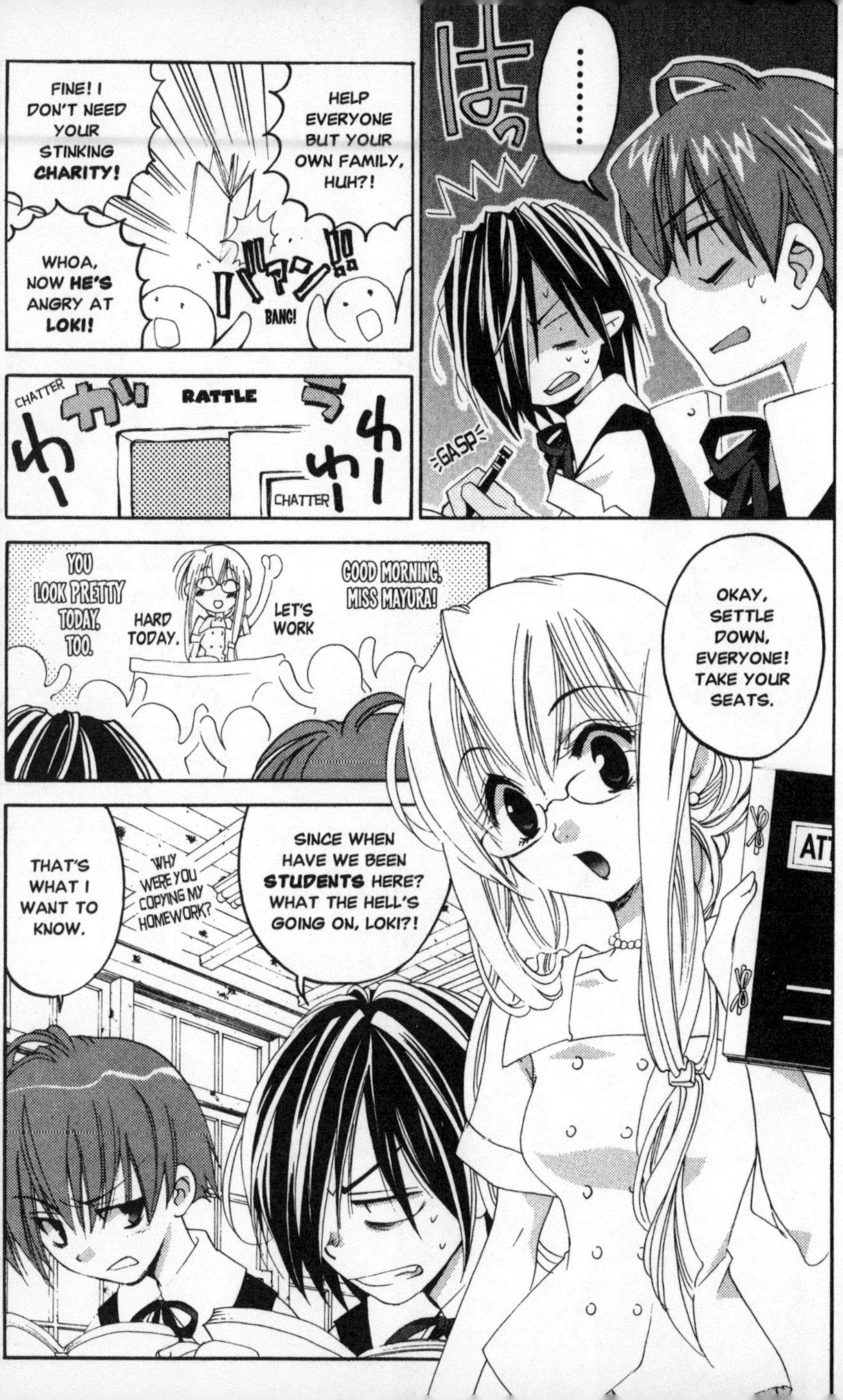
はっ
......
GASP
FINE! I DON'T NEED YOUR STINKING CHARITY!
HELP EVERYONE BUT YOUR OWN FAMILY, HUH?!
BANG!
WHOA, NOW HE'S ANGRY AT LOKI!
RATTLE
CHATTER
CHATTER
OKAY, SETTLE DOWN, EVERYONE! TAKE YOUR SEATS.
GOOD MORNING, MISS MAYURA!
LET'S WORK
HARD TODAY.
YOU LOOK PRETTY TODAY, TOO.
ATT
SINCE WHEN HAVE WE BEEN STUDENTS HERE? WHAT THE HELL'S GOING ON, LOKI?!
WHY WERE YOU COPYING MY HOMEWORK?
THAT'S WHAT I WANT TO KNOW.

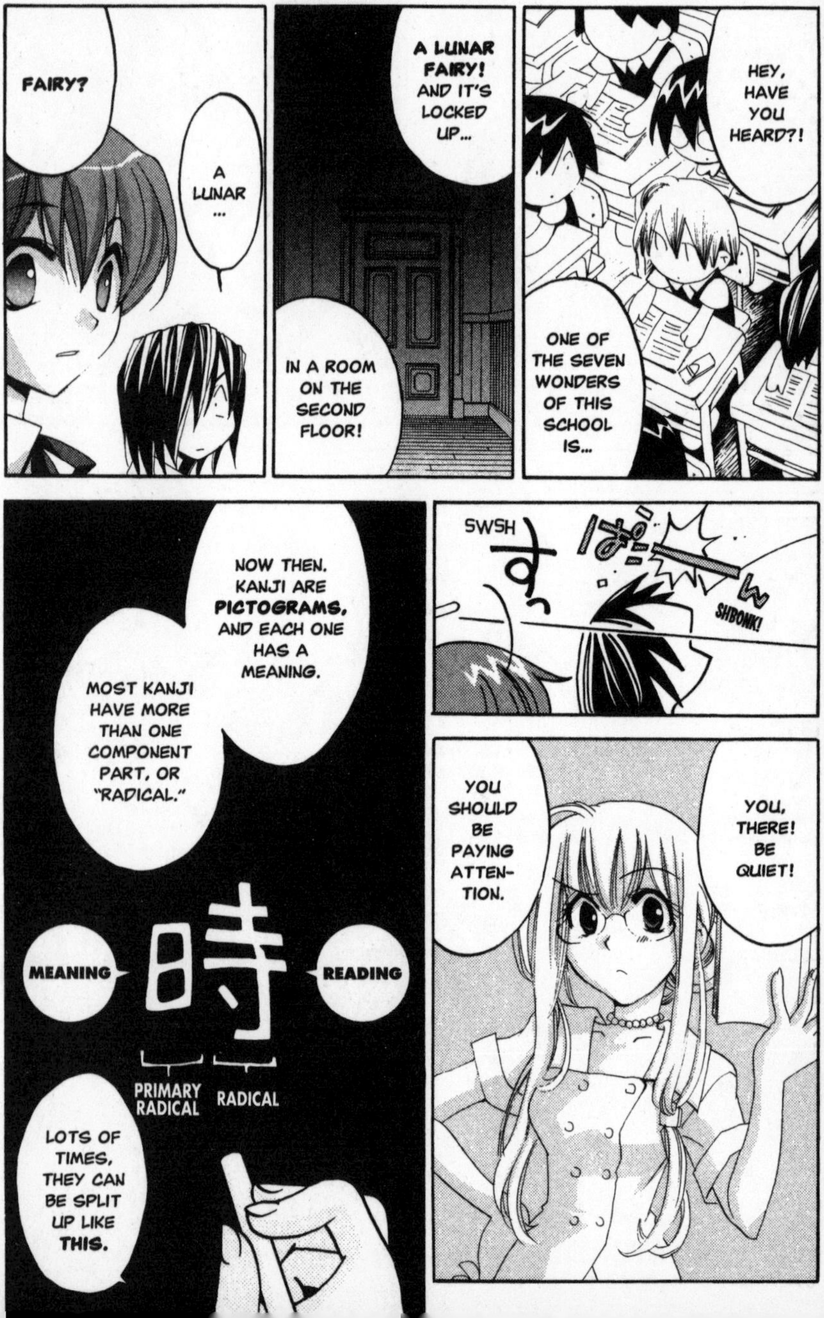

HEY, HAVE YOU HEARD?!
ONE OF THE SEVEN WONDERS OF THIS SCHOOL IS...
A LUNAR FAIRY! AND IT'S LOCKED UP...
IN A ROOM ON THE SECOND FLOOR!
A LUNAR...
FAIRY?
SWSH
すっ
SHBONK!
YOU, THERE! BE QUIET!
YOU SHOULD BE PAYING ATTEN-TION.
NOW THEN. KANJI ARE PICTOGRAMS, AND EACH ONE HAS A MEANING.
MOST KANJI HAVE MORE THAN ONE COMPONENT PART, OR "RADICAL."
MEANING
時
READING
PRIMARY RADICAL
RADICAL
LOTS OF TIMES, THEY CAN BE SPLIT UP LIKE THIS.

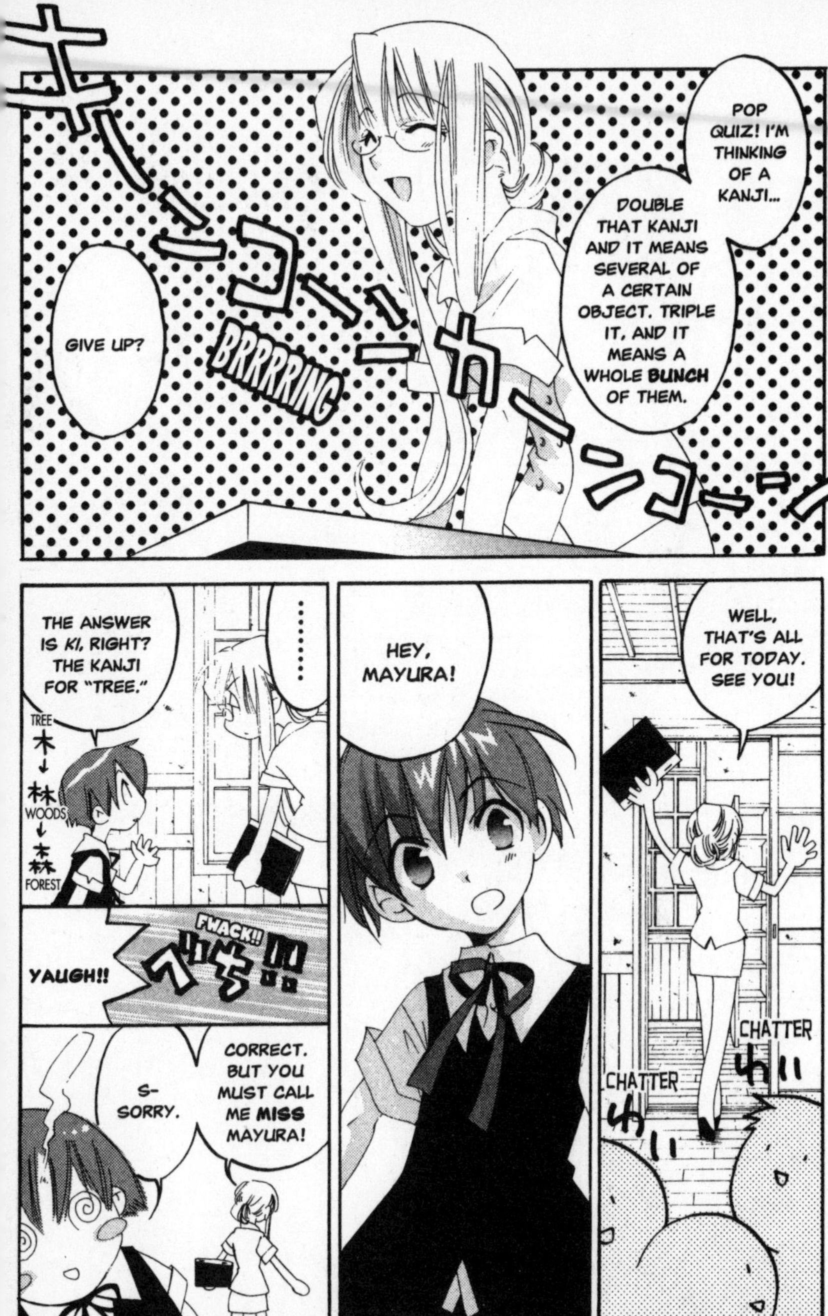
POP QUIZ! I'M THINKING OF A KANJI...
DOUBLE THAT KANJI AND IT MEANS SEVERAL OF A CERTAIN OBJECT. TRIPLE IT, AND IT MEANS A WHOLE **BUNCH** OF THEM.
BRRRRRING
GIVE UP?
WELL, THAT'S ALL FOR TODAY. SEE YOU!
CHATTER
CHATTER
HEY, MAYURA!
......
THE ANSWER IS *KI*, RIGHT? THE KANJI FOR "TREE."
TREE 木
林 WOODS
森 FOREST
FWACK!!
YAUGH!!
CORRECT. BUT YOU MUST CALL ME **MISS** MAYURA!
S- SORRY.

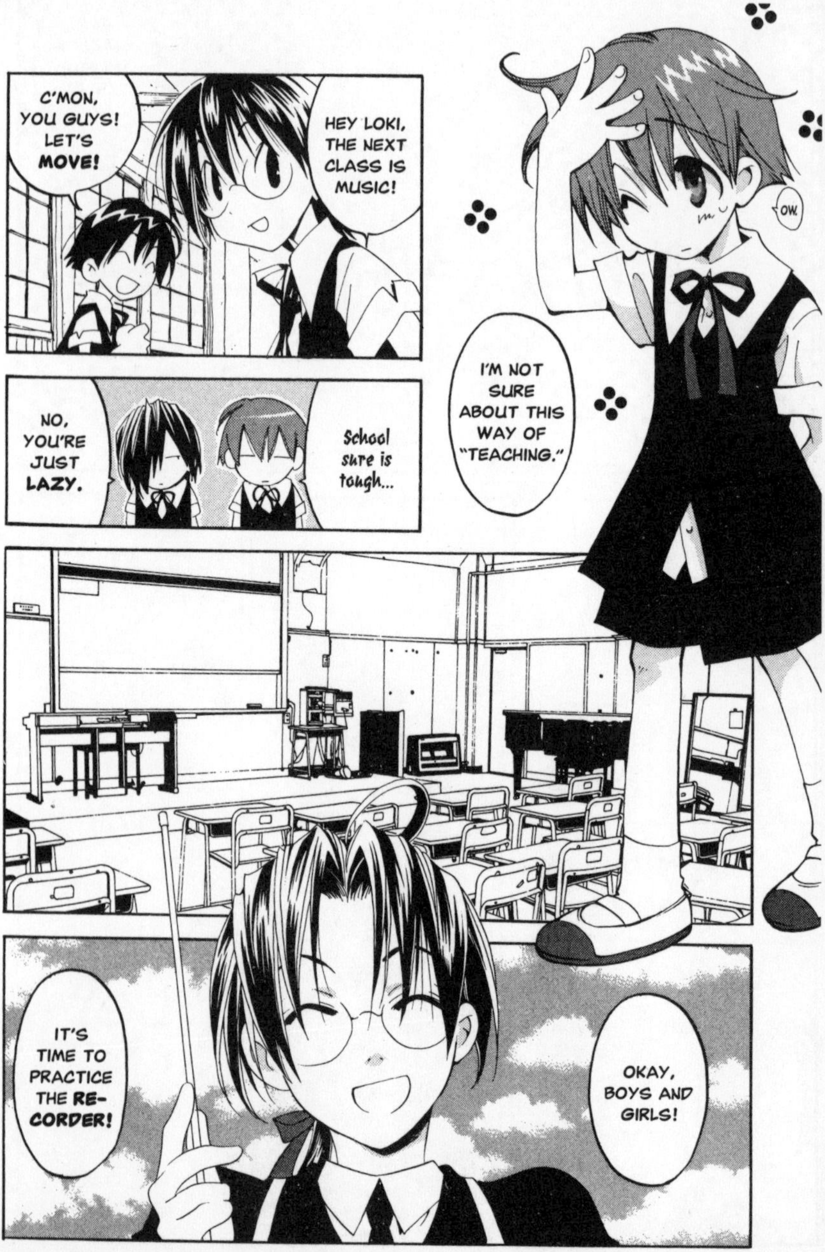
OW.
I'M NOT SURE ABOUT THIS WAY OF "TEACHING."
HEY LOKI, THE NEXT CLASS IS MUSIC!
C'MON, YOU GUYS! LET'S MOVE!
School sure is tough...
NO, YOU'RE JUST LAZY.
OKAY, BOYS AND GIRLS!
IT'S TIME TO PRACTICE THE RE-CORDER!

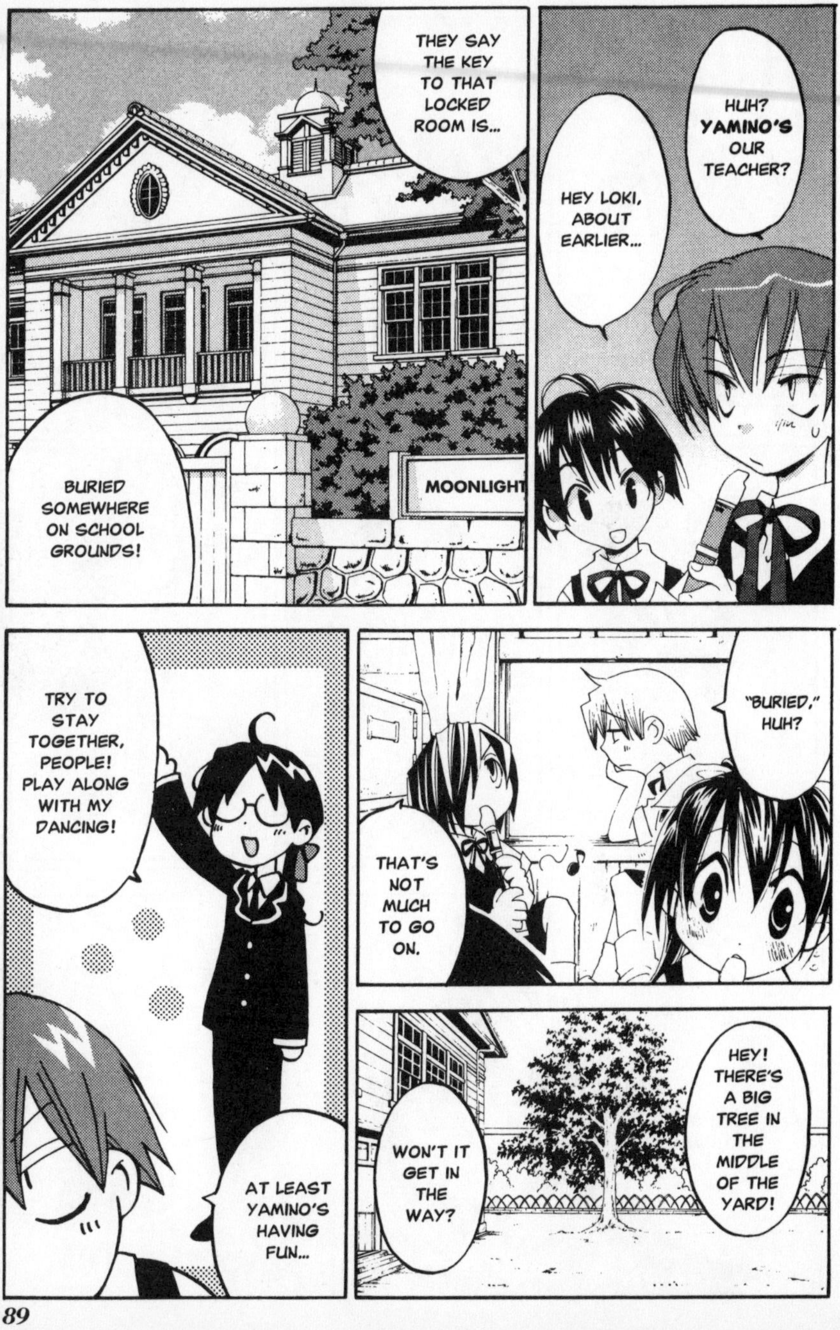
HEY LOKI, ABOUT EARLIER...
HUH? YAMINO'S OUR TEACHER?
THEY SAY THE KEY TO THAT LOCKED ROOM IS...
MOONLIGHT
BURIED SOMEWHERE ON SCHOOL GROUNDS!
"BURIED," HUH?
THAT'S NOT MUCH TO GO ON.
HEY! THERE'S A BIG TREE IN THE MIDDLE OF THE YARD!
WON'T IT GET IN THE WAY?
TRY TO STAY TOGETHER, PEOPLE! PLAY ALONG WITH MY DANCING!
AT LEAST YAMINO'S HAVING FUN...

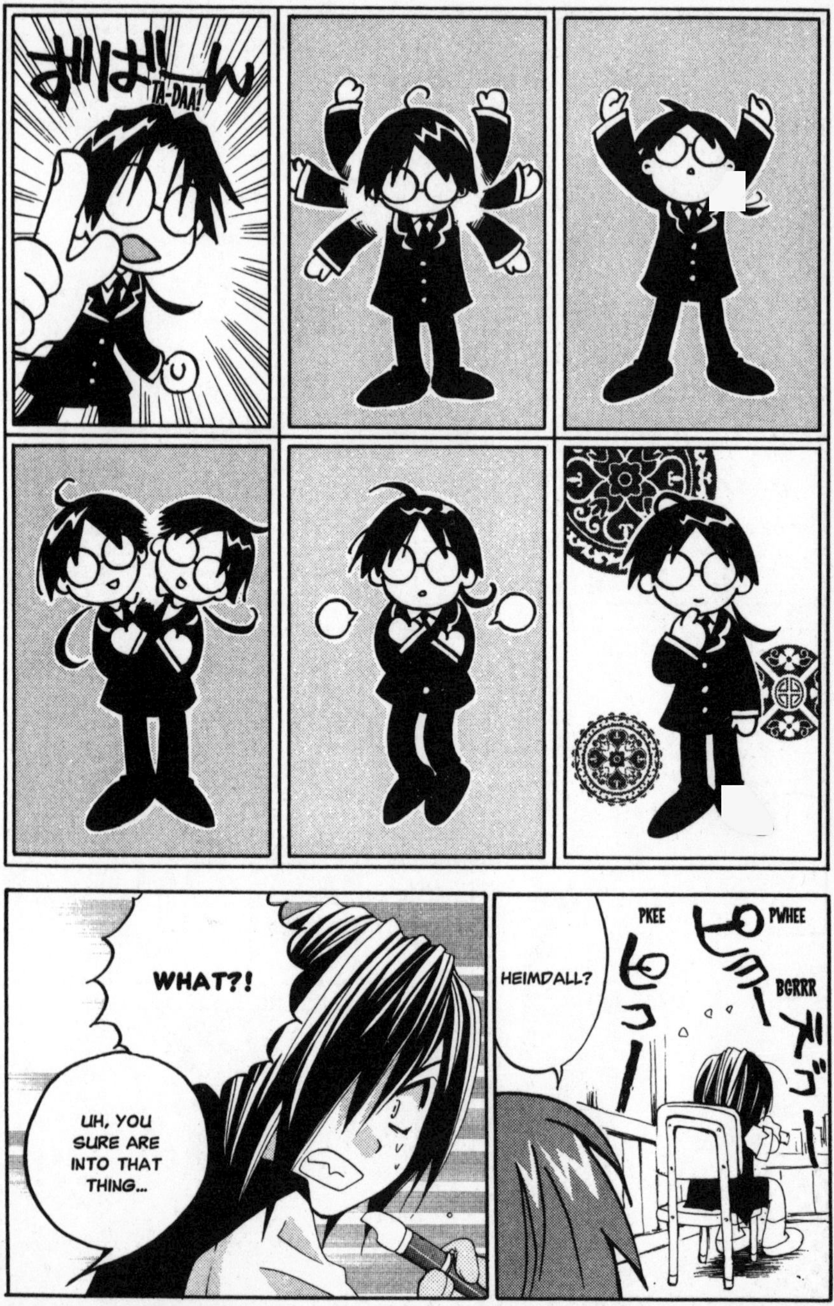
TA-DAA!
HEIMDALL?
PKEE
PWHEE
BGRRR
WHAT?!
UH, YOU SURE ARE INTO THAT THING...

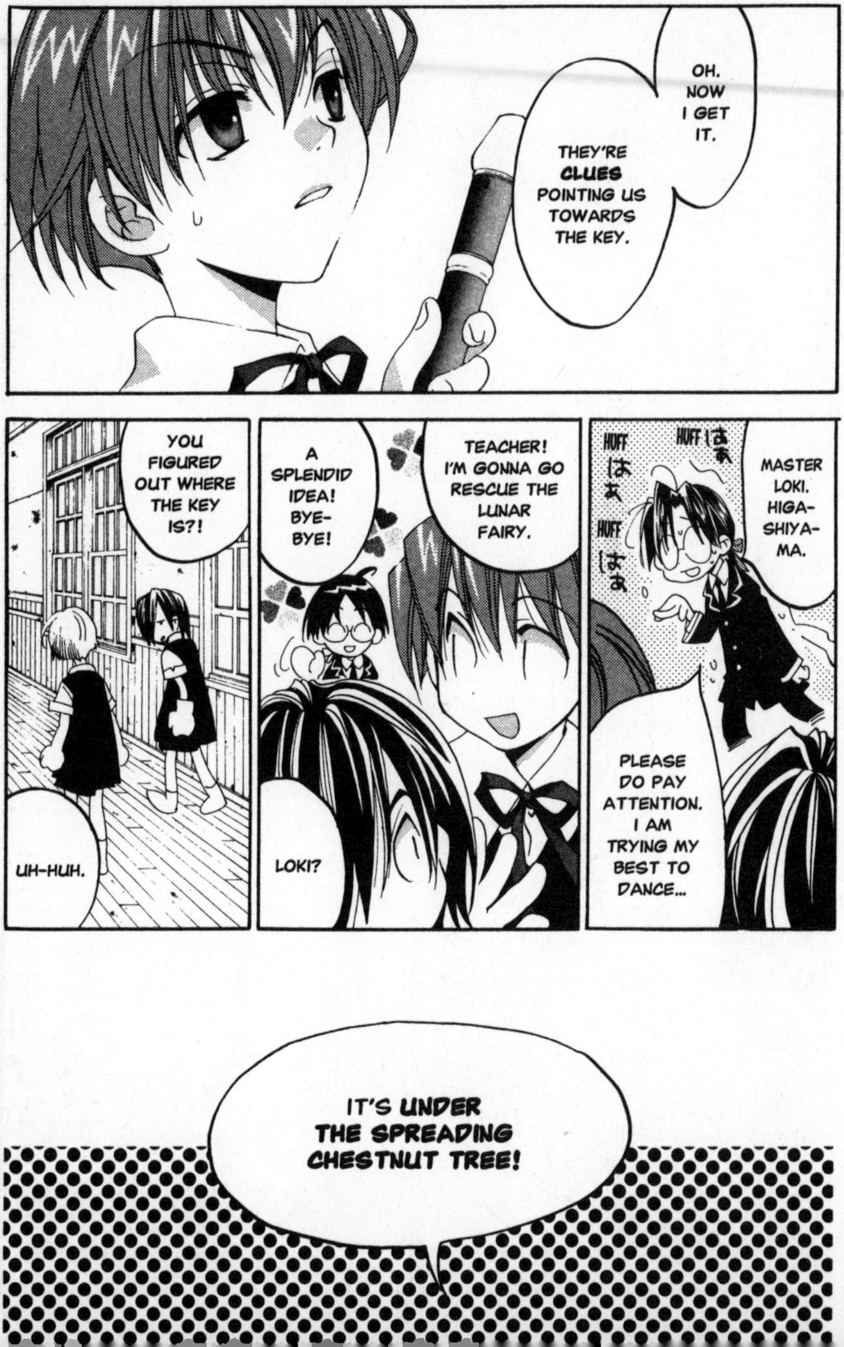
OH. NOW I GET IT.
THEY'RE **CLUES** POINTING US TOWARDS THE KEY.
MASTER LOKI. HIGA-SHIYA-MA.
HUFF はぁ
HUFF はぁ
HUFF はぁ
PLEASE DO PAY ATTENTION. I AM TRYING MY BEST TO DANCE...
TEACHER! I'M GONNA GO RESCUE THE LUNAR FAIRY.
A SPLENDID IDEA! BYE-BYE!
LOKI?
YOU FIGURED OUT WHERE THE KEY IS?!
UH-HUH.
IT'S **UNDER THE SPREADING CHESTNUT TREE!**

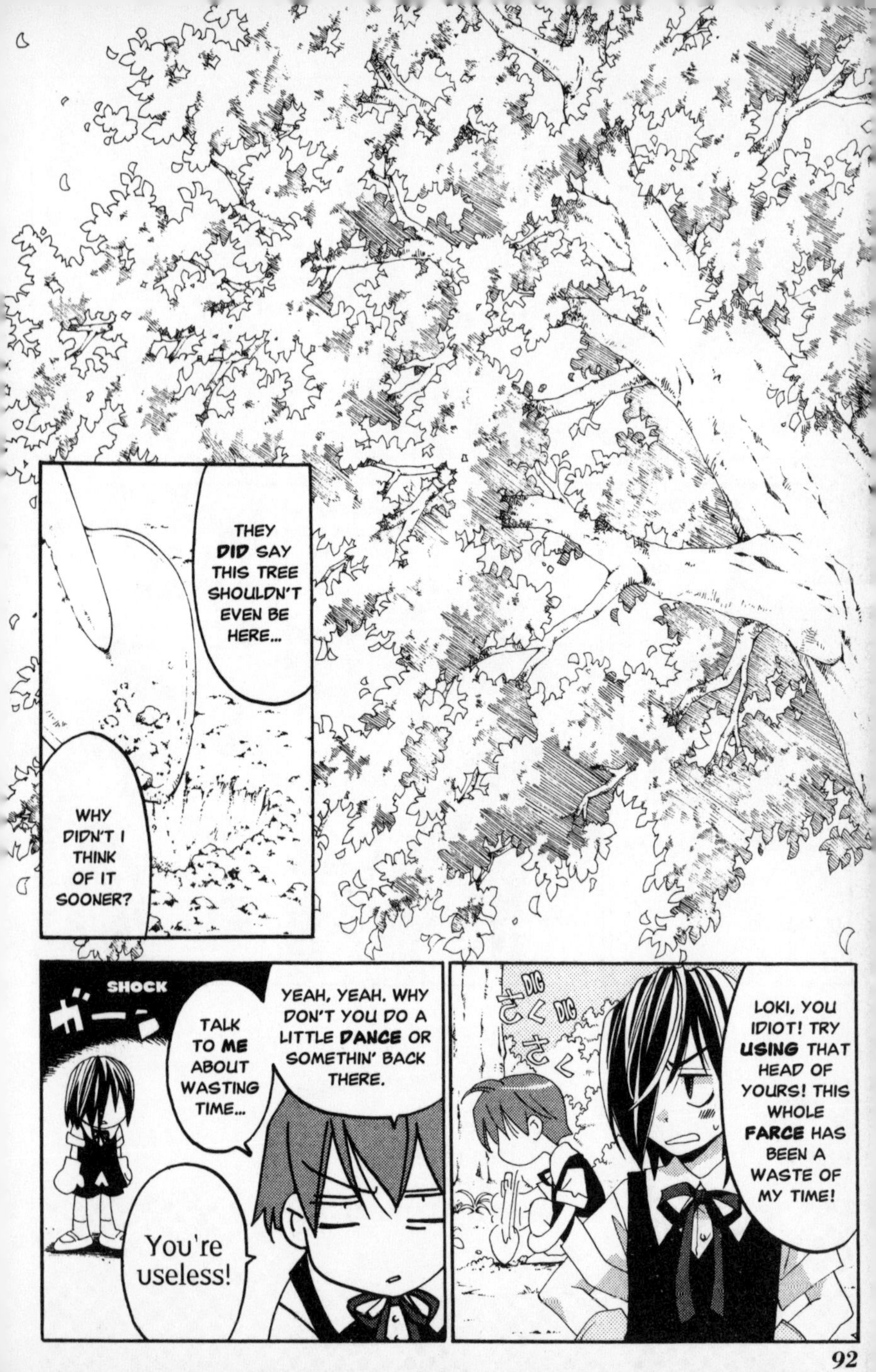
THEY DID SAY THIS TREE SHOULDN'T EVEN BE HERE...
WHY DIDN'T I THINK OF IT SOONER?
DIG さく DIG さく
LOKI, YOU IDIOT! TRY USING THAT HEAD OF YOURS! THIS WHOLE FARCE HAS BEEN A WASTE OF MY TIME!
YEAH, YEAH. WHY DON'T YOU DO A LITTLE DANCE OR SOMETHIN' BACK THERE.
TALK TO ME ABOUT WASTING TIME...
SHOCK
ガーン
You're useless!

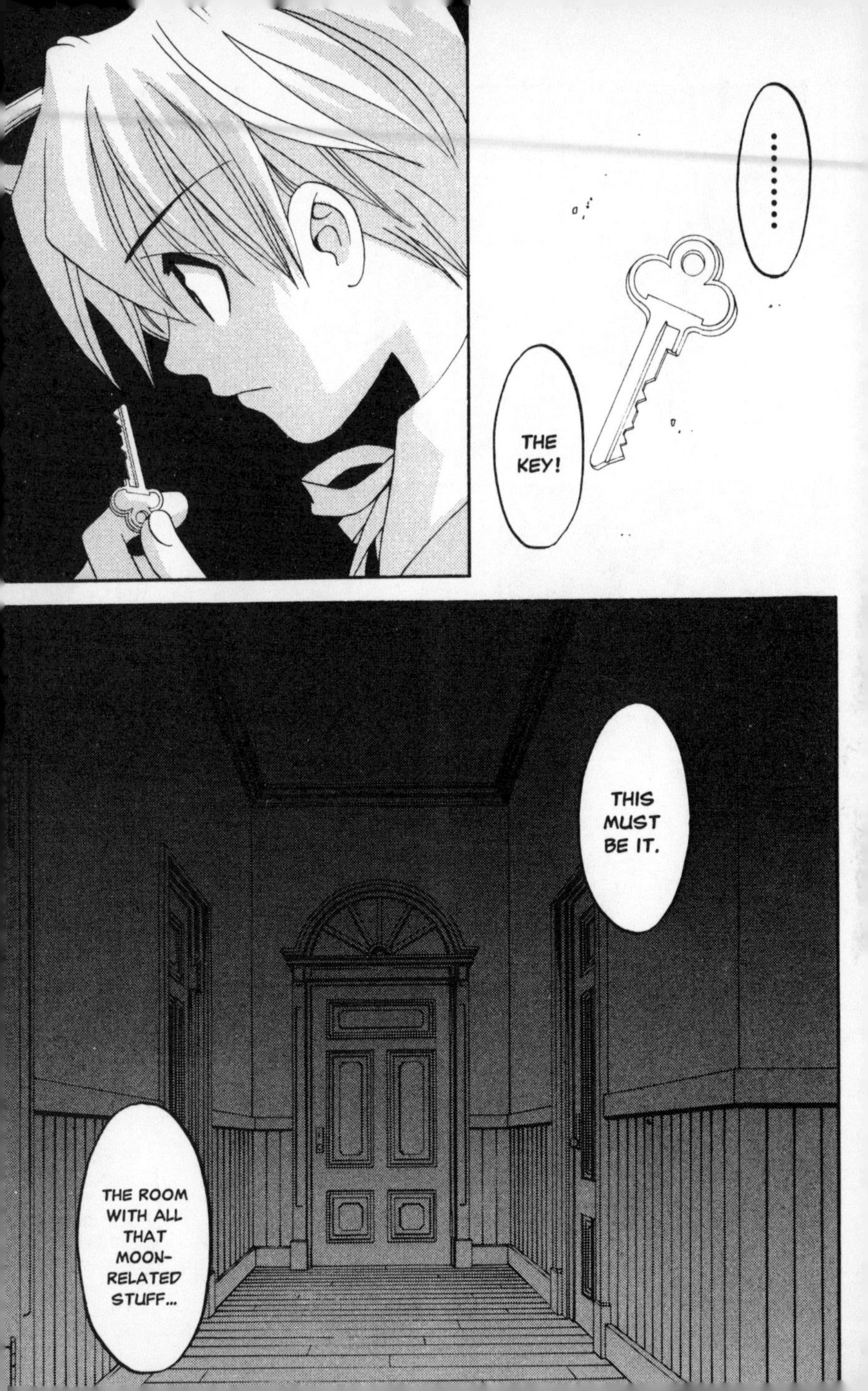

......
THE KEY!
THIS MUST BE IT.
THE ROOM WITH ALL THAT MOON-RELATED STUFF...

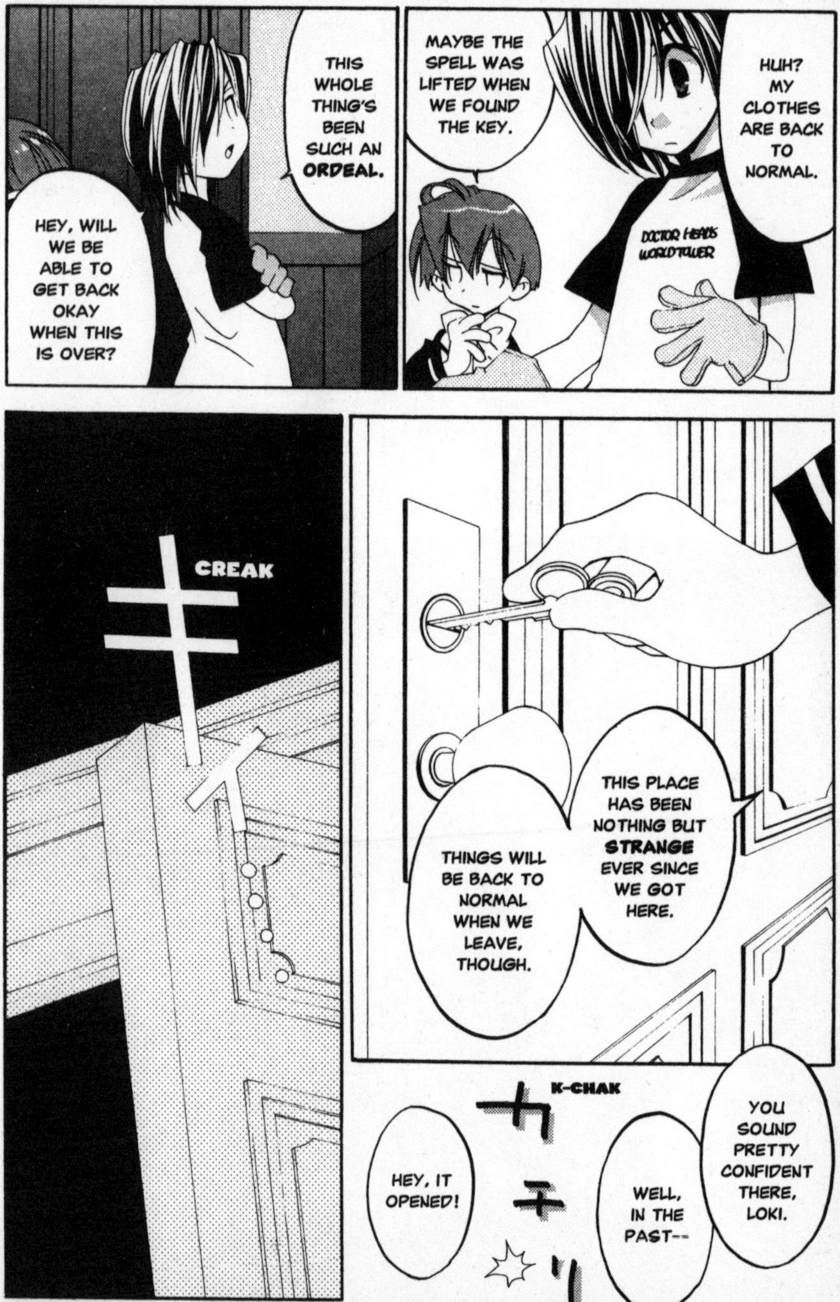
HUH? MY CLOTHES ARE BACK TO NORMAL.
DOCTOR HEAD'S WORLDTOWER
MAYBE THE SPELL WAS LIFTED WHEN WE FOUND THE KEY.
THIS WHOLE THING'S BEEN SUCH AN **ORDEAL.**
HEY, WILL WE BE ABLE TO GET BACK OKAY WHEN THIS IS OVER?
THIS PLACE HAS BEEN NOTHING BUT **STRANGE** EVER SINCE WE GOT HERE.
THINGS WILL BE BACK TO NORMAL WHEN WE LEAVE, THOUGH.
YOU SOUND PRETTY CONFIDENT THERE, LOKI.
WELL, IN THE PAST--
K-CHAK
HEY, IT OPENED!
CREAK

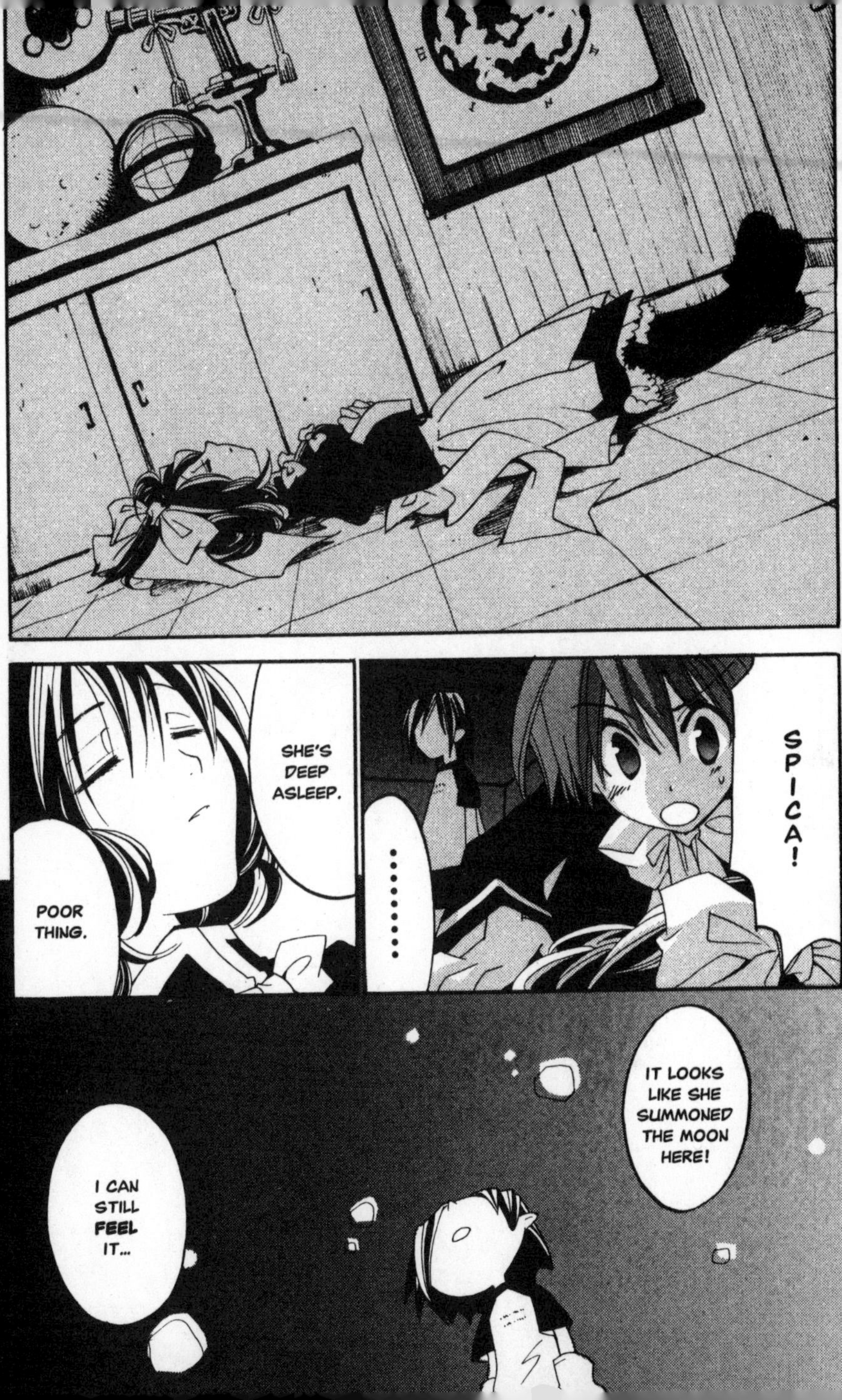
SPICA!
......
SHE'S DEEP ASLEEP.
POOR THING.
IT LOOKS LIKE SHE SUMMONED THE MOON HERE!
I CAN STILL FEEL IT...

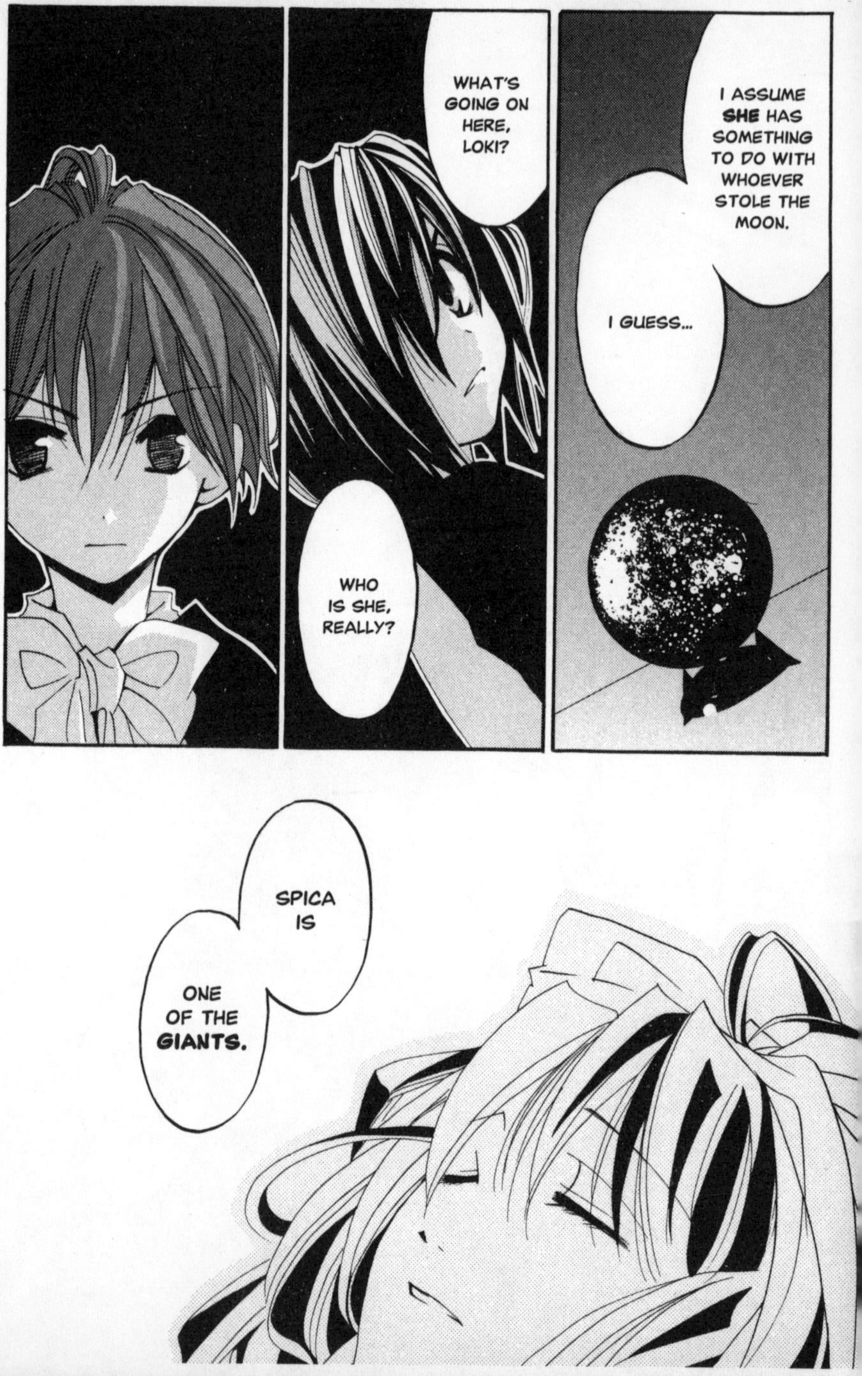
I ASSUME **SHE** HAS SOMETHING TO DO WITH WHOEVER STOLE THE MOON.
I GUESS...
WHAT'S GOING ON HERE, LOKI?
WHO IS SHE, REALLY?
SPICA IS
ONE OF THE **GIANTS.**

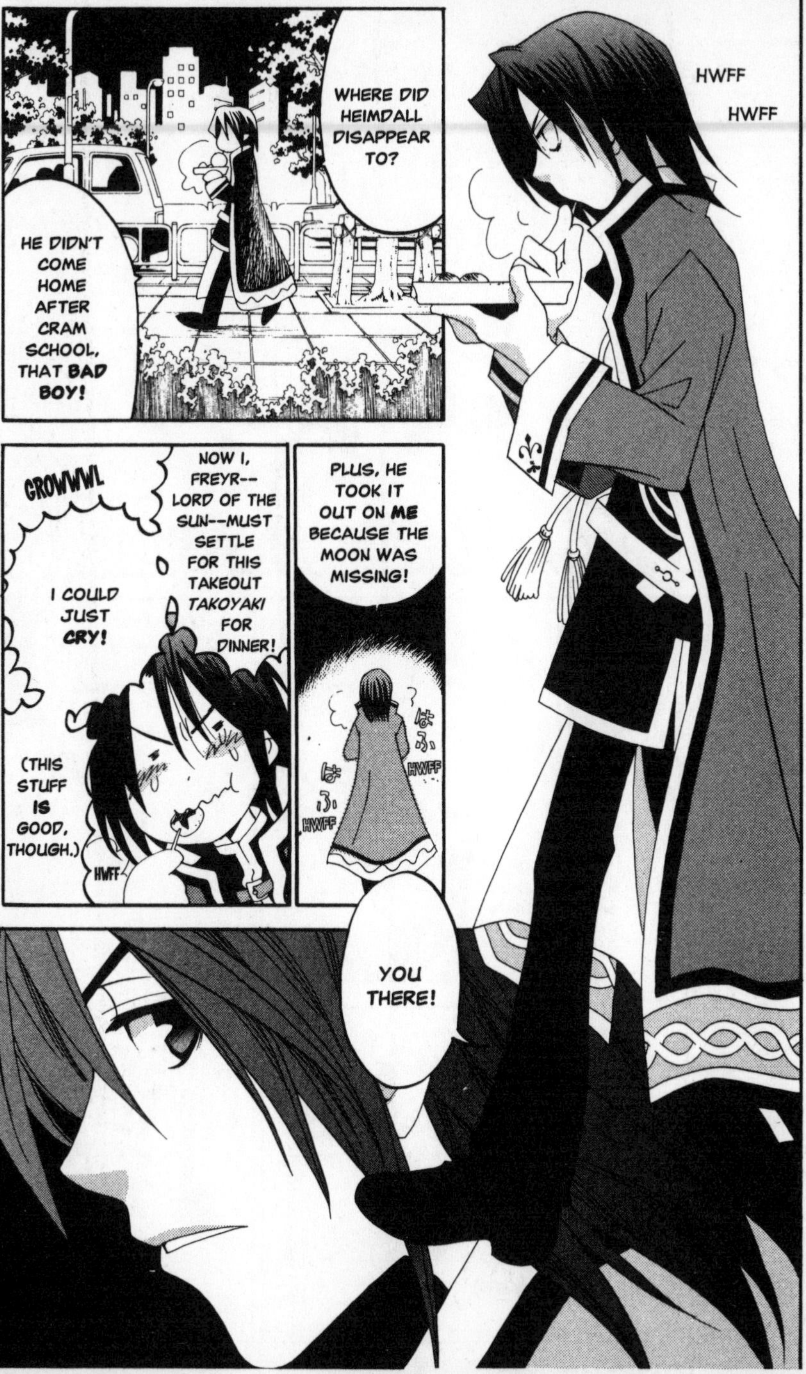
HWFF
HWFF
WHERE DID HEIMDALL DISAPPEAR TO?
HE DIDN'T COME HOME AFTER CRAM SCHOOL, THAT BAD BOY!
PLUS, HE TOOK IT OUT ON ME BECAUSE THE MOON WAS MISSING!
はふ
HWFF
はふ
HWFF
NOW I, FREYR--LORD OF THE SUN--MUST SETTLE FOR THIS TAKEOUT *TAKOYAKI* FOR DINNER!
GROWWWL
I COULD JUST CRY!
(THIS STUFF IS GOOD, THOUGH.)
HWFF
YOU THERE!

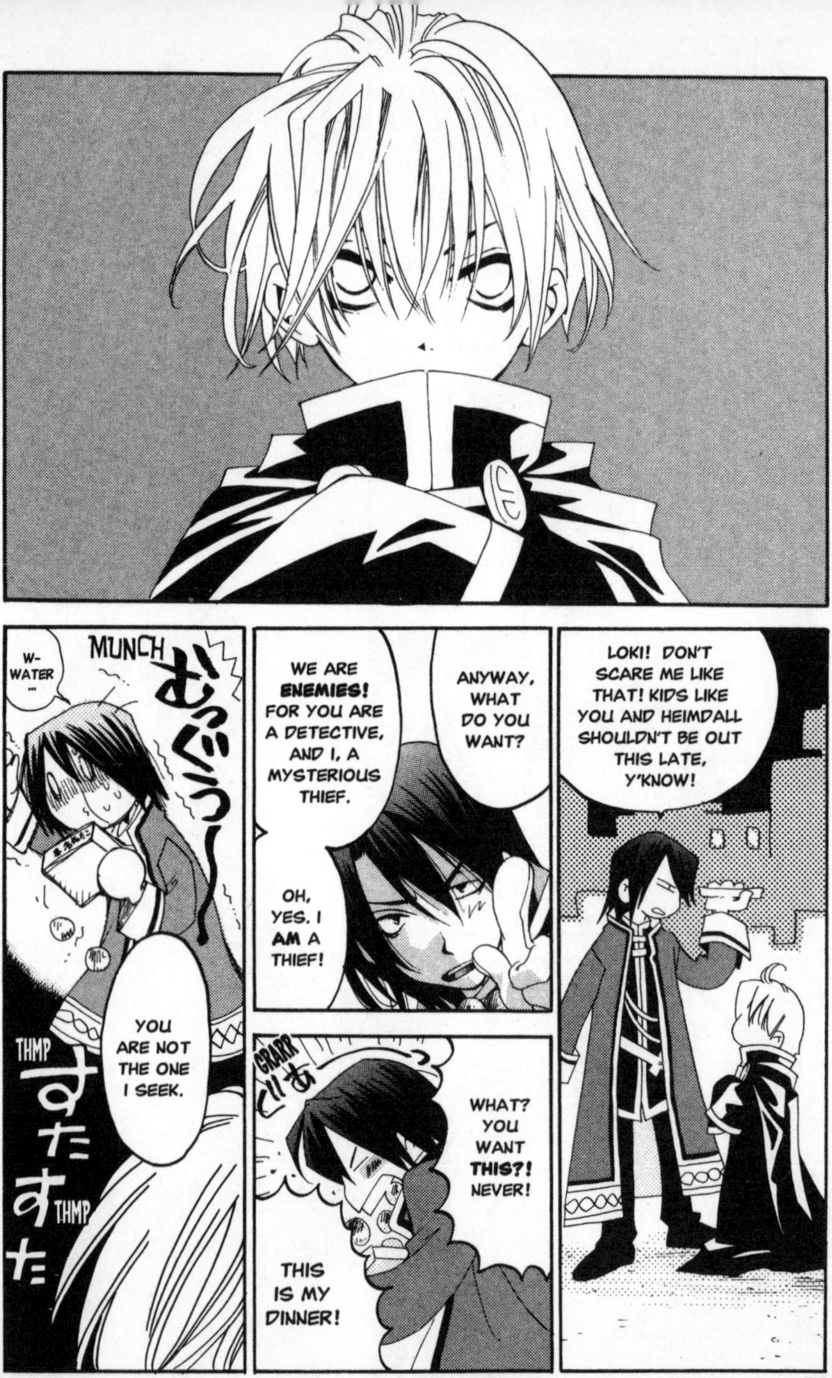
LOKI! DON'T SCARE ME LIKE THAT! KIDS LIKE YOU AND HEIMDALL SHOULDN'T BE OUT THIS LATE, Y'KNOW!
ANYWAY, WHAT DO YOU WANT?
WE ARE **ENEMIES!** FOR YOU ARE A DETECTIVE, AND I, A MYSTERIOUS THIEF.
OH, YES. I **AM** A THIEF!
GRARR
WHAT? YOU WANT **THIS?!** NEVER!
THIS IS MY DINNER!
MUNCH
W-WATER...
YOU ARE NOT THE ONE I SEEK.
THMP
すたすた
THMP

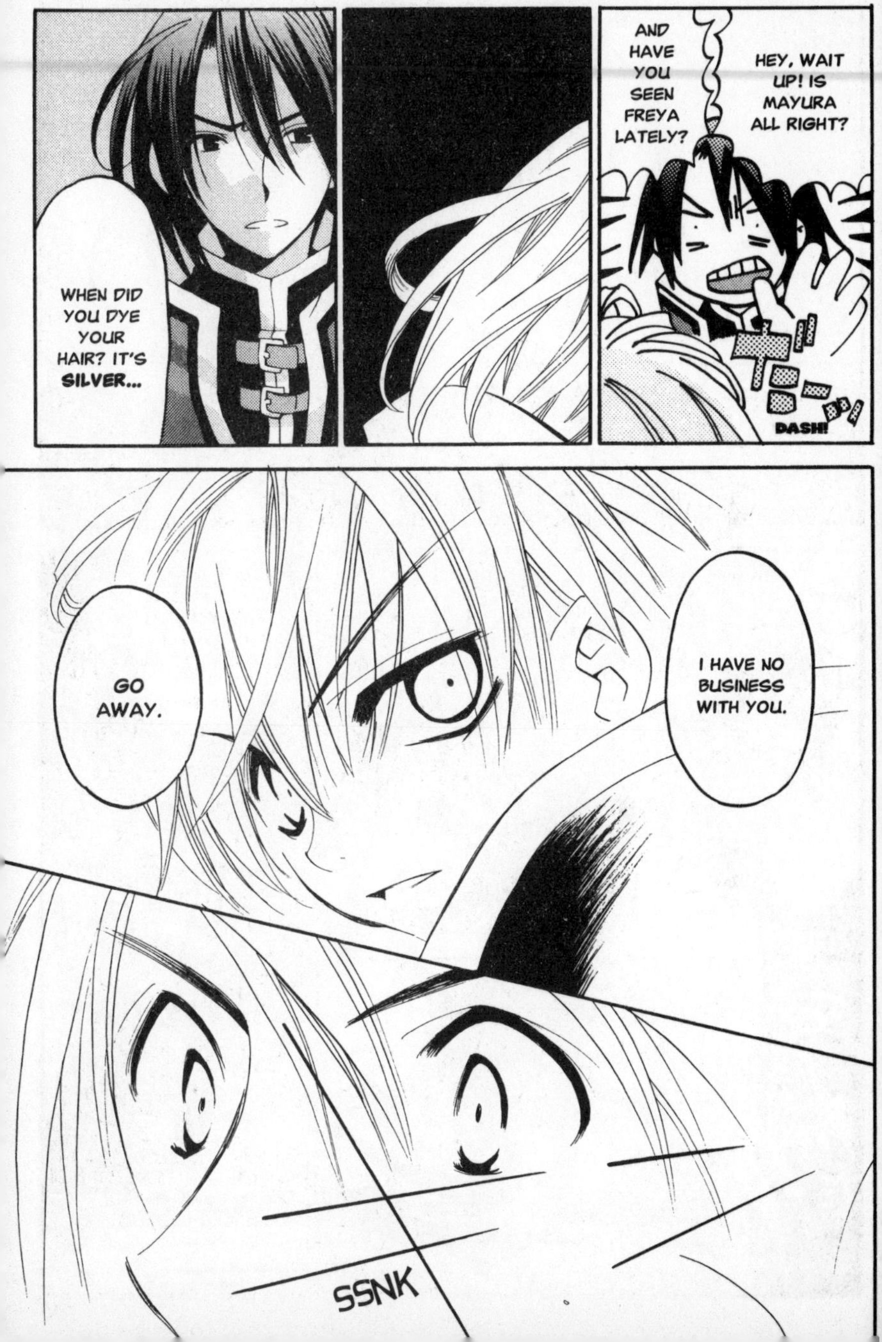
HEY, WAIT UP! IS MAYURA ALL RIGHT?
AND HAVE YOU SEEN FREYA LATELY?
DASH!
WHEN DID YOU DYE YOUR HAIR? IT'S **SILVER...**
I HAVE NO BUSINESS WITH YOU.
GO AWAY.
SSNK

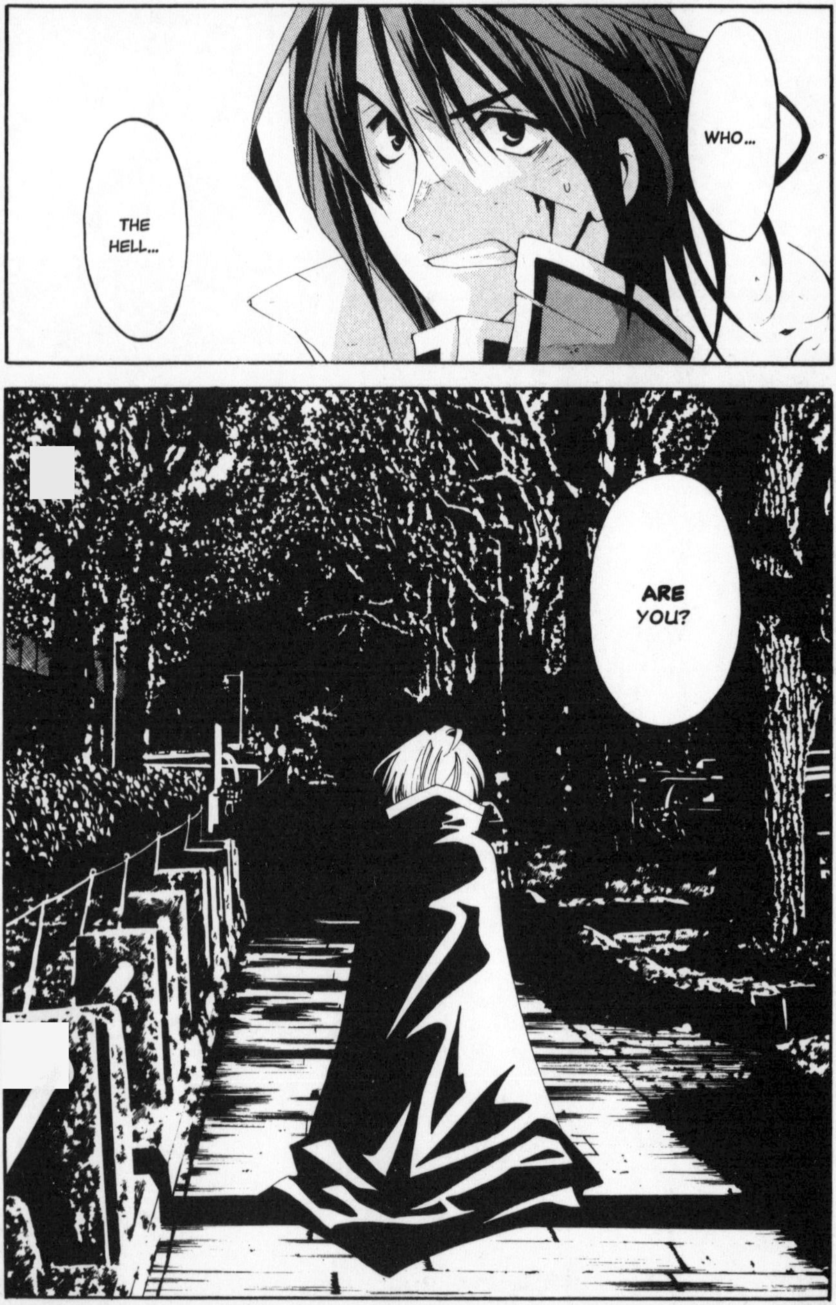
WHO...
THE HELL...
ARE YOU?

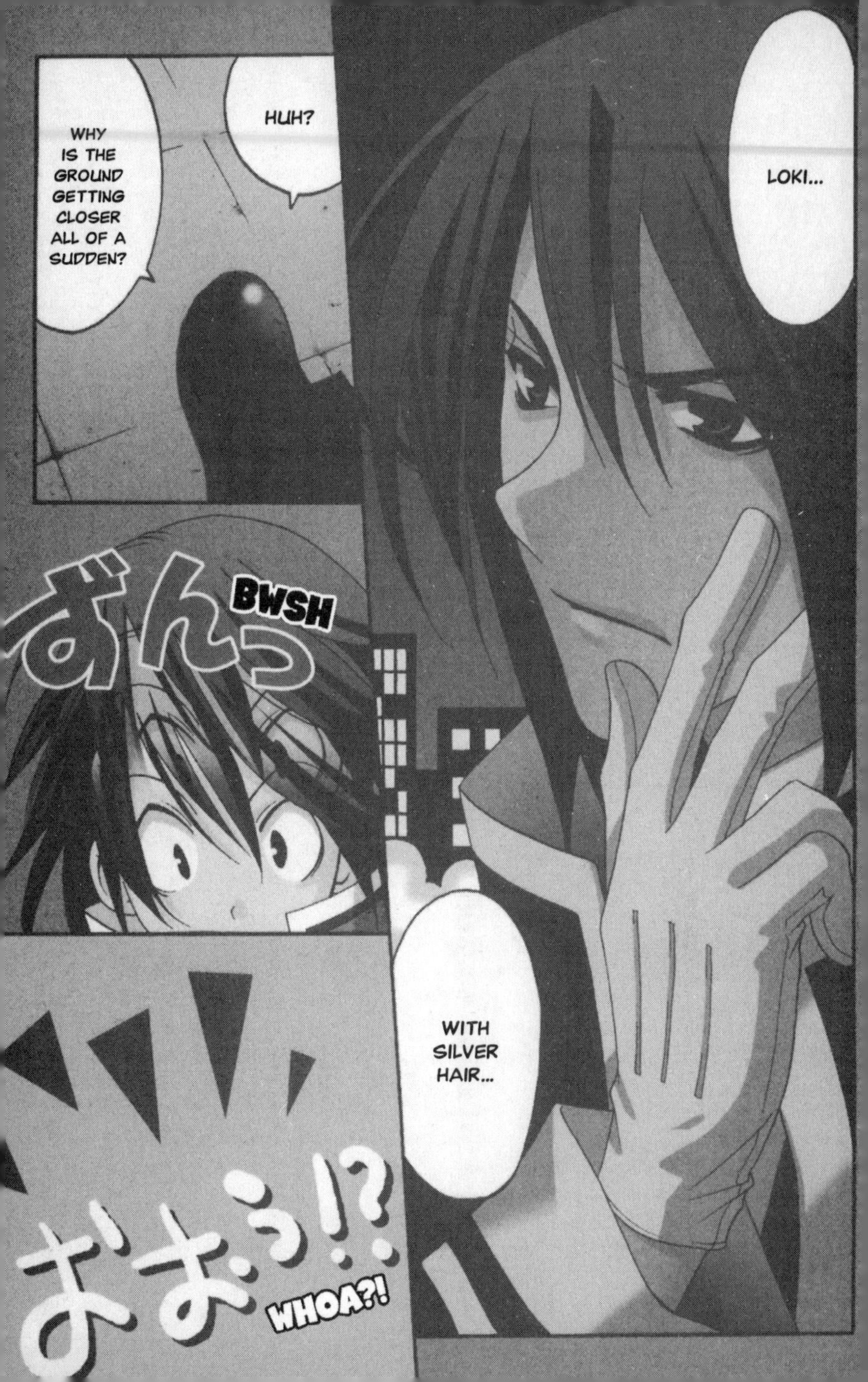
LOKI...
HUH?
WHY IS THE GROUND GETTING CLOSER ALL OF A SUDDEN?
ざんっ
BWSH
WITH SILVER HAIR...
おおぅ!?
WHOA?!

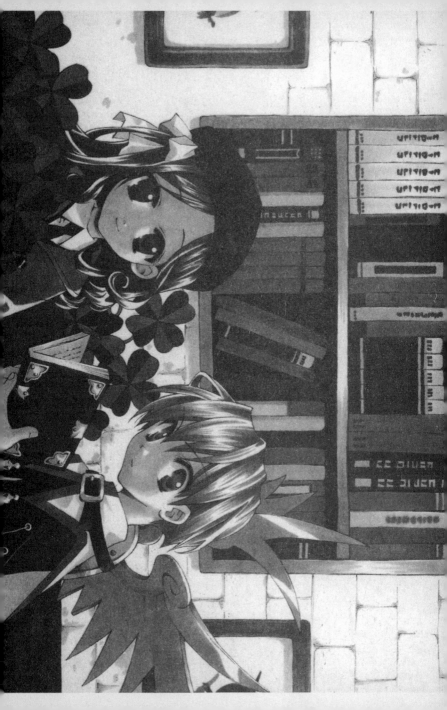

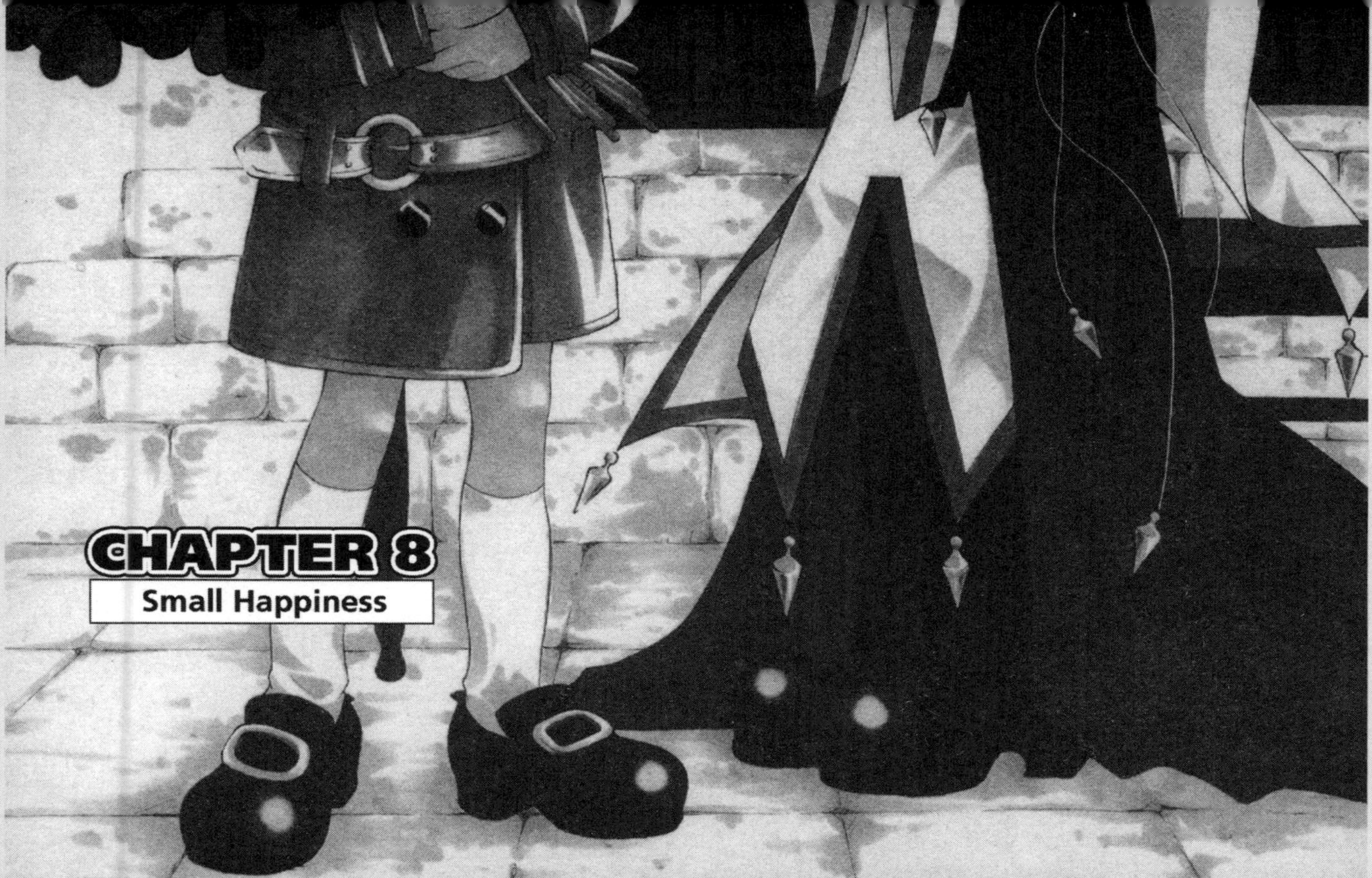
CHAPTER 8
Small Happiness

Random Thoughts (Part 2)

Sudden Self-Promotion!

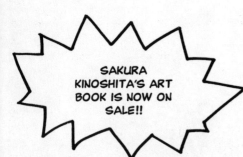

SAKURA KINOSHITA'S ART BOOK IS NOW ON SALE!!

Thanks, everyone! ♥

Includes both color *and* black and white illustrations! I came across many of my past drawings while working on this collection. It brought a tear to my eye, and also brought back a lot of memories of things I sacrificed in order to work on serial manga... But enough of that!

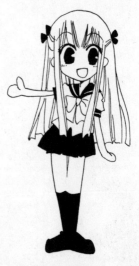

Please buy it! ♥
It's got a nice happy ending!

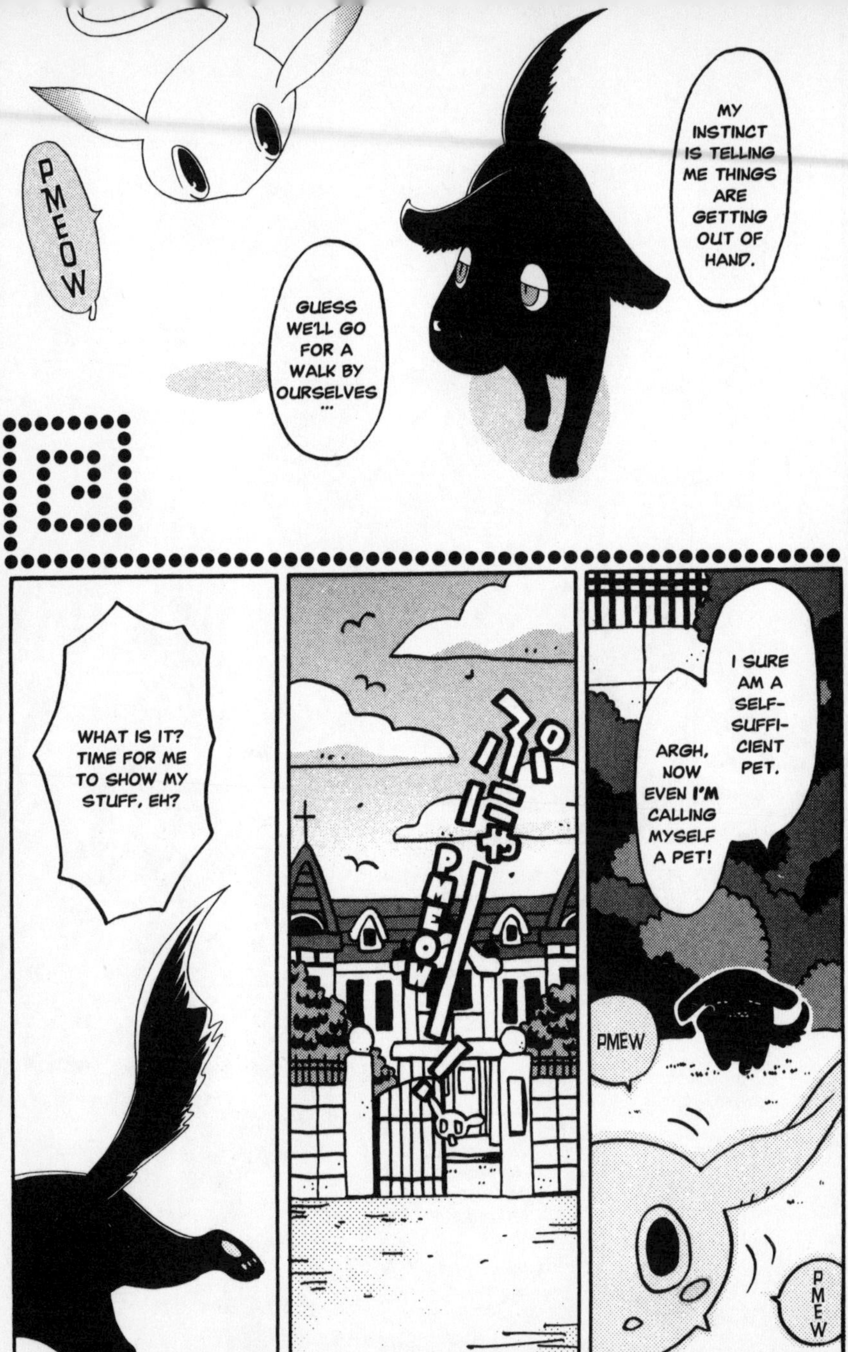
MY INSTINCT IS TELLING ME THINGS ARE GETTING OUT OF HAND.
GUESS WE'LL GO FOR A WALK BY OURSELVES...
PMEOW
I SURE AM A SELF-SUFFICIENT PET.
ARGH, NOW EVEN I'M CALLING MYSELF A PET!
PMEW
PMEW
ぷにゃー
PMEOW!
WHAT IS IT? TIME FOR ME TO SHOW MY STUFF, EH?

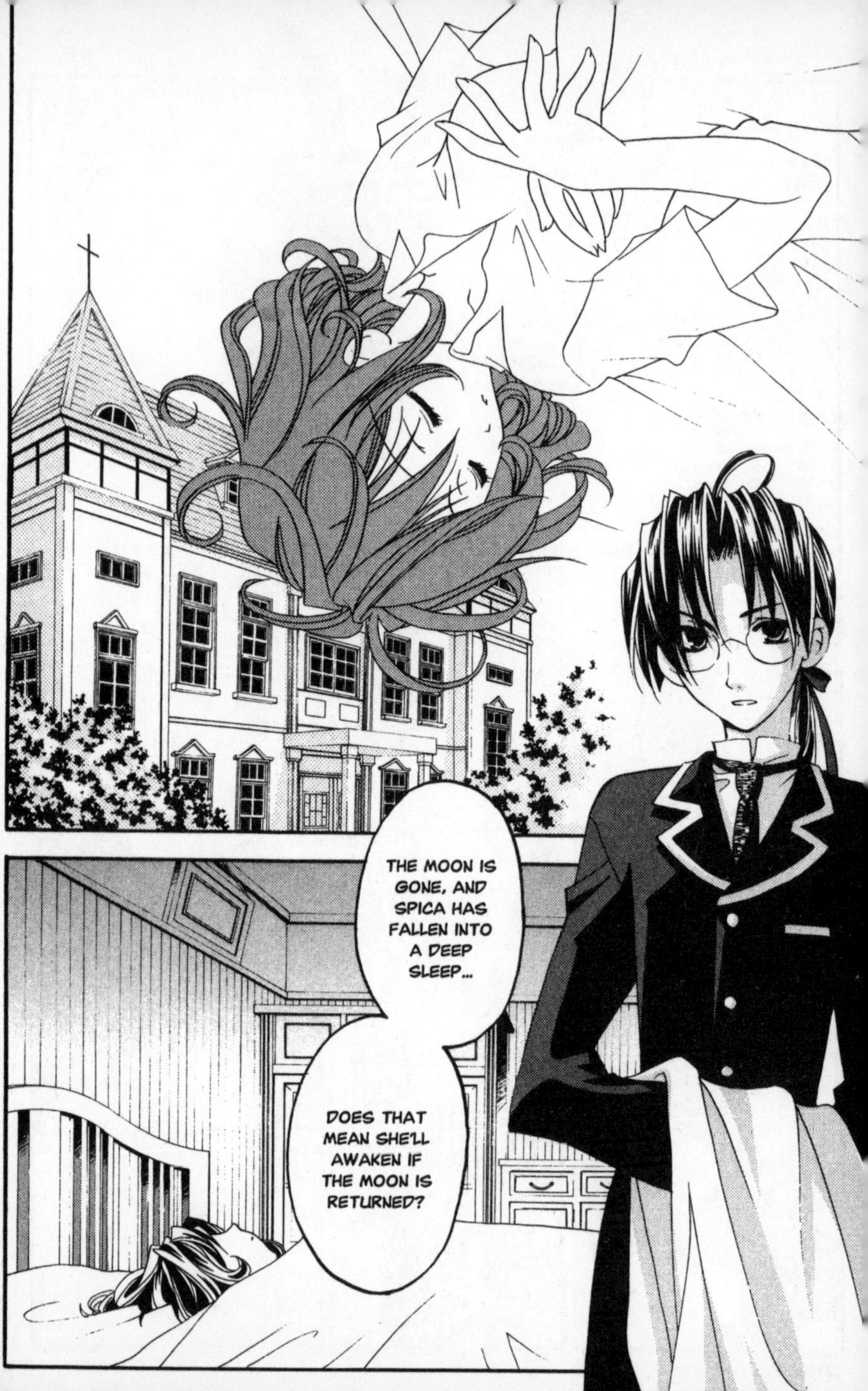
THE MOON IS GONE, AND SPICA HAS FALLEN INTO A DEEP SLEEP...
DOES THAT MEAN SHE'LL AWAKEN IF THE MOON IS RETURNED?

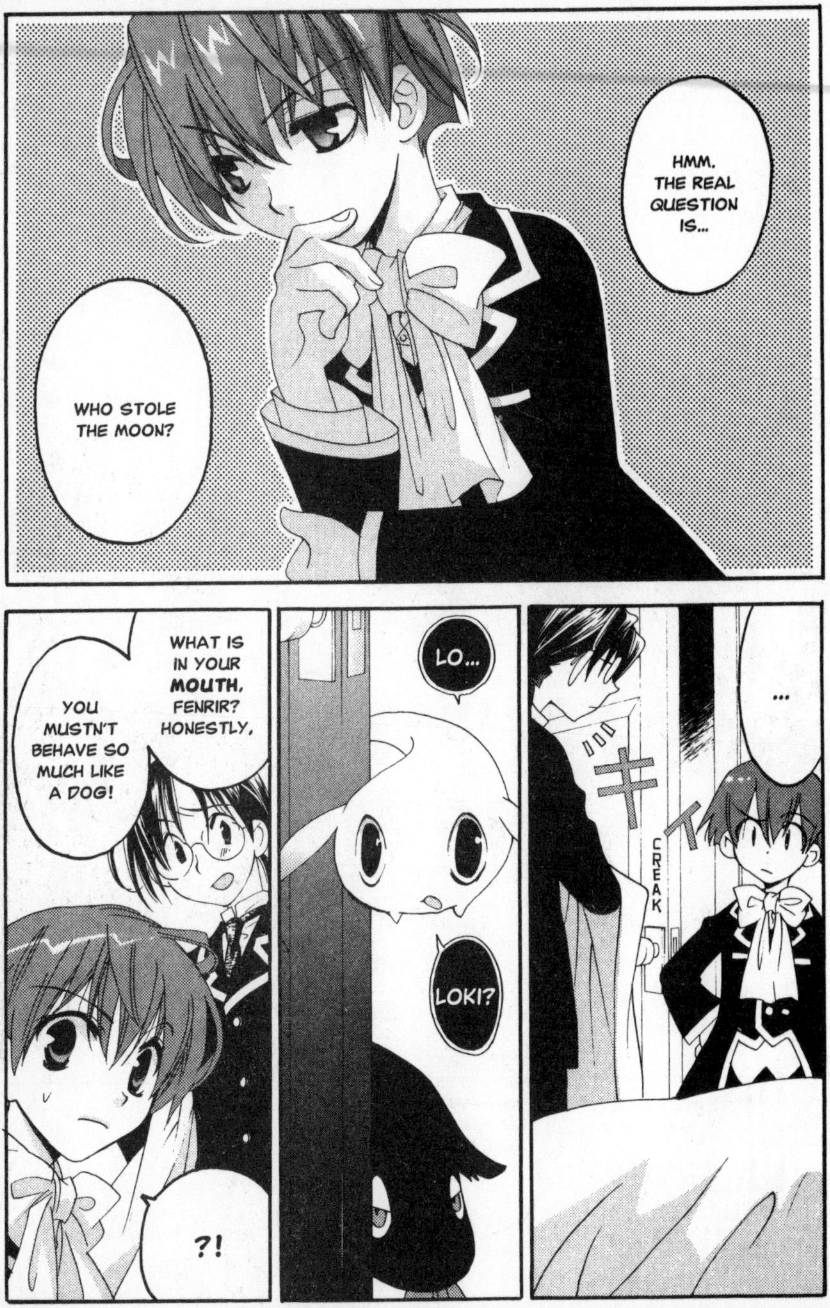
HMM. THE REAL QUESTION IS...
WHO STOLE THE MOON?
...
キィ
CREAK
LO...
LOKI?
WHAT IS IN YOUR MOUTH, FENRIR? HONESTLY,
YOU MUSTN'T BEHAVE SO MUCH LIKE A DOG!
?!

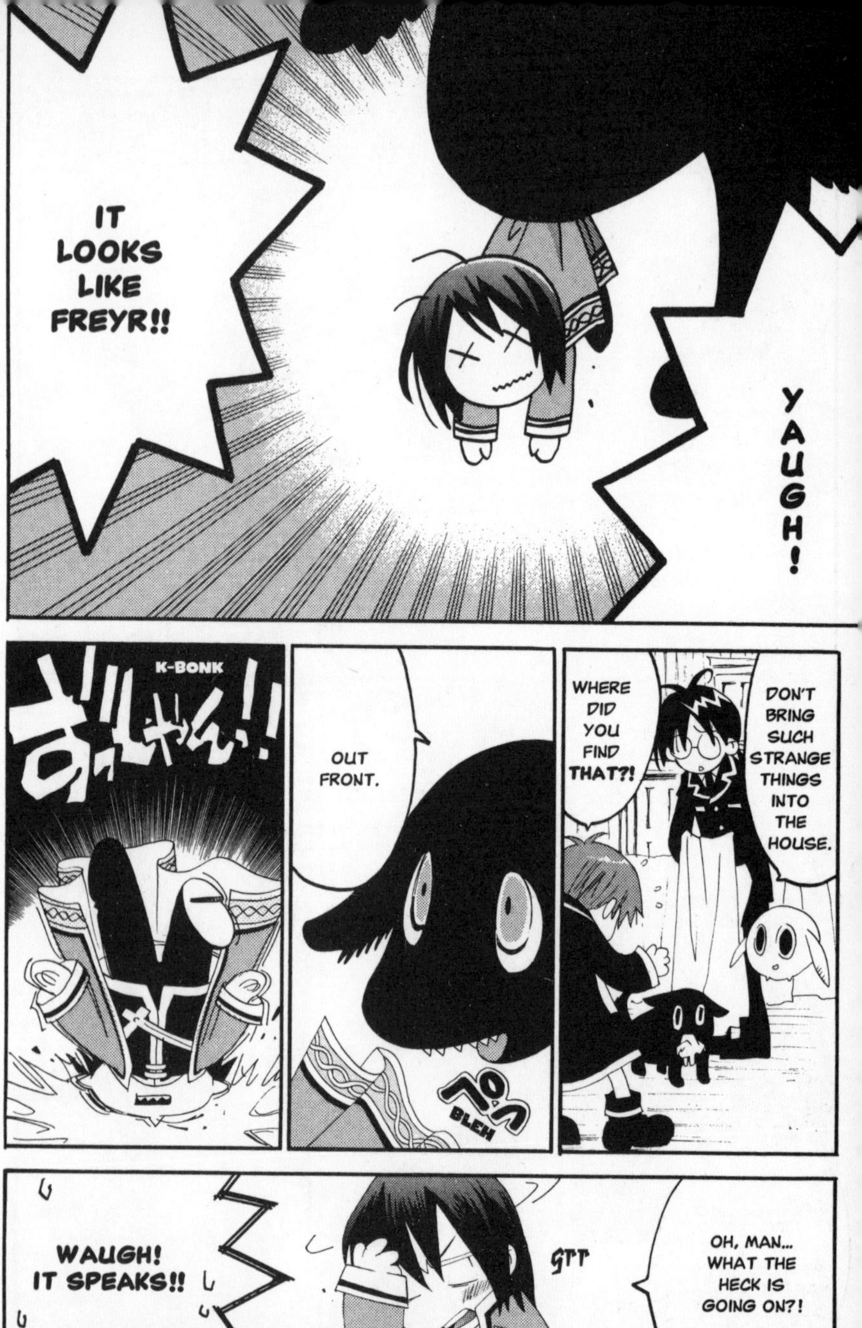
YAUGH!
IT LOOKS LIKE FREYR!!
DON'T BRING SUCH STRANGE THINGS INTO THE HOUSE.
WHERE DID YOU FIND THAT?!
OUT FRONT.
BLEH
K-BONK
OH, MAN... WHAT THE HECK IS GOING ON?!
GTT
WAUGH! IT SPEAKS!!

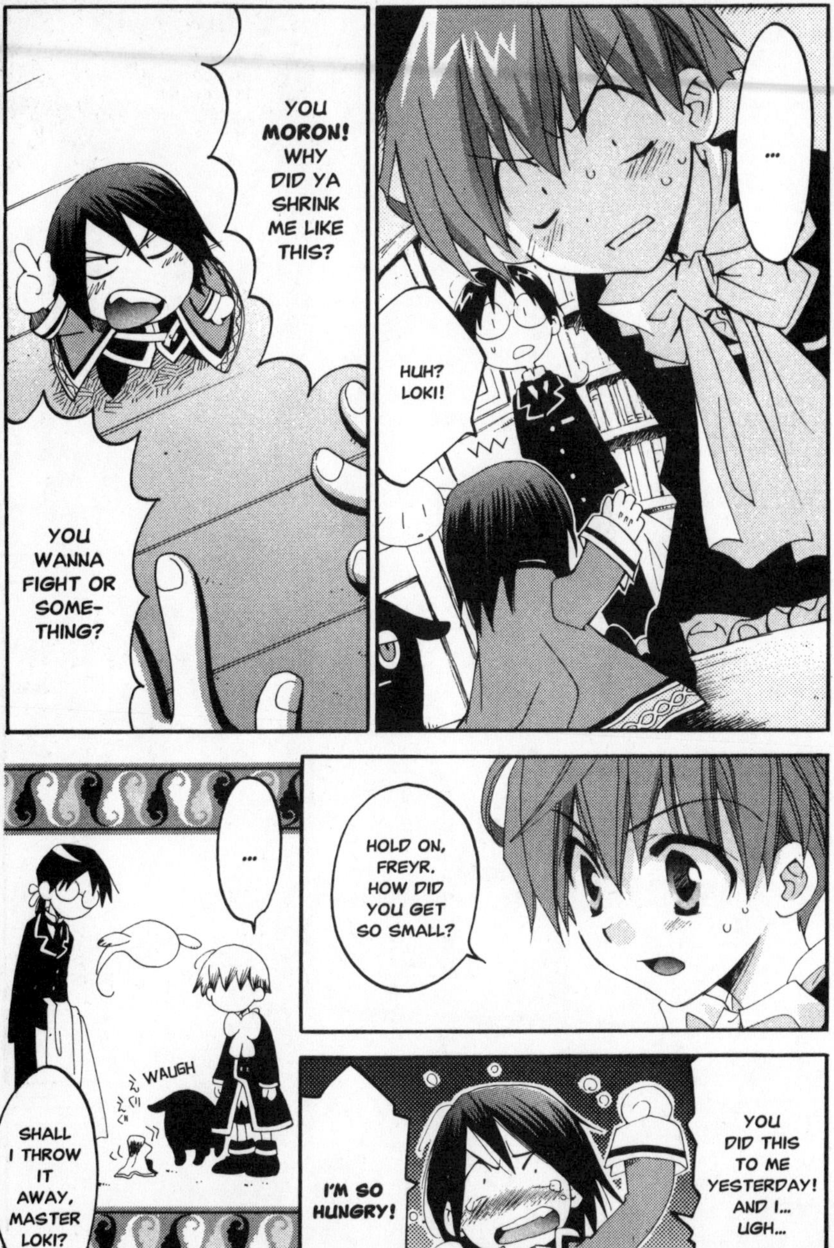
...
HUH? LOKI!
YOU MORON! WHY DID YA SHRINK ME LIKE THIS?
YOU WANNA FIGHT OR SOME-THING?
HOLD ON, FREYR. HOW DID YOU GET SO SMALL?
YOU DID THIS TO ME YESTERDAY! AND I... UGH...
I'M SO HUNGRY!
...
WAUGH
SHALL I THROW IT AWAY, MASTER LOKI?

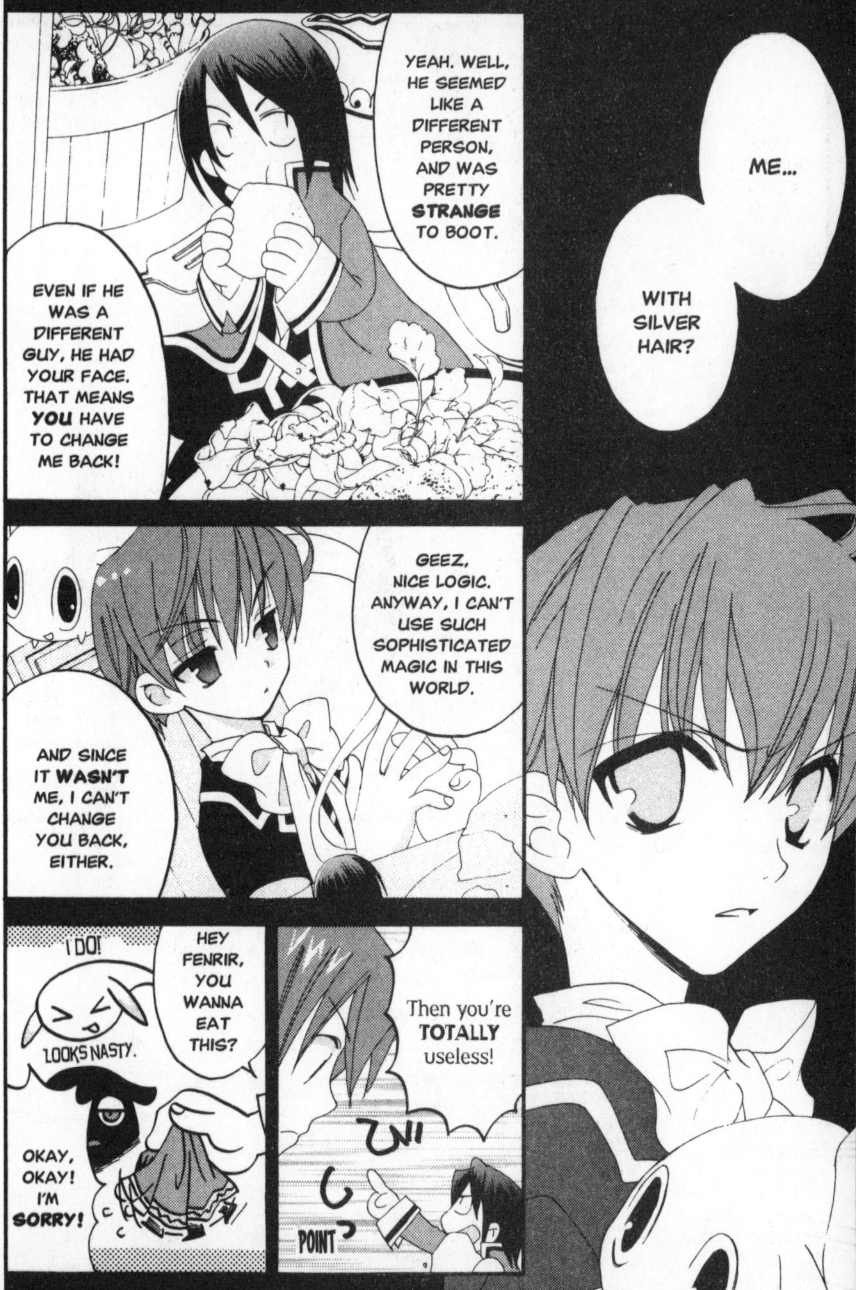
ME...
WITH SILVER HAIR?
YEAH. WELL, HE SEEMED LIKE A DIFFERENT PERSON, AND WAS PRETTY STRANGE TO BOOT.
EVEN IF HE WAS A DIFFERENT GUY, HE HAD YOUR FACE. THAT MEANS YOU HAVE TO CHANGE ME BACK!
GEEZ, NICE LOGIC. ANYWAY, I CAN'T USE SUCH SOPHISTICATED MAGIC IN THIS WORLD.
AND SINCE IT WASN'T ME, I CAN'T CHANGE YOU BACK, EITHER.
Then you're TOTALLY useless!
POINT
HEY FENRIR, YOU WANNA EAT THIS?
I DO!
LOOKS NASTY.
OKAY, OKAY! I'M SORRY!

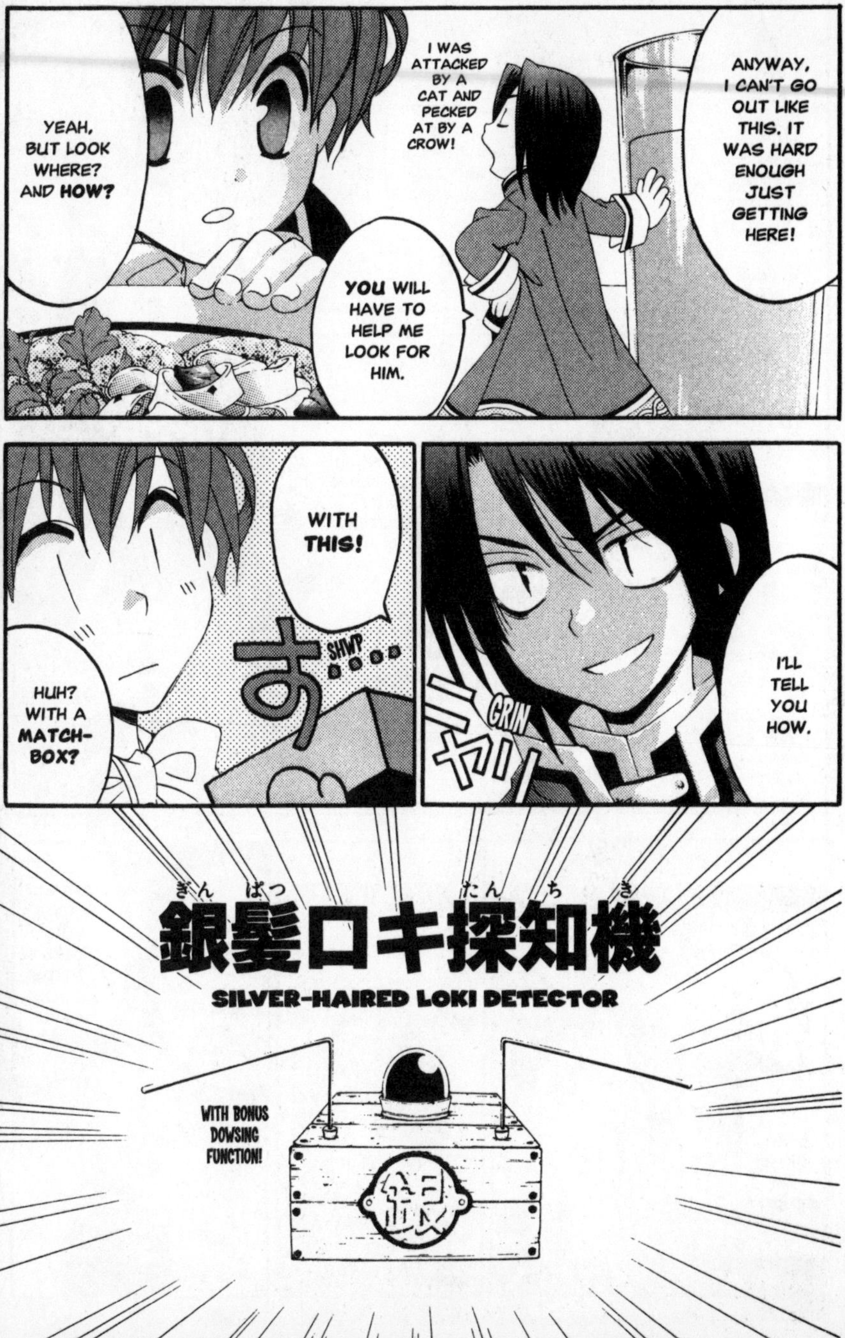
ANYWAY, I CAN'T GO OUT LIKE THIS. IT WAS HARD ENOUGH JUST GETTING HERE!
I WAS ATTACKED BY A CAT AND PECKED AT BY A CROW!
YOU WILL HAVE TO HELP ME LOOK FOR HIM.
YEAH, BUT LOOK WHERE? AND HOW?
I'LL TELL YOU HOW.
GRIN
WITH THIS!
SHWP
HUH? WITH A MATCH-BOX?
銀髪ロキ探知機
SILVER-HAIRED LOKI DETECTOR
WITH BONUS DOWSING FUNCTION!

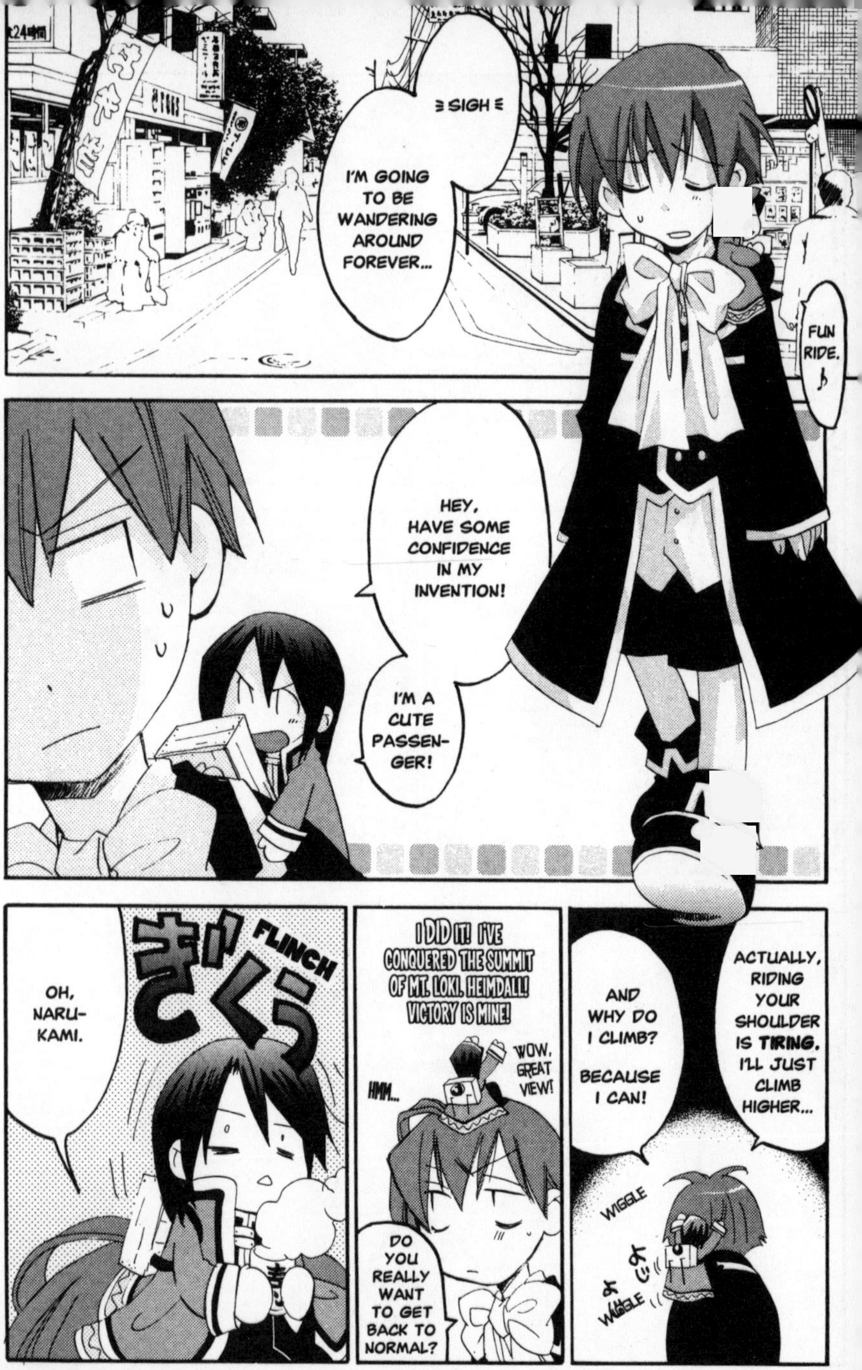

≡ SIGH ≡
I'M GOING TO BE WANDERING AROUND FOREVER...
FUN RIDE. ♪
HEY, HAVE SOME CONFIDENCE IN MY INVENTION!
I'M A CUTE PASSENGER!
ACTUALLY, RIDING YOUR SHOULDER IS TIRING. I'LL JUST CLIMB HIGHER...
AND WHY DO I CLIMB? BECAUSE I CAN!
WIGGLE
WIGGLE
I DID IT! I'VE CONQUERED THE SUMMIT OF MT. LOKI, HEIMDALL! VICTORY IS MINE!
WOW, GREAT VIEW!
HMM...
DO YOU REALLY WANT TO GET BACK TO NORMAL?
FLINCH
OH, NARU-KAMI.

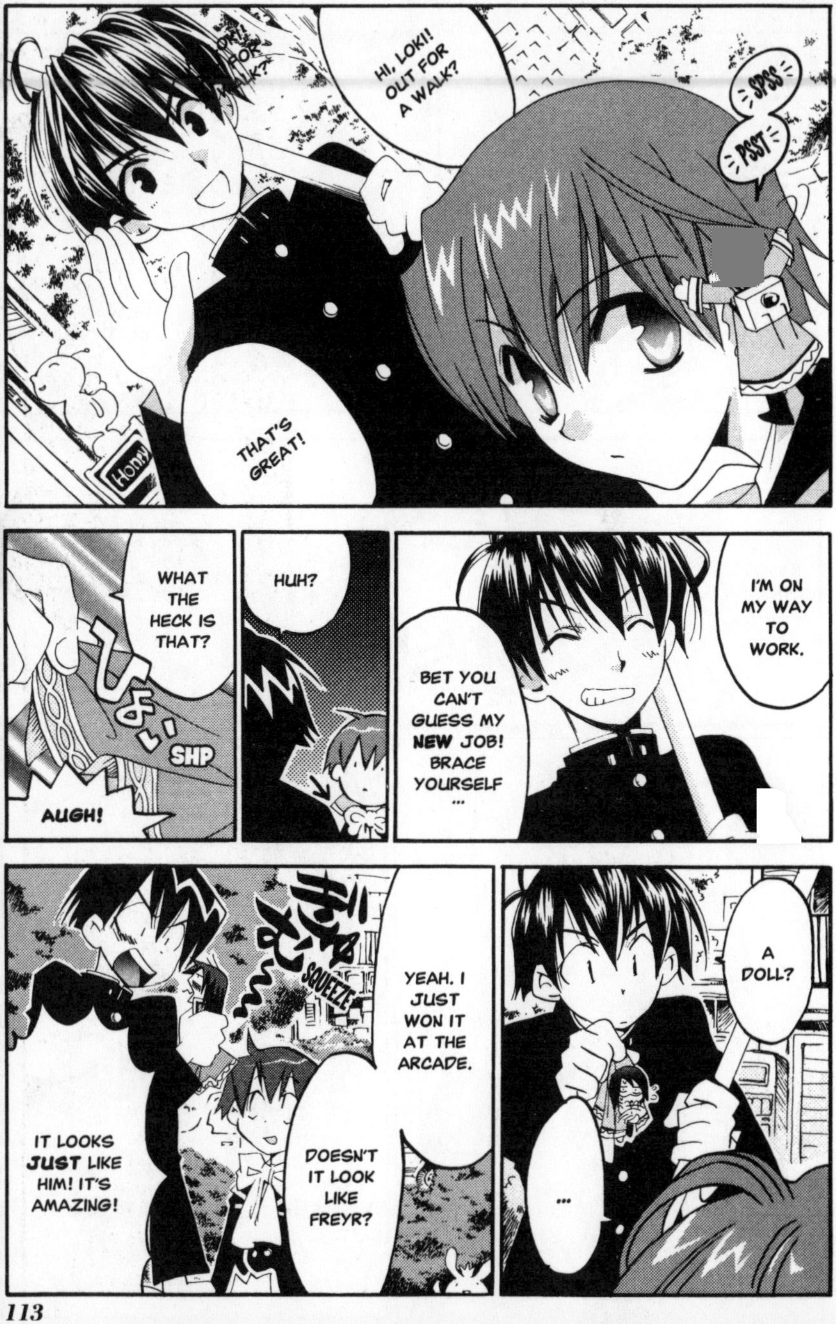
SPSS
PSST
HI, LOKI! OUT FOR A WALK?
THAT'S GREAT!
I'M ON MY WAY TO WORK.
BET YOU CAN'T GUESS MY NEW JOB! BRACE YOURSELF ...
HUH?
WHAT THE HECK IS THAT?
SHP
AUGH!
A DOLL?
...
YEAH. I JUST WON IT AT THE ARCADE.
SQUEEZE
DOESN'T IT LOOK LIKE FREYR?
IT LOOKS JUST LIKE HIM! IT'S AMAZING!

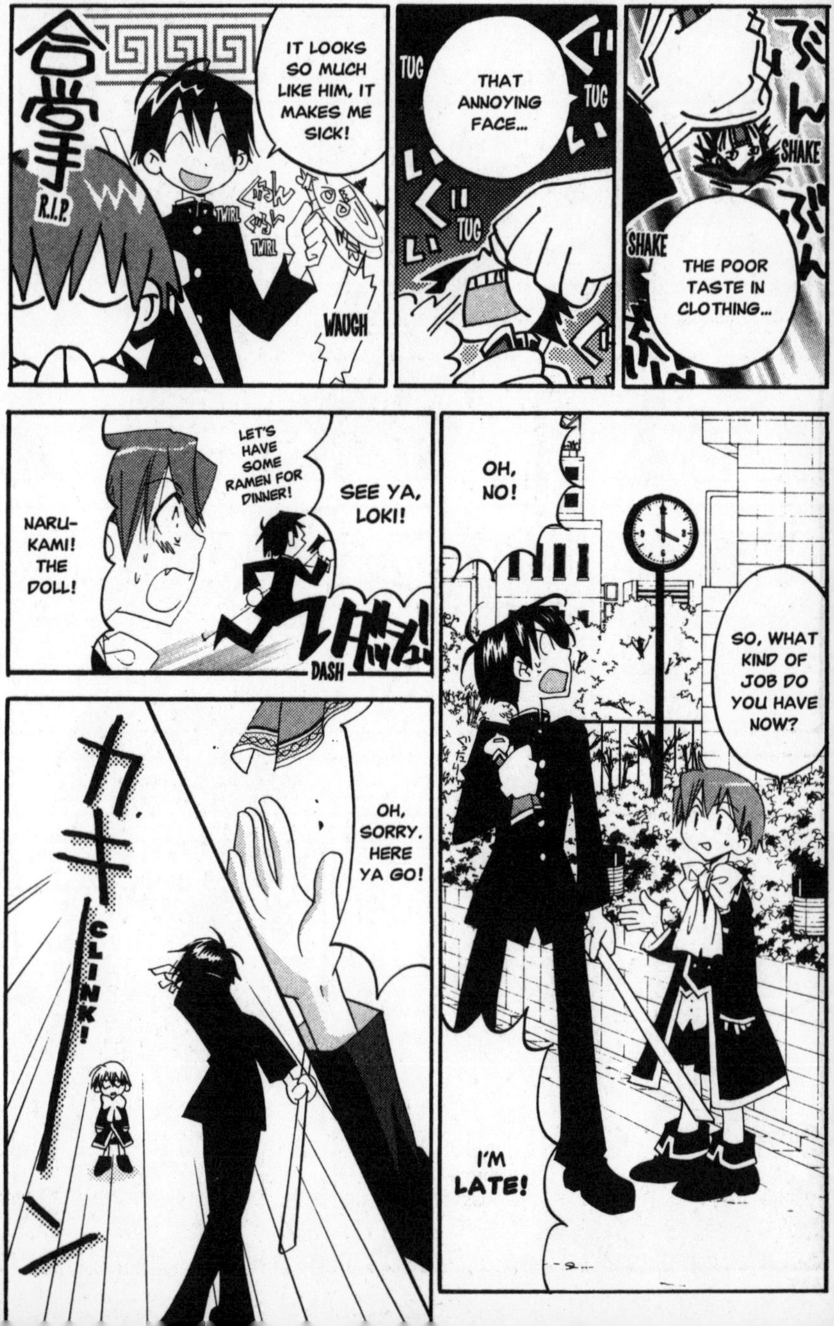
SHAKE
THE POOR TASTE IN CLOTHING...
SHAKE
TUG
THAT ANNOYING FACE...
TUG
TUG
IT LOOKS SO MUCH LIKE HIM, IT MAKES ME SICK!
TWIRL
TWIRL
WAUGH
R.I.P.
SO, WHAT KIND OF JOB DO YOU HAVE NOW?
OH, NO!
I'M LATE!
SEE YA, LOKI!
LET'S HAVE SOME RAMEN FOR DINNER!
NARU-KAMI! THE DOLL!
DASH
OH, SORRY. HERE YA GO!
CLINK!

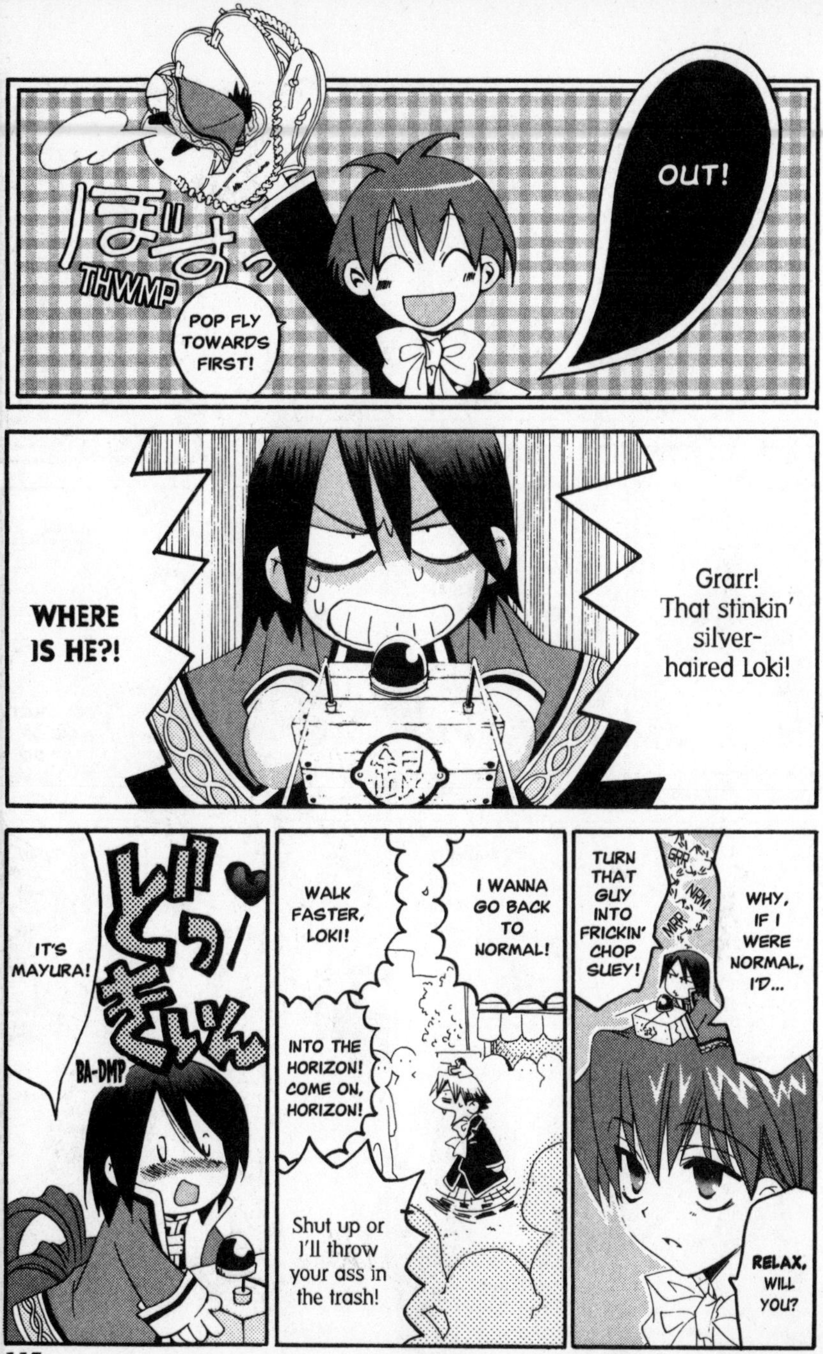

OUT!
THWMP
POP FLY TOWARDS FIRST!
Grarr! That stinkin' silver-haired Loki!
WHERE IS HE?!
WHY, IF I WERE NORMAL, I'D...
TURN THAT GUY INTO FRICKIN' CHOP SUEY!
RELAX, WILL YOU?
I WANNA GO BACK TO NORMAL!
WALK FASTER, LOKI!
INTO THE HORIZON! COME ON, HORIZON!
Shut up or I'll throw your ass in the trash!
IT'S MAYURA!
BA-DMP

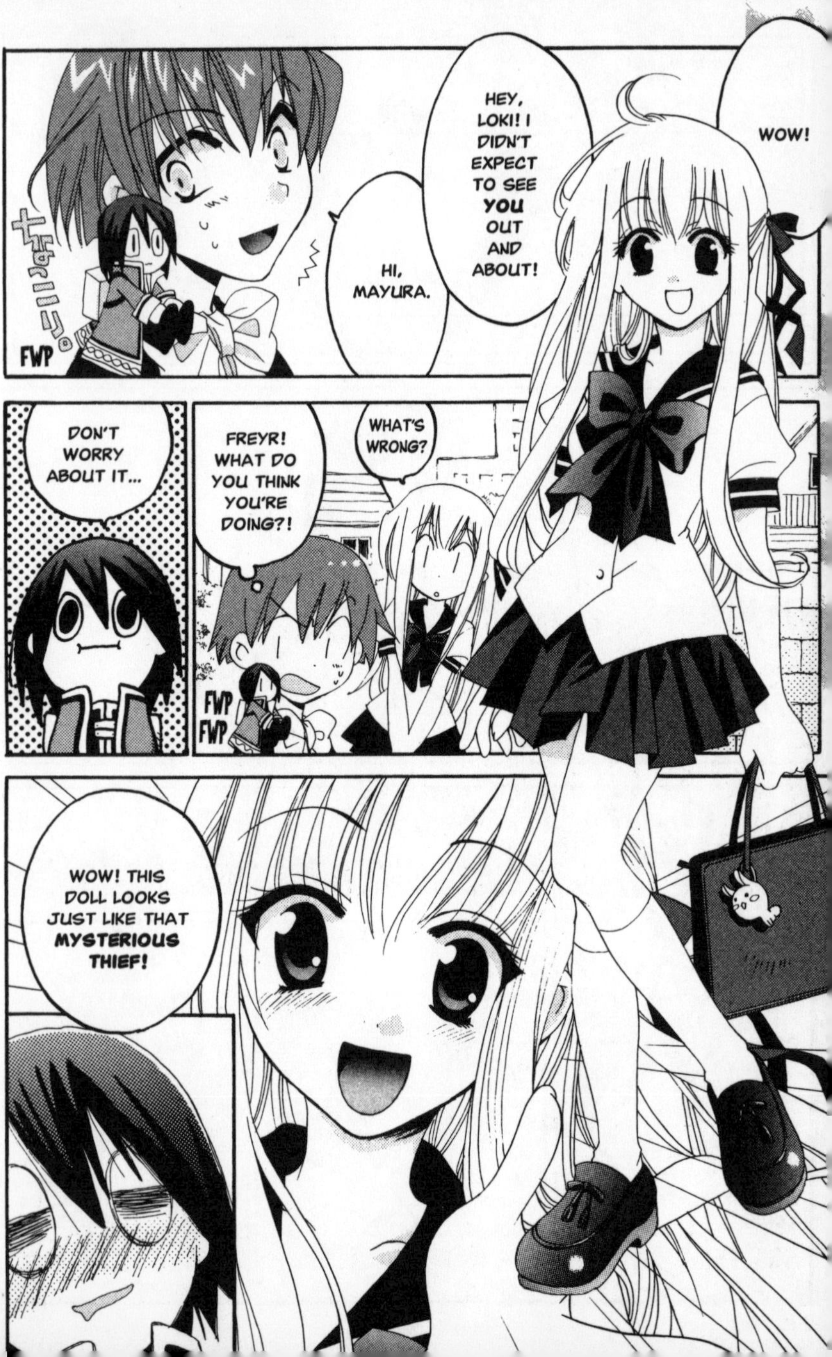
WOW!
HEY, LOKI! I DIDN'T EXPECT TO SEE YOU OUT AND ABOUT!
HI, MAYURA.
FWP
WHAT'S WRONG?
FREYR! WHAT DO YOU THINK YOU'RE DOING?!
FWP FWP
DON'T WORRY ABOUT IT...
WOW! THIS DOLL LOOKS JUST LIKE THAT MYSTERIOUS THIEF!

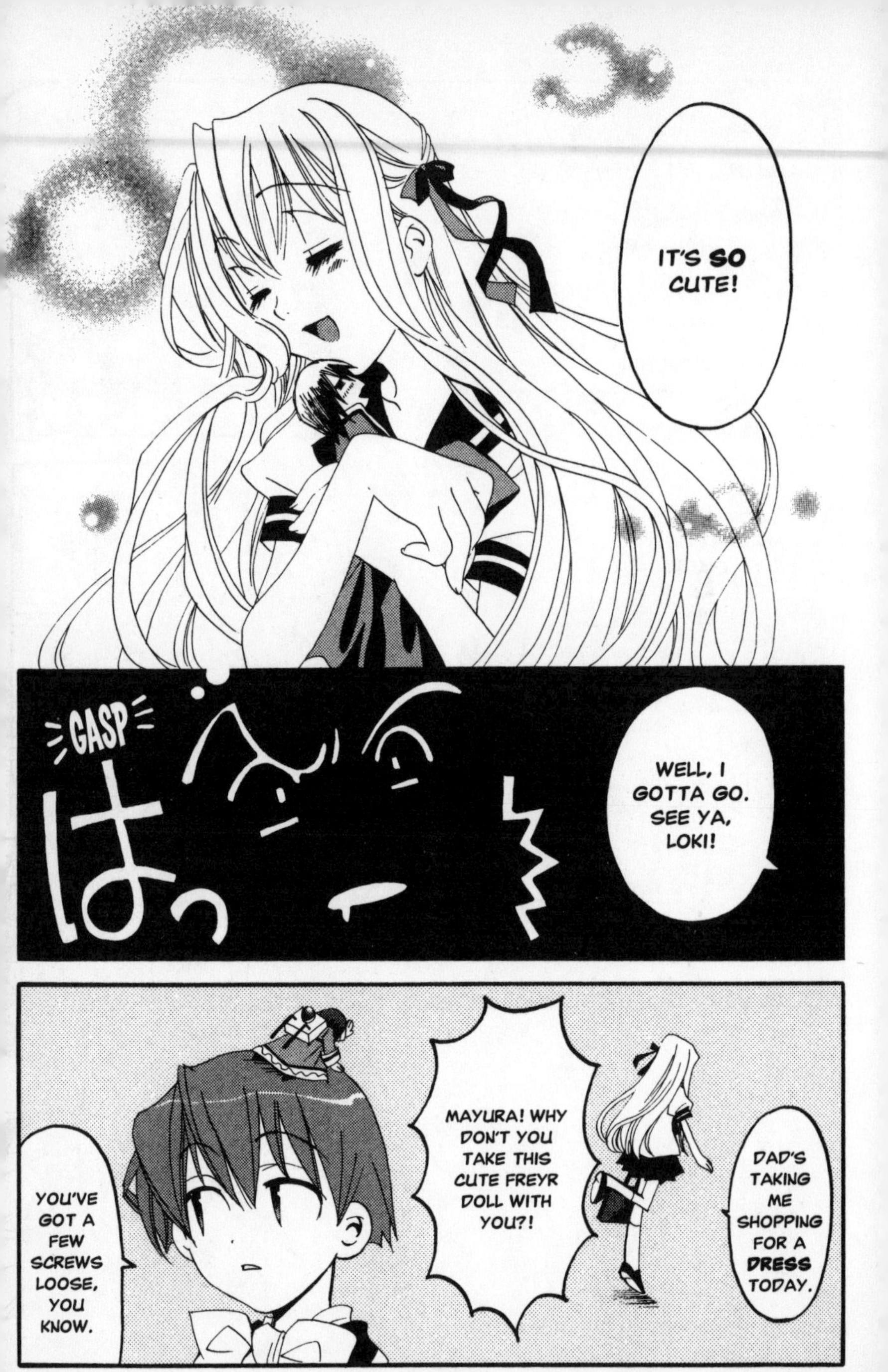
IT'S SO CUTE!
WELL, I GOTTA GO. SEE YA, LOKI!
GASP
はっ
DAD'S TAKING ME SHOPPING FOR A DRESS TODAY.
MAYURA! WHY DON'T YOU TAKE THIS CUTE FREYR DOLL WITH YOU?!
YOU'VE GOT A FEW SCREWS LOOSE, YOU KNOW.

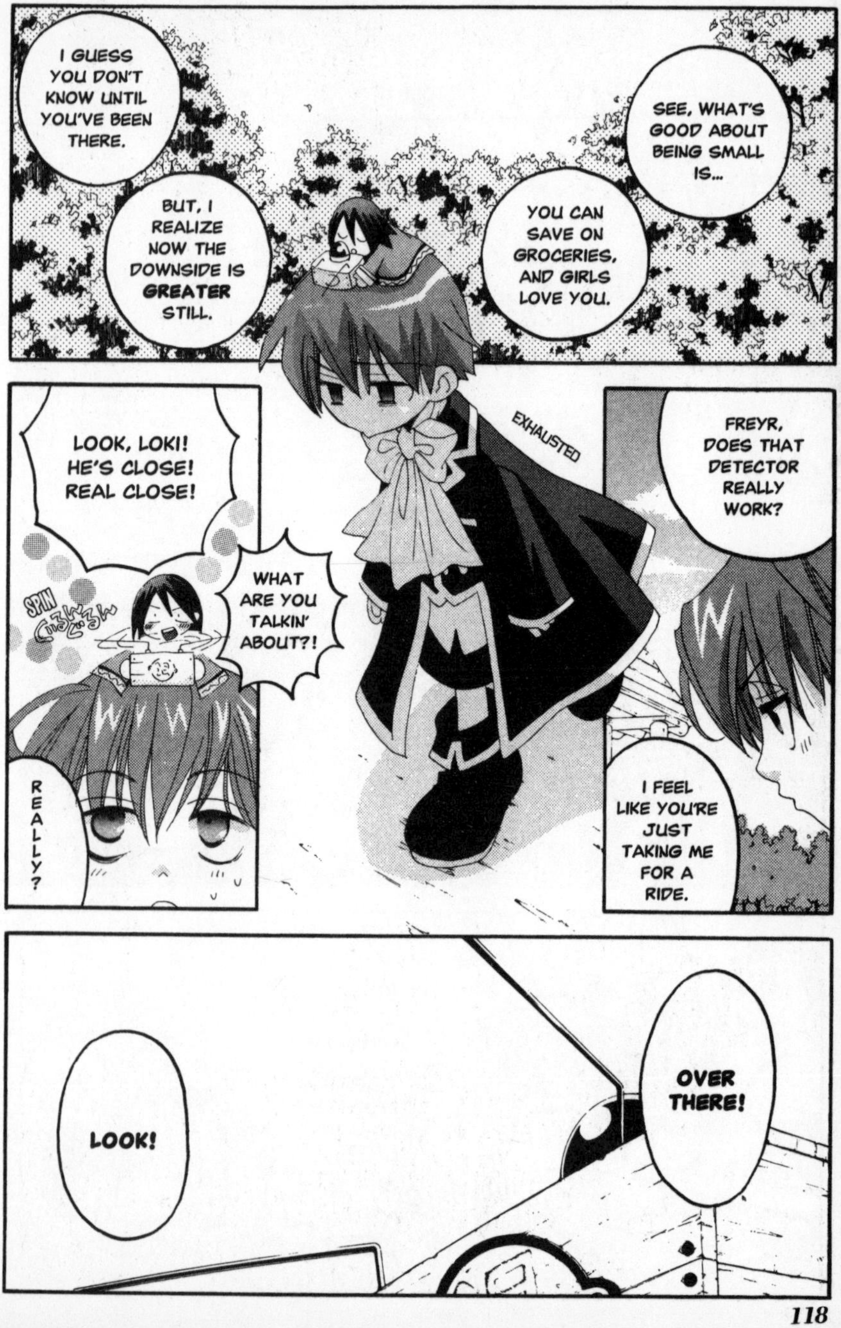
SEE, WHAT'S GOOD ABOUT BEING SMALL IS...
YOU CAN SAVE ON GROCERIES, AND GIRLS LOVE YOU.
I GUESS YOU DON'T KNOW UNTIL YOU'VE BEEN THERE.
BUT, I REALIZE NOW THE DOWNSIDE IS **GREATER** STILL.
EXHAUSTED
FREYR, DOES THAT DETECTOR REALLY WORK?
I FEEL LIKE YOU'RE JUST TAKING ME FOR A RIDE.
LOOK, LOKI! HE'S CLOSE! REAL CLOSE!
WHAT ARE YOU TALKIN' ABOUT?!
SPIN
REALLY?
OVER THERE!
LOOK!

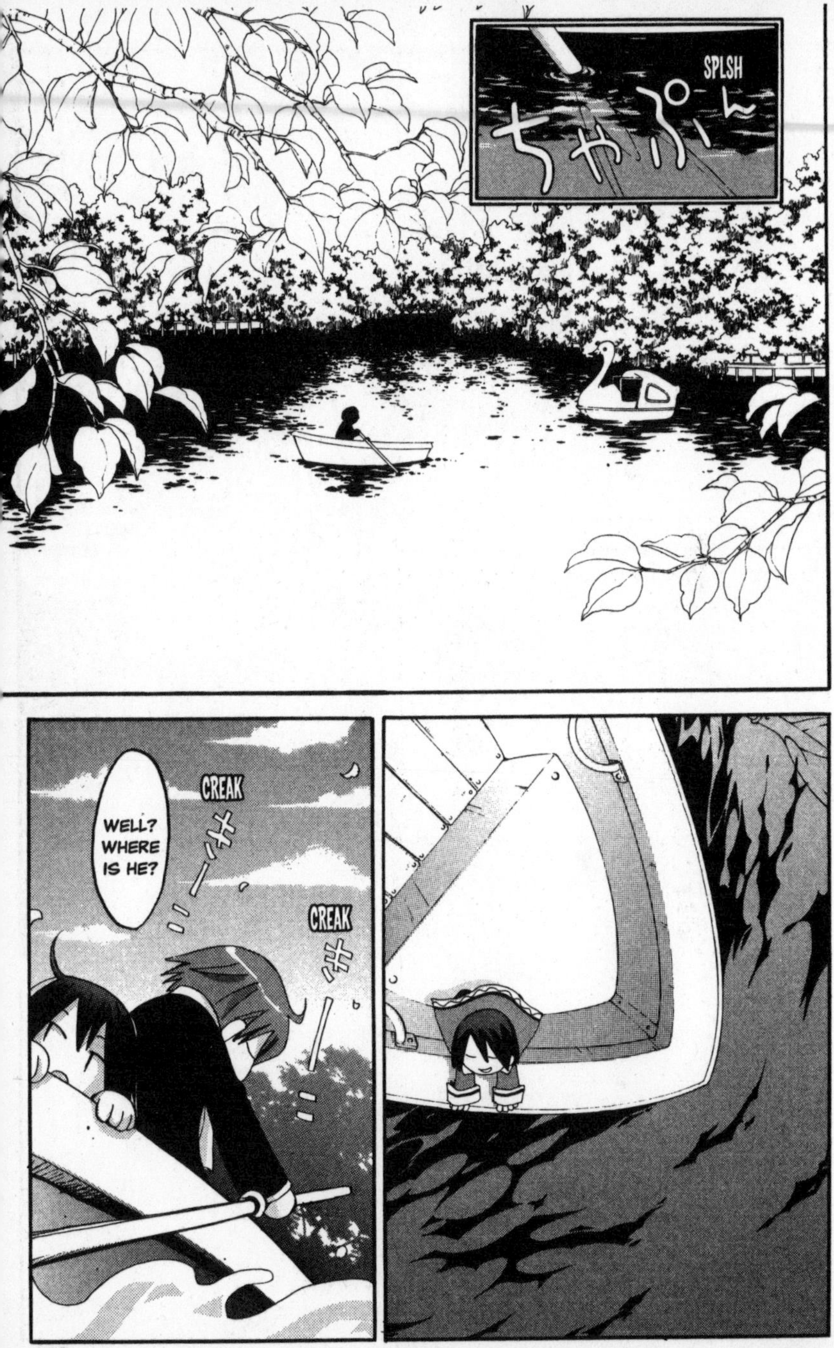
SPLSH
ちゃぷん
WELL? WHERE IS HE?
CREAK
CREAK

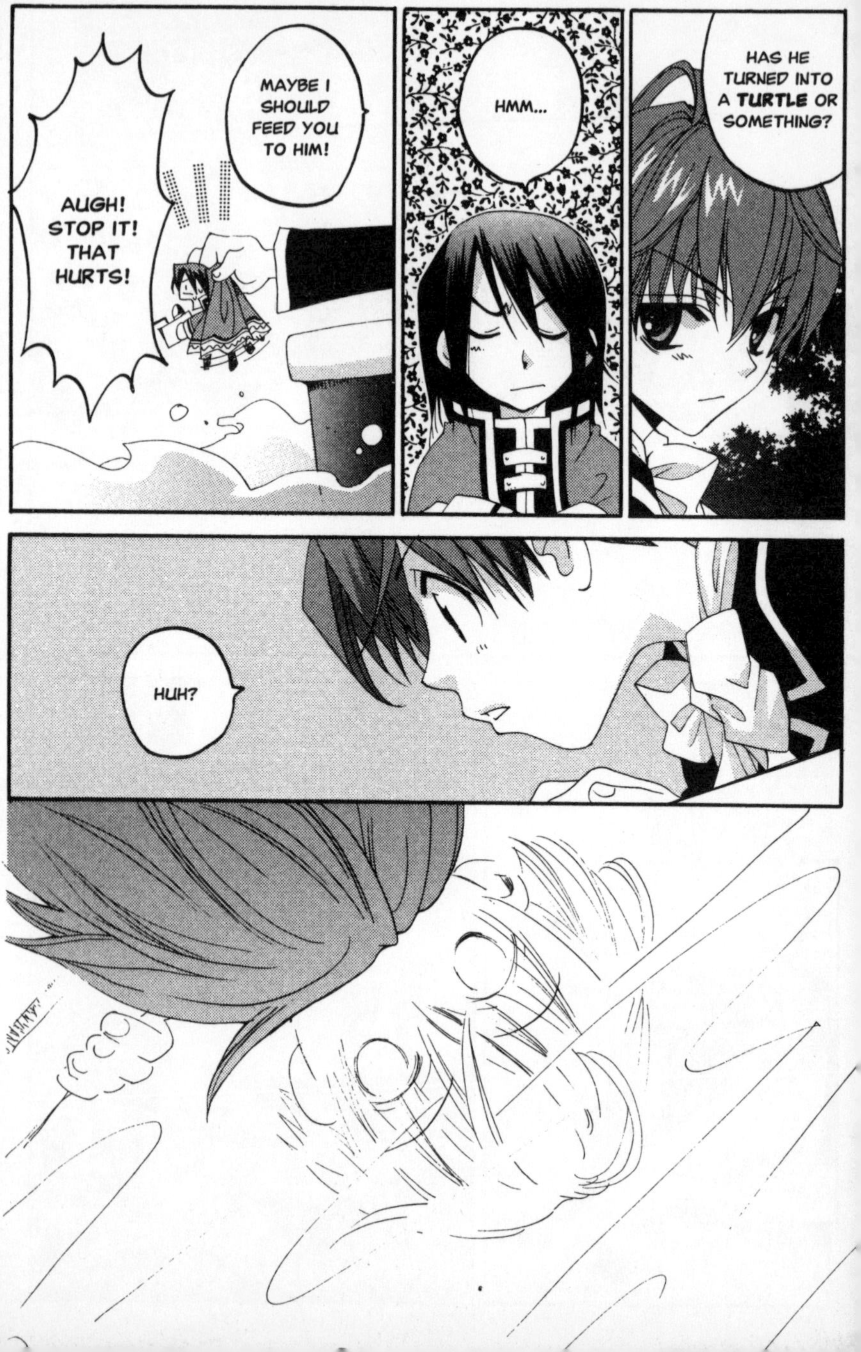
HAS HE TURNED INTO A TURTLE OR SOMETHING?
HMM...
MAYBE I SHOULD FEED YOU TO HIM!
AUGH! STOP IT! THAT HURTS!
HUH?

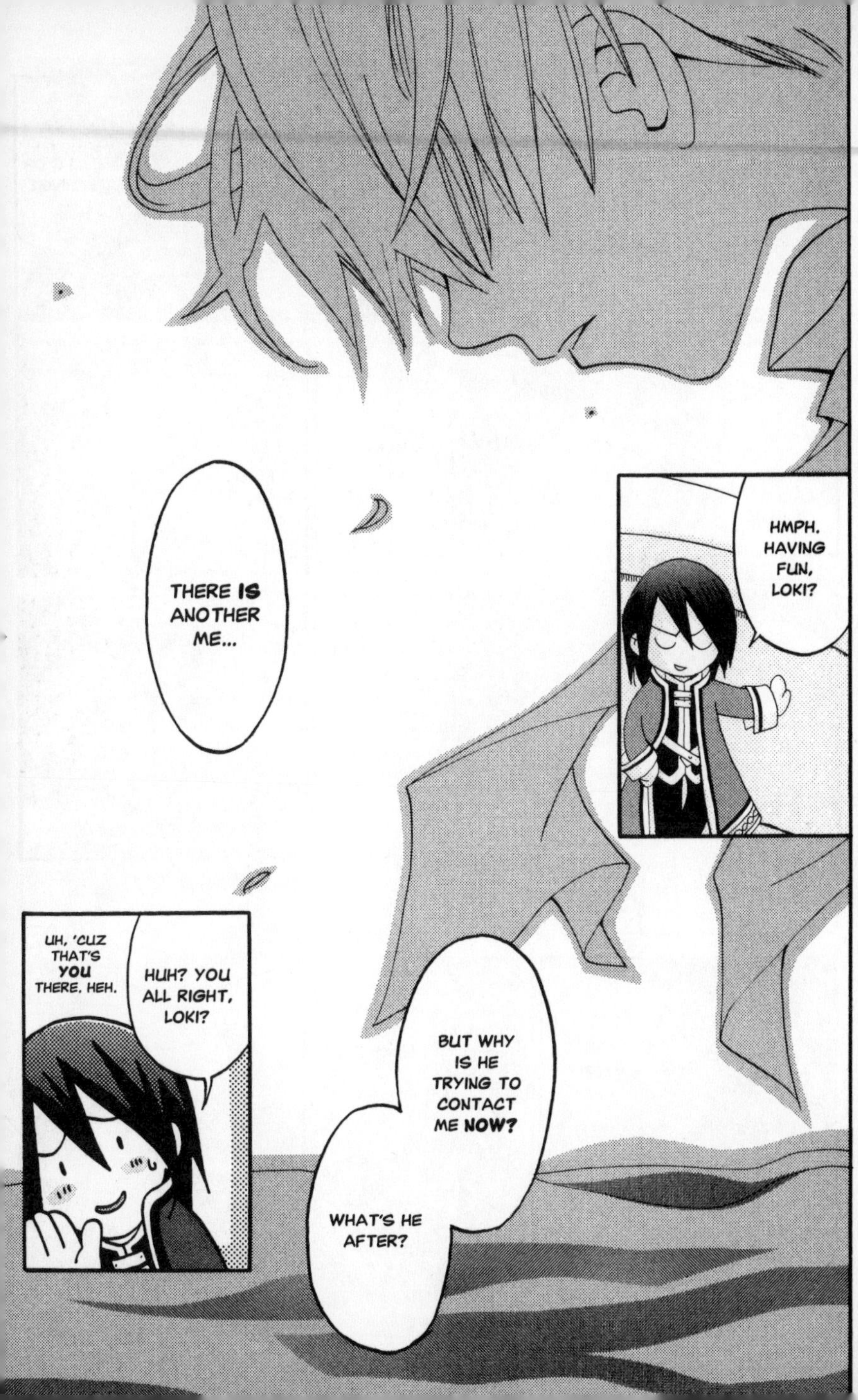
THERE IS ANOTHER ME...
HMPH. HAVING FUN, LOKI?
BUT WHY IS HE TRYING TO CONTACT ME NOW?
WHAT'S HE AFTER?
HUH? YOU ALL RIGHT, LOKI?
UH, 'CUZ THAT'S YOU THERE. HEH.

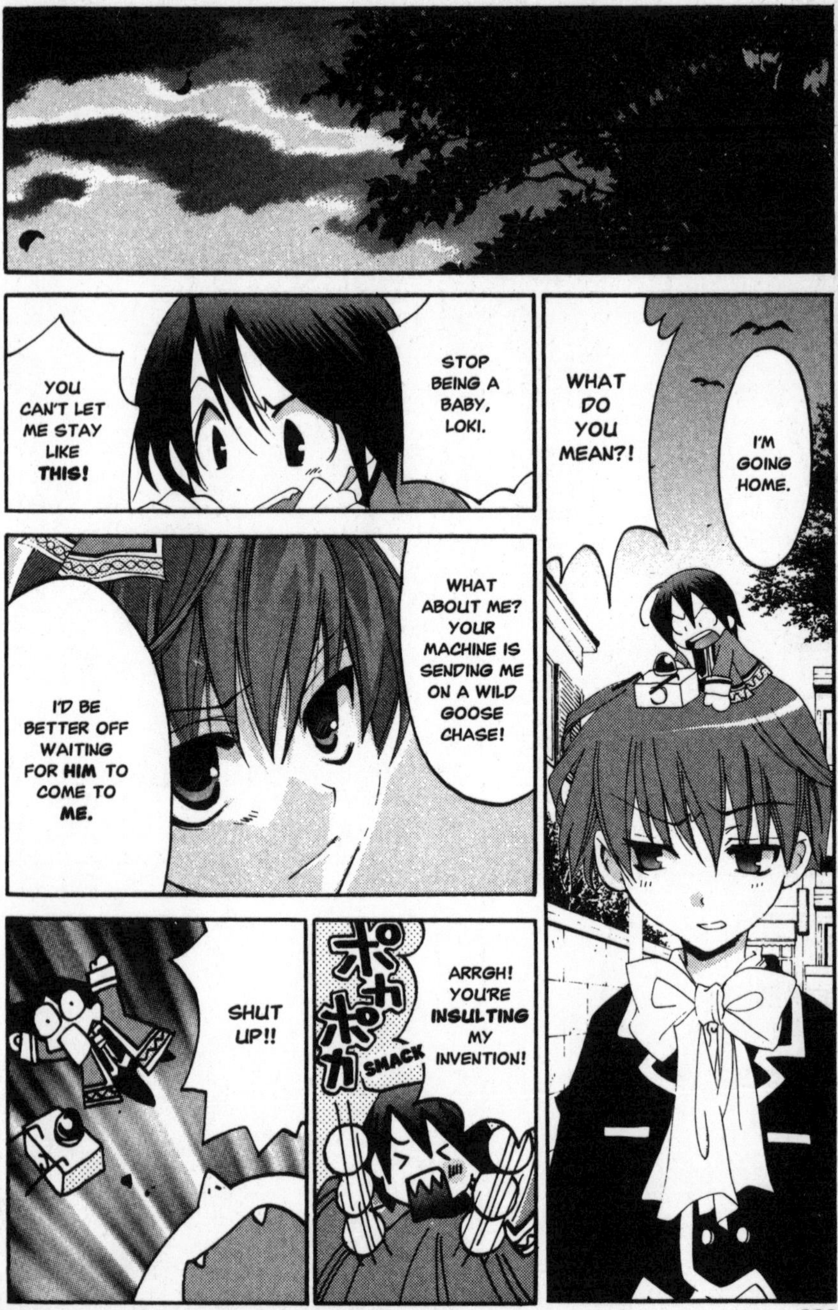
I'M GOING HOME.
WHAT DO YOU MEAN?!
STOP BEING A BABY, LOKI.
YOU CAN'T LET ME STAY LIKE THIS!
WHAT ABOUT ME? YOUR MACHINE IS SENDING ME ON A WILD GOOSE CHASE!
I'D BE BETTER OFF WAITING FOR HIM TO COME TO ME.
ARRGH! YOU'RE INSULTING MY INVENTION!
ポカポカ
SMACK
SHUT UP!!

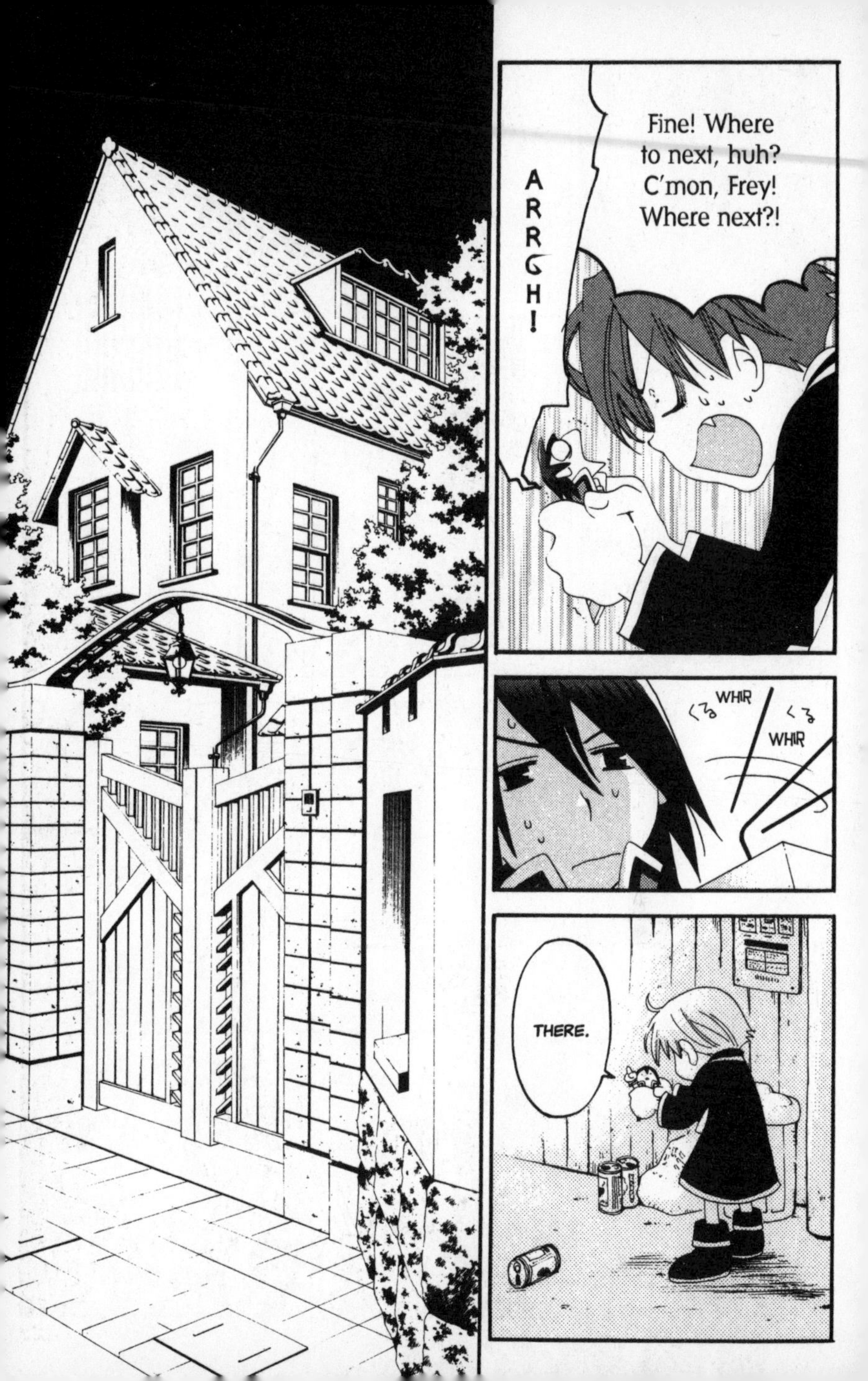

Fine! Where to next, huh? C'mon, Frey! Where next?!
ARRGH!
くる WHIR
くる WHIR
THERE.

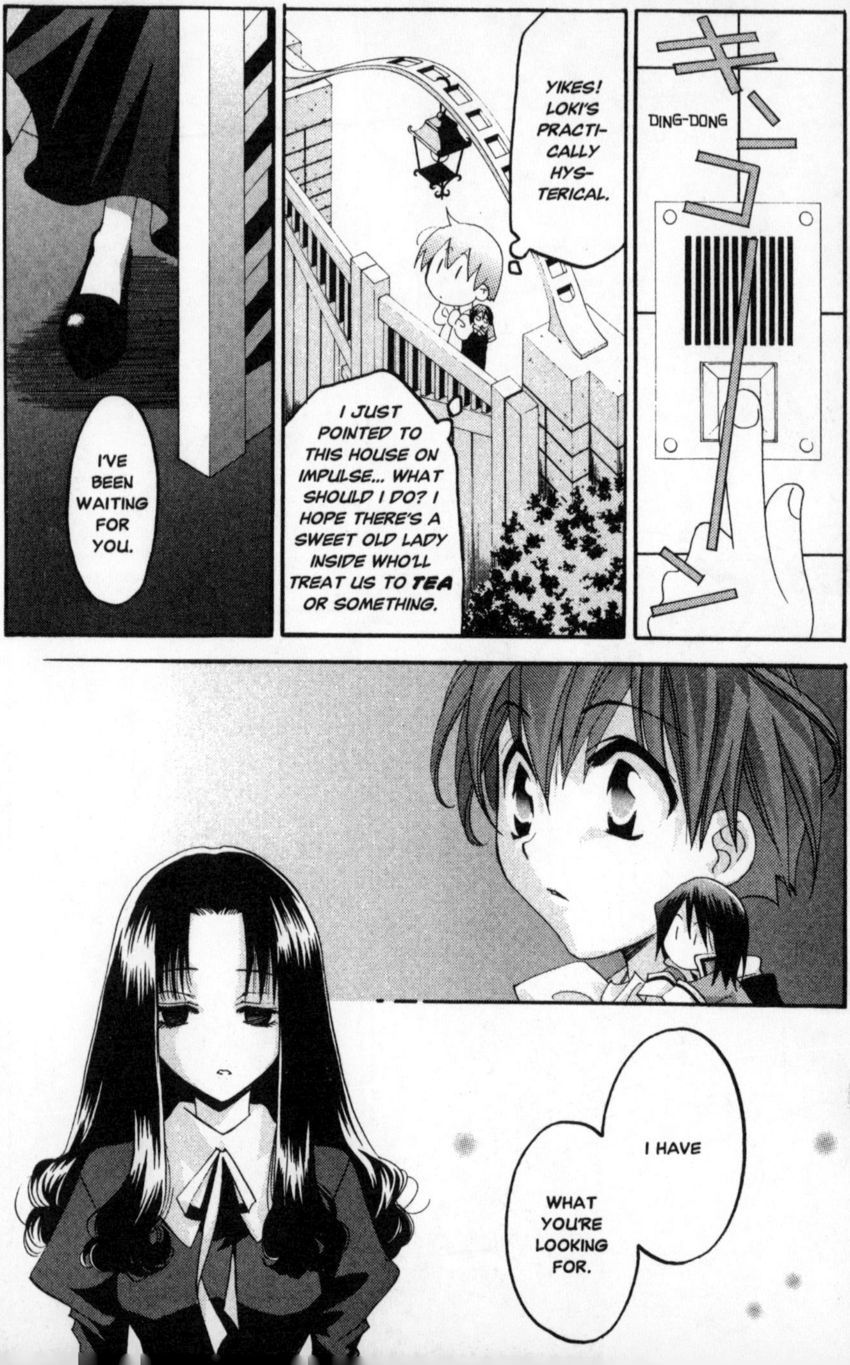
DING-DONG
YIKES! LOKI'S PRACTI-CALLY HYS-TERICAL.
I JUST POINTED TO THIS HOUSE ON IMPULSE... WHAT SHOULD I DO? I HOPE THERE'S A SWEET OLD LADY INSIDE WHO'LL TREAT US TO TEA OR SOMETHING.
I'VE BEEN WAITING FOR YOU.
I HAVE
WHAT YOU'RE LOOKING FOR.

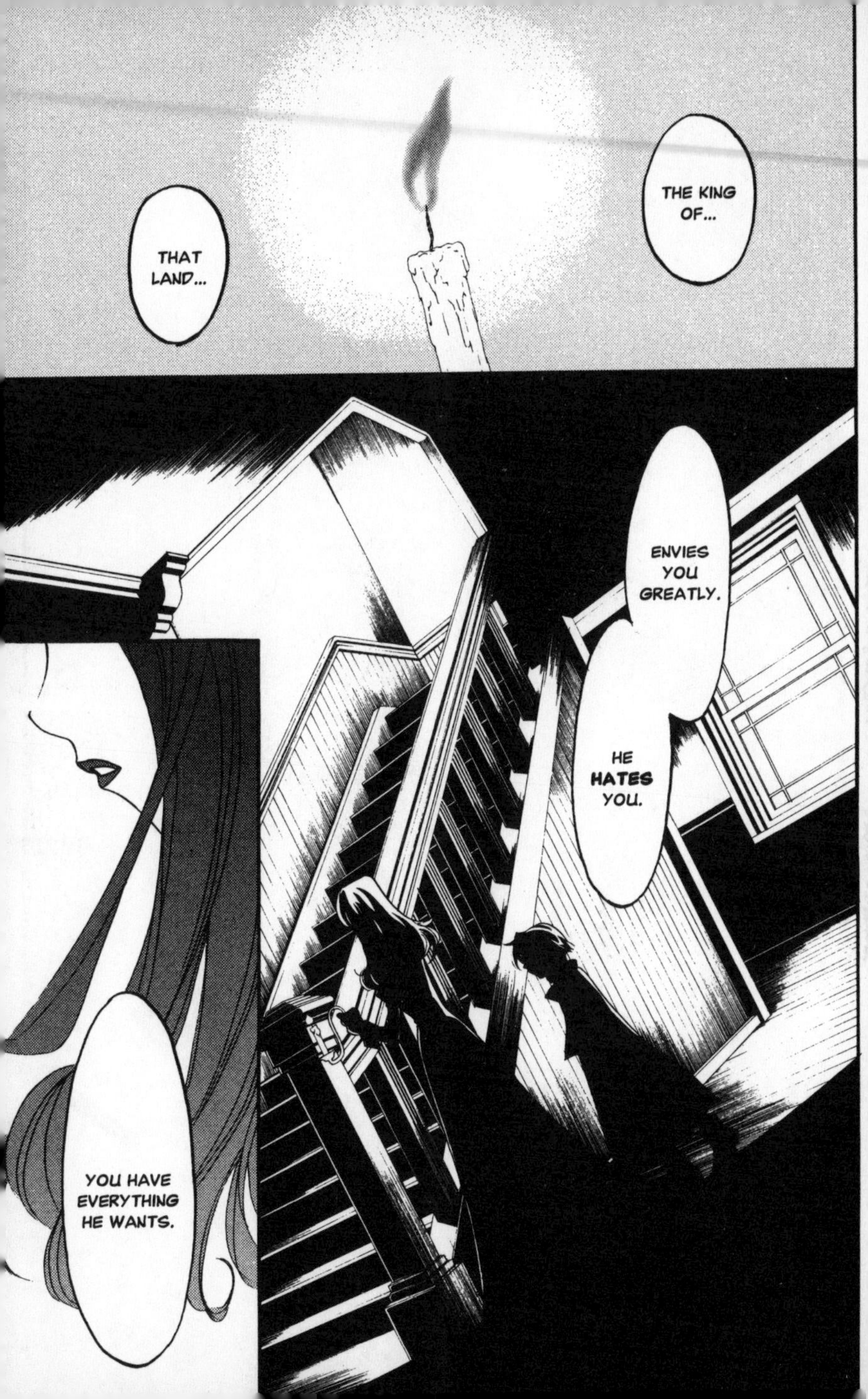
THE KING OF...
THAT LAND...
ENVIES YOU GREATLY.
HE HATES YOU.
YOU HAVE EVERYTHING HE WANTS.

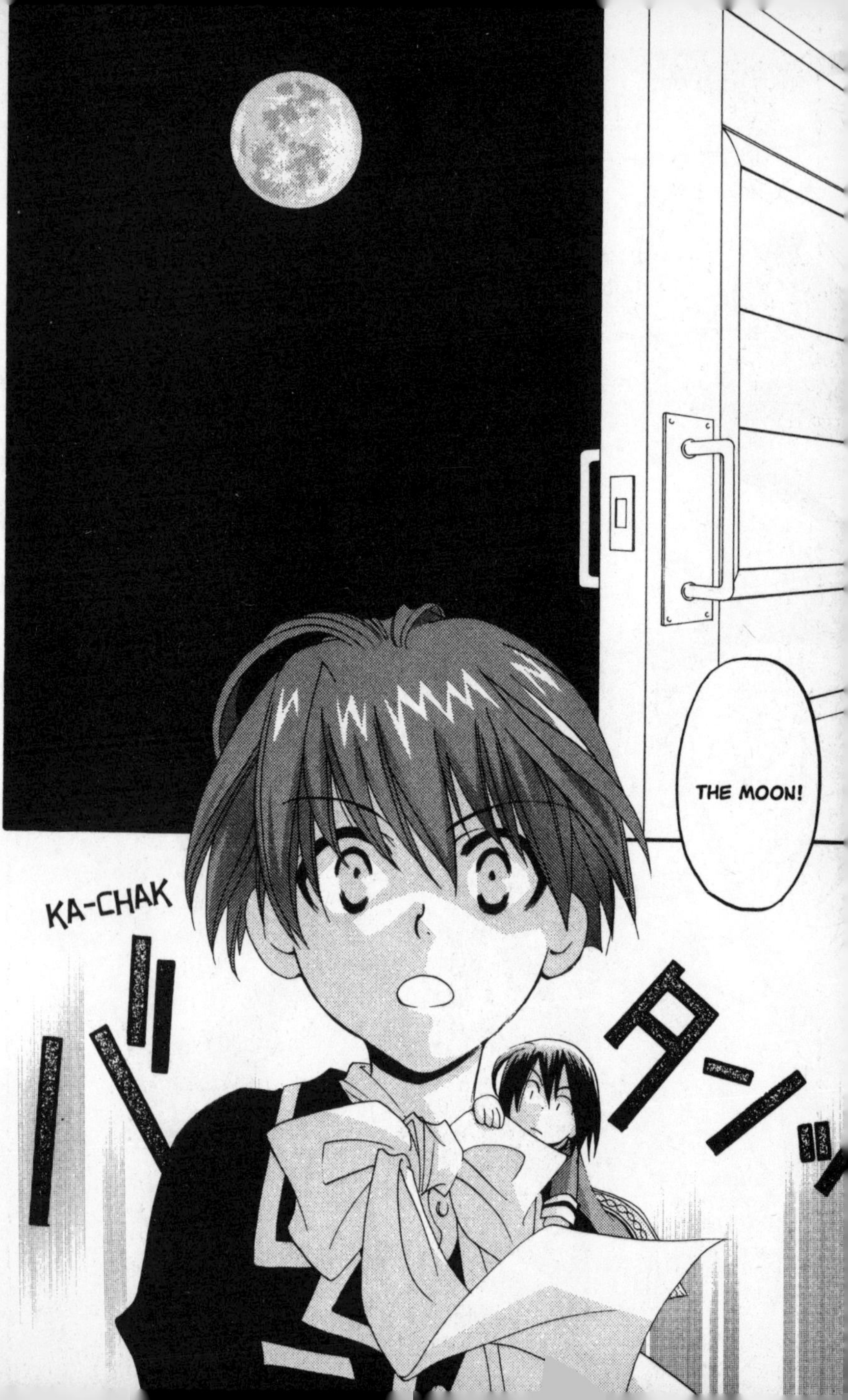
THE MOON!
KA-CHAK

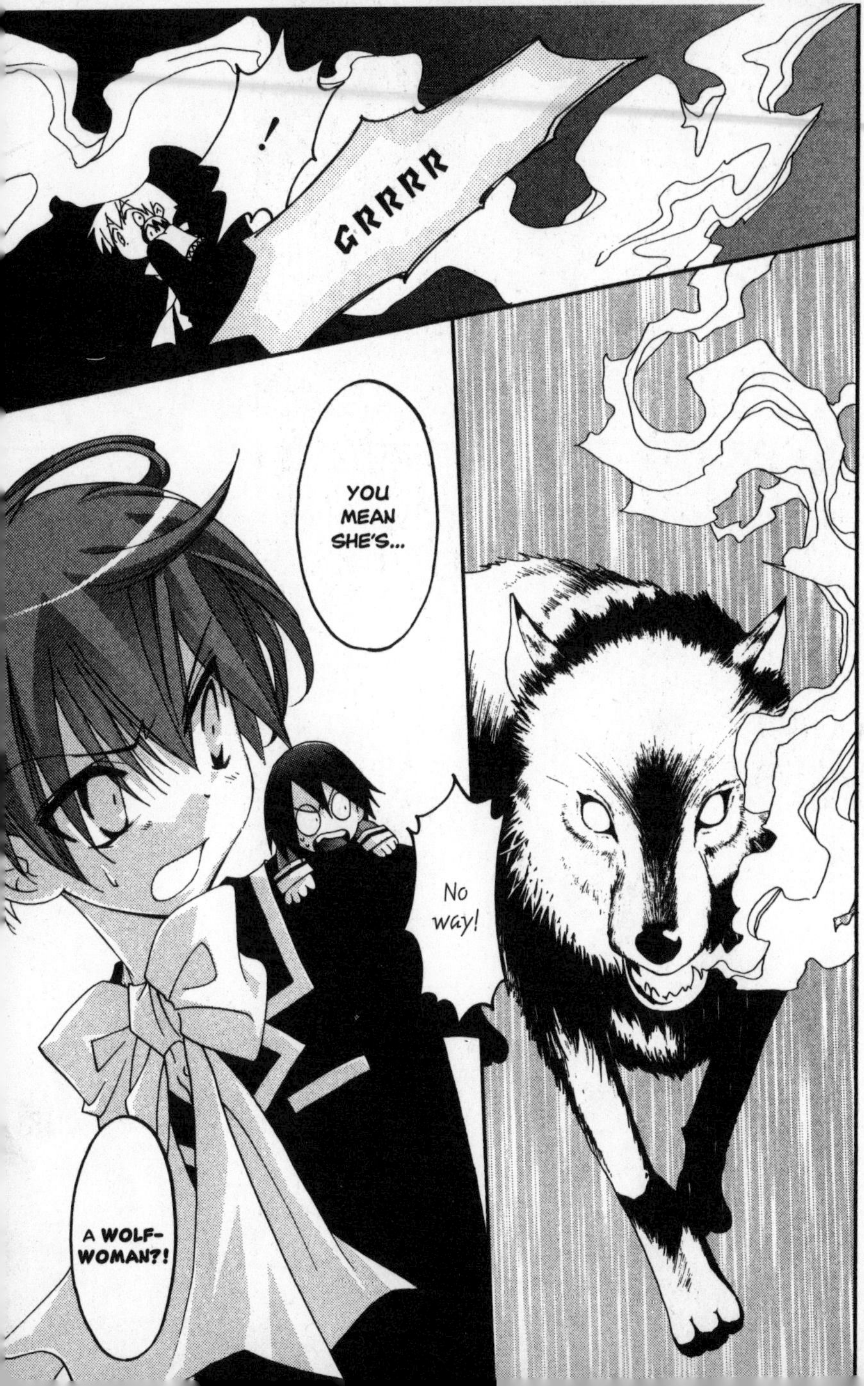
GRRRR
!
YOU MEAN SHE'S...
No way!
A WOLF-WOMAN?!

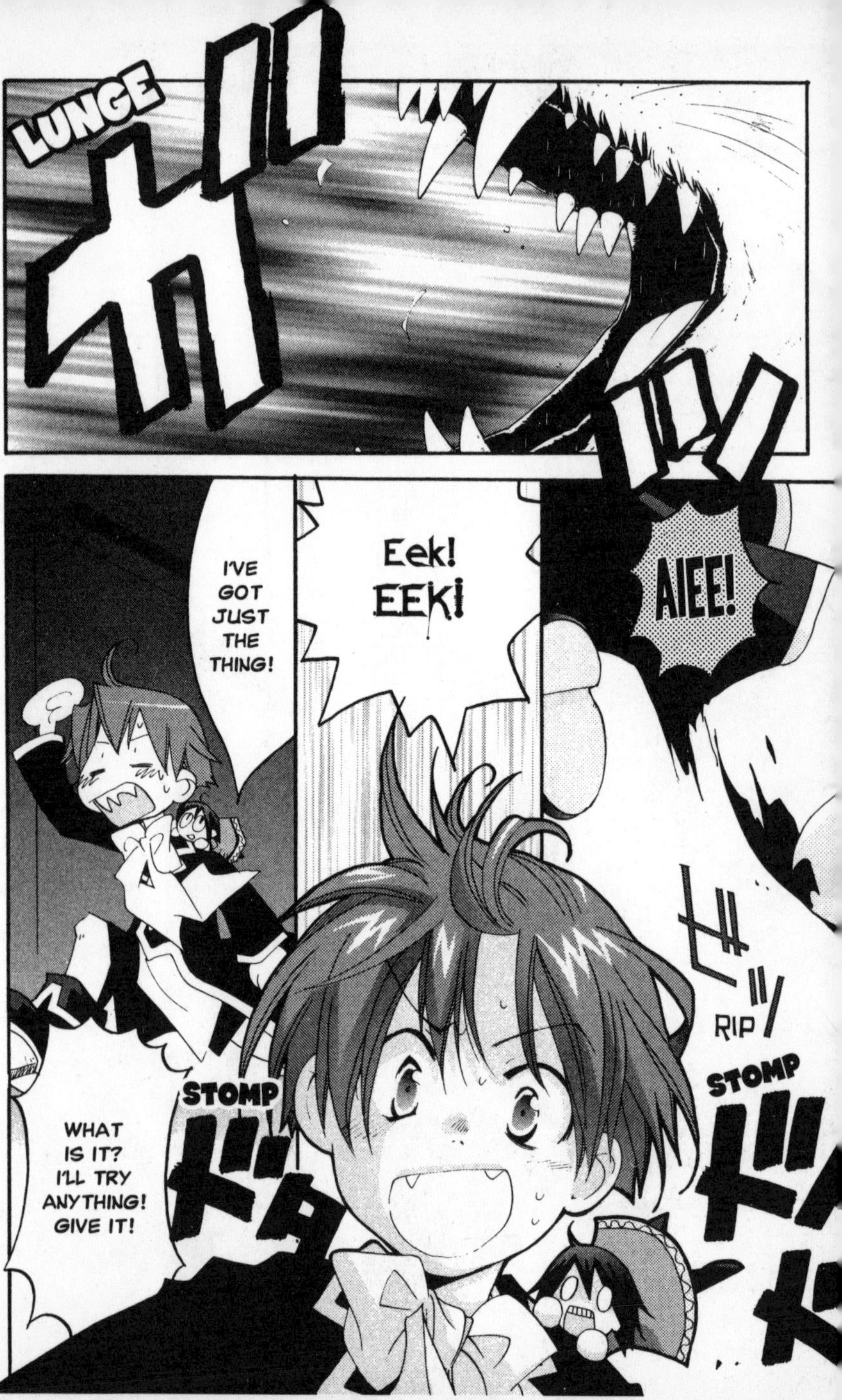
LUNGE
AIEE!
Eek! EEK!
I'VE GOT JUST THE THING!
RIP
STOMP
STOMP
WHAT IS IT? I'LL TRY ANYTHING! GIVE IT!

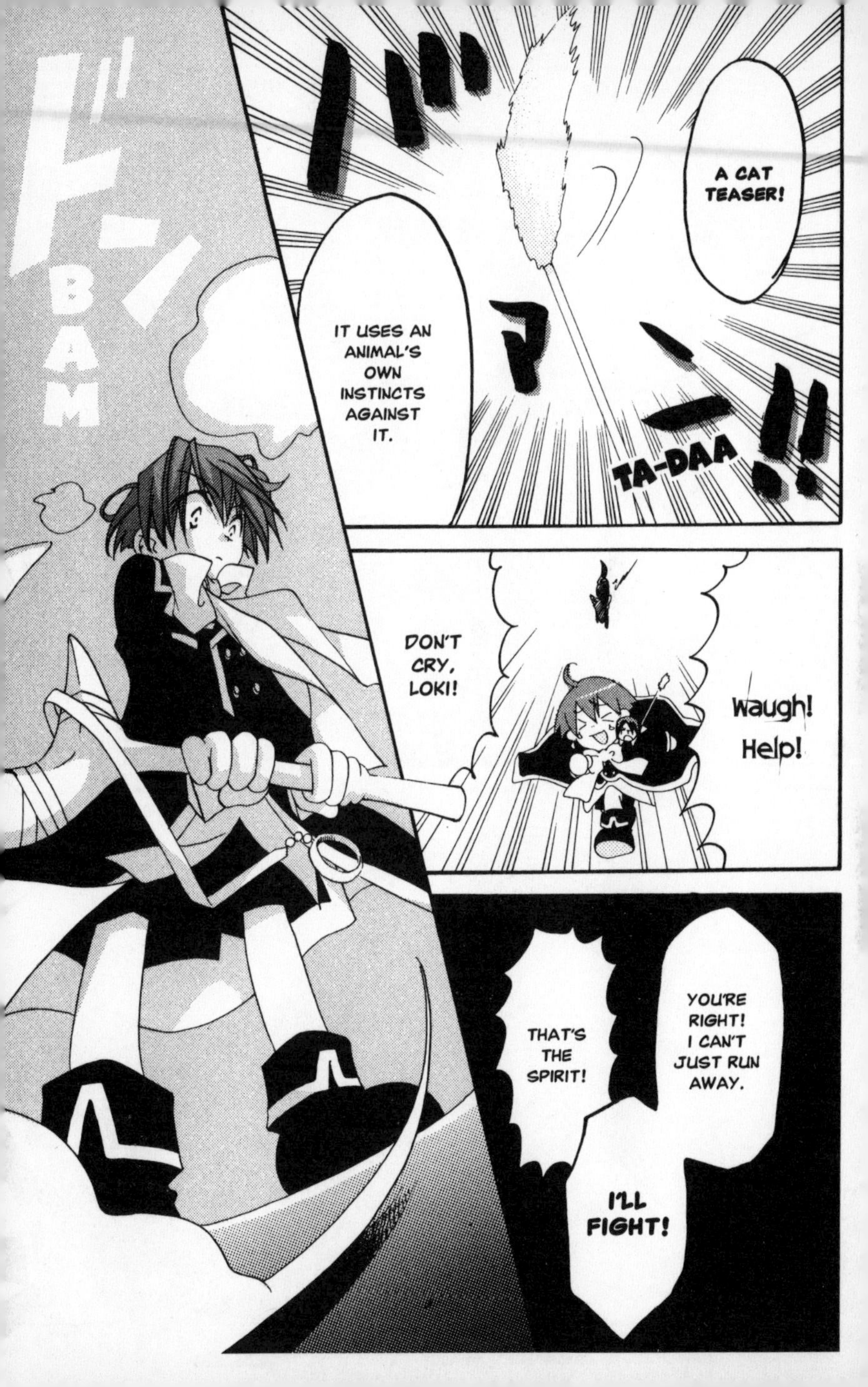
A CAT TEASER!
IT USES AN ANIMAL'S OWN INSTINCTS AGAINST IT.
TA-DAA!!
BAM
Waugh! Help!
DON'T CRY, LOKI!
YOU'RE RIGHT! I CAN'T JUST RUN AWAY.
I'LL FIGHT!
THAT'S THE SPIRIT!

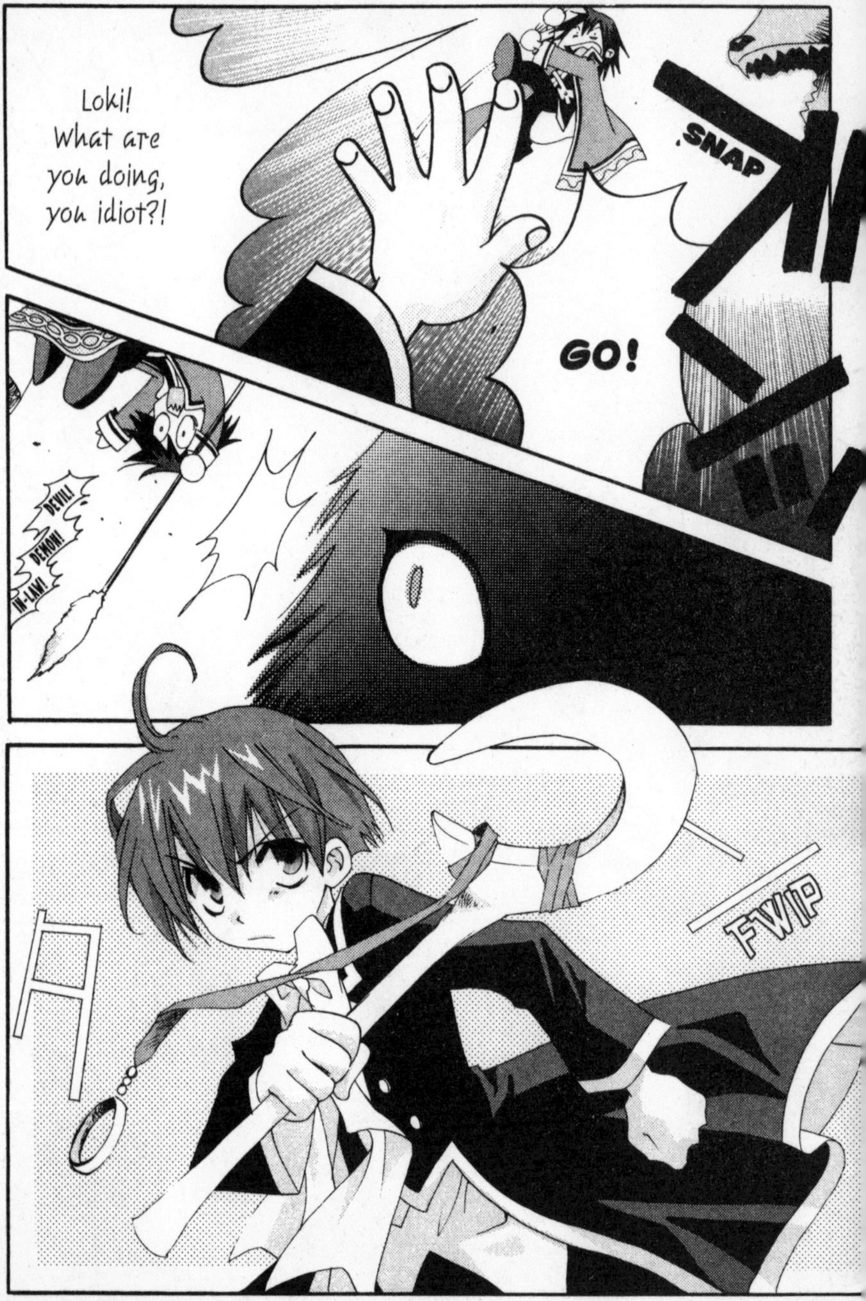
SNAP
Loki!
What are you doing, you idiot?!
GO!
DEVIL!
DEMON!
IN-LAW!
FWIP

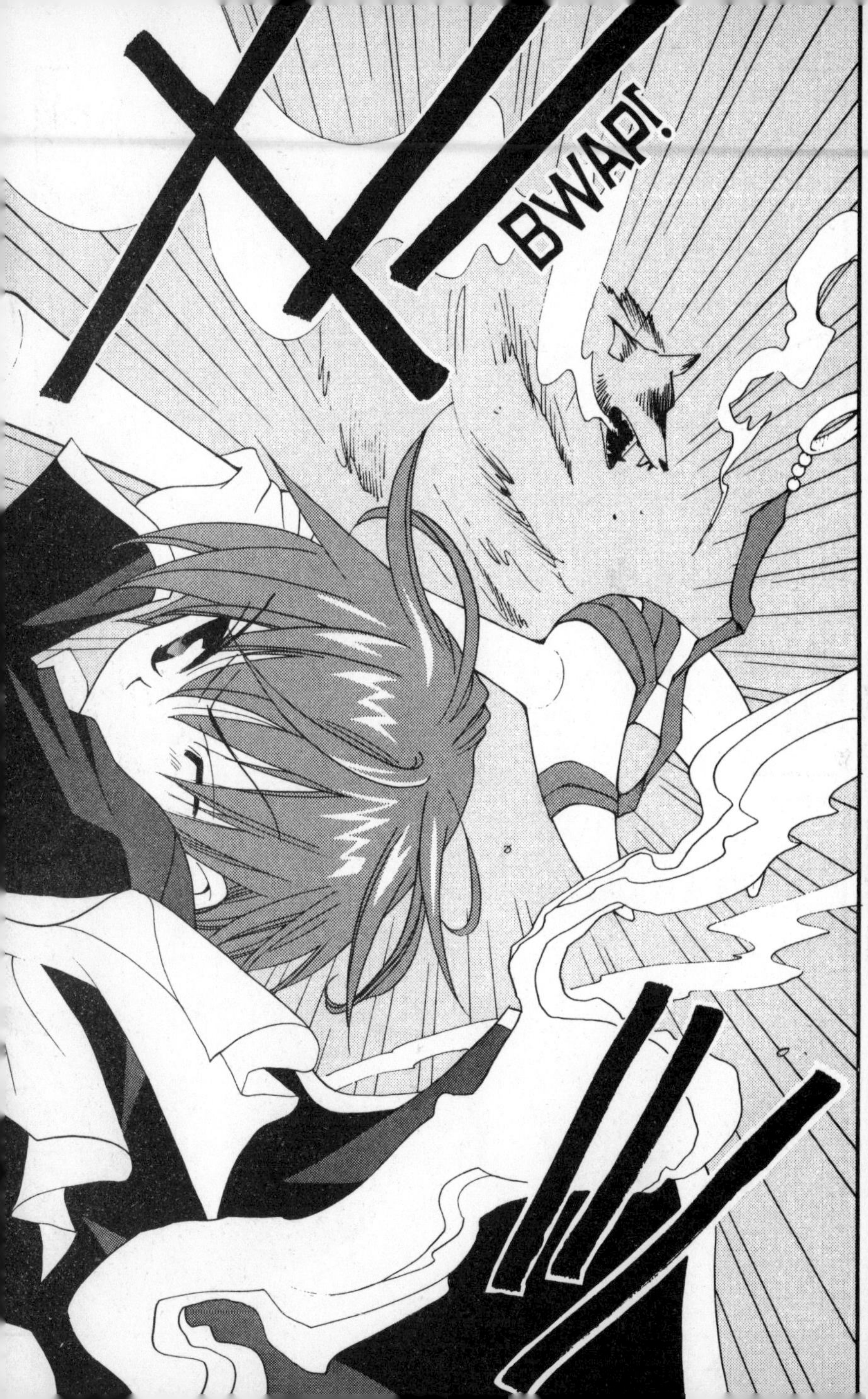
BWAP!

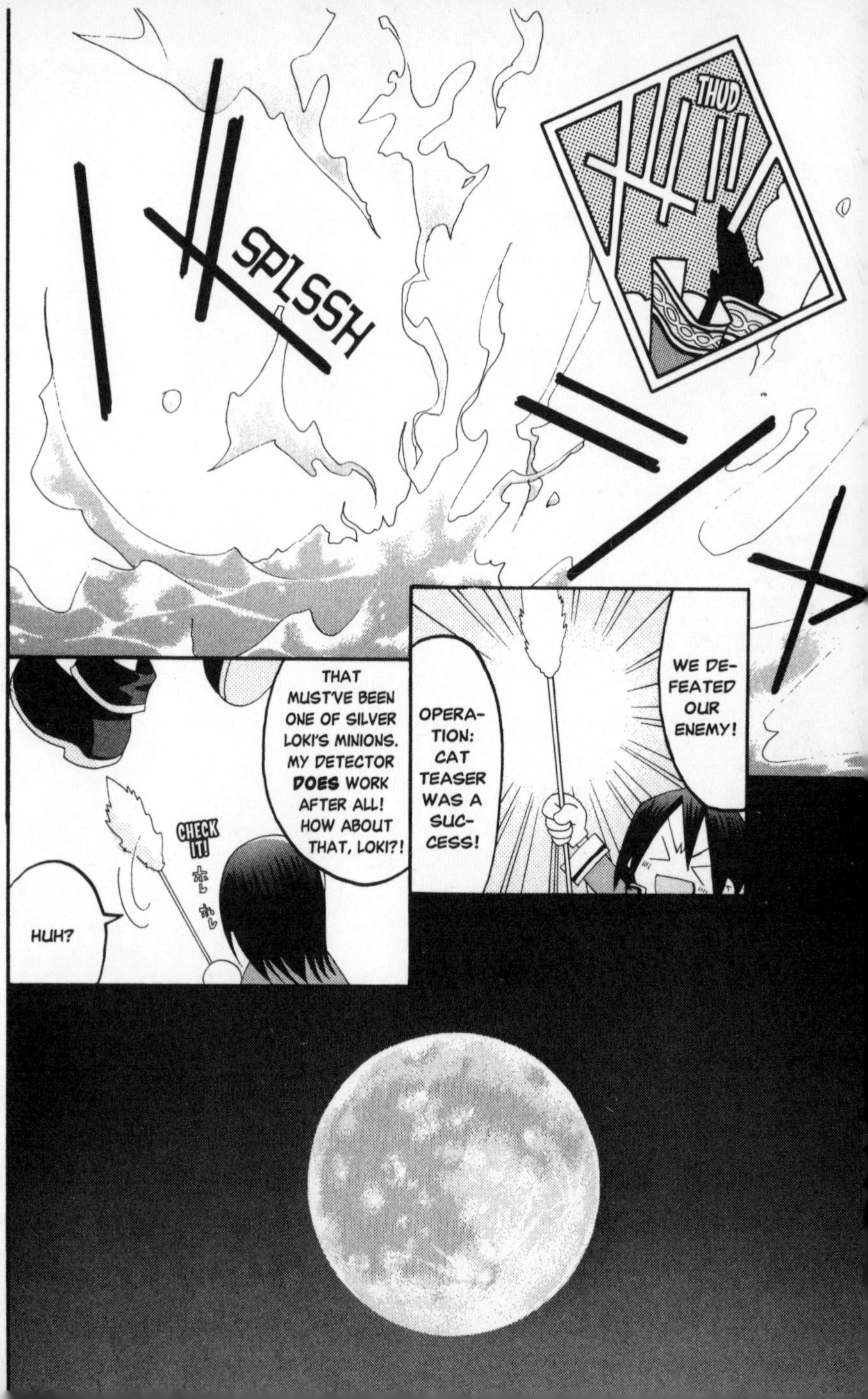
THUD
SPLSSH
WE DE-FEATED OUR ENEMY!
OPERA-TION: CAT TEASER WAS A SUC-CESS!
THAT MUST'VE BEEN ONE OF SILVER LOKI'S MINIONS. MY DETECTOR **DOES** WORK AFTER ALL! HOW ABOUT THAT, LOKI?!
CHECK IT!
HUH?

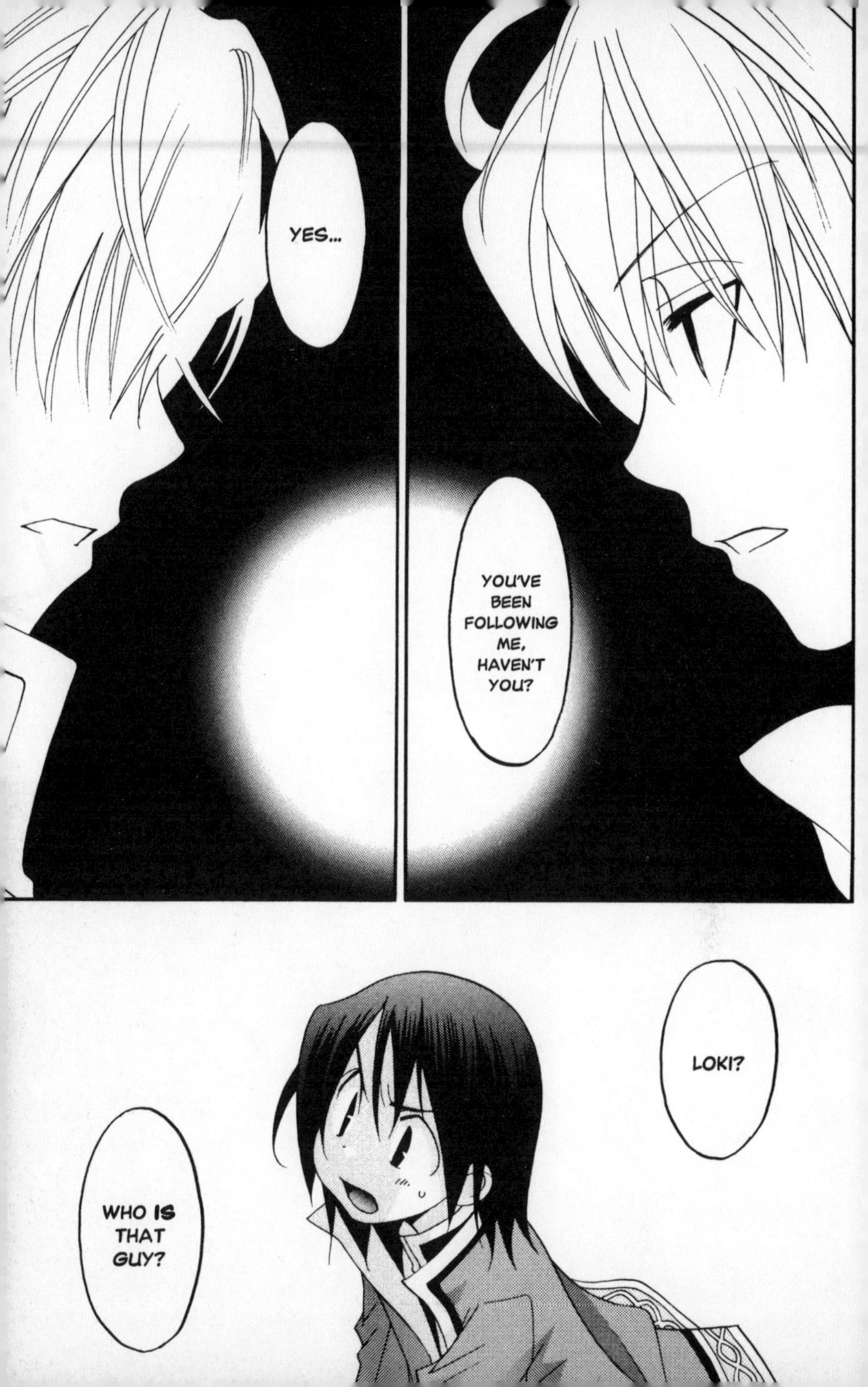

YOU'VE BEEN FOLLOWING ME, HAVEN'T YOU?
YES...
LOKI?
WHO IS THAT GUY?

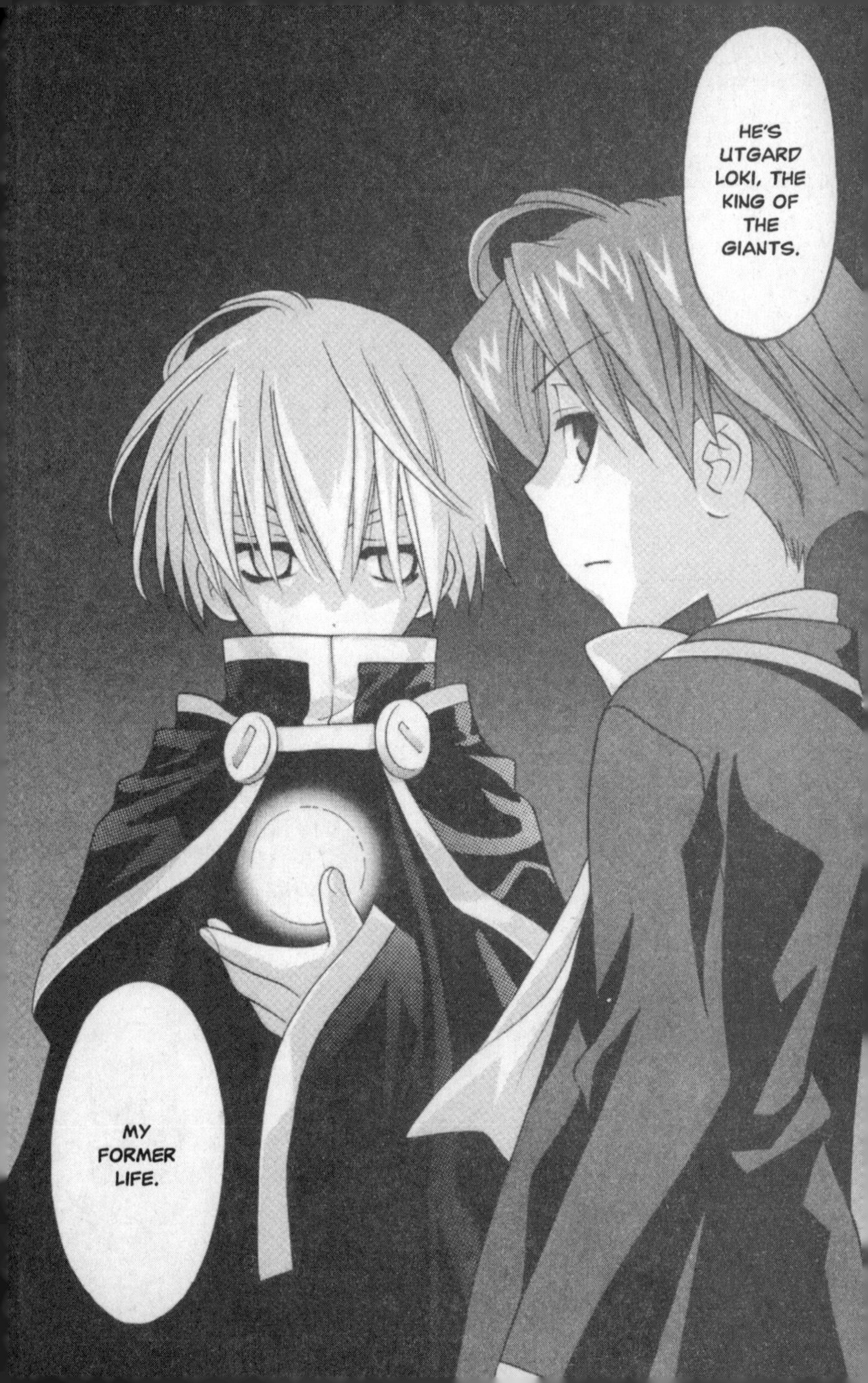
HE'S UTGARD LOKI, THE KING OF THE GIANTS.
MY FORMER LIFE.

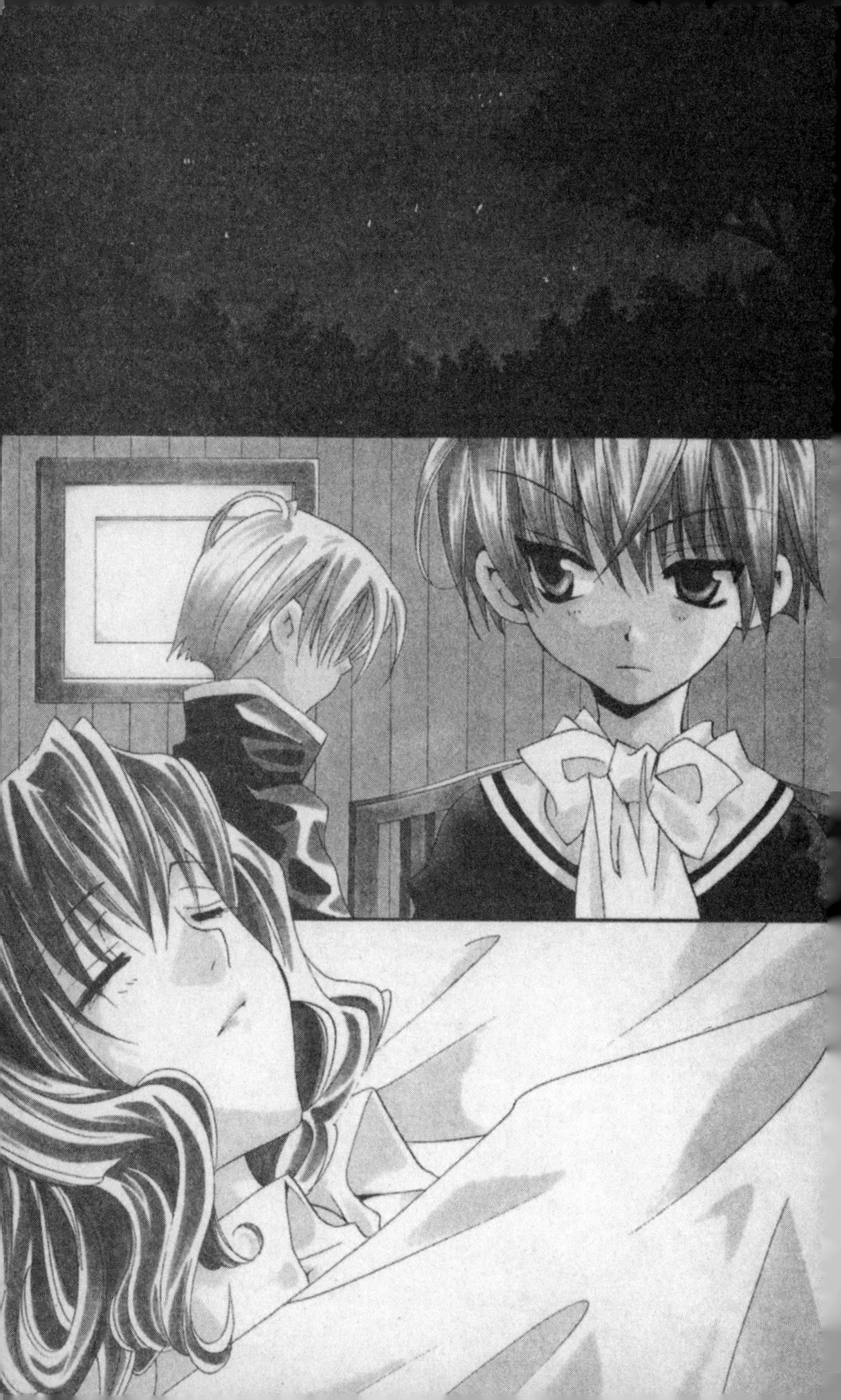

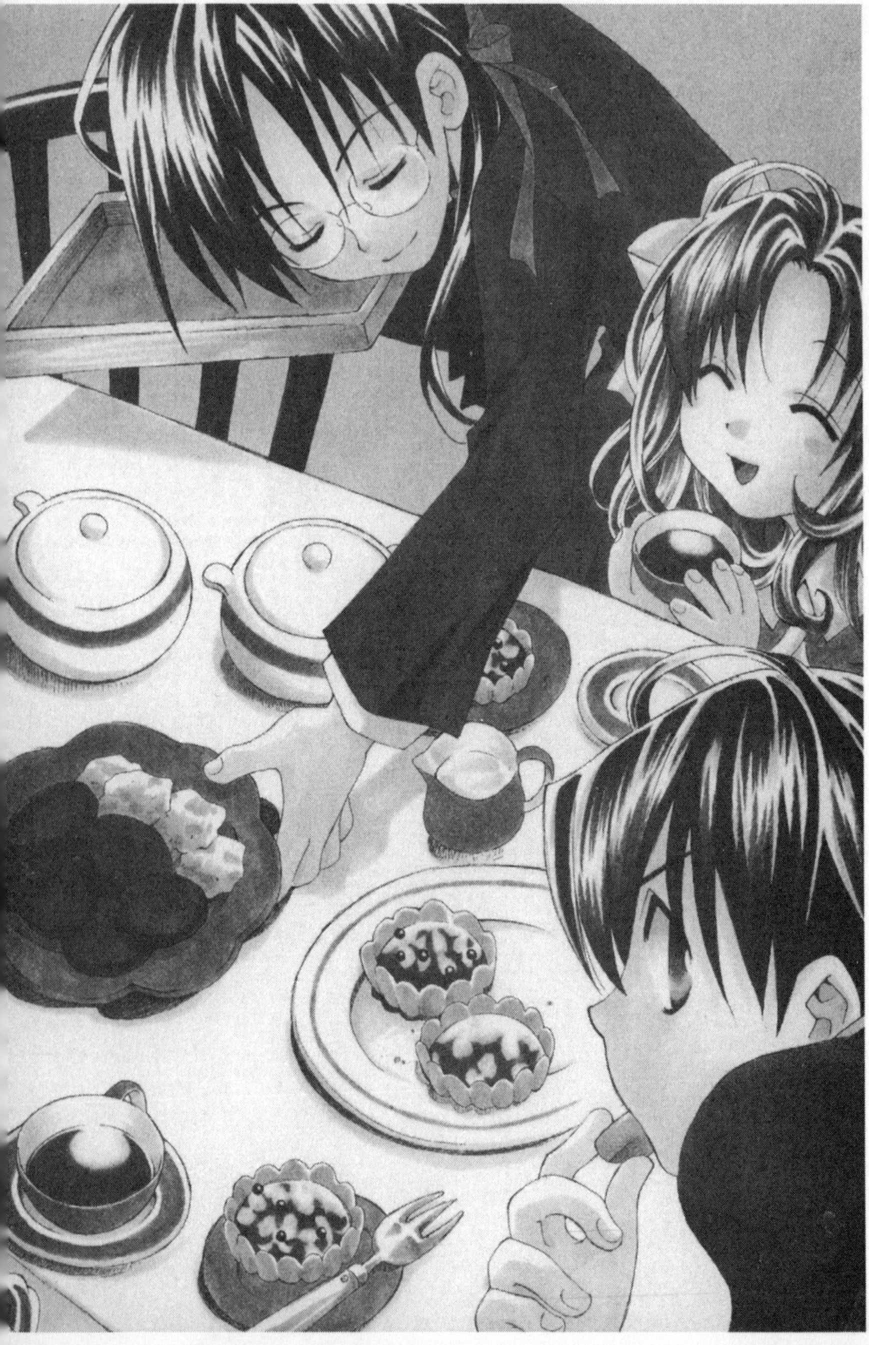

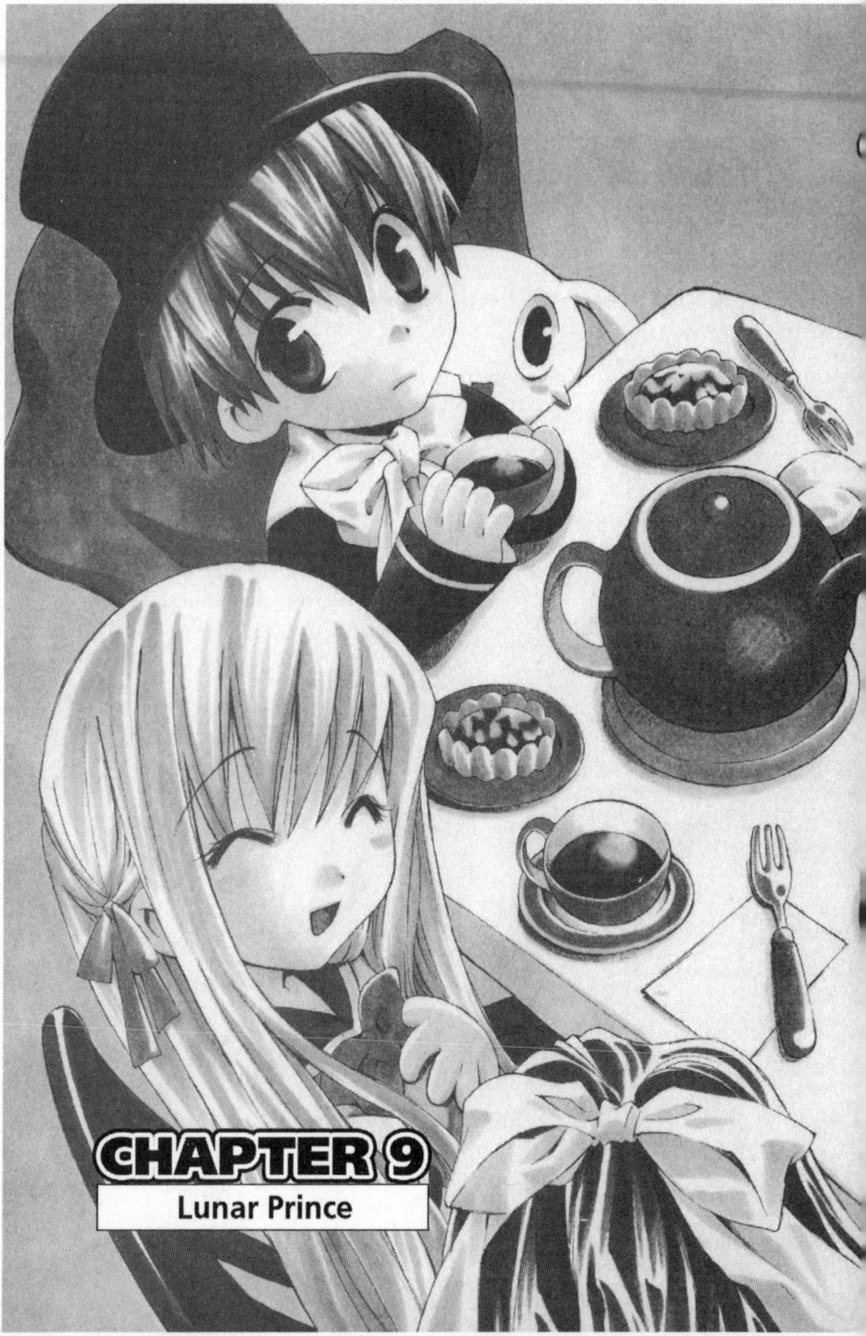
CHAPTER 9
Lunar Prince

Random Thoughts (Part 3)

(I wonder how long this section will last...)

Don't you just feel **HAPPY** when you draw pictures of girls? I especially like working on their waistlines, hair and so on. Anyway, let's talk about *Ragnarok*. As opposed to the previous series, this time around I'm focusing on the gods themselves. Since I'm not so good at serious stories (What, ME, serious?!), I tend to overthink things. I always plan on having more female characters, but for some reason when things get serious, I end up with nothing but male characters. Why? WHY? Where did you go to, Mayura?!

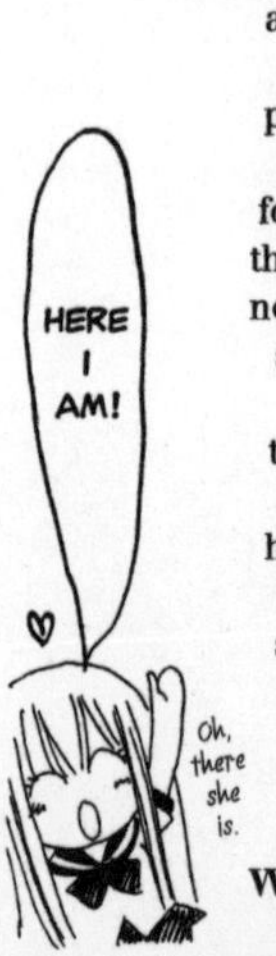
HERE I AM!
Oh, there she is.

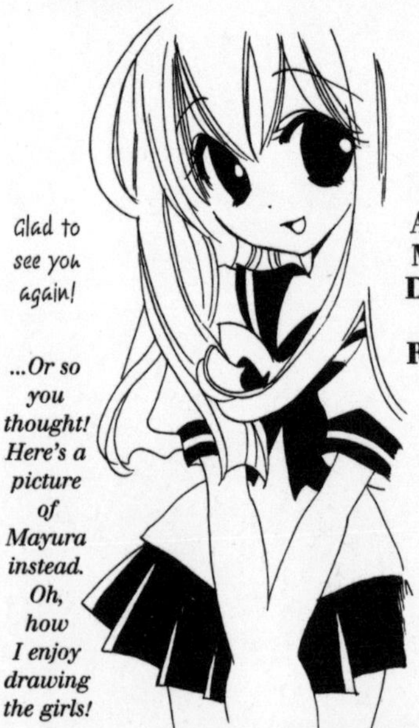
Glad to see you again!

...Or so you thought! Here's a picture of Mayura instead. Oh, how I enjoy drawing the girls!

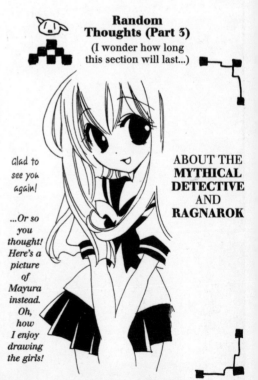

ABOUT THE **MYTHICAL DETECTIVE** AND **RAGNAROK**

Y'KNOW, I'VE REALIZED THAT THE GIRLS I DRAW TURN OUT TO BE AIRHEADS. NO WAIT--COME TO THINK OF IT, **ALL** OF MY CHARACTERS DO! [DIES]

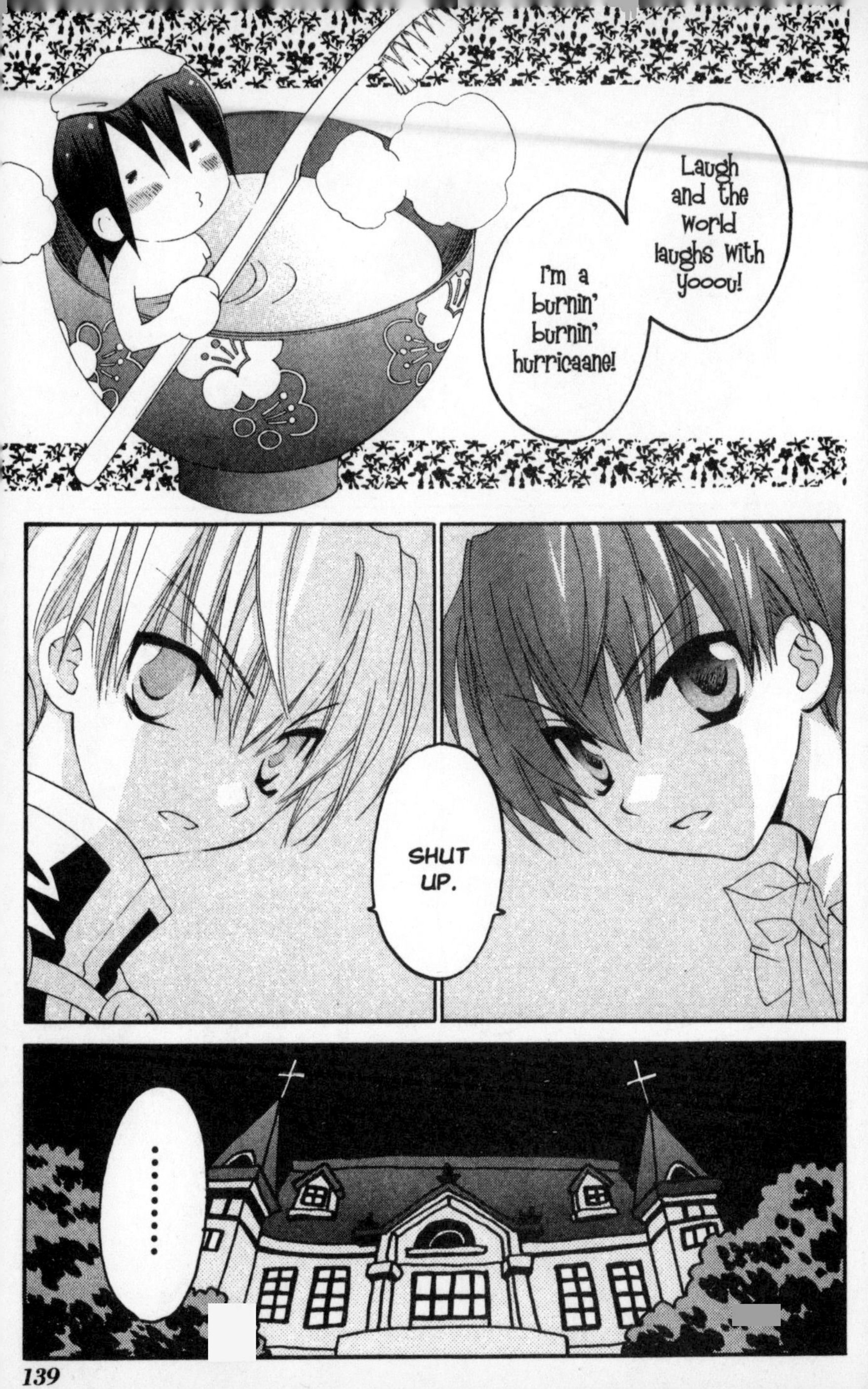
Laugh and the world laughs with yooou!
I'm a burnin' burnin' hurricaane!
SHUT UP.
....

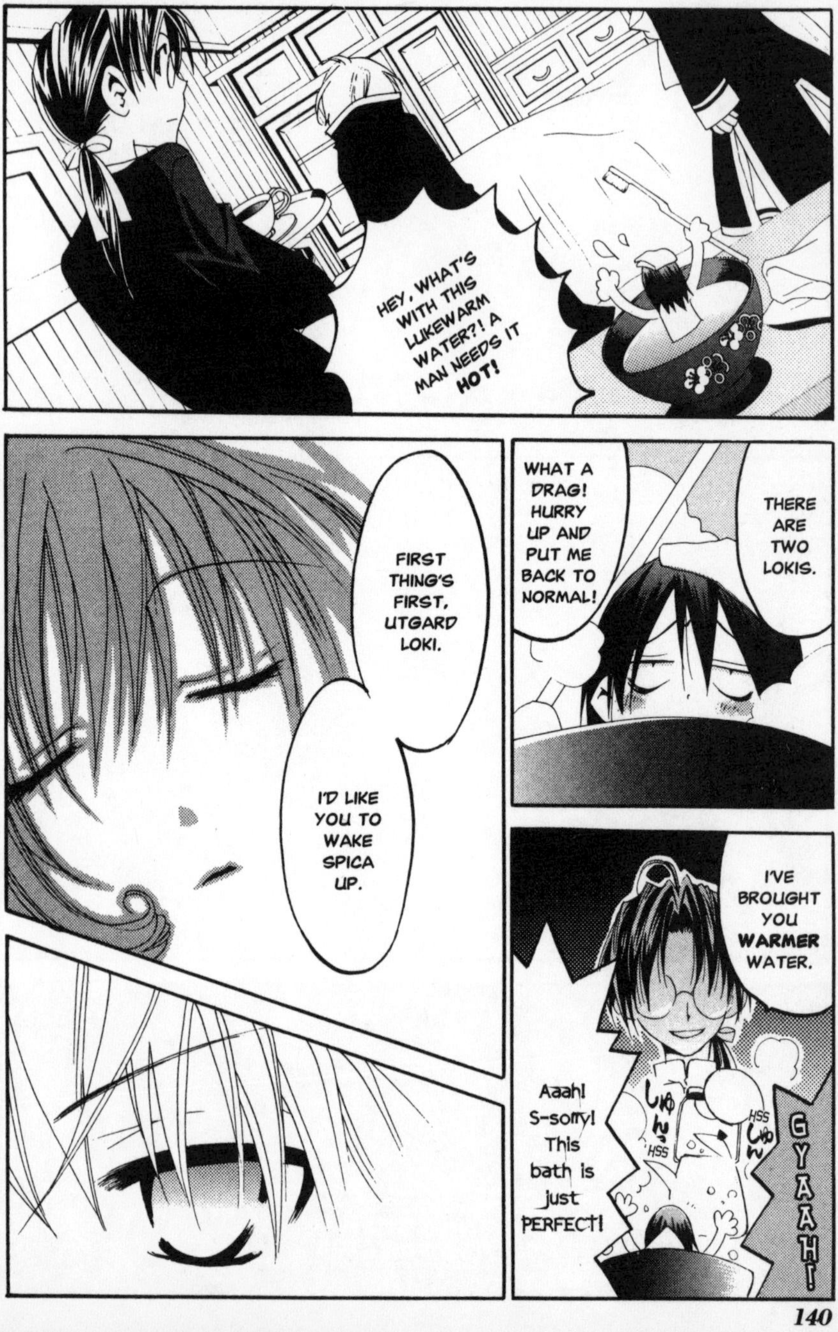
HEY, WHAT'S WITH THIS LUKEWARM WATER?! A MAN NEEDS IT **HOT!**
THERE ARE TWO LOKIS.
WHAT A DRAG! HURRY UP AND PUT ME BACK TO NORMAL!
FIRST THING'S FIRST, UTGARD LOKI.
I'D LIKE YOU TO WAKE SPICA UP.
I'VE BROUGHT YOU **WARMER** WATER.
Aaah! S-sorry! This bath is just PERFECT!
HSS
HSS
GYAAAH!

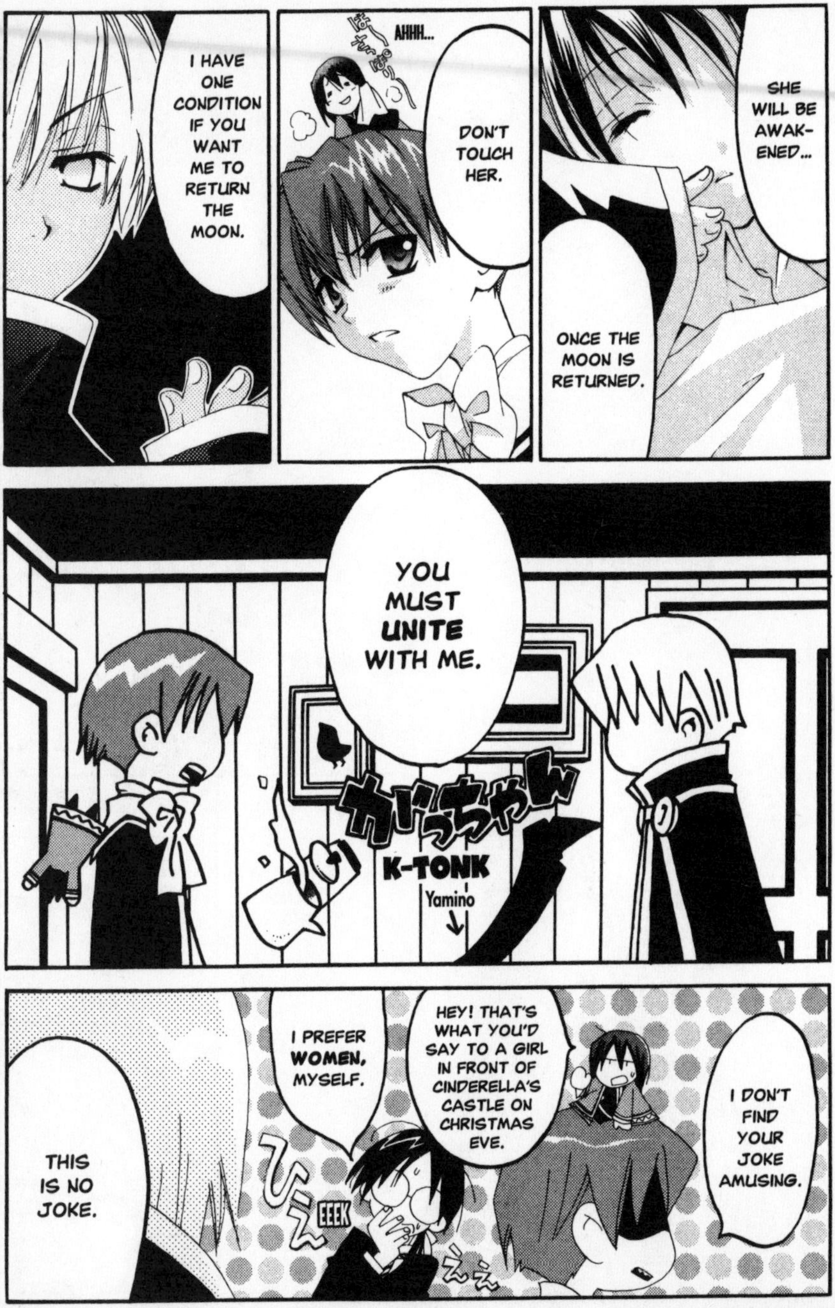
SHE WILL BE AWAKENED...
ONCE THE MOON IS RETURNED.
AHHH...
DON'T TOUCH HER.
I HAVE ONE CONDITION IF YOU WANT ME TO RETURN THE MOON.
YOU MUST **UNITE** WITH ME.
K-TONK
Yamino
I DON'T FIND YOUR JOKE AMUSING.
HEY! THAT'S WHAT YOU'D SAY TO A GIRL IN FRONT OF CINDERELLA'S CASTLE ON CHRISTMAS EVE.
I PREFER **WOMEN,** MYSELF.
EEEK
THIS IS NO JOKE.

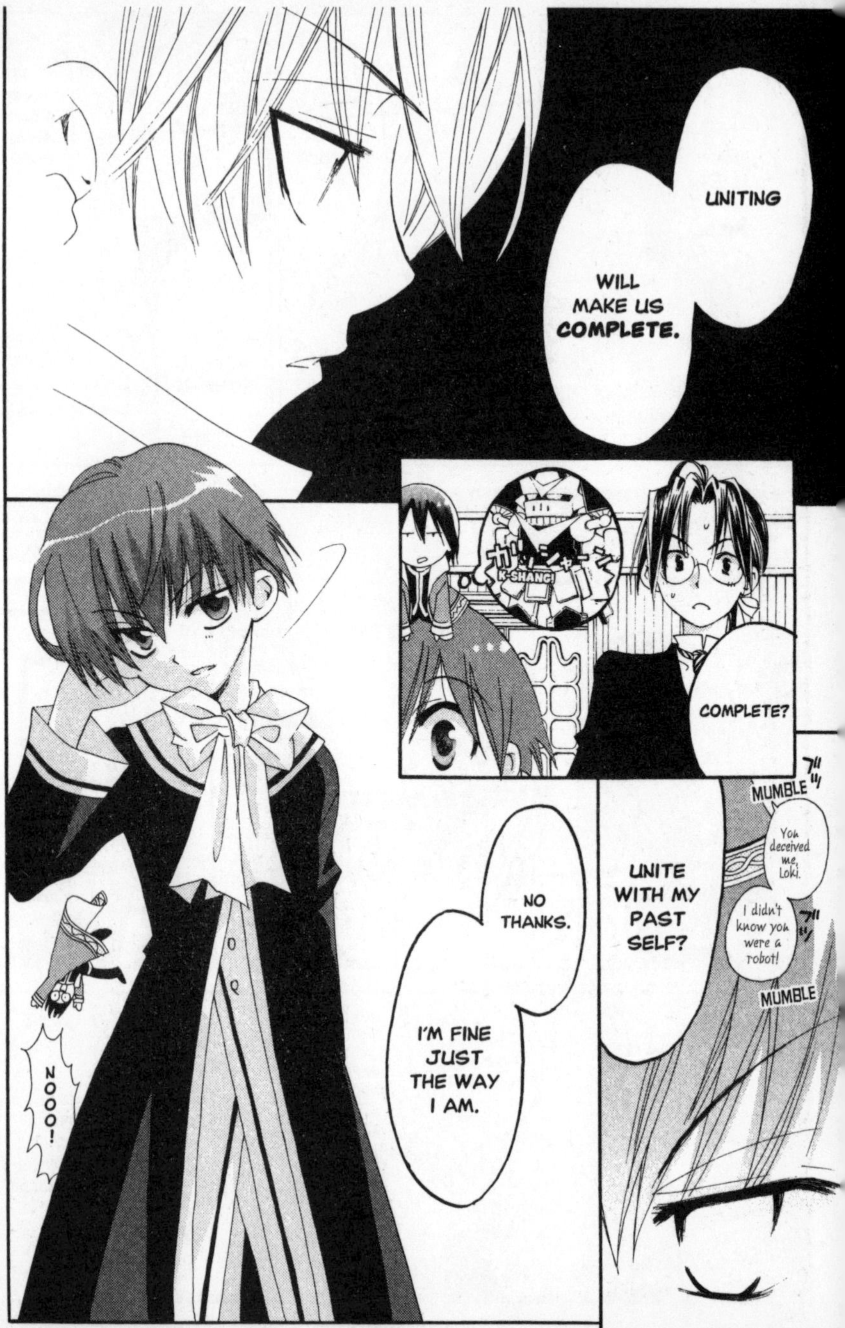
UNITING
WILL MAKE US COMPLETE.
K-SHANG!
COMPLETE?
MUMBLE
You deceived me, Loki.
I didn't know you were a robot!
MUMBLE
UNITE WITH MY PAST SELF?
NO THANKS.
I'M FINE JUST THE WAY I AM.
NOOO!

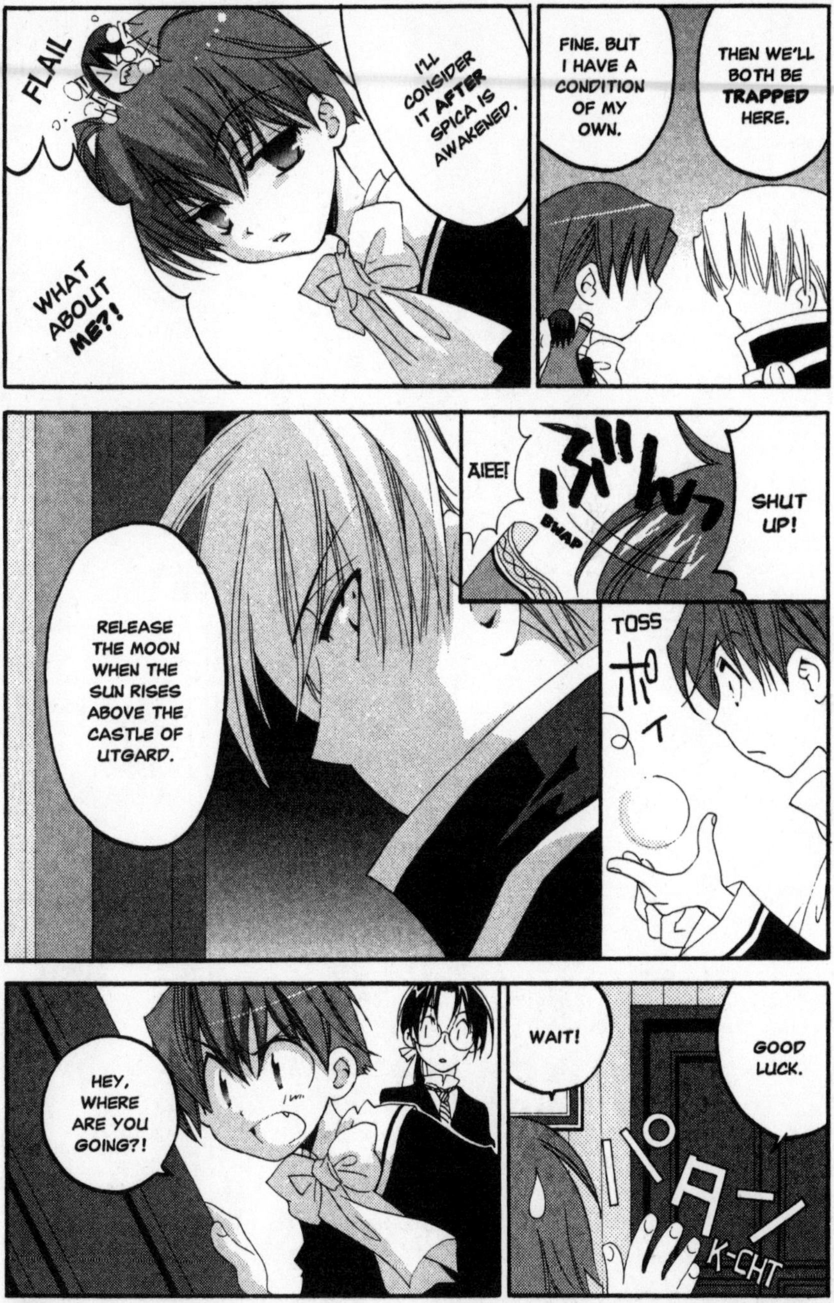
THEN WE'LL BOTH BE TRAPPED HERE.
FINE. BUT I HAVE A CONDITION OF MY OWN.
I'LL CONSIDER IT AFTER SPICA IS AWAKENED.
FLAIL
WHAT ABOUT ME?!
SHUT UP!
ぶんっ
BWAP
AIEE!
TOSS
ポイ
RELEASE THE MOON WHEN THE SUN RISES ABOVE THE CASTLE OF UTGARD.
GOOD LUCK.
WAIT!
パター
K-CHT
HEY, WHERE ARE YOU GOING?!

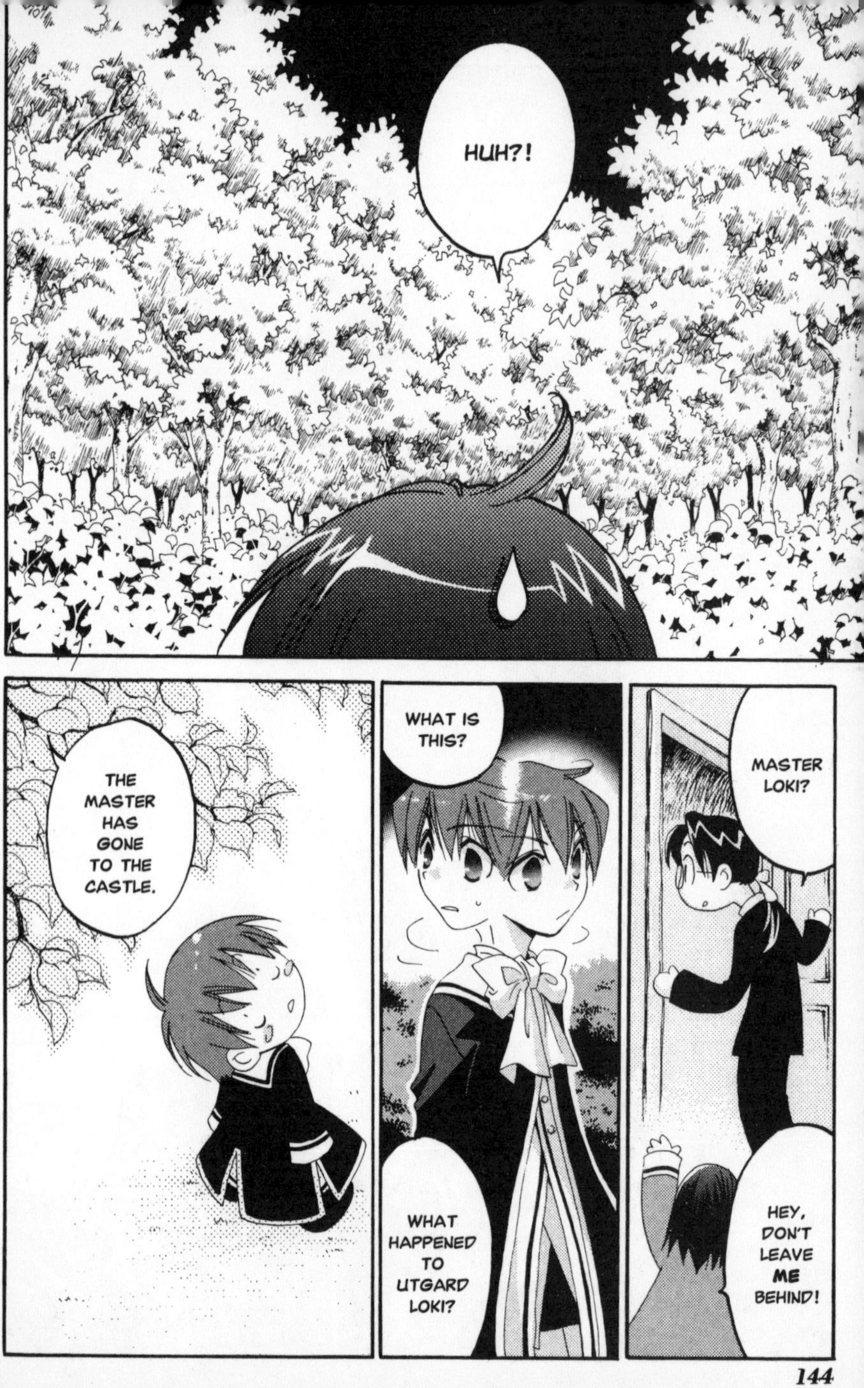
HUH?!
MASTER LOKI?
HEY, DON'T LEAVE ME BEHIND!
WHAT IS THIS?
WHAT HAPPENED TO UTGARD LOKI?
THE MASTER HAS GONE TO THE CASTLE.

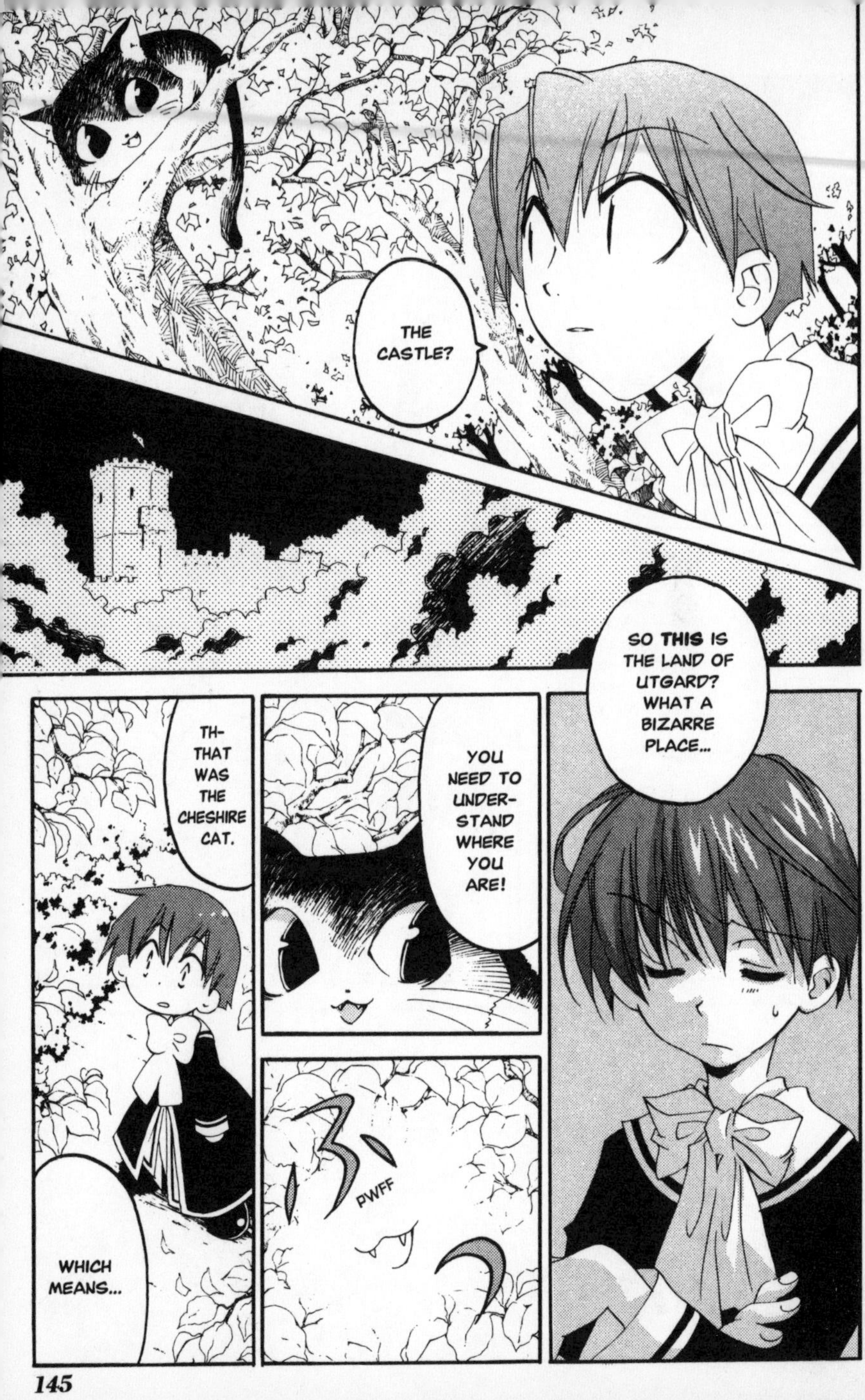
THE CASTLE?
SO **THIS** IS THE LAND OF UTGARD? WHAT A BIZARRE PLACE...
YOU NEED TO UNDER-STAND WHERE YOU ARE!
PWFF
TH-THAT WAS THE CHESHIRE CAT.
WHICH MEANS...

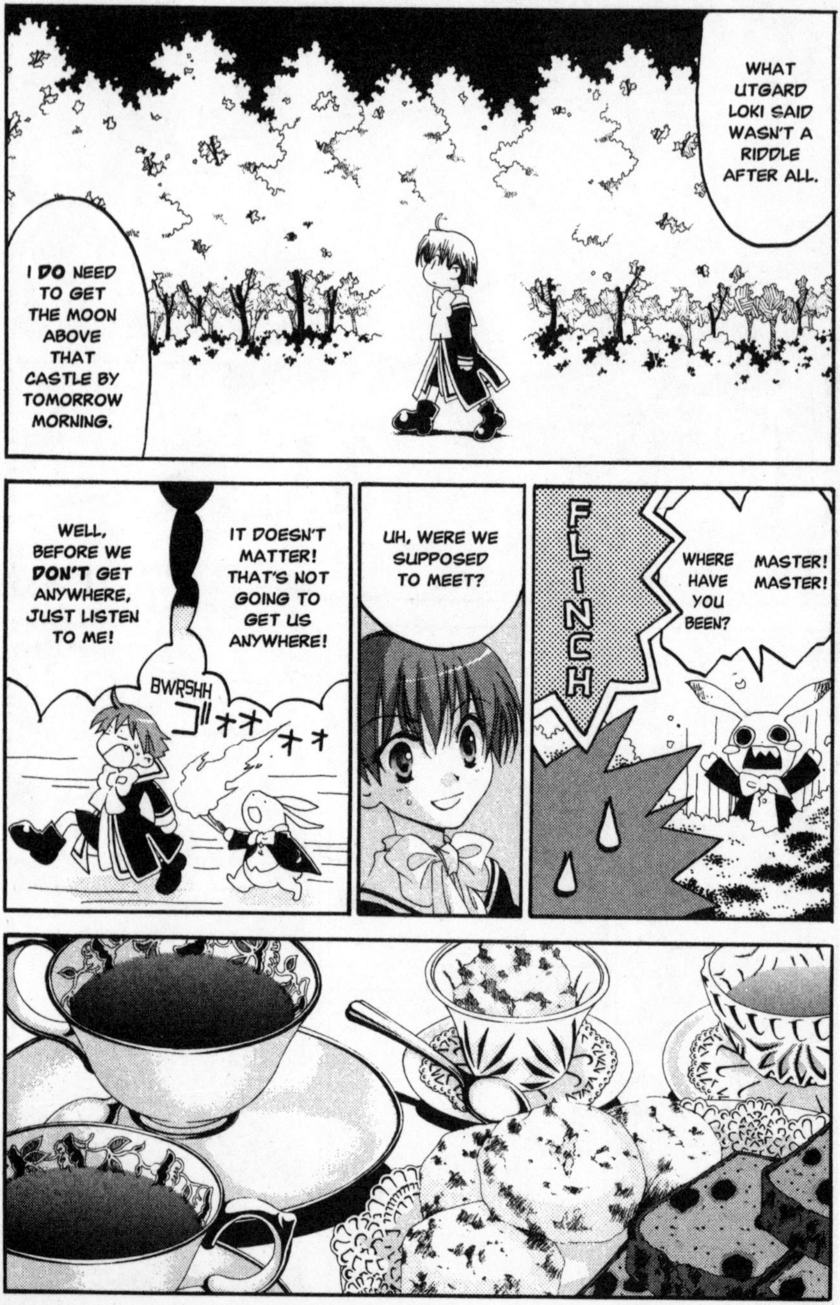
WHAT UTGARD LOKI SAID WASN'T A RIDDLE AFTER ALL.
I DO NEED TO GET THE MOON ABOVE THAT CASTLE BY TOMORROW MORNING.
FLINCH
MASTER! MASTER!
WHERE HAVE YOU BEEN?
UH, WERE WE SUPPOSED TO MEET?
IT DOESN'T MATTER! THAT'S NOT GOING TO GET US ANYWHERE!
WELL, BEFORE WE DON'T GET ANYWHERE, JUST LISTEN TO ME!
BWRSHH
ゴオオオオ

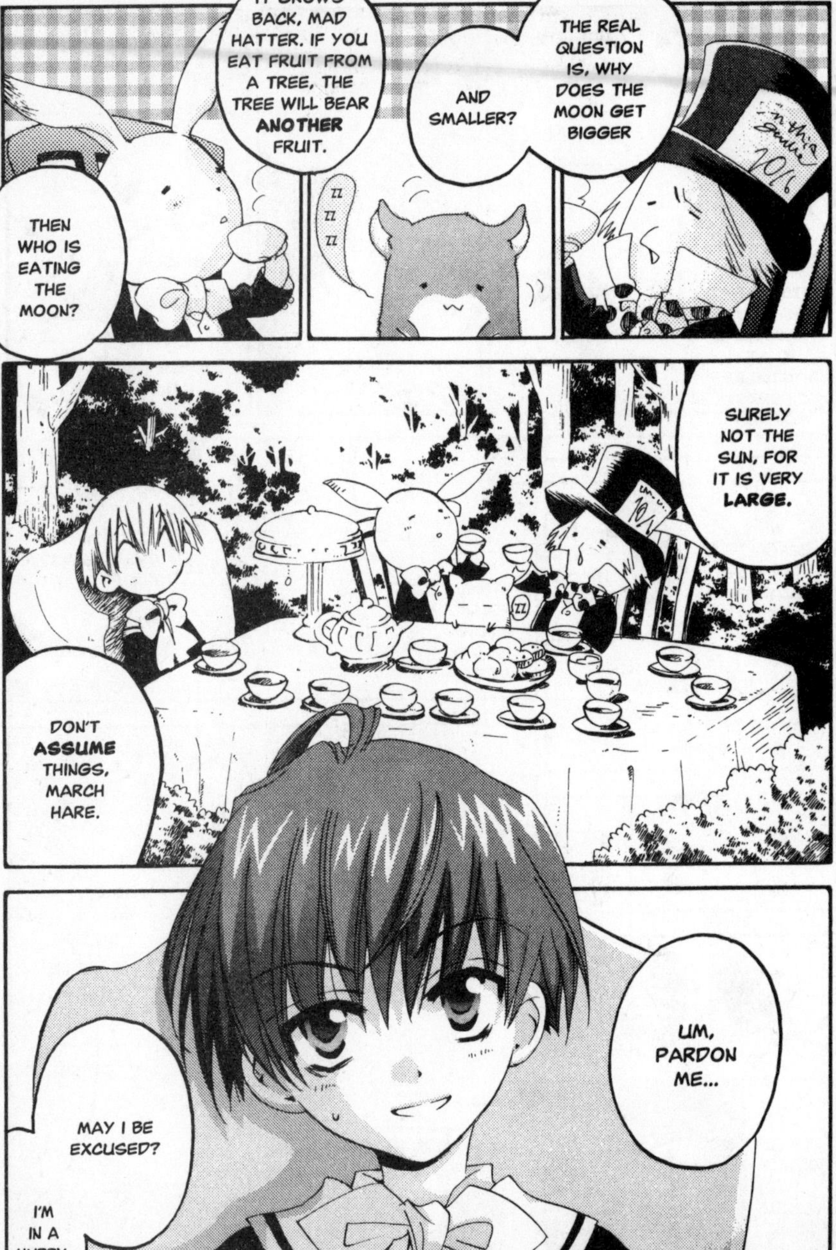

THE REAL QUESTION IS, WHY DOES THE MOON GET BIGGER AND SMALLER?
IT GROWS BACK, MAD HATTER. IF YOU EAT FRUIT FROM A TREE, THE TREE WILL BEAR **ANOTHER** FRUIT.
ZZ ZZ ZZ
THEN WHO IS EATING THE MOON?
SURELY NOT THE SUN, FOR IT IS VERY **LARGE.**
DON'T **ASSUME** THINGS, MARCH HARE.
UM, PARDON ME...
MAY I BE EXCUSED?
I'M IN A HURRY.

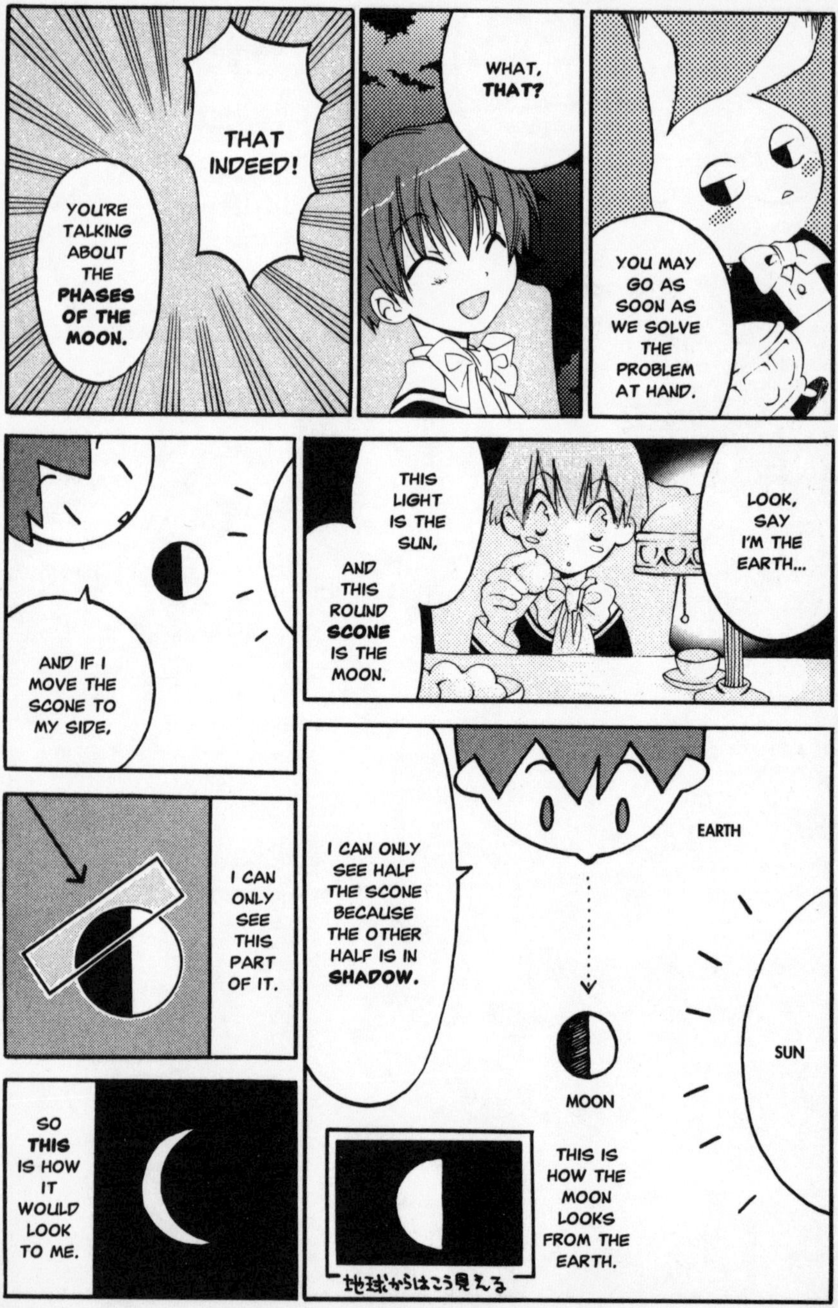
YOU MAY GO AS SOON AS WE SOLVE THE PROBLEM AT HAND.
WHAT, THAT?
THAT INDEED!
YOU'RE TALKING ABOUT THE PHASES OF THE MOON.
LOOK, SAY I'M THE EARTH...
THIS LIGHT IS THE SUN,
AND THIS ROUND SCONE IS THE MOON.
AND IF I MOVE THE SCONE TO MY SIDE,
I CAN ONLY SEE HALF THE SCONE BECAUSE THE OTHER HALF IS IN SHADOW.
EARTH
SUN
MOON
THIS IS HOW THE MOON LOOKS FROM THE EARTH.
地球からはこう見える
I CAN ONLY SEE THIS PART OF IT.
SO THIS IS HOW IT WOULD LOOK TO ME.

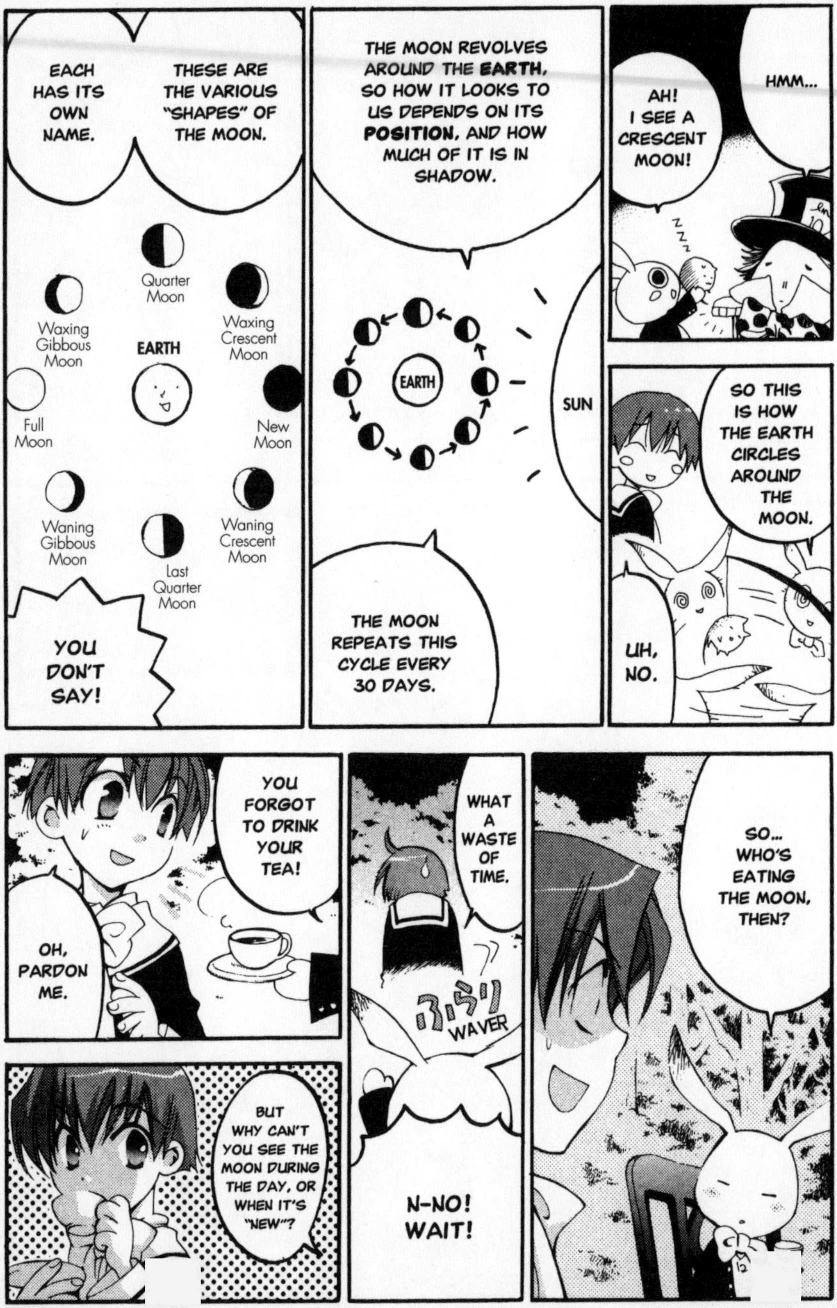

THESE ARE THE VARIOUS "SHAPES" OF THE MOON.
EACH HAS ITS OWN NAME.
Quarter Moon
Waxing Gibbous Moon
Waxing Crescent Moon
EARTH
Full Moon
New Moon
Waning Gibbous Moon
Waning Crescent Moon
Last Quarter Moon
YOU DON'T SAY!
THE MOON REVOLVES AROUND THE **EARTH**, SO HOW IT LOOKS TO US DEPENDS ON ITS **POSITION**, AND HOW MUCH OF IT IS IN SHADOW.
EARTH
SUN
THE MOON REPEATS THIS CYCLE EVERY 30 DAYS.
AH! I SEE A CRESCENT MOON!
HMM...
SO THIS IS HOW THE EARTH CIRCLES AROUND THE MOON.
UH, NO.
YOU FORGOT TO DRINK YOUR TEA!
OH, PARDON ME.
BUT WHY CAN'T YOU SEE THE MOON DURING THE DAY, OR WHEN IT'S "NEW"?
WHAT A WASTE OF TIME.
ふらり
WAVER
N-NO! WAIT!
SO... WHO'S EATING THE MOON, THEN?

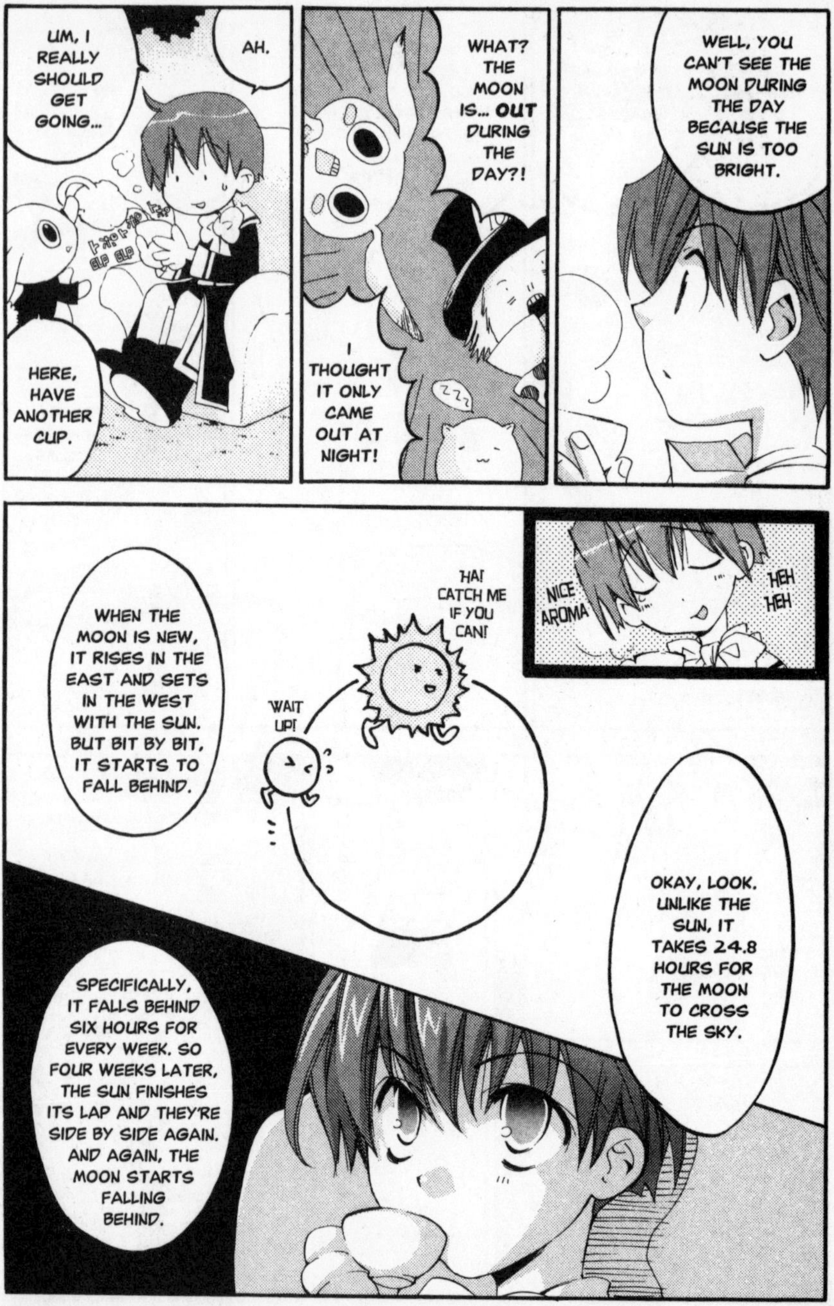
UM, I REALLY SHOULD GET GOING...
AH.
GLP GLP
HERE, HAVE ANOTHER CUP.
WHAT? THE MOON IS... OUT DURING THE DAY?!
I THOUGHT IT ONLY CAME OUT AT NIGHT!
WELL, YOU CAN'T SEE THE MOON DURING THE DAY BECAUSE THE SUN IS TOO BRIGHT.
NICE AROMA
HEH HEH
OKAY, LOOK. UNLIKE THE SUN, IT TAKES 24.8 HOURS FOR THE MOON TO CROSS THE SKY.
WHEN THE MOON IS NEW, IT RISES IN THE EAST AND SETS IN THE WEST WITH THE SUN. BUT BIT BY BIT, IT STARTS TO FALL BEHIND.
HA! CATCH ME IF YOU CAN!
WAIT UP!
SPECIFICALLY, IT FALLS BEHIND SIX HOURS FOR EVERY WEEK. SO FOUR WEEKS LATER, THE SUN FINISHES ITS LAP AND THEY'RE SIDE BY SIDE AGAIN. AND AGAIN, THE MOON STARTS FALLING BEHIND.

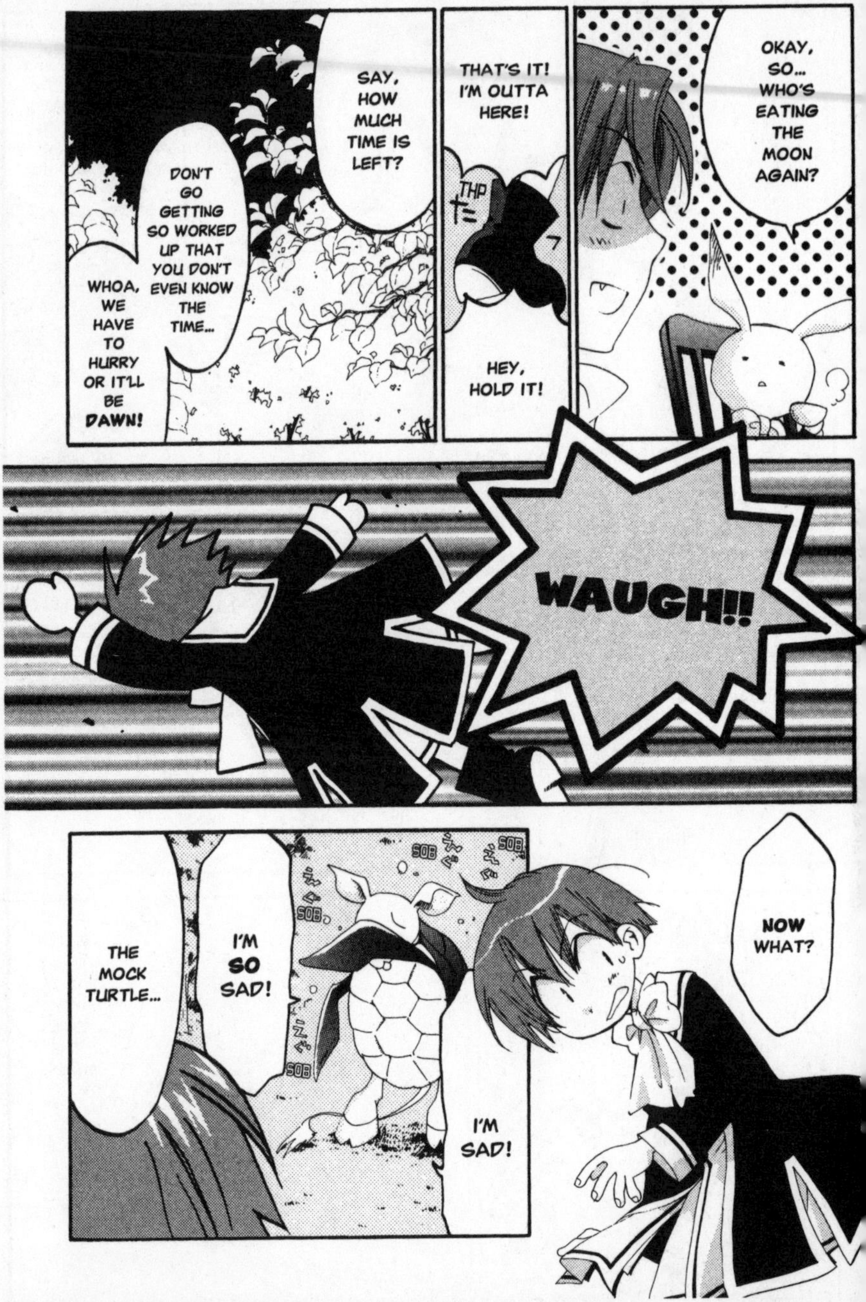
OKAY, SO... WHO'S EATING THE MOON AGAIN?
THAT'S IT! I'M OUTTA HERE!
THP
HEY, HOLD IT!
SAY, HOW MUCH TIME IS LEFT?
DON'T GO GETTING SO WORKED UP THAT YOU DON'T EVEN KNOW THE TIME...
WHOA, WE HAVE TO HURRY OR IT'LL BE DAWN!
WAUGH!!
NOW WHAT?
SOB
SOB
I'M SAD!
I'M SO SAD!
SOB
SOB
THE MOCK TURTLE...

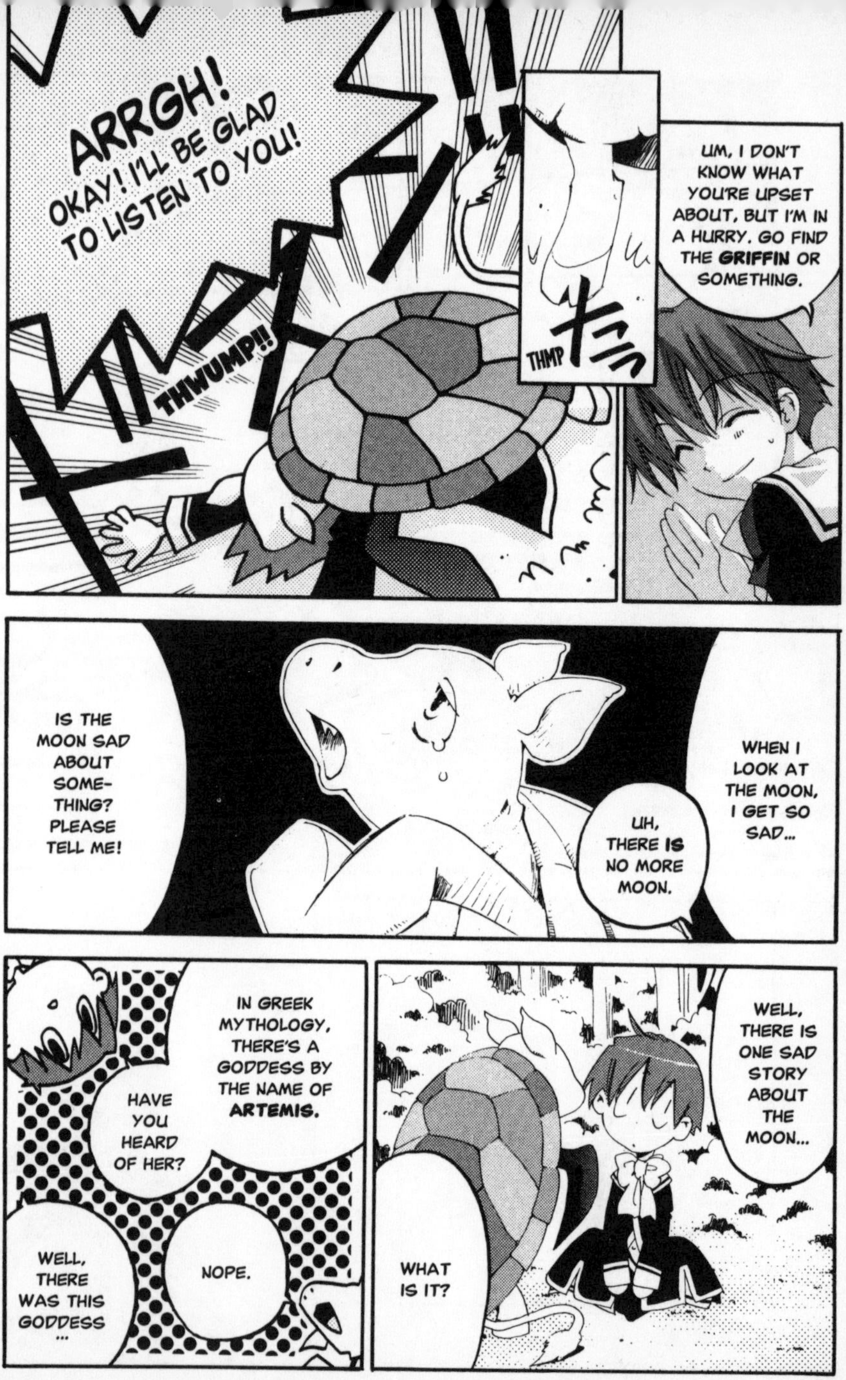
UM, I DON'T KNOW WHAT YOU'RE UPSET ABOUT, BUT I'M IN A HURRY. GO FIND THE GRIFFIN OR SOMETHING.
THMP
ARRGH!
OKAY! I'LL BE GLAD TO LISTEN TO YOU!
THWUMP!!
WHEN I LOOK AT THE MOON, I GET SO SAD...
UH, THERE IS NO MORE MOON.
IS THE MOON SAD ABOUT SOME-THING? PLEASE TELL ME!
WELL, THERE IS ONE SAD STORY ABOUT THE MOON...
WHAT IS IT?
IN GREEK MYTHOLOGY, THERE'S A GODDESS BY THE NAME OF ARTEMIS.
HAVE YOU HEARD OF HER?
NOPE.
WELL, THERE WAS THIS GODDESS...

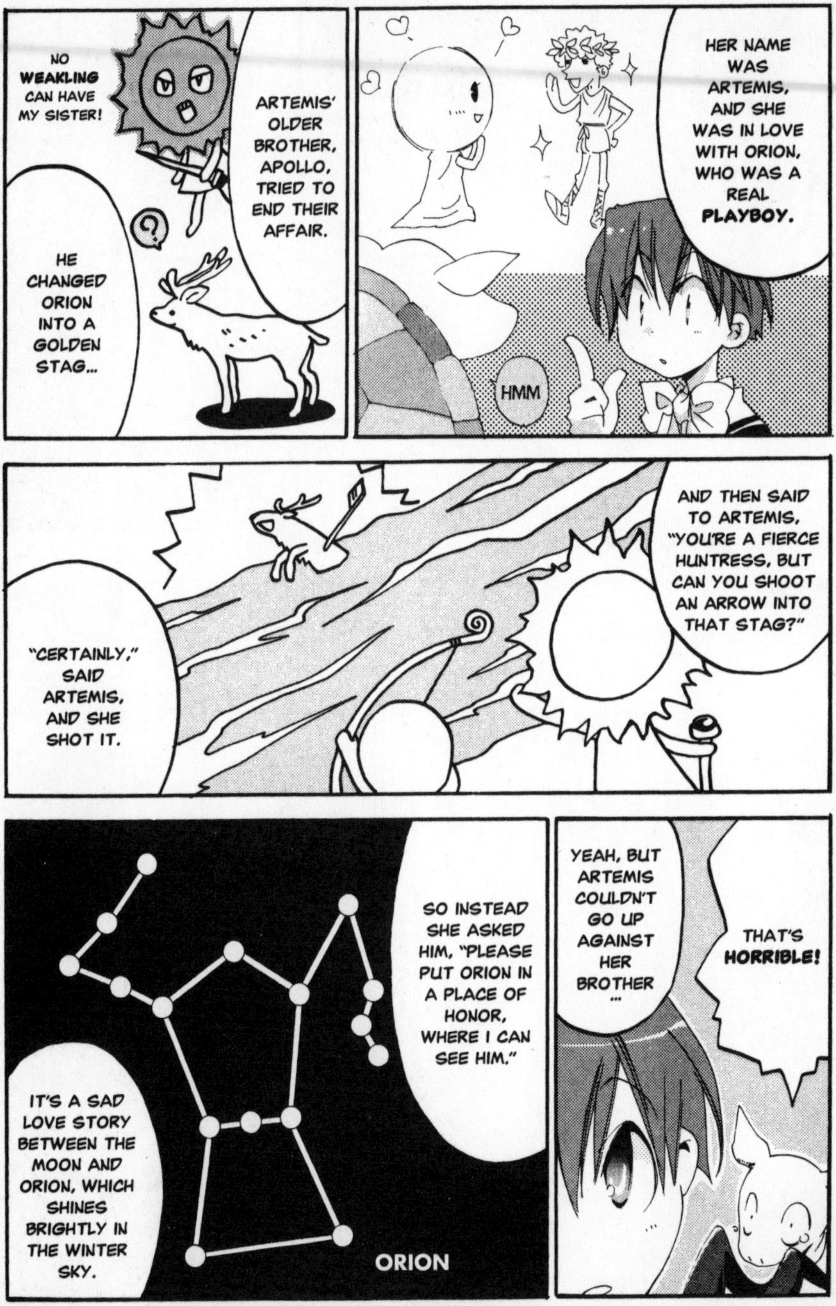
HER NAME WAS ARTEMIS, AND SHE WAS IN LOVE WITH ORION, WHO WAS A REAL **PLAYBOY.**
HMM
ARTEMIS' OLDER BROTHER, APOLLO, TRIED TO END THEIR AFFAIR.
NO **WEAKLING** CAN HAVE MY SISTER!
?
HE CHANGED ORION INTO A GOLDEN STAG...
AND THEN SAID TO ARTEMIS, "YOU'RE A FIERCE HUNTRESS, BUT CAN YOU SHOOT AN ARROW INTO THAT STAG?"
"CERTAINLY," SAID ARTEMIS, AND SHE SHOT IT.
THAT'S **HORRIBLE!**
YEAH, BUT ARTEMIS COULDN'T GO UP AGAINST HER BROTHER ...
SO INSTEAD SHE ASKED HIM, "PLEASE PUT ORION IN A PLACE OF HONOR, WHERE I CAN SEE HIM."
IT'S A SAD LOVE STORY BETWEEN THE MOON AND ORION, WHICH SHINES BRIGHTLY IN THE WINTER SKY.
ORION

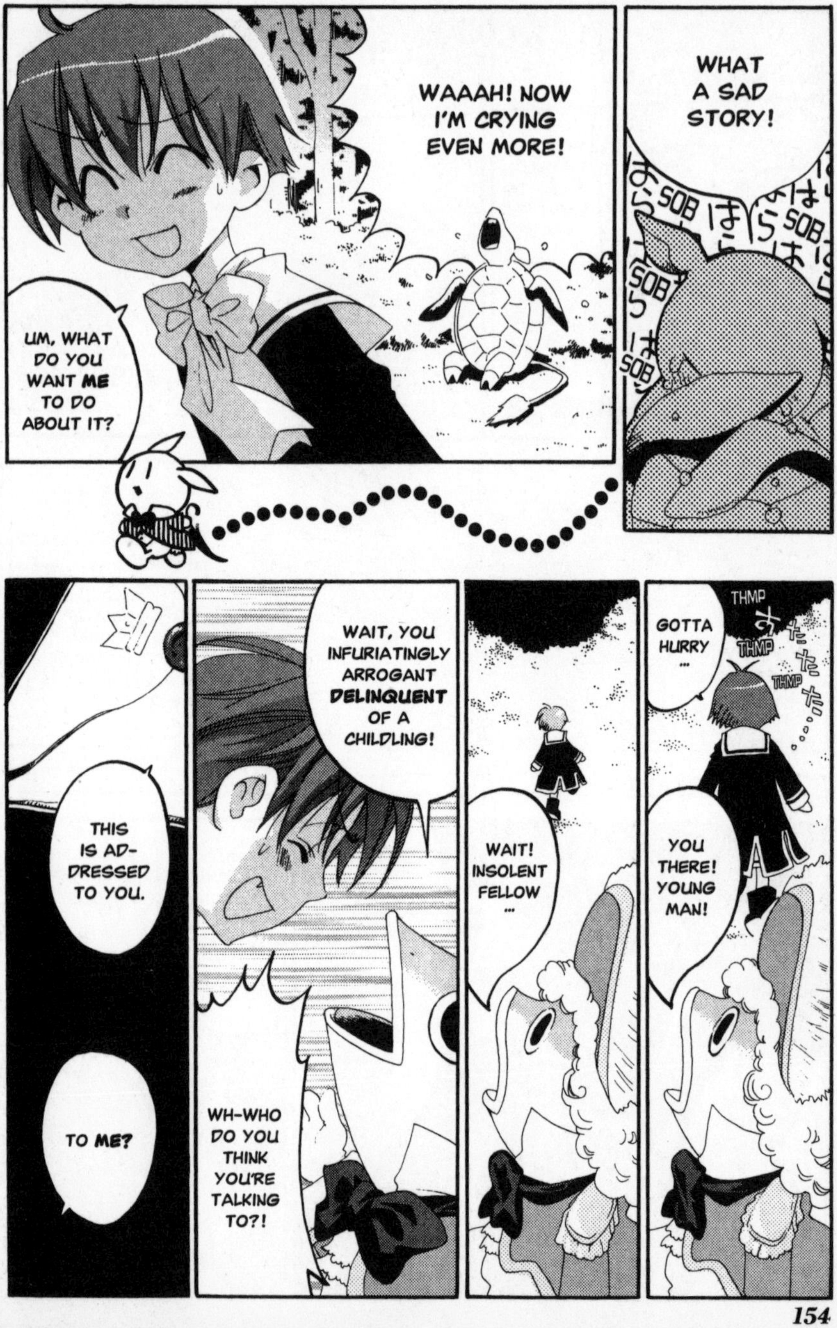
WHAT A SAD STORY!
SOB SOB SOB SOB
WAAAH! NOW I'M CRYING EVEN MORE!
UM, WHAT DO YOU WANT ME TO DO ABOUT IT?
THMP THMP THMP
GOTTA HURRY ...
YOU THERE! YOUNG MAN!
WAIT! INSOLENT FELLOW ...
WAIT, YOU INFURIATINGLY ARROGANT DELINQUENT OF A CHILDLING!
WH-WHO DO YOU THINK YOU'RE TALKING TO?!
THIS IS AD-DRESSED TO YOU.
TO ME?

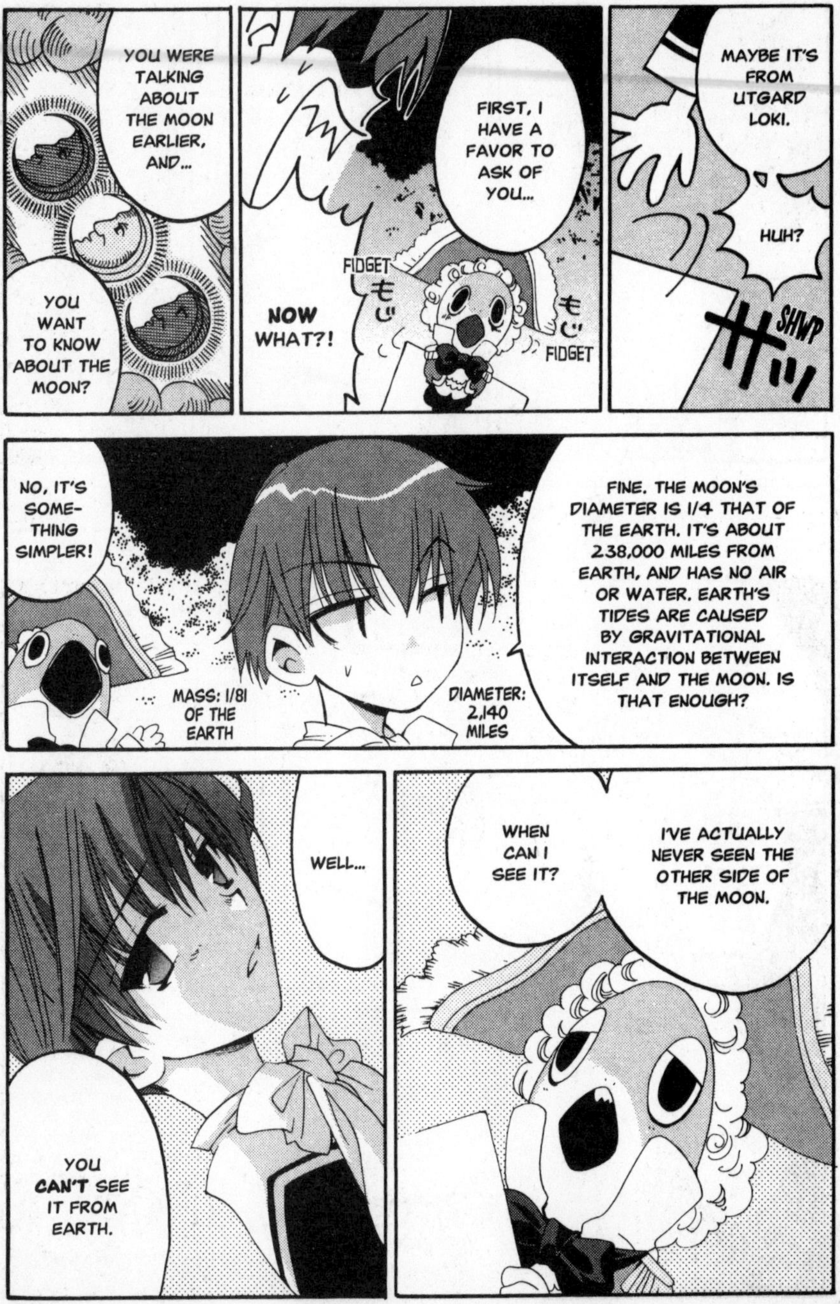
MAYBE IT'S FROM UTGARD LOKI.
HUH?
SHWP
FIRST, I HAVE A FAVOR TO ASK OF YOU...
NOW WHAT?!
FIDGET
FIDGET
YOU WERE TALKING ABOUT THE MOON EARLIER, AND...
YOU WANT TO KNOW ABOUT THE MOON?
FINE. THE MOON'S DIAMETER IS 1/4 THAT OF THE EARTH. IT'S ABOUT 238,000 MILES FROM EARTH, AND HAS NO AIR OR WATER. EARTH'S TIDES ARE CAUSED BY GRAVITATIONAL INTERACTION BETWEEN ITSELF AND THE MOON. IS THAT ENOUGH?
DIAMETER: 2,140 MILES
MASS: 1/81 OF THE EARTH
NO, IT'S SOME-THING SIMPLER!
I'VE ACTUALLY NEVER SEEN THE OTHER SIDE OF THE MOON.
WHEN CAN I SEE IT?
WELL...
YOU **CAN'T** SEE IT FROM EARTH.

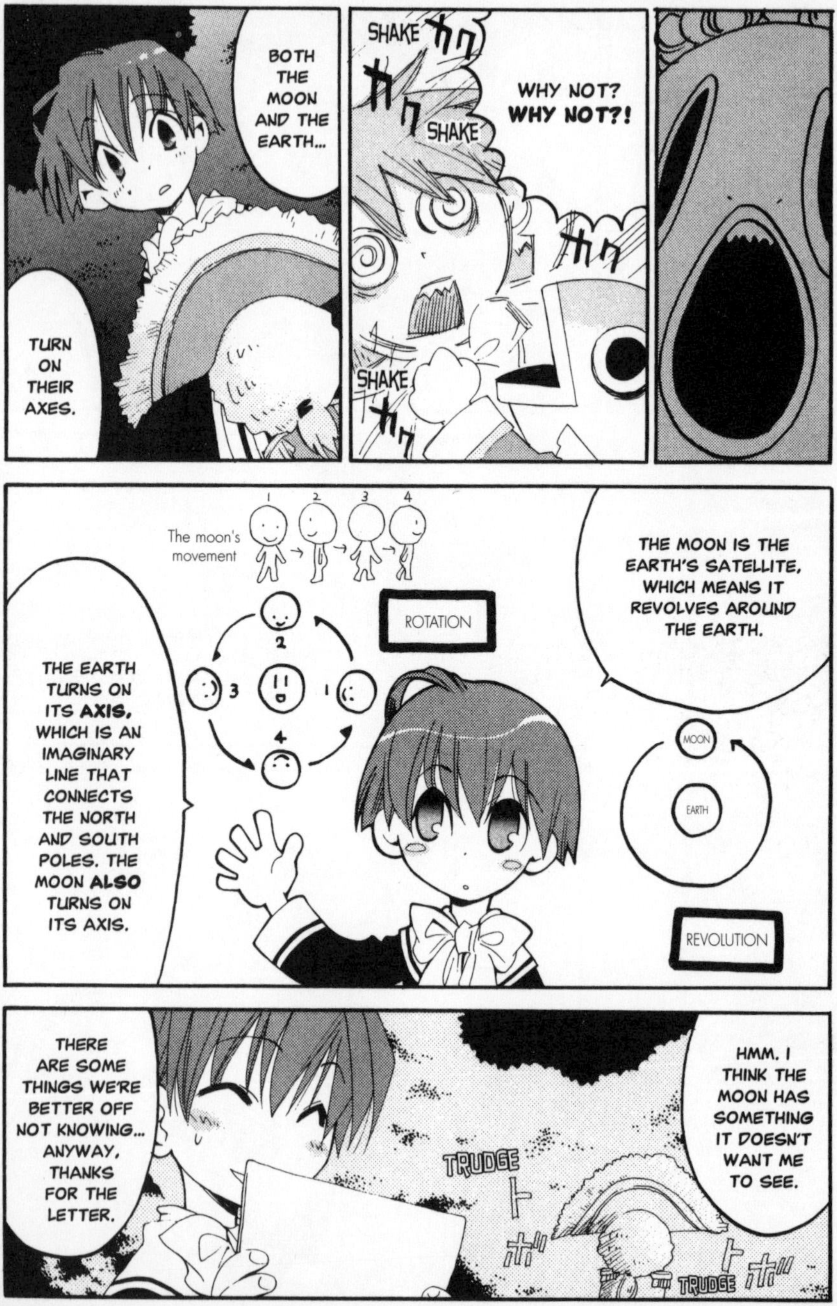
BOTH THE MOON AND THE EARTH...
TURN ON THEIR AXES.
SHAKE カク
カク SHAKE
WHY NOT? WHY NOT?!
カク
SHAKE カク
The moon's movement
1 2 3 4
ROTATION
2 3 1 4
THE EARTH TURNS ON ITS AXIS, WHICH IS AN IMAGINARY LINE THAT CONNECTS THE NORTH AND SOUTH POLES. THE MOON ALSO TURNS ON ITS AXIS.
THE MOON IS THE EARTH'S SATELLITE, WHICH MEANS IT REVOLVES AROUND THE EARTH.
MOON
EARTH
REVOLUTION
THERE ARE SOME THINGS WE'RE BETTER OFF NOT KNOWING... ANYWAY, THANKS FOR THE LETTER.
TRUDGE
TRUDGE
HMM. I THINK THE MOON HAS SOMETHING IT DOESN'T WANT ME TO SEE.

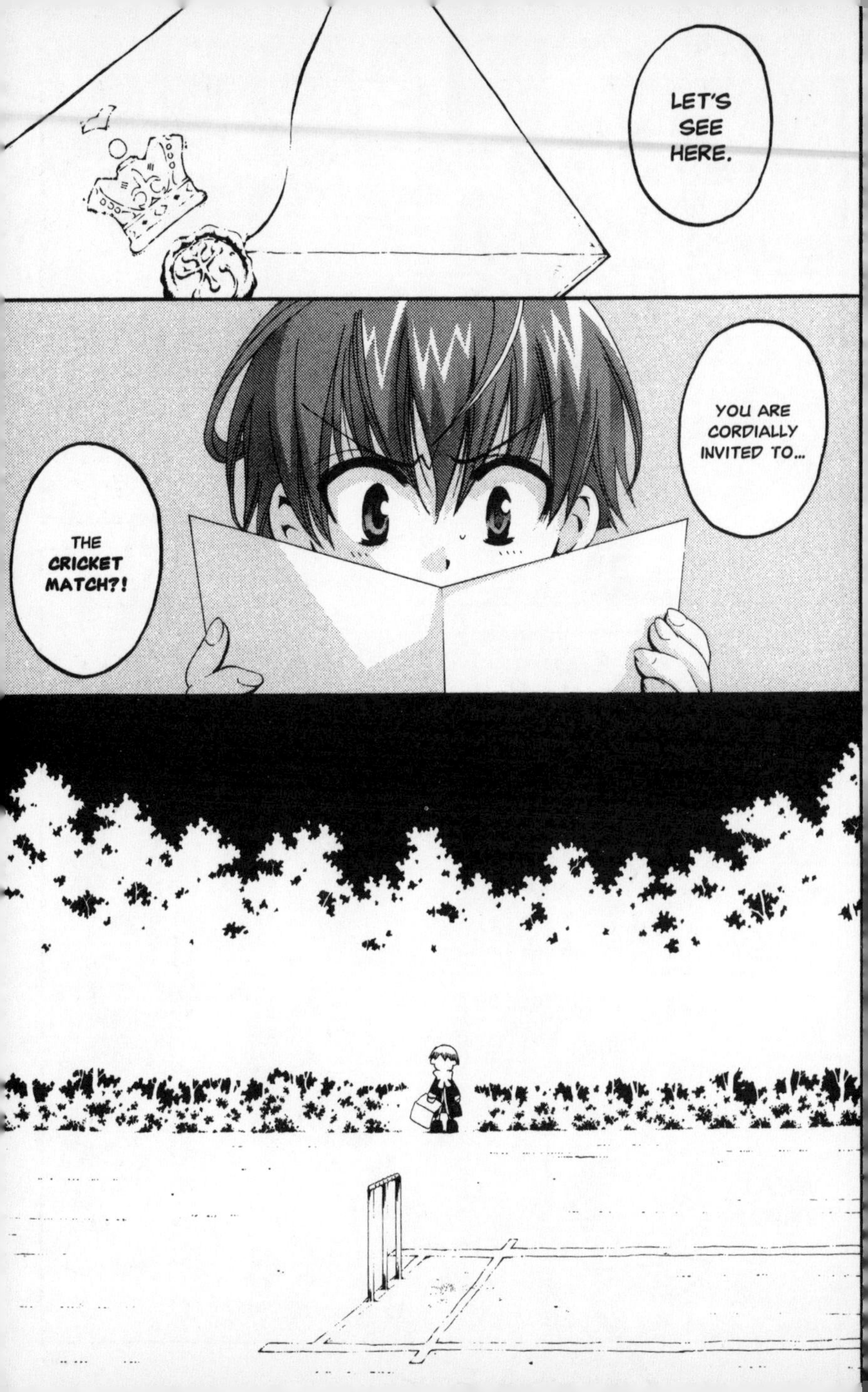
LET'S SEE HERE.
YOU ARE CORDIALLY INVITED TO...
THE CRICKET MATCH?!

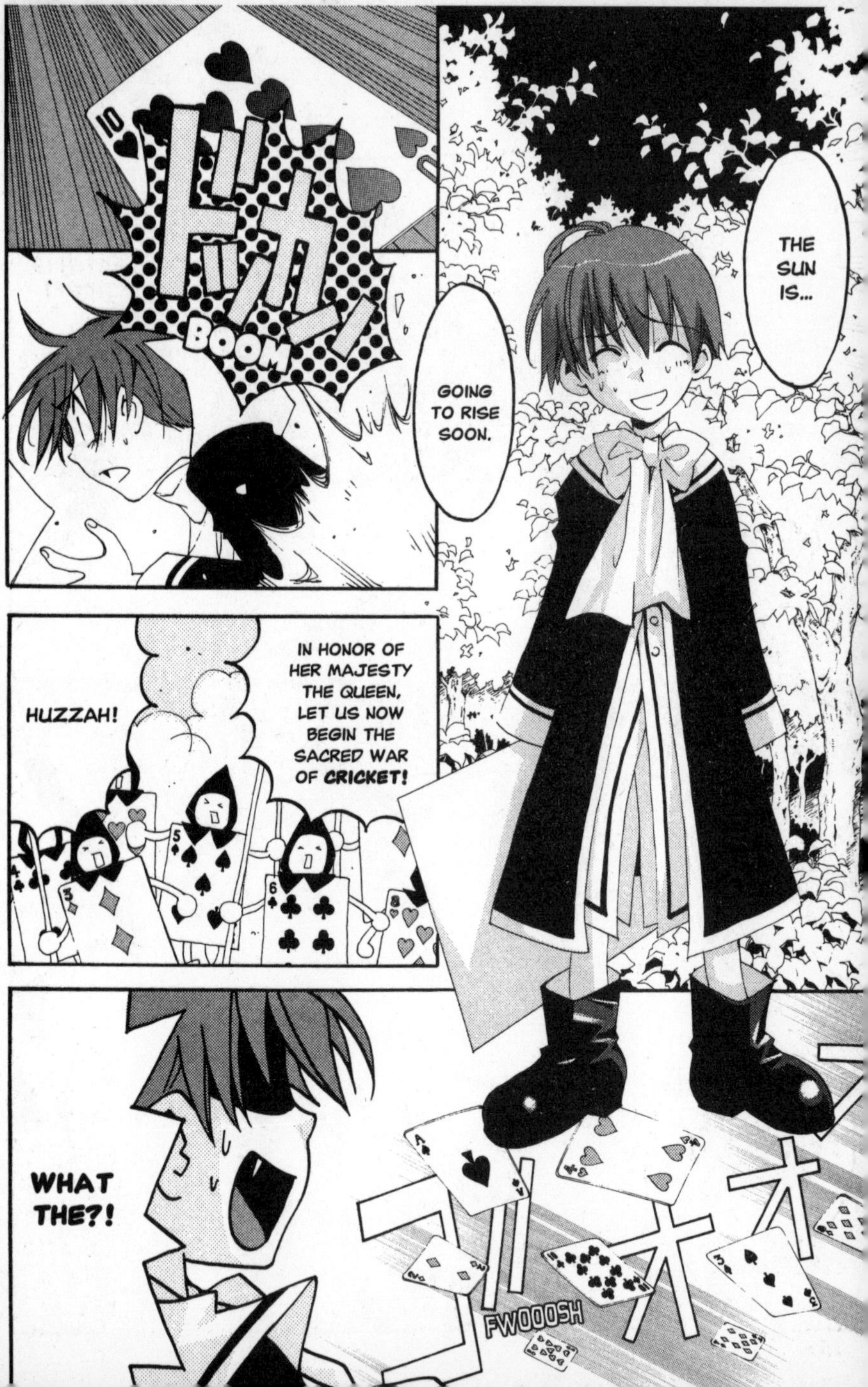
THE SUN IS...
GOING TO RISE SOON.
ドッカーン
BOOM
IN HONOR OF HER MAJESTY THE QUEEN, LET US NOW BEGIN THE SACRED WAR OF CRICKET!
HUZZAH!
WHAT THE?!
FWOOOSH

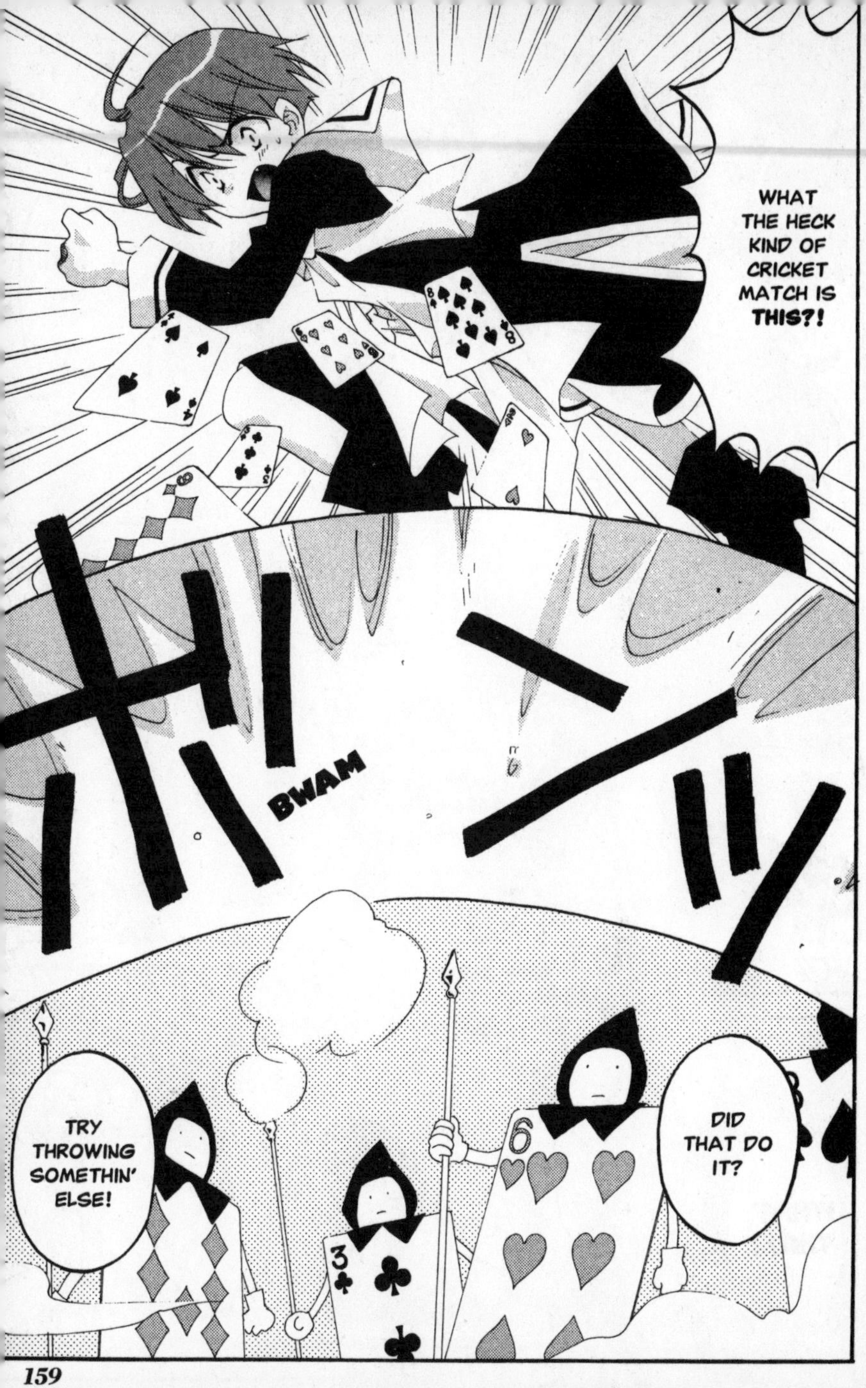
WHAT THE HECK KIND OF CRICKET MATCH IS THIS?!
BWAM
DID THAT DO IT?
TRY THROWING SOMETHIN' ELSE!

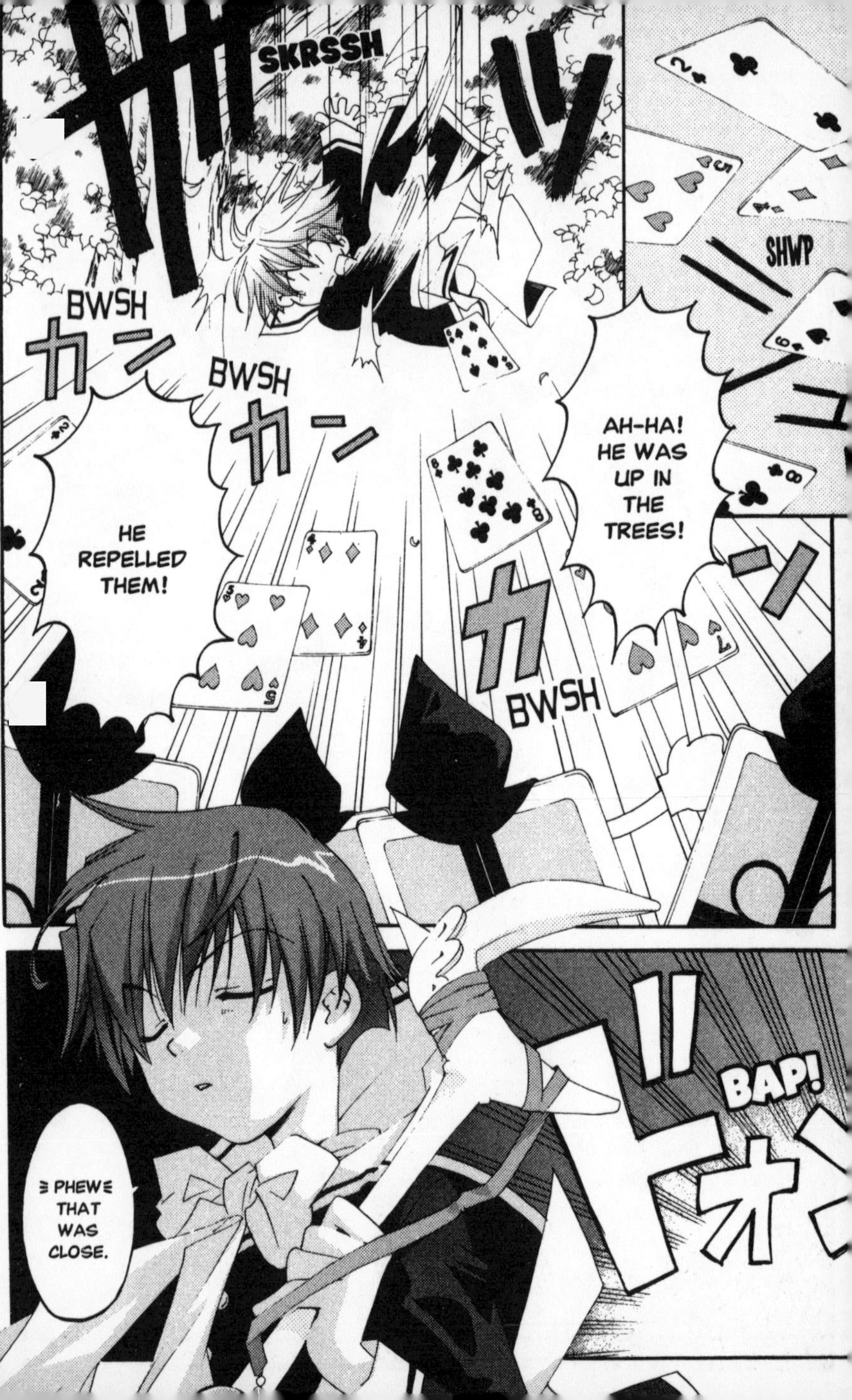
SKRSSH
SHWP
AH-HA! HE WAS UP IN THE TREES!
BWSH
BWSH
BWSH
HE REPELLED THEM!
BAP!
≡PHEW≡ THAT WAS CLOSE.

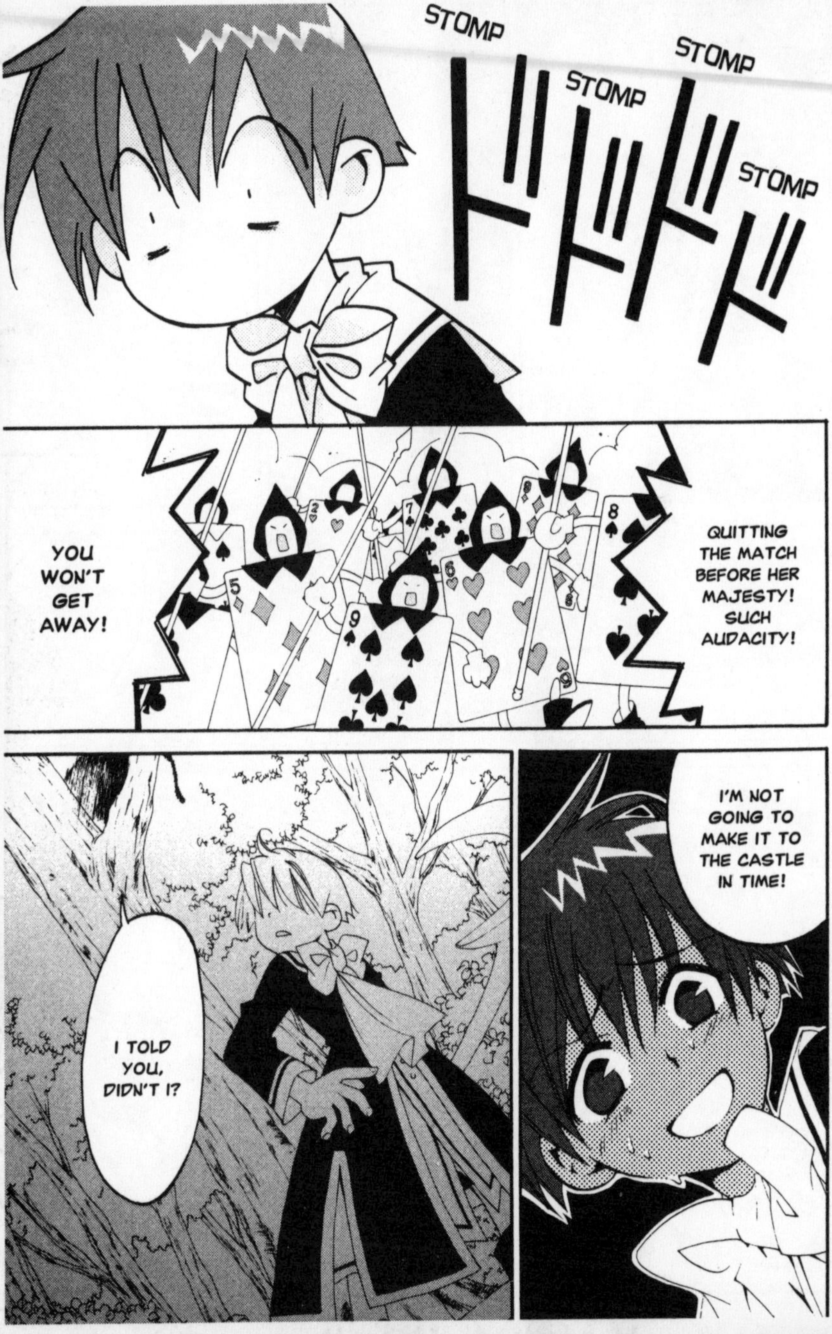
STOMP
STOMP
STOMP
STOMP
ドドドド
QUITTING THE MATCH BEFORE HER MAJESTY! SUCH AUDACITY!
YOU WON'T GET AWAY!
I'M NOT GOING TO MAKE IT TO THE CASTLE IN TIME!
I TOLD YOU, DIDN'T I?

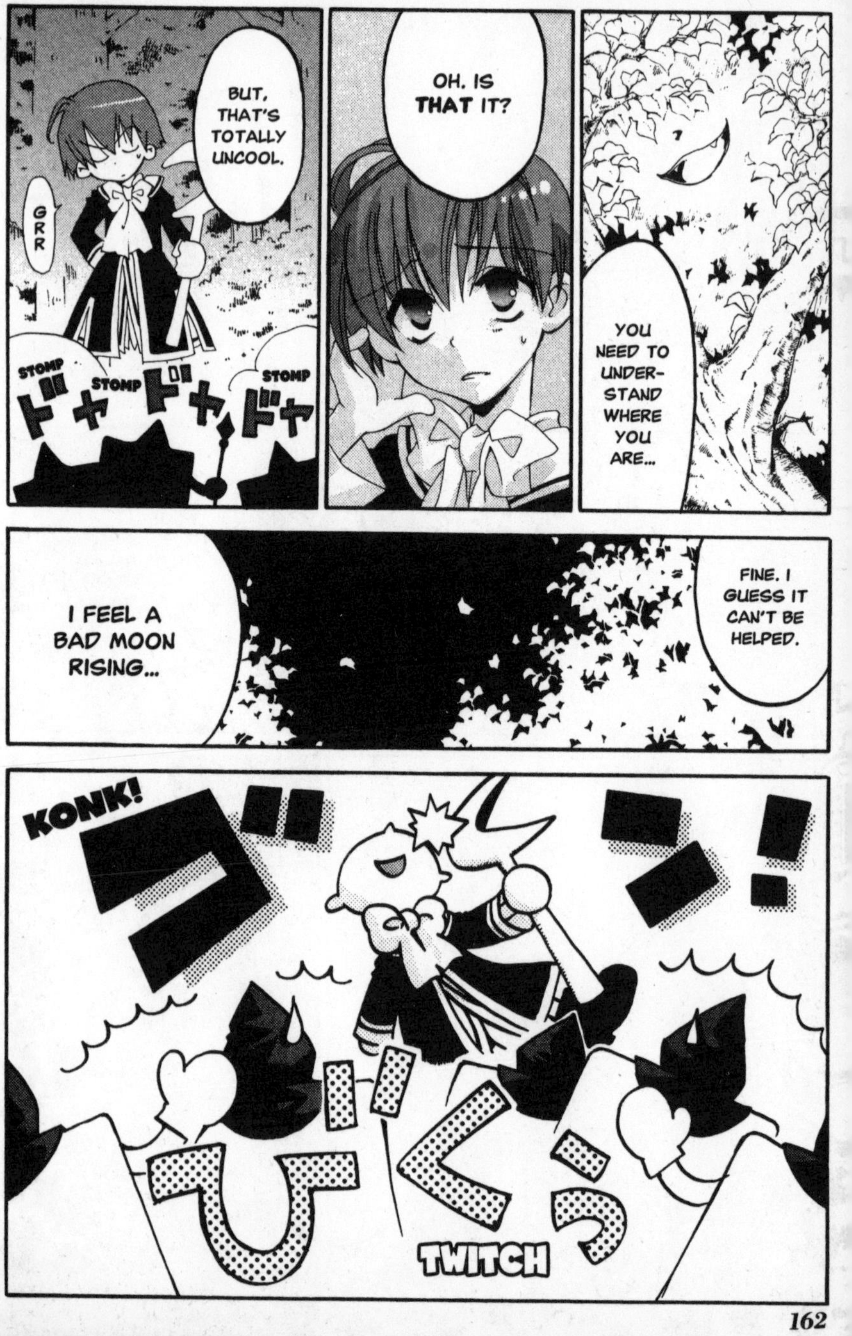
YOU NEED TO UNDER-STAND WHERE YOU ARE...
OH. IS THAT IT?
BUT, THAT'S TOTALLY UNCOOL.
GRR
STOMP
STOMP
STOMP
FINE. I GUESS IT CAN'T BE HELPED.
I FEEL A BAD MOON RISING...
KONK!
TWITCH

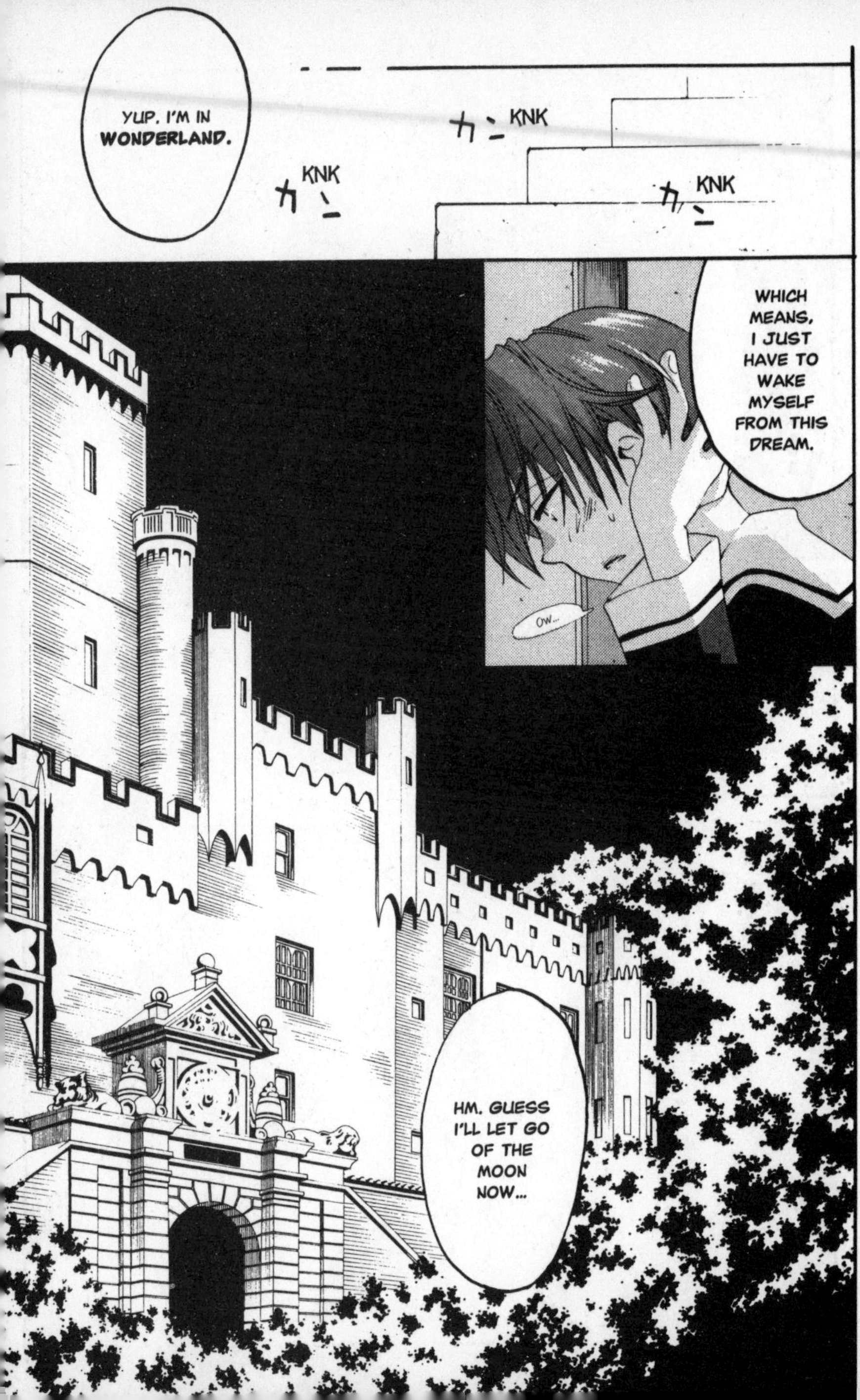
KNK
KNK
KNK
YUP. I'M IN WONDERLAND.
WHICH MEANS, I JUST HAVE TO WAKE MYSELF FROM THIS DREAM.
OW...
HM. GUESS I'LL LET GO OF THE MOON NOW...

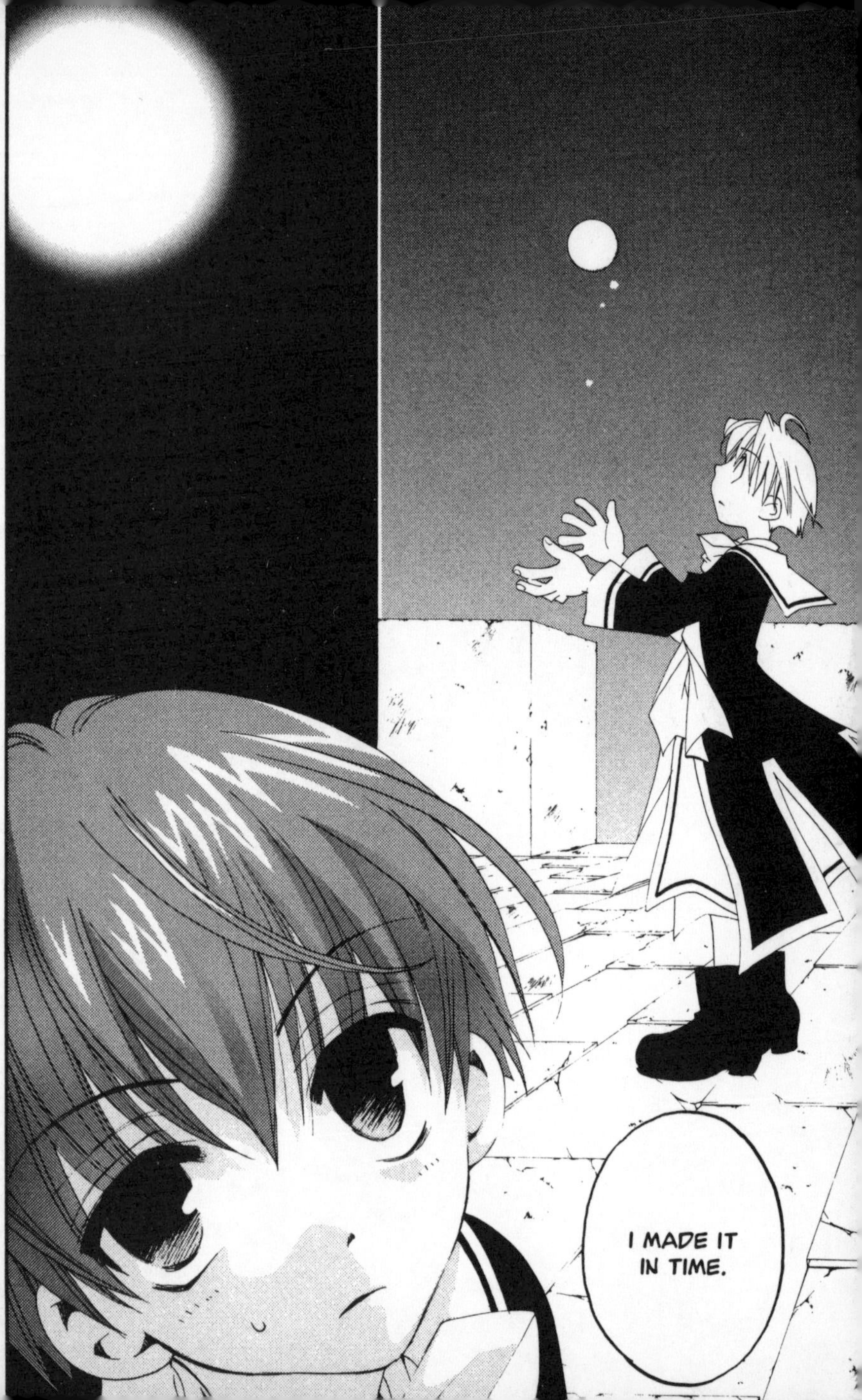
I MADE IT IN TIME.

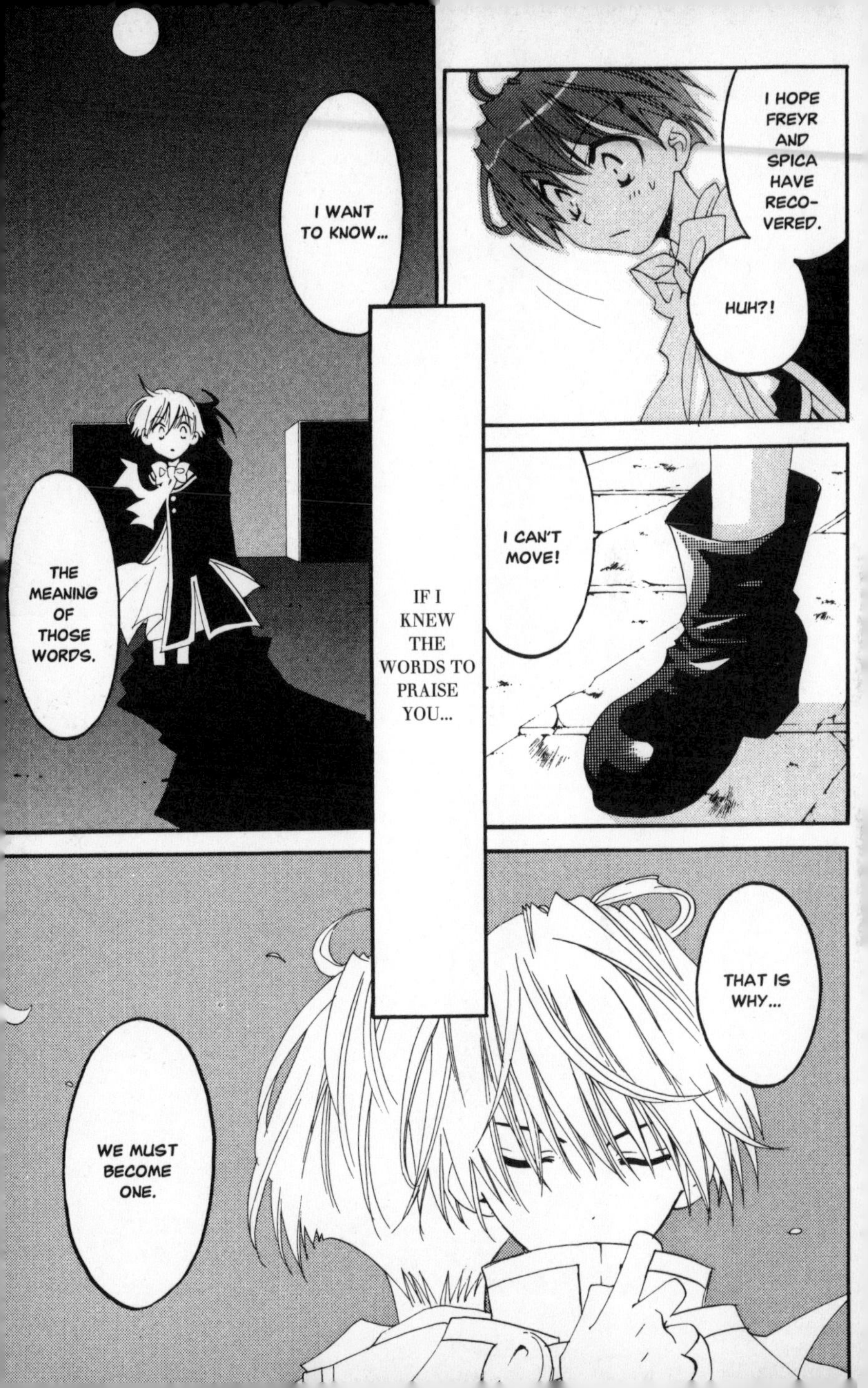
I HOPE FREYR AND SPICA HAVE RECOVERED.
HUH?!
I CAN'T MOVE!
I WANT TO KNOW...
THE MEANING OF THOSE WORDS.
IF I KNEW THE WORDS TO PRAISE YOU...
THAT IS WHY...
WE MUST BECOME ONE.

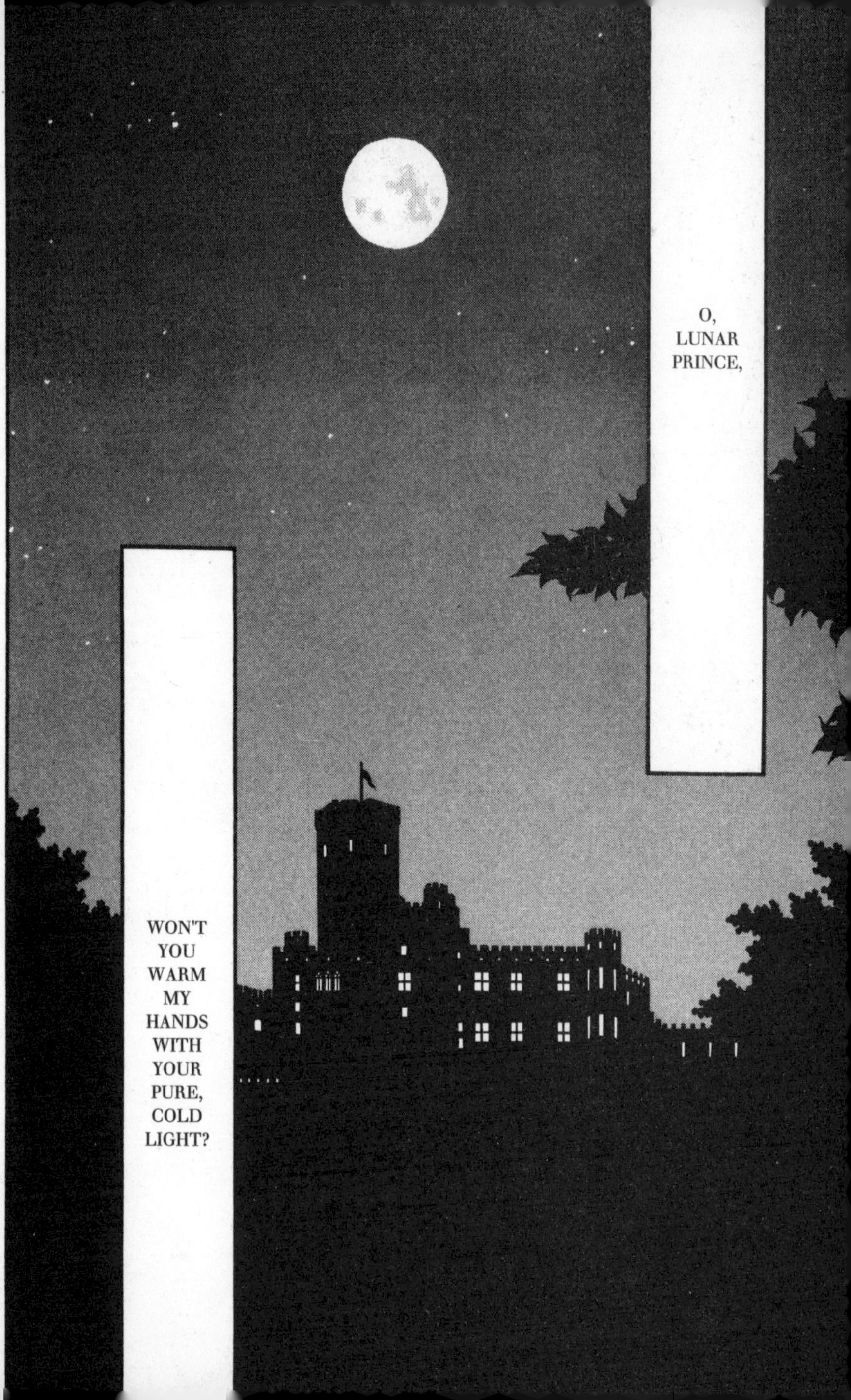
O, LUNAR PRINCE,
WON'T YOU WARM MY HANDS WITH YOUR PURE, COLD LIGHT?

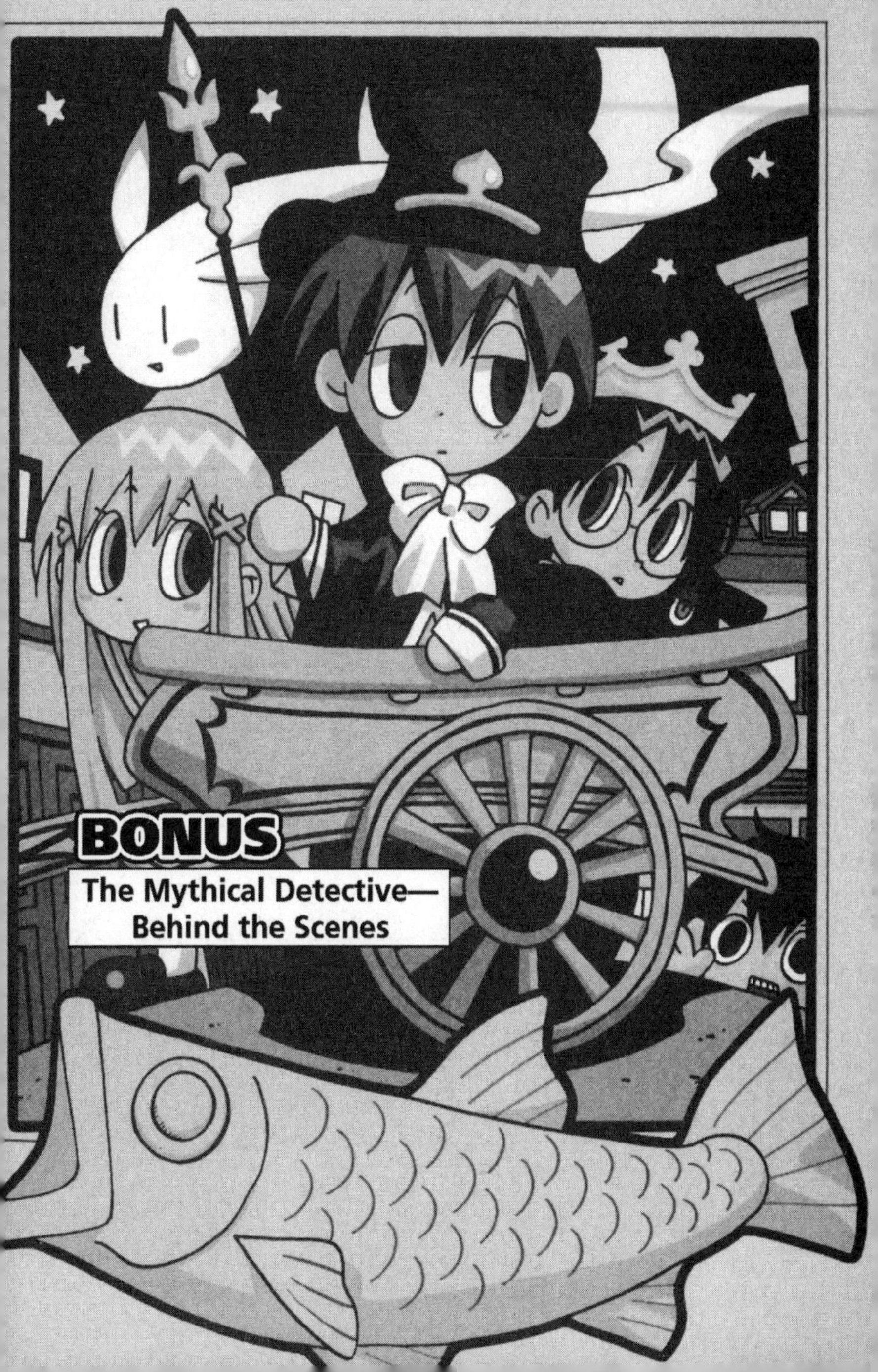
BONUS
The Mythical Detective—
Behind the Scenes

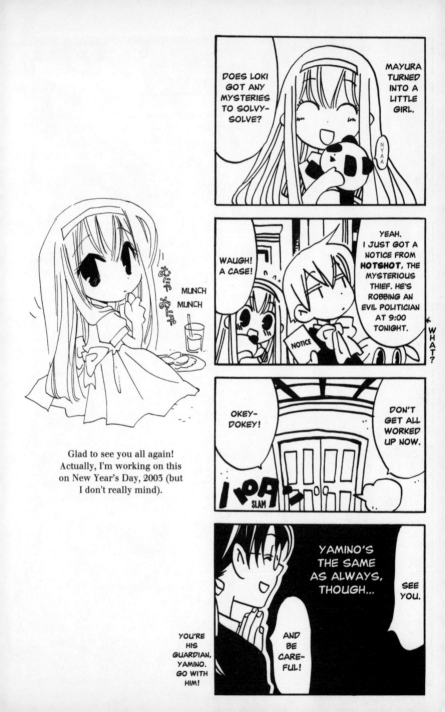

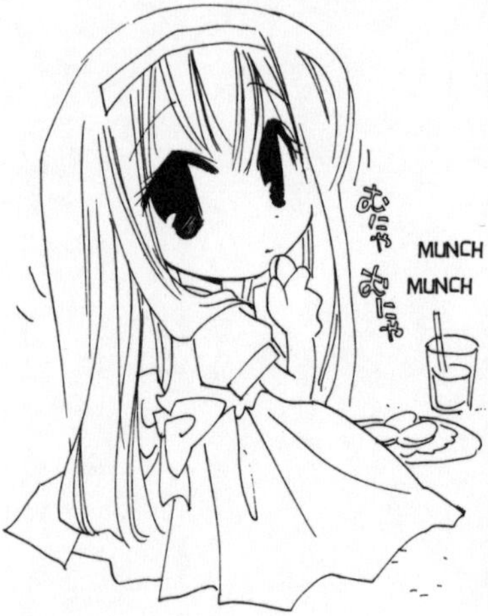
MUNCH
MUNCH

Glad to see you all again! Actually, I'm working on this on New Year's Day, 2003 (but I don't really mind).

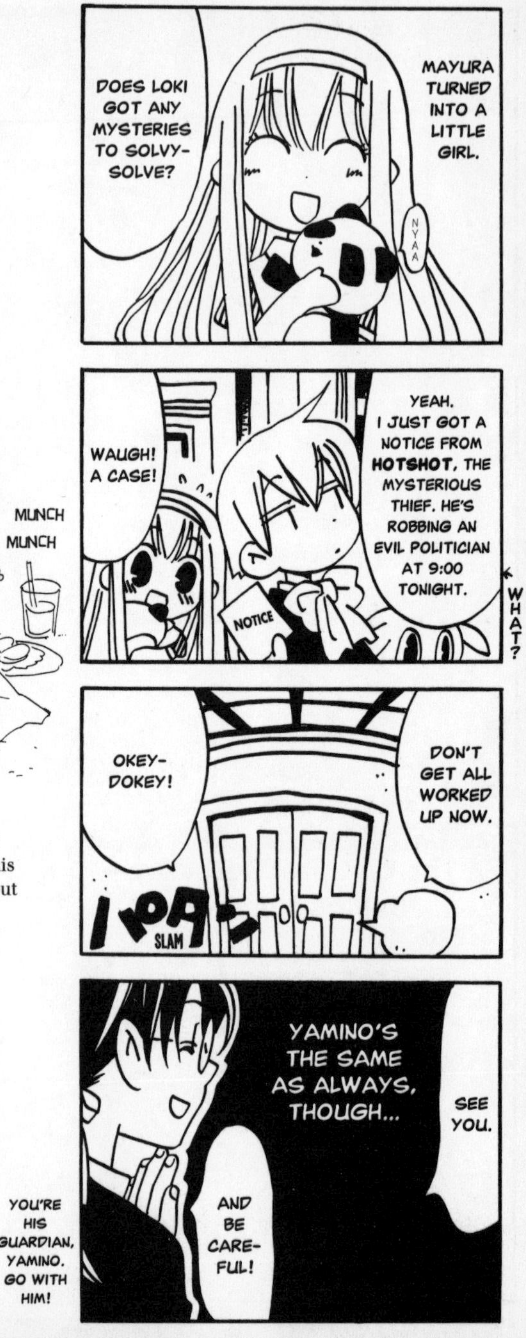
MAYURA TURNED INTO A LITTLE GIRL.
NYAA
DOES LOKI GOT ANY MYSTERIES TO SOLVY-SOLVE?
WHAT?
YEAH. I JUST GOT A NOTICE FROM HOTSHOT, THE MYSTERIOUS THIEF. HE'S ROBBING AN EVIL POLITICIAN AT 9:00 TONIGHT.
NOTICE
WAUGH! A CASE!
DON'T GET ALL WORKED UP NOW.
OKEY-DOKEY!
SLAM
YAMINO'S THE SAME AS ALWAYS, THOUGH...
SEE YOU.
AND BE CARE-FUL!
YOU'RE HIS GUARDIAN, YAMINO. GO WITH HIM!

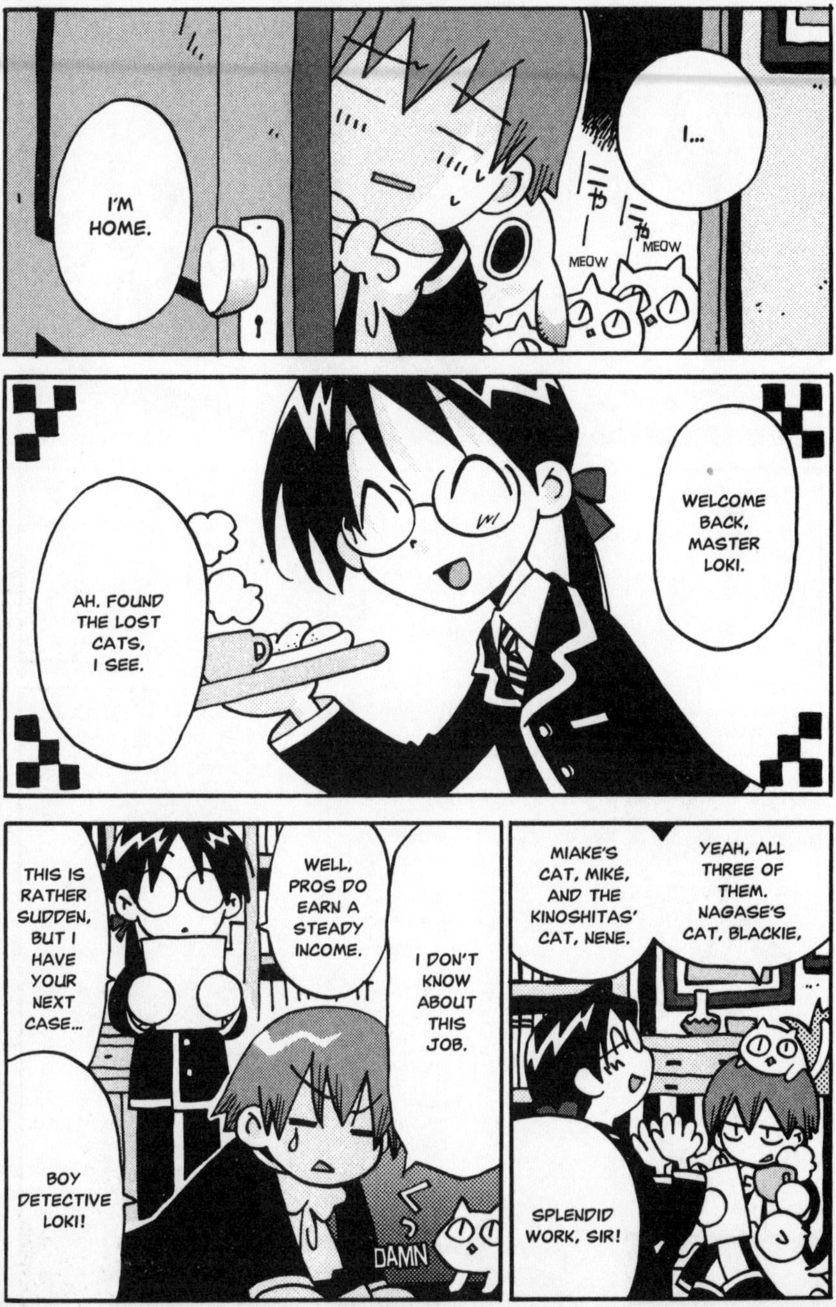
I...
MEOW
MEOW
I'M HOME.
WELCOME BACK, MASTER LOKI.
AH. FOUND THE LOST CATS, I SEE.
YEAH, ALL THREE OF THEM. NAGASE'S CAT, BLACKIE,
MIAKE'S CAT, MIKÉ, AND THE KINOSHITAS' CAT, NENE.
SPLENDID WORK, SIR!
I DON'T KNOW ABOUT THIS JOB.
WELL, PROS DO EARN A STEADY INCOME.
THIS IS RATHER SUDDEN, BUT I HAVE YOUR NEXT CASE...
BOY DETECTIVE LOKI!
DAMN

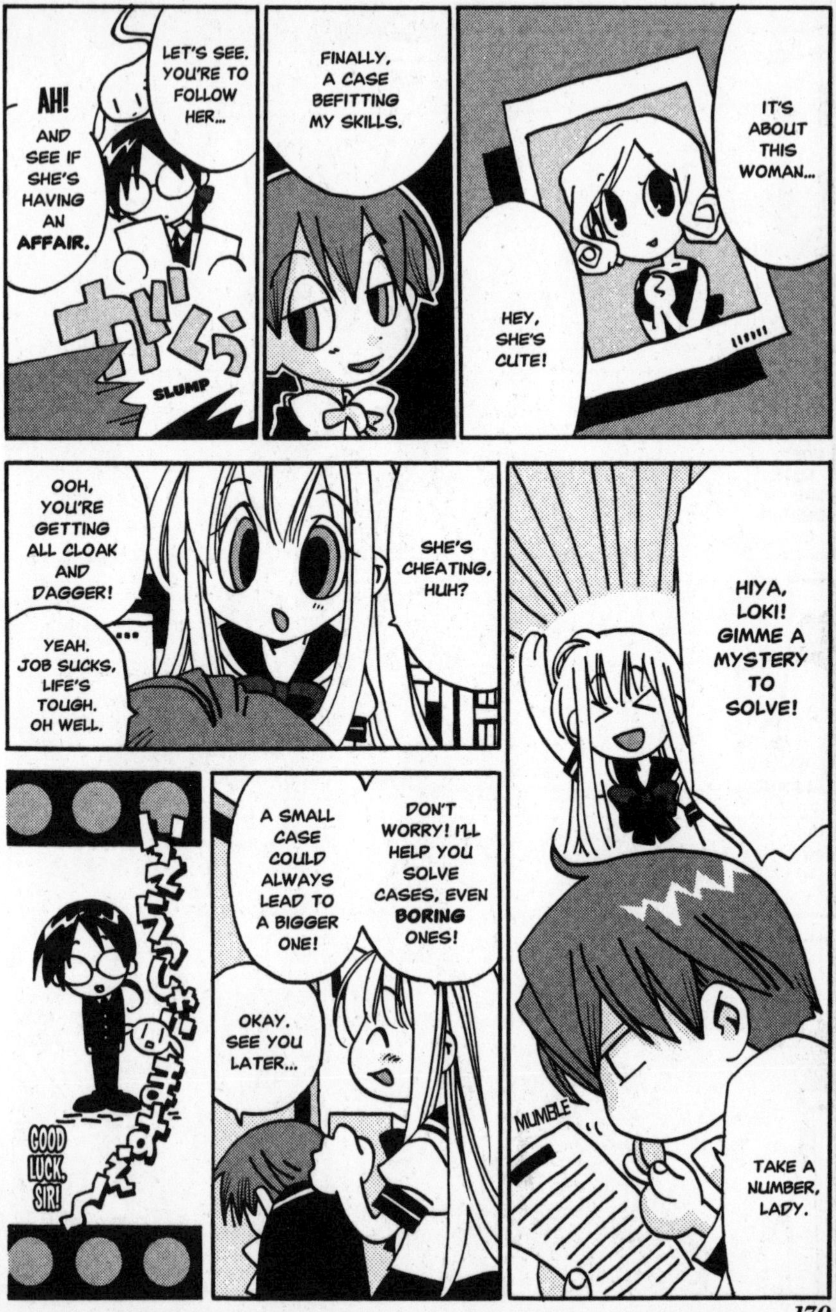
IT'S ABOUT THIS WOMAN...
HEY, SHE'S CUTE!
FINALLY, A CASE BEFITTING MY SKILLS.
LET'S SEE. YOU'RE TO FOLLOW HER...
AH! AND SEE IF SHE'S HAVING AN AFFAIR.
SLUMP
HIYA, LOKI! GIMME A MYSTERY TO SOLVE!
TAKE A NUMBER, LADY.
MUMBLE
SHE'S CHEATING, HUH?
OOH, YOU'RE GETTING ALL CLOAK AND DAGGER!
YEAH. JOB SUCKS, LIFE'S TOUGH. OH WELL.
DON'T WORRY! I'LL HELP YOU SOLVE CASES, EVEN BORING ONES!
A SMALL CASE COULD ALWAYS LEAD TO A BIGGER ONE!
OKAY. SEE YOU LATER...
GOOD LUCK, SIR!

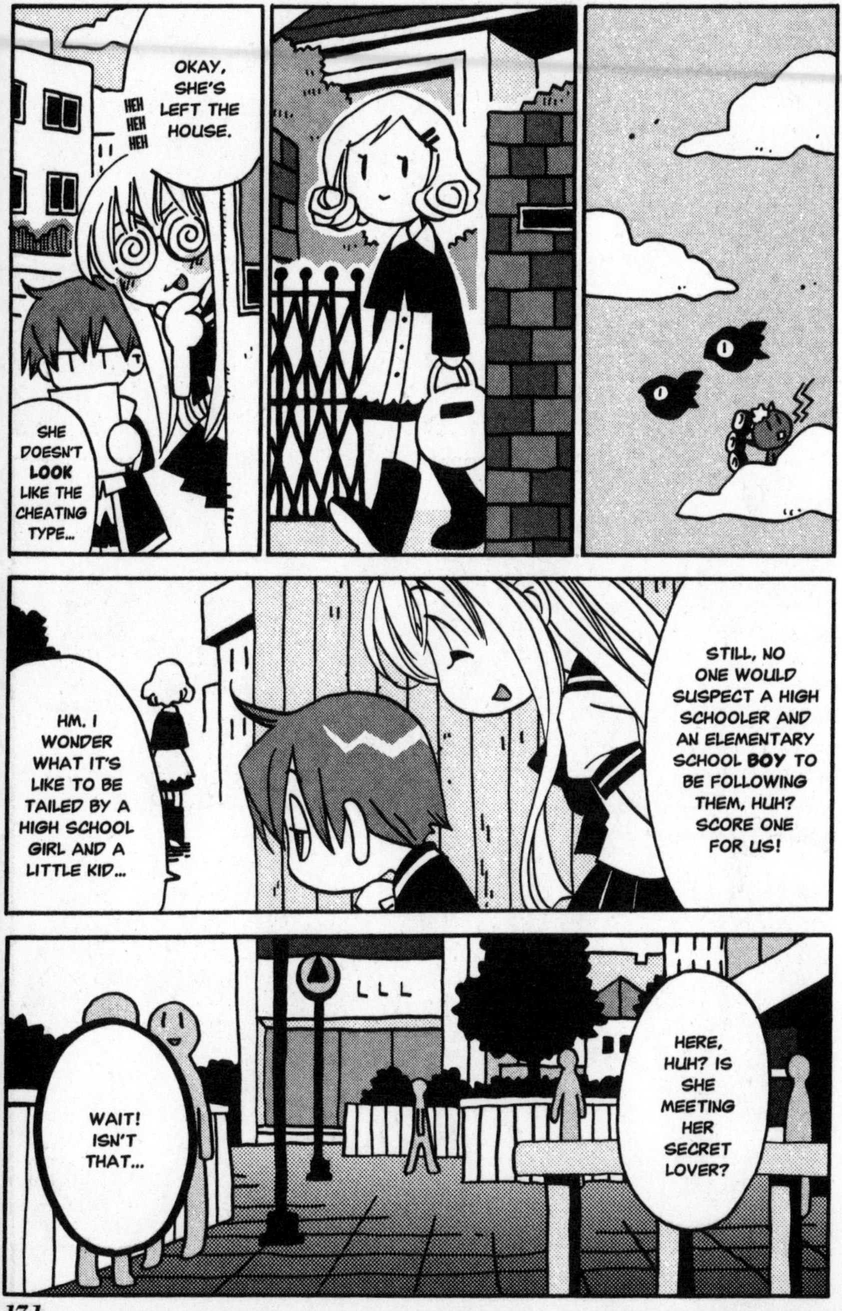
OKAY, SHE'S LEFT THE HOUSE.
HEH HEH HEH
SHE DOESN'T **LOOK** LIKE THE CHEATING TYPE...
STILL, NO ONE WOULD SUSPECT A HIGH SCHOOLER AND AN ELEMENTARY SCHOOL **BOY** TO BE FOLLOWING THEM, HUH? SCORE ONE FOR US!
HM. I WONDER WHAT IT'S LIKE TO BE TAILED BY A HIGH SCHOOL GIRL AND A LITTLE KID...
HERE, HUH? IS SHE MEETING HER SECRET LOVER?
WAIT! ISN'T THAT...

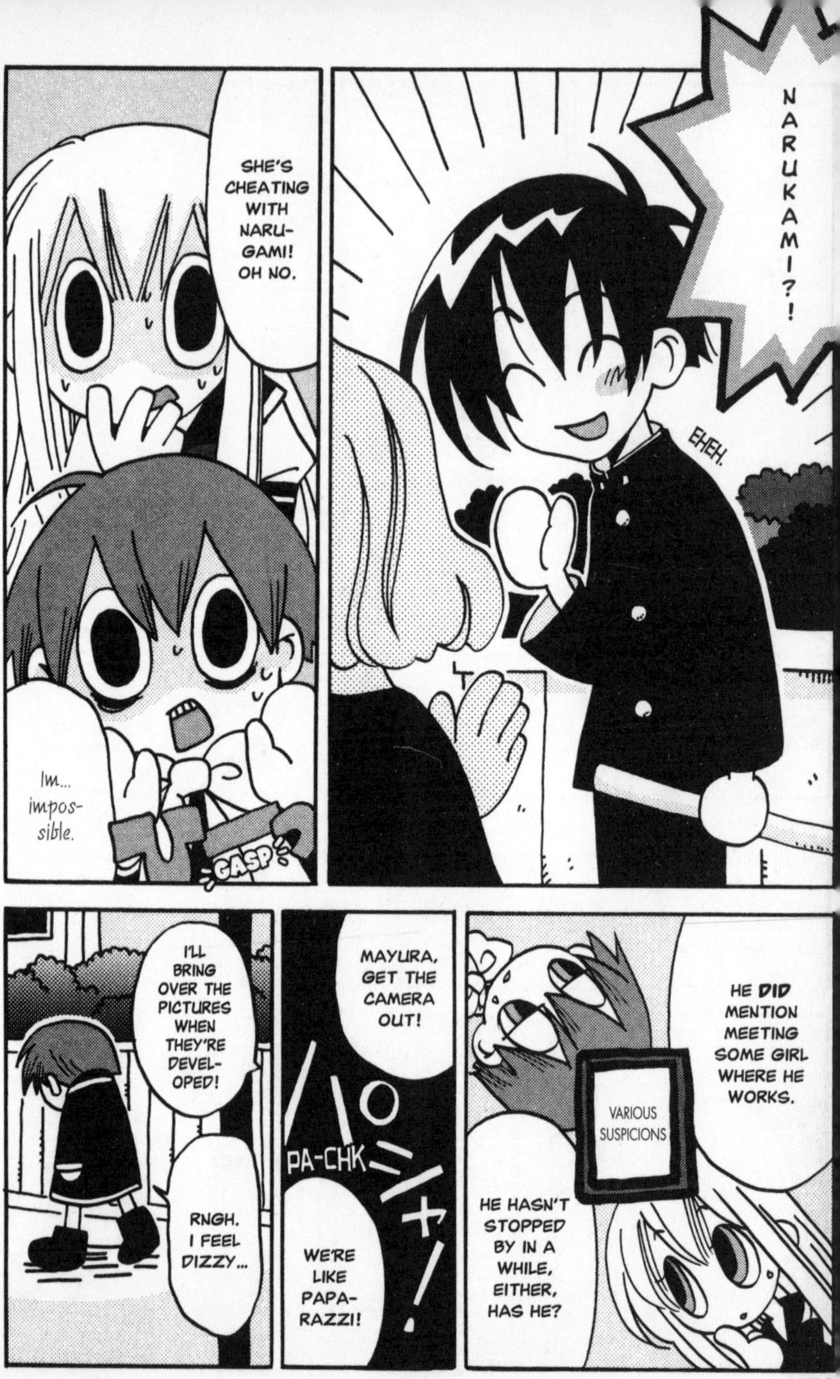
NARUKAMI?!
EHEH.
SHE'S CHEATING WITH NARUGAMI! OH NO.
Im... impossible.
GASP
HE DID MENTION MEETING SOME GIRL WHERE HE WORKS.
VARIOUS SUSPICIONS
HE HASN'T STOPPED BY IN A WHILE, EITHER, HAS HE?
MAYURA, GET THE CAMERA OUT!
PA-CHK
WE'RE LIKE PAPARAZZI!
I'LL BRING OVER THE PICTURES WHEN THEY'RE DEVELOPED!
RNGH. I FEEL DIZZY...

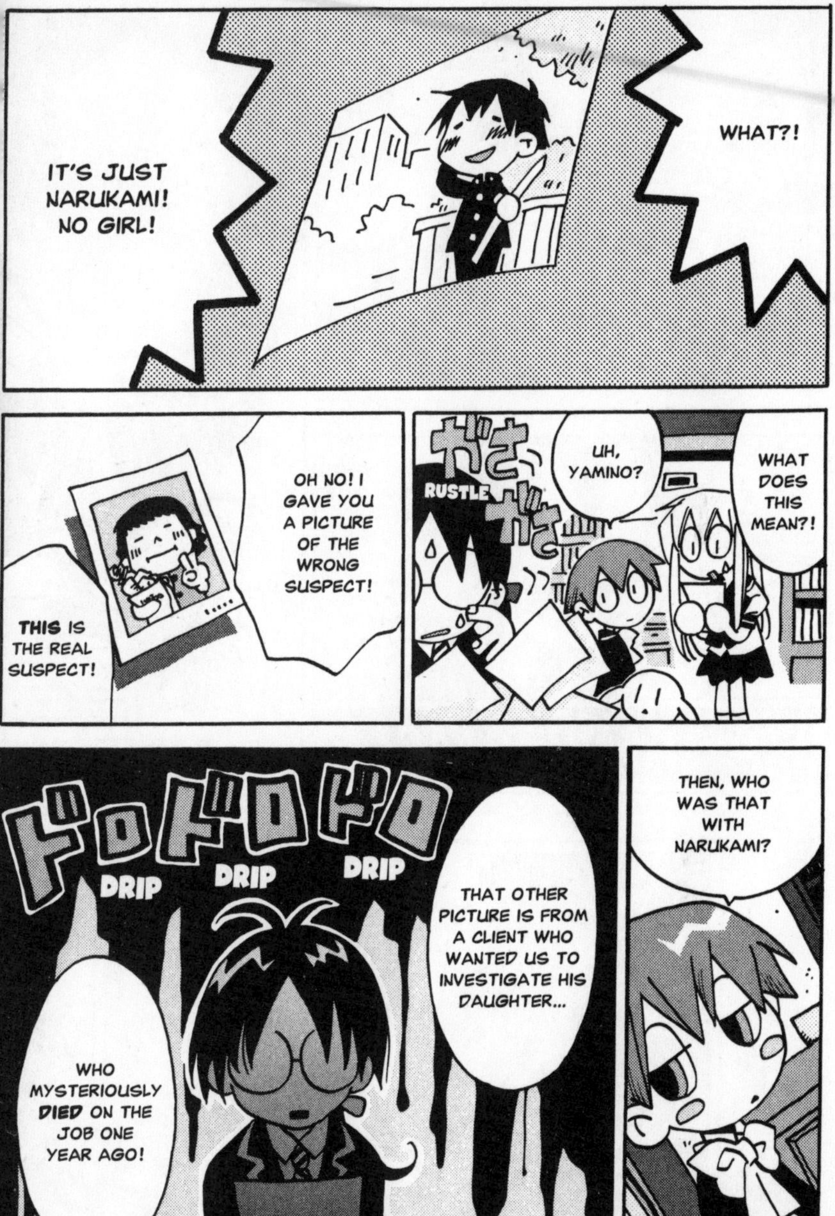
WHAT?!
IT'S JUST NARUKAMI! NO GIRL!
WHAT DOES THIS MEAN?!
UH, YAMINO?
RUSTLE
OH NO! I GAVE YOU A PICTURE OF THE WRONG SUSPECT!
THIS IS THE REAL SUSPECT!
THEN, WHO WAS THAT WITH NARUKAMI?
THAT OTHER PICTURE IS FROM A CLIENT WHO WANTED US TO INVESTIGATE HIS DAUGHTER...
DRIP DRIP DRIP
WHO MYSTERIOUSLY DIED ON THE JOB ONE YEAR AGO!

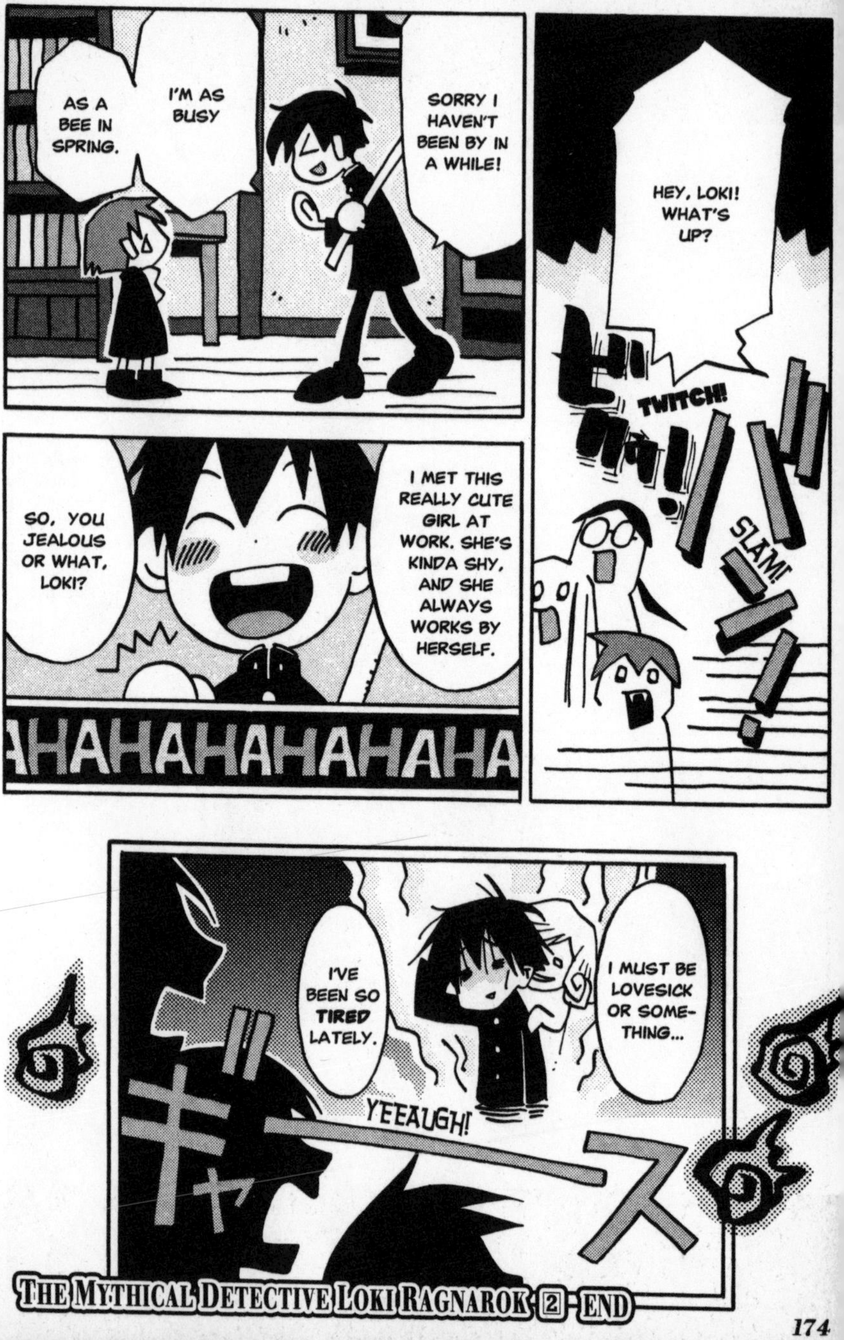
HEY, LOKI! WHAT'S UP?
TWITCH!
SLAM!
SORRY I HAVEN'T BEEN BY IN A WHILE!
I'M AS BUSY
AS A BEE IN SPRING.
I MET THIS REALLY CUTE GIRL AT WORK. SHE'S KINDA SHY, AND SHE ALWAYS WORKS BY HERSELF.
SO, YOU JEALOUS OR WHAT, LOKI?
AHAHAHAHAHAHAHA
I MUST BE LOVESICK OR SOME-THING...
I'VE BEEN SO TIRED LATELY.
YEEAUGH!

THE MYTHICAL DETECTIVE LOKI RAGNAROK 2 END

Hello! Sakura Kinoshita here. Thank you very much for buying *The Mythical Detective Loki Ragnarok* Volume 2. Things are so hectic these days and I am totally stressed out. My brain is like a melting pot, and I can't remember things. I wonder why. Maybe I'm getting old... Oh well!

By the way, *Loki* is being made into an anime! I'm a little nervous, but also very happy—even if a little-known author like me doesn't deserve such an honor.

The director, script writers and character designers are all very talented people and inspire a lot of confidence. The voice actors are also talented and are perfect fits for the characters. I can't wait to see the anime! I hope you enjoy the TV show as well as the manga. So, bye for now, but I look forward to seeing you again soon!

Sakura Kinoshita, 2003

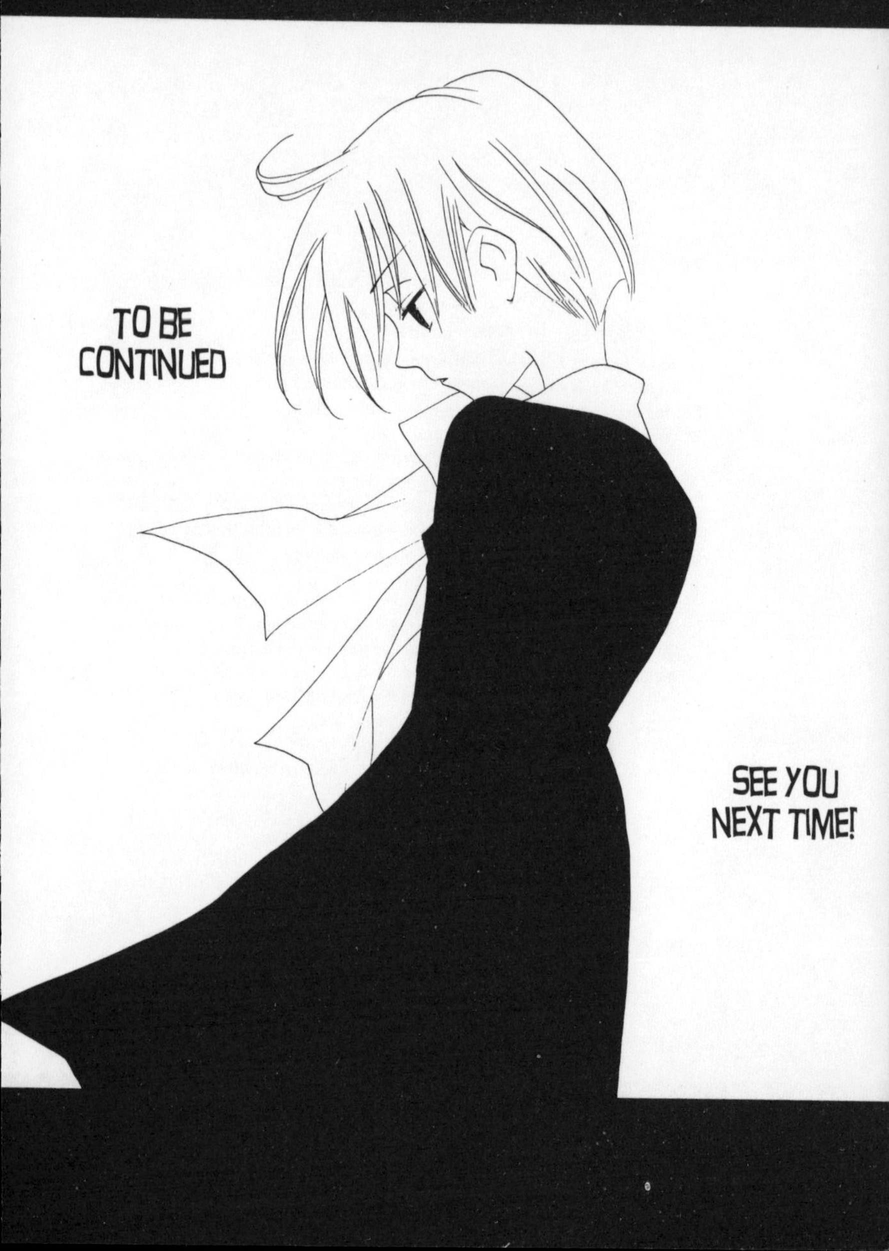
TO BE CONTINUED
SEE YOU NEXT TIME!

THE MYTHICAL DETECTIVE LOKI RAGNAROK VOLUME 2

First published in 2003 by MAG Garden Corporation.
English translation rights arranged with MAG Garden Corporation.

Translator **EIKO McGREGOR**
Lead Translator/Translation Supervisor **JAVIER LOPEZ**
Translation Staff **KAY BERTRAND,**
AMY FORSYTH and **BRENDAN FRAYNE**

Print Production/Art Studio Manager **LISA PUCKETT**
Pre-press Manager **KLYS REEDYK**
Sr. Designer/Creative Manager **JORGE ALVARADO**
Graphic Designer/Group Leader **GEORGE REYNOLDS**
Graphic Artists **NATALIA MORALES** and **HEATHER GARY**
Graphic Intern **MARK MEZA**

International Coordinators **TORU IWAKAMI,**
ATSUSHI KANBAYASHI & KYOKO DRUMHELLER

Publishing Editor **SUSAN ITIN**
Assistant Editor **MARGARET SCHAROLD**
Editorial Assistant **SHERIDAN JACOBS**
Research/Traffic Coordinator **MARSHA ARNOLD**
Editorial Intern **MIKE ESSMYER**

Executive VP, CFO, COO **KEVIN CORCORAN**

President, CEO & Publisher **JOHN LEDFORD**

Email: editor@adv-manga.com
www.adv-manga.com
www.advfilms.com

For sales and distribution inquiries please call 1.800.282.7202

ADV MANGA™ is a division of A.D. Vision, Inc.
10114 W. Sam Houston Parkway, Suite 200, Houston, Texas 77099

English text © 2005 published by A.D. Vision, Inc. under exclusive license.
ADV MANGA is a trademark of A.D. Vision, Inc.

ISBN: 1-4139-0184-0
First printing, March 2005
10 9 8 7 6 5 4 3 2 1
Printed in Canada

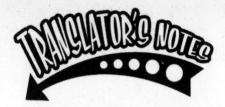

TRANSLATOR'S NOTES

PG. 4 **Cockatrice**
In European mythology, a hodgepodge of a beastie with the head and feet of a rooster, but with lizard-like wings and a serpentine body and tail. The gaze and even the breath of this creature (which was said to be laid by a rooster, and then nursed by a lizard or toad) were purported to be lethal. Unfortunately, no references exist of blue cockatrices.

PG. 36 **Narukami vs. Narugami**
As was explained by the author, Loki's continual pronunciation of Thor's name here on Earth is actually a pun. Thor is the god of thunder—in Japanese, "god" is *kami* and "thunder" is *kaminari*, which gives Loki two reasons to stress the *kami* aspect of this name.

PG. 41 **Midgardsormr**
Yamino is in actuality the great serpent Jormungand (or Jormungandr). In Norse mythology, he was believed to encircle Midgard (the world of the humans), and was thus also referred to as Midgardsormr, which means "the serpent of Midgard."

PG. 42 **One-room apartment**
Specifically, this would be a 4.5 *tatami* apartment, or roughly 75 square feet. *Tatami* are a kind of woven straw mat used in traditional houses and "Japanese-style rooms," and are used to measure the space of living quarters.

PG. 52 **Big bro**
Aniki, a respectful word for "big brother," can also be used to indicate a senior member of an organization one belongs to (as opposed to any sort of familial relation). Masaru's use of this word, the gun, and his parents' comment to the effect that they thought he had a real job all point toward Masaru having fallen in with a criminal organization.

PG. 91 **Under the spreading chestnut tree**
This is a reference to the poem "The Village Blacksmith" by Henry Wadsworth Longfellow, which opens with a description of the "mighty smithy" standing beneath the tree. Fans of George Orwell's *1984* will also recognize this line (though "re-interpreted" through the principles of Ingsoc) as the inspiration behind the Chestnut Tree Café.

PG. 97 **Takoyaki**
Originally created in Osaka, this simple dish consisting of a piece of octopus dropped into a small amount of batter and shaped into small, gooey balls has since spread all over Japan. Takoyaki is commonly sold by street vendors, but sit-down restaurants such as Osaka's famous "Takomasa" exist as well.

PG. 141 **Cinderella's Castle on Christmas Eve**
In Japan, Christmas is considered a time for couples, much as Valentine's Day is so considered abroad. Standing in front of Cinderella's Castle (the one in Tokyo Disneyland, that is) and sharing words of love is considered quite romantic.

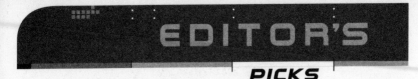

EDITOR'S PICKS

If you liked *MYTHICAL DETECTIVE LOKI RAGNAROK* Volume 2, then you'll love these!

PICK 1

tactics
Sakura Kinoshita × Kazuko Higashiyama 1

TACTICS

Kantaro Ichinomiya studies folklore, and he takes his knowledge of ghouls and goblins to the streets of Japan, in hopes of bringing the worlds of beasts and humans together. This is no smooth transition, but with the help of the powerful demon-eater Haruka, Kantaro might be able to steer a course of collision between two groups of rivals that keep this bi-species referee on his toes!

PICK 2

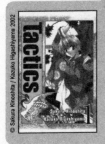

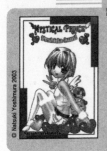

MYSTICAL PRINCE

MYSTICAL PRINCE YOSHIDA-KUN!

In the dark realm, one man rules—King Dark Fleet. But such power begins to wear on the aging ruler, and he suddenly declares his intention to retire by naming his replacement, Yoshida. Now the minions of the Dark Fleet will seek to destroy young Kaoru Yoshida, and this kid's passion for magic might not level the playing field! His world is about to turn upside down, and he'll be taking a few friends along for the ride!

PICK 3

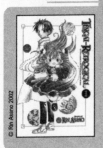

TENGAI-RETROGICAL
RIN ASANO

TENGAI-RETROGICAL

The fog of strange and spooky rumors that hovers over Tengai-ya is about to be lifted by a curious teenager and a twist of fate. After his father agrees to become its property manager, Ryohei's curiosity will force him beyond the unwelcoming gates, where mysteries wait to be uncovered and memories wait to be remembered. And a boy who seeks to breathe life into an abandoned neighborhood will soon find company hidden in the shadows of Tengai-ya.

CHECK'EM OUT TODAY!

ADV Manga™

www.adv-manga.com

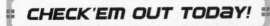

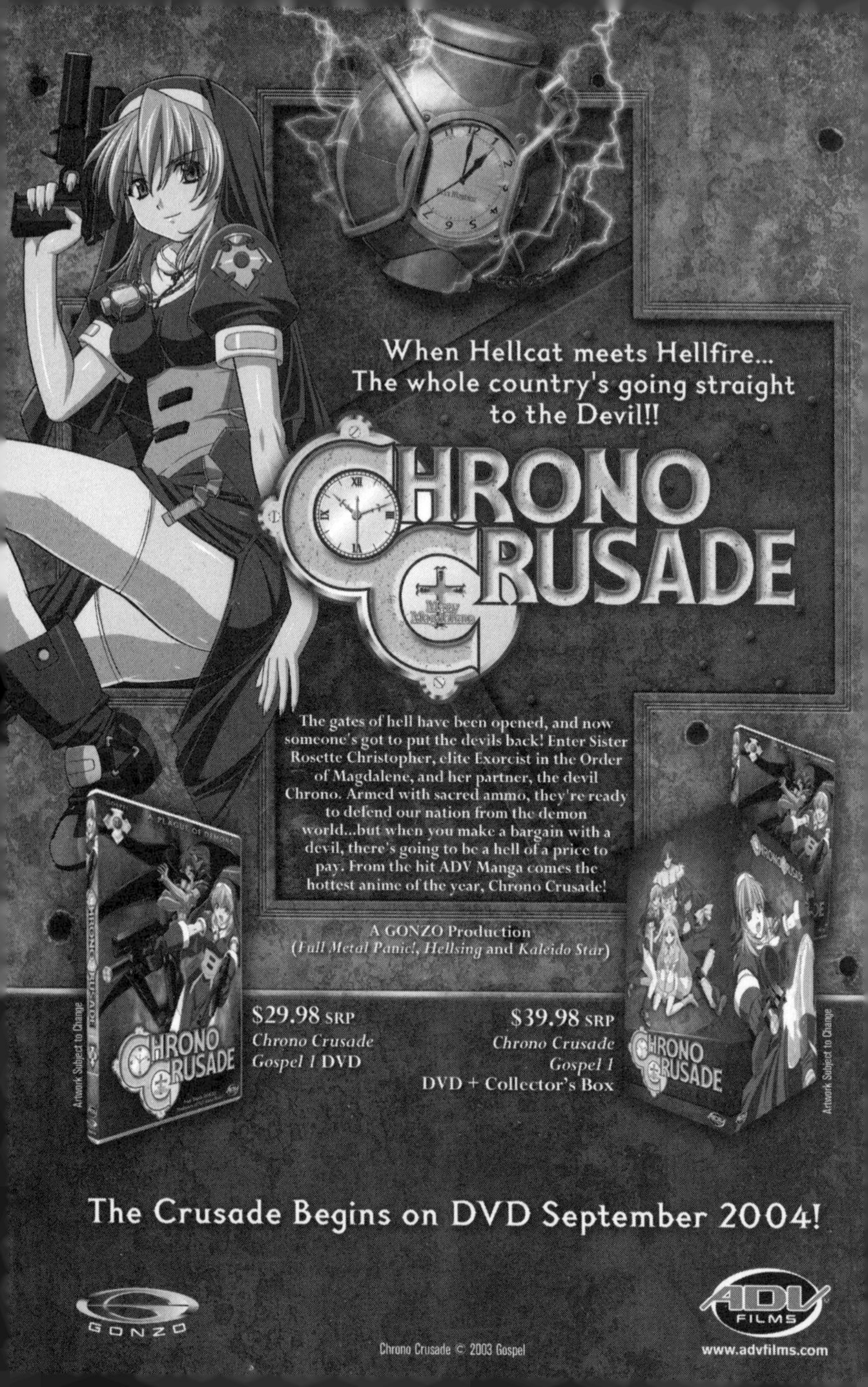
When Hellcat meets Hellfire...
The whole country's going straight to the Devil!!
CHRONO CRUSADE
The gates of hell have been opened, and now someone's got to put the devils back! Enter Sister Rosette Christopher, elite Exorcist in the Order of Magdalene, and her partner, the devil Chrono. Armed with sacred ammo, they're ready to defend our nation from the demon world...but when you make a bargain with a devil, there's going to be a hell of a price to pay. From the hit ADV Manga comes the hottest anime of the year, Chrono Crusade!
A GONZO Production
(Full Metal Panic!, Hellsing and Kaleido Star)
$29.98 SRP
Chrono Crusade
Gospel 1 DVD
$39.98 SRP
Chrono Crusade
Gospel 1
DVD + Collector's Box
Artwork Subject to Change
Artwork Subject to Change
The Crusade Begins on DVD September 2004!
GONZO
ADV FILMS
Chrono Crusade © 2003 Gospel
www.advfilms.com

DO YOU HAVE WHAT IT TAKES TO MAKE IT IN CROMARTIE HIGH?

Do you have a tough nickname?

❑ Yes ❑ No

How many fights have you been in?

❑ None ❑ More than 100

❑ 5-10 ❑ None – no one ever had the stones to challenge me

What's in your bookbag?

❑ My homework ❑ Porn ❑ A metal plate

How tough do you look? Check all that apply.

❑ Pompadour ❑ Handlebar mustache ❑ Shaved eyebrows

❑ Carpet of chest hair ❑ Lazy swagger ❑ Menacing glare

Say you checked out eleven adult videos. Three of those were new releases, so you had to return them the next day. How many videos do you have left?

❑ 3 ❑ 8 ❑ 11 – I would never give them back.

How did you rate?

10 points or less	**Errand Boy**
10 – 15	**Wannabe Punk**
30 – 40	**One Badass Dude**
More than 100	**Champ by Default**

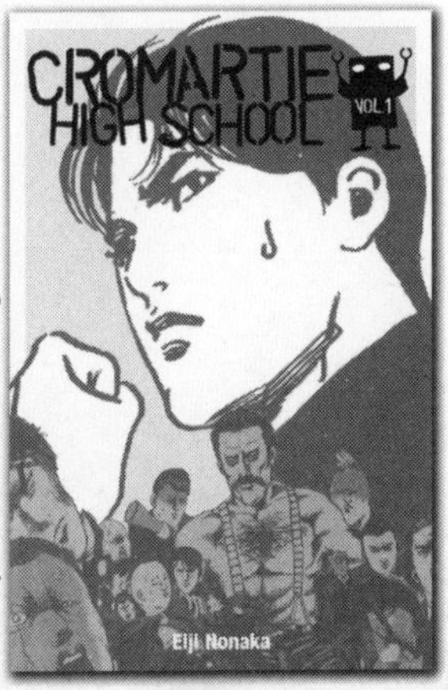

CROMARTIE HIGH SCHOOL
VOL.1
Eiji Nonaka

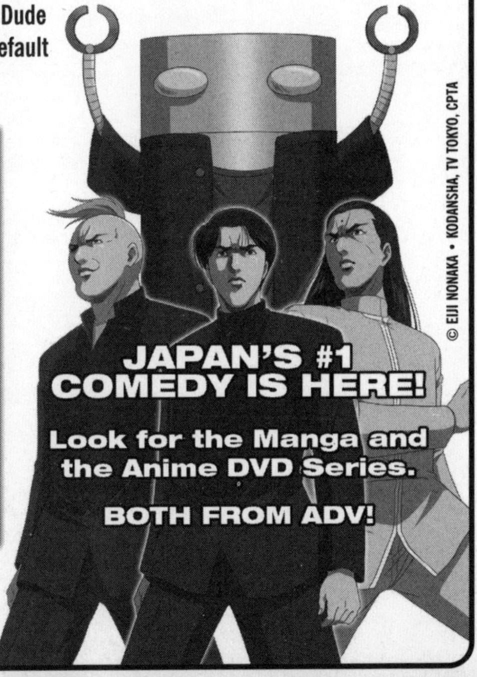

JAPAN'S #1 COMEDY IS HERE!
Look for the Manga and the Anime DVD Series.
BOTH FROM ADV!

ADV MANGA™

www.adv-manga.com

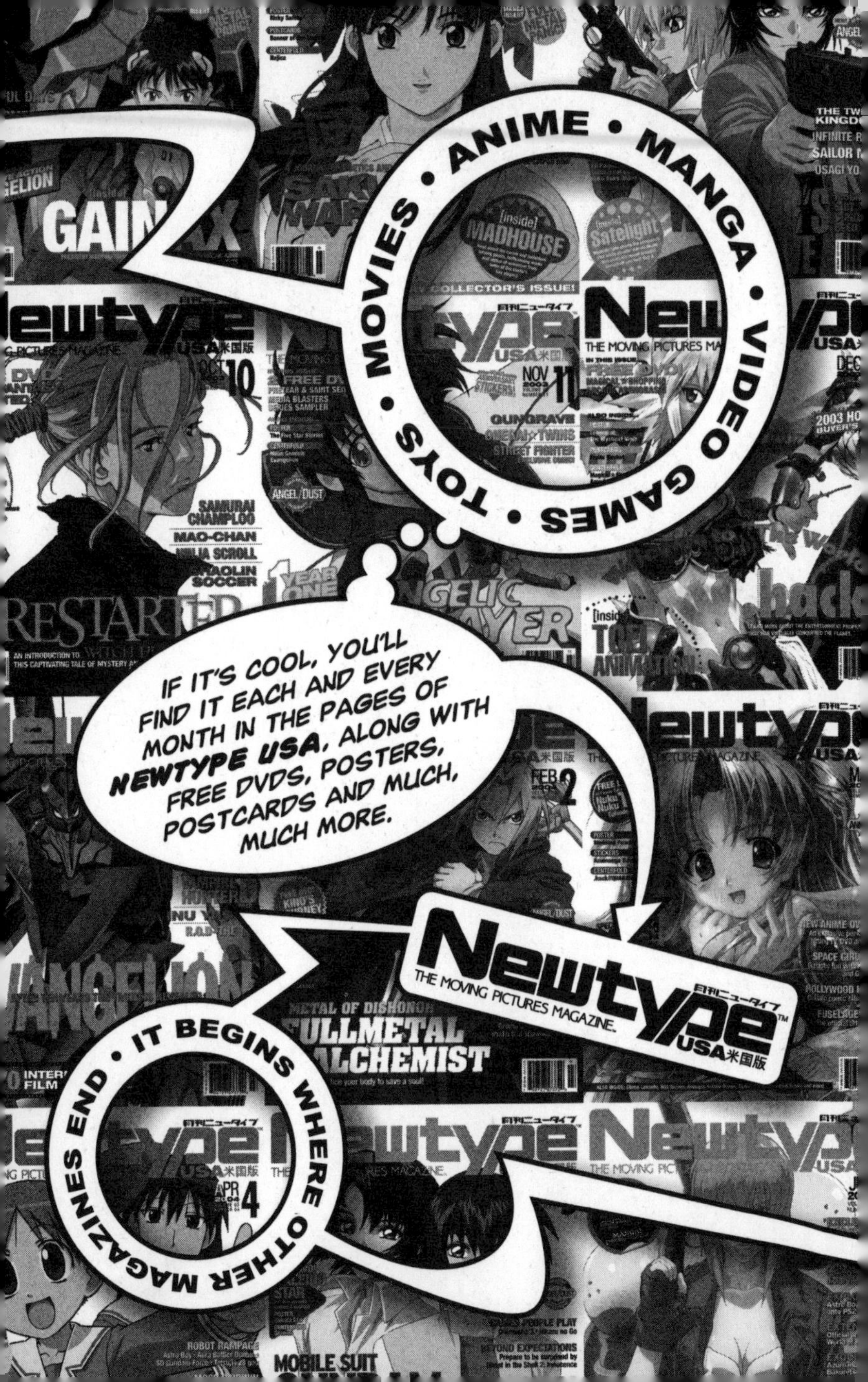
ANIME • MANGA • VIDEO GAMES • TOYS • MOVIES •
IF IT'S COOL, YOU'LL FIND IT EACH AND EVERY MONTH IN THE PAGES OF NEWTYPE USA, ALONG WITH FREE DVDS, POSTERS, POSTCARDS AND MUCH, MUCH MORE.
Newtype USA 米国版
THE MOVING PICTURES MAGAZINE.
IT BEGINS WHERE OTHER MAGAZINES END •